12

INTERNATIONAL AGRICULTURAL
TRADE
DISPUTES
CASE STUDIES IN NORTH AMERICA

International Agricultural Trade Disputes: Case Studies in North America

EDITED BY

Andrew Schmitz

Department of Food and Resource Economics
University of Florida—Gainesville, Florida

Charles B. Moss

Department of Food and Resource Economics
University of Florida—Gainesville, Florida

Troy G. Schmitz

Morrison School of Agribusiness and
Resource Management
Arizona State University East—Mesa, Arizona

Won W. Koo

Department of Agribusiness and Applied Economics
North Dakota State University

© 2005 Andrew Schmitz
Published by the University of Calgary Press
2500 University Drive NW, Calgary, Alberta, Canada T2N 1N4
www.uofcpress.com

LIBRARY AND ARCHIVES CANADA CATALOGUING IN PUBLICATION

International agricultural trade disputes : case studies in
America / edited by Andrew Schmitz ... [et al.].

Proceedings of a conference held at University of Florida, Gainesville,
    March 20, 2003.
Includes bibliographical references and index.
ISBN 1-55238-152-8

    1. Food industry and trade—North America—Congresses.
2. Produce trade—North America—Congresses. 3. Dispute resolution (Law)—
North America—Congresses. 4. Free trade—North America—Congresses.
I. Schmitz, Andrew

HF1453.I68 2004   343'.70871   C2004-906619-6

We acknowledge the financial support of the Government of Canada through the Book
Publishing Industry Development Program (BPIDP) the Alberta Foundation for the
Arts and the Alberta Lottery Fund—Community Initiatives Program for our publishing
activities.

Printed and bound in Canada by Houghton Boston
∞This book is printed on Enviro 100, acid free. post consumer paper
Cover design by Mieka West

Contents

Section III: Trade Disputes—Case Studies (Canada and the United States)

Section IV: Trade Disputes—Case Studies (The United States and Other Countries)

Contributors

Charles Adams
Department of Food and Resource Economics, University of Florida, Gainesville, Florida, USA

Flynn J. Adcock
Center for North American Studies, Texas A&M University, College Station, Texas, USA

Janaki R. R. Alavalapati
School of Forest Resources and Conservation, University of Florida, Gainesville, Florida, USA

Mel Annand
College of Agriculture, University of Saskatchewan, Saskatoon, Saskatchewan, Canada

Richard R. Barichello
Food and Resource Economics, University of British Columbia, Vancouver, British Columbia, Canada

Peter Berck
Department of Agricultural and Resource Economics and Policy, University of California, Berkeley, California, USA

Colin A. Carter
Department of Agricultural and Resource Economics, University of California, Davis, California, USA

W. Hartley Furtan
Department of Agricultural Economics, University of Saskatchewan, Saskatoon, Saskatchewan, Canada

Carol Goodloe
Office of Chief Economist, U.S. Department of Agriculture,
Washington, DC, USA

Caroline Gunning-Trant
Department of Agricultural and Resource Economics, University of
California, Davis, California, USA

Cathy Jabara
U.S. International Trade Commission,
Washington, DC, USA

Walter J. Keithly
Coastal Fisheries Institute, Louisiana State University,
Baton Rouge, Louisiana, USA

Won W. Koo
Department of Agribusiness and Applied Economics,
North Dakota State University, Fargo, North Dakota, USA

Shiv Mehrotra
School of Forest Resources and Conservation, University of Florida,
Gainesville, Florida, USA

Charles B. Moss
Department of Food and Resource Economics, University of Florida,
Gainesville, Florida, USA

Al Mussell
George Morris Centre,
Guelph, Ontario, Canada

David Orden
Agricultural and Applied Economics, Virginia Polytechnic Institute
and State University, Blacksburg, Virginia, USA

Mechel S. Paggi
Center for Agricultural Business, Fresno State University,
Fresno, California, USA

Warren Payne
U.S. International Trade Commission,
Washington, DC, USA

Stephen J. Powell
Levin College of Law, University of Florida,
Gainesville, Florida, USA

Robert F. Romain
Department of Agricultural Economics, Université Laval,
Sainte-Foy, Quebec, Canada

C. Parr Rosson, III
Center for North American Studies, Texas A&M University,
College Station, Texas, USA

Andrew Schmitz
Department of Food and Resource Economics, University of Florida,
Gainesville, Florida, USA

Troy G. Schmitz
Morrison School of Agribusiness and Resource Management, Arizona State
University East, Mesa, Arizona, USA

James L. Seale, Jr.
Department of Food and Resource Economics, University of Florida,
Gainesville, Florida, USA

Thomas Spreen
Department of Food and Resource Economics, University of Florida,
Gainesville, Florida, USA

Ihn H. Uhm
Canadian International Trade Tribunal,
Ottawa, Ontario, Canada

Sal Versaggi
Versaggi Shrimp Corporation,
Tampa, Florida USA

Michael Wohlgenant
College of Agriculture and Life Sciences, North Carolina State University,
Raleigh, North Carolina, USA

Fumiko Yamazaki
Center for Agricultural Business, Fresno State University,
Fresno, California, USA

Acknowledgements

The editors thank all who attended and participated in the conference entitled "International Agricultural Trade Disputes: Case Studies on North America," from which this book is derived. The conference was hosted by the University of Florida, and was held in Gainesville, Florida from March 20–21, 2003. Special thanks go to the authors of the chapters in this book who put forth great effort to produce a thoughtful and innovative set of selected papers. We deeply appreciate the thoughtful contributions of the discussants whose ideas improved the papers as they evolved into book chapters.

A grateful acknowledgement is extended to the various agencies and institutions that provided the financial support to organize the conference and to prepare this book for publication. Included as financial supporters are Agriculture and Agri-Food Canada; the Farm Foundation; the Ben Hill Griffin, Jr. Endowed Chair at the University of Florida; the Center for Agricultural Policy and Trade Studies, North Dakota State University; the American Farm Bureau Federation; the Center for Agricultural Business, Fresno State University; the Center for North American Studies, Texas A&M University; the Centre for Studies in Agriculture, Law and the Environment, University of Saskatchewan; the Florida Farm Bureau; the International Agricultural Trade and Policy Center, University of Florida; and the University of Saskatchewan, College of Law.

A special thank you goes to H. Carole Schmitz and Kjërstin Terry for their invaluable assistance organizing the conference, editing the papers into chapters, reformatting the tables and figures, formatting the book, and carrying out the copy-editing and indexing.

Foreword

Andrew Schmitz
University of Florida

INTERNATIONAL AGRICULTURAL TRADE DISPUTES

Numerous border disputes in agricultural products, including lumber, continue between the United States, Canada, and Mexico and their numbers appear to be escalating. This was the subject of a conference of economists, lawyers, and private-industry representatives that was hosted by the University of Florida, Gainesville, on March 20–22, 2003. Selected papers from this conference are presented in this volume as chapters. This conference was sponsored by Agriculture and Agri-Food Canada; the Farm Foundation; the Ben Hill Griffin, Jr. Endowed Chair at the University of Florida; the Center for Agricultural Policy and Trade Studies, North Dakota State University; the American Farm Bureau Federation; the Center for Agricultural Business, Fresno State University; the Center for North American Studies, Texas A&M University; the Centre for Studies in Agriculture, Law and the Environment, University of Saskatchewan; the Florida Farm Bureau; the International Agricultural Trade and Policy Center, University of Florida; and the University of Saskatchewan, College of Law.

Little scholarly work has been written on this topic since the 1990 book by Lermer and Klein (eds), entitled *Canadian Agricultural Trade: Disputes, Actions, and Prospects* that was published by the University of Calgary Press. Our book updates much of their material and adds more dimension to their volume, including various legal aspects concerning trade disputes, rent-seeking behaviour on the part of producers and processors under the so called Byrd Amendment (in which tariff revenues are given to the private sector and are not retained by the government), and the possible resolution of the lumber war between the United States and Canada. We also include a discussion of Country of Origin Labelling (COOL), that was passed under the 2002 U.S. Farm Bill, even though this is not specific to dumping and countervail actions per se. COOL, in conjunction with the finding of Mad Cow Disease in Canada in May of 2003, and in the United States in December of that same year, presents formidable challenges when estimating the associated added transaction costs and the resolution of food-safety concerns. Along with the other dimensions of the 2002

U.S. Farm Bill, COOL has led trading partners to argue that U.S. farm policy is a vehicle by which the United States is dumping export products abroad. This concept was certainly a major stumbling block in the failure of the Cancun Round of trade negotiations in 2003.

Trade remedy measures, including antidumping, countervailing duty, and safeguard remedies, are used by the United States, Canada, and Mexico to resolve international trade disputes. These measures provide a means for governments to protect domestic industries from competition due to alleged "unfair imports" and from import surges. The positive and normative aspects discussed in this volume, which are used to explain how the international trading system has evolved, will hopefully yield new solutions that will more quickly resolve agricultural-trade disputes.

These trade remedy measures are contentious because they can be used to block trade unfairly. Trade remedies can be applied based on findings by relevant government agencies that a domestic industry is injured or is facing threat of injury due to unfair trading practices. Included in this volume is a discussion of industries affected that include lumber, tomatoes, live cattle, shrimp, high fructose corn syrup (HFCS), wheat, and dairy products. For example, based on findings of material injury, Mexico has implemented a number of trade remedy actions, including dumping duties, especially over the exportation of HFCS by the United States to the Mexican market. When evidence of a dumping and/or a countervail case is found, a country can appeal the findings and actions to a dispute panel of the World Trade Organization (WTO).

Attorneys, economists, and private industry representatives who participated in the International Agricultural Trade Disputes Conference in 2003 generally agreed on the following:

- There is a wide discrepancy between trade law and economics. Trade in agricultural products is often quite different from trade in manufactured goods. Trade law for example, cannot deal adequately with perishable agricultural products. Often, as a normal business practice, U.S. farmers (like foreign competitors) sell below the cost of production, especially for perishable agricultural products. As a result, a normal business-practice criterion should be used as a basis for determining whether or not dumping has occurred, rather than the standard full cost-of-production criterion, which is in use today that has been adopted essentially from cases involving manufacturing.

- There is considerable debate over the methodology that countries use to determine injury. If there is no injury from alleged dumping, tariffs are not imposed. There are many cases in this volume that discuss the material-injury question. And politics plays a role in trade-dispute resolution. For example, consider the case by Mexico against U.S. exports of HFCS to Mexico. This case was initiated not necessarily because HFCS was being dumped in the Mexican market, but rather because of the allegations by Mexico that the

United States had not honoured the so called NAFTA side agreement on U.S. sugar imports from Mexico. Consider other commodities. For U.S. garlic imports, the finding of injury is extremely contentious, since cost-of-production data by country are not readily available. The U.S. finding that Canadian exports of spring wheat cause material injury to U.S. farmers but Canadian durum exports do not is far from obvious largely because the Canadian Wheat Board (CWB), a state-trading enterprise, is the sole exporter of both types of wheat.

- An increase in U.S. agricultural imports, coupled with a slowness of U.S. agricultural exports, has led to increased interest about the imposition of border measures to block trade. At the same time, less-developed countries argue that U.S. farm policy is being used as a vehicle to dump export products abroad.

Other issues highlighted by conference presenters include:

- Trade-dispute resolution frequently benefits producers in both countries because of formal and/or informal price agreements. This was certainly the case with the suspension agreement between the United States and Mexico on tomato imports, for which the two countries agreed on a minimum price floor.
- Trade practices of state-trading enterprises are a common and continuing basis of disputes. They are not well understood, nor is the law clear on how to deal with trading accomplished by the use of state-trading enterprises.
- The *Continued Dumping and Subsidy Offset Act* of 2000 allows producers and manufacturers, who successfully petition the United States to impose antidumping tariffs on imports, to keep the proceeds of those tariffs. These windfalls from countervailing tariffs create unusual incentives for those lobby groups who gain from protection.
- There is discontinuity of U.S. agricultural-trade policy relative to U.S. domestic laws. U.S. agricultural-trade policy results in reduced subsidies and increased market access, while U.S. law continues to subsidize agriculture at significant levels, and often operates to limit market access for imports. This ensues in part from the U.S. Constitution, which grants the Executive Branch the power to negotiate treaties while giving Congress sole power to set duties and regulate commerce with foreign nations.
- Differences exist in the dispute-settlement systems of the WTO and the North American Free Trade Agreement (NAFTA). One example is Mexico's imposition of antidumping duties on U.S. imports of HFCS to Mexico. The two trade agreements differ on

how the process is invoked; how a panel is formed; what the panel's jurisdiction is; what standard of review is used; how precedent is treated; what role private counsel plays in the process; what the nature of an appeal of a panel decision is; and how the panel decision will be implemented.

- Antidumping duties in agriculture have merits as a means to deal with trade-distorting structural domestic subsidies and to prevent the long-term dumping of agricultural products at prices below the cost of production.

- Trade remedy laws, considered a major vehicle for protection in U.S. agriculture, generally do not yield the desired results for the United States because countries turn to alternative sources for their imports.

- There are extensive inconsistencies and misconceptions regarding the COOL provisions of the 2002 Farm Bill. COOL also presents the potential for trade retaliation and will have varied impacts on selected regions, consumers, and the food-supply chain. There is also debate on whether or not suppliers or retailers should bear the cost of compliance, which the USDA estimates at U.S. $2 billion in the first year of mandatory labelling that began on October 1, 2004.

Section I:
Economic Considerations

Chapter 1

NAFTA Trade Disputes and U.S. Agriculture

Cathy Jabara and Warren Payne[*]

U.S. International Trade Commission

INTRODUCTION

Trade remedy measures, including antidumping (AD), countervailing duty (CVD), and safeguard actions, are used by the United States, Canada, and Mexico in international trade. These measures provide a means for governments to protect domestic industries from competition due to allegedly "unfair imports" and from import surges. These trade remedies are World Trade Organization (WTO) legal mechanisms, but are contentious due to concerns that they can be used to block trade unfairly. In the United States, trade remedy measures can be applied based on findings of relevant government agencies that a domestic industry is injured, or is facing threat of injury, due to the effects of imports on prices and production. The use of trade remedy actions affects a very small part of U.S. agricultural trade with North American partners. Globalization, and the integration of U.S. agricultural industries with import and export sectors, will further reduce the use of trade remedy actions in the long run. However, Mexico has implemented a number of trade remedy actions in recent years. As tariff and other barriers fall due to trade liberalization, increasing use of trade remedy measures by developing countries may provide significant threats to the expansion of agricultural exports in future years.

This chapter examines some of the economic considerations behind the use of AD and CVD measures in the United States and other North American Free Trade Agreement (NAFTA) countries. It particularly examines the role of the U.S. International Trade Commission (USITC), the independent U.S. agency that determines injury in AD and CVD cases, and some of the economic factors analyzed in these determinations. The role of the U.S. Department of Commerce (USDOC), which determines margins in AD and CVD cases, is also discussed.

TYPES OF TRADE REMEDY ACTIONS

The agreements under the WTO and for U.S. implementing legislation provide for three trade remedy actions:

- antidumping;
- countervailing duty; and
- safeguard actions (Sections 201 to 204 of the *Trade Act of 1974*).

These actions are discussed below.

Antidumping

Antidumping (USITC 2002a) actions can be imposed when two conditions are met: (1) the USDOC determines that foreign goods are sold, or likely to be sold, at less than fair value (LTFV); and (2) the USITC determines that an industry in the United States is injured materially, or threatened with injury, from the sale of the goods. Dumping, or sales at LTFV, typically occurs when a company exports a product at a price lower than the price it normally charges in its own home market. However, a foreign producer selling imports at prices below those of American products is not necessarily considered to be dumping.

The WTO agreement allows governments to act against dumping when there is genuine material injury. The government institutions must show that dumping is taking place, calculate the extent of dumping (the dumping margin), and show that dumping is causing injury. Typically an AD action means charging extra import duties in order to bring the price closer to normal value. The dumping margin is the difference between the price or cost in the home market (the normal value) and the price in the export market.

The WTO agreement stipulates three methods for calculating the normal value:

- a comparison of the export price with the price in the exporter's home market;
- a comparison of the export price with the price charged in a third-country market; or
- a calculation based on the combination of the exporter's production costs, other expenses, and normal profit (constructed value).

For nonmarket economy countries, such as the People's Republic of China (PRC), the normal methodology for calculating normal value is not generally used (USDOC 2003a). Instead, the USDOC constructs a normal value using factors of production such as labour hours, raw materials used, and representative capital costs, including depreciation. The factors of production are then valued in a market-economy country, which has a comparable level of economic development and is a significant producer of the subject products. For example,

India is often used as the comparable country for the PRC. Dumping margins for merchandise from the PRC tend to be relatively high. For example, in a 1994 case, the weighted average dumping margin imposed on fresh garlic from the PRC was 376.67 percent. In 2001, dumping margins on honey from the PRC ranged from 25.88 percent to 183.8 percent, whereas dumping margins for Argentina in the same investigation ranged from 32.56 percent to 60.67 percent (USDOC 2003b).

Countervailing Duties

CV duties can be imposed when: (1) the USDOC determines that the government of a country, or any public entity within a country, provides a countervailable subsidy on the manufacture, production, or export of goods sold into the United States; and (2) the USITC determines that an industry in the United States is injured materially or threatened with injury by reason of these imports. The types of subsidies covered by CVD actions are specified in the WTO Agreement on Subsidies and Countervailing Measures (ASCM) (WTO 2003). Only specific subsidies that apply to a specific enterprise or industry group are usually actionable. The WTO Agreement identifies three types of actionable subsidies. They are:

- subsidies that provide an advantage over rival exporters in a third-country market;
- subsidies that advantage the domestic industry over exporters to that country; or
- subsidies that damage the domestic industry in the importing country.

If the domestic industry suffers material injury as a result of the subsidies, then CVDs can be imposed.

Article 13 of the Peace Clause of the GATT Agreement on Agriculture (WTO 2003) stipulates that countries will not bring CVD cases against another country's agricultural subsidies provided that the subsidy conforms to the Green Box category, and that due restraint will be exercised when initiating CVD actions on other programs notified in a WTO member's schedule (Office of the United States Trade Representative 1994). Due to the Peace Clause, in the United States few CVD actions have been initiated against foreign agricultural programs in recent years. In addition, following the *Uruguay Round Agreements Act* (URAA) of the General Agreement on Tariffs and Trade (GATT), many countries changed their programs to become more generally available so as to fit into the Green Box category and to avoid potential CVD actions (GATT 1994). U.S. CVD actions include the imposition of a 4.53 percent CVD on imports of honey from Argentina[1] in 2001. Further, the 2002 investigation of Canadian durum and hard red spring wheat resulted in a CVD of 5.29 on hard red spring wheat.[2] Also, a case initiated in 1999 by U.S. live-cattle producers against Canada resulted in the USDOC dismissing CVD allegations. The USITC, in a finding of no injury, later dismissed the U.S. live-cattle producers against Canada AD case.

Global Safeguards

Under the WTO Agreement on Safeguards (WTO 2003) a country may apply a global safeguard measure if it is determined that a product is being imported in such increased quantities to cause or threaten to cause serious injury to that industry. Sections 201 to 204 of the *Trade Act* of 1974 allows the United States to take action, including import relief, to facilitate efforts by a domestic industry that has been found to be seriously injured by imports, in order to make a positive adjustment to import competition (*Trade Act* 1974). Such action may include the imposition of higher tariffs or tariff-rate quotas, or other action. The relief provided, if any, is determined by the President of the United States, upon a finding of serious injury by the USITC. Imports from NAFTA countries can be excluded from global safeguard actions, provided the total imports from NAFTA countries do not contribute importantly to the injury found by the USITC, or do not account for a substantial share of imports. As a result, no safeguard actions have been taken under this WTO provision enforced by the United States against NAFTA countries in recent years.

Recent Antidumping and Countervailing Duty Investigations Involving NAFTA Countries

Tables 1.1, 1.2, and 1.3 provide information on recent AD and CVD cases involving NAFTA countries and the United States. For products traded between the United States and Canada, data in the tables indicate a trend toward duties being removed and/or cases being terminated. In recent years, duties have been applied on softwood lumber following the lapse of the Softwood Lumber Agreement in 2002. The only ongoing investigation between these two countries affecting agricultural products is the case on wheat, which is a long-standing issue between the two countries involving the Canadian Wheat Board (CWB) (USITC 2001).

The only trade remedy in force against Mexico by the United States for an agricultural product concerns the suspended 1996 AD investigation on fresh tomatoes. This investigation did not result in the application of duties, which would have ranged from 4.16 to 188.45 percent based on preliminary calculations, but rather it resulted in an agreement under which Mexican producers/exporters agreed to sell into the United States at or above a predetermined price (USDOC 2003c). On the other hand, there have been five cases involving duties placed on U.S. agricultural products to Mexico since 1997. Among the NAFTA countries, the upswing in the use of AD/CVD remedies appears to be in Mexico. Activity in Canada and the United States appears to be declining except where there are long-running trade-dispute issues, such as in wheat and lumber in the United States.

Table 1.1: Antidumping (AD) and Countervailing Duty (CVD) Cases Instituted by Canada against the United States, 1984 to 2001

Product	Initiation	Final Measures	Current Status
Whole potatoes (AD)	1984	Product exported from Washington State to British Columbia	Reviewed in 2000 and continued
Yellow onions (AD)	1986	Import volume of 400,000 per hundred weight (1995)	Reviewed in 1997 and discontinued
Fresh iceberg lettuce (AD)	1992	Imports into British Columbia	Reviewed in 2002 and discontinued
Apples, red and golden delicious (AD)	1994	AD measure revoked: import quota of 83 million pounds	Reviewed in 2000 and rescinded
Refined sugar (AD)	1995	Duty 43.86 percent	Reviewed in 2000 and continued
Baby food (AD)	1997	Duty 59.76 percent or 18.7 percent	Reviewed in 2003 and discontinued
Certain grain corn (AD/CVD)	2000	CITT[a] finds no injury	Case dismissed
Fresh tomatoes (AD)	2001	CITT[a] finds no injury	Case dismissed

[a] Canadian International Trade Tribunal.
Source: Import Administration (2003); USITC (2003).

Table 1.2: Antidumping (AD) and Countervailing Duty (CVD) Cases Instituted by the United States against Agriculture and Food Products from Canada, 1999 to 2002

Product	Initiation	Final Measures	Current Status
Live cattle (AD/CVD)	1999	USITC[a] finding of no injury	Terminated
Mussels (AD)	2001	None	Terminated
Greenhouse tomatoes (AD)	2001	USITC finding of no injury	Terminated
Softwood lumber (AD/CVD)	2001	AD duties: 5.96 percent to 15.83 percent CVDs: 19.34 percent	In force
IQF[b] coldwater pink shrimp (CVD)	2002	None	Terminated
Durum and hard red spring wheat (CVD/AD)	2002	CVD margin of 5.29 percent; AD duty of 8.86 percent (hard red spring wheat only)	In force

[a] U.S. International Trade Commission.
[b] Individually Quick Frozen.
Source: Import Administration (2003); USITC (2003).

Table 1.3: Antidumping (AD) and Countervailing Duty (CVD) Investigations by the United States against Agriculture and Food Products from Mexico, 1996 to 2001

Product	Initiation	Final Measures	Current Status
Fresh tomatoes (AD)	1996	Producer/Exporters in Mexico agreed to sell subject products to U.S. customers at or above a reference price	Suspended
Live cattle (AD)	1999	USITC[a] finding of no injury	Terminated
Spring table grapes (AD)	2001	USITC[a] finding of no injury	Terminated

[a] U.S. International Trade Commission.
Source: Import Administration (2003); USITC (2003).

Economic Analysis in the Determination of Injury in AD/CVD Cases

As noted earlier, the USITC determines whether an industry in the United States is injured materially, or threatened with material injury, by imports that are the subject of an AD/CVD investigation. U.S. antidumping law requires the USITC to look at a number of statutory factors to determine injury (USITC 2002a). Material injury is "harm which is not inconsequential, immaterial, or unimportant." Under the statutes, the USITC is directed to consider:

- the volume of imports of the subject merchandise;
- the effect of imports of that merchandise on prices in the United States for domestic-like products; and
- the impact of imports of such merchandise on domestic producers of domestic-like products in the context of the production operations within the United States.

When evaluating the effect of imports of subject merchandise on prices, the USITC is directed to consider:

- whether there has been significant price underselling of the imported merchandise as compared with the price of domestic-like product in the United States; and
- whether the effect of imports of such merchandise otherwise depresses prices to a significant degree or prevents price increases, which otherwise would have occurred, to a significant degree.

The USITC examines all relevant economic factors to evaluate injury. Such factors include, but are not limited to:

- actual and potential declines in output, sales, market share, profits, productivity, return on investment, and capacity utilization;
- factors affecting domestic prices;

- actual and potential negative effects on cash flow, inventories, employment, wages, growth, ability to raise capital, and investment;
- actual and potential negative effects in the development and production efforts of the domestic industry, including efforts to develop a derivative or more advanced version of the domestic-like product;
- the magnitude of the margin of dumping in AD investigations; and
- the nature of the subsidy in CVD investigations.

The USITC has often included the results of a partial equilibrium supply and demand model to analyze the likely effect of unfair pricing or subsidies on subject imports on the domestic industry. This model, known as the COMPAS model, is based on Armington (1969) specifications of goods differentiated by country of origin. The model requires several exogenous parameters to be determined and requires input that is separate from the model: the elasticity of demand, the elasticity of supply for both domestic and each country in the analysis, and the elasticity of substitution. The model is significantly more sensitive to the elasticity of substitution and the margin of dumping or subsidy than to any other parameter.

The COMPAS model results, as well as the presence or absence of any of the other factors, do not necessarily determine the outcome of an investigation, but rather each factor is considered in its turn. More recently, the COMPAS-model results have not been included in the reports prepared by the USITC staff on each investigation. The absence of the COMPAS results follows a remand to the USITC on an investigation in which a party questioned the use of the COMPAS results by the USITC.[3]

Other Factors Affecting the Use of AD/CV Remedies

Macroeconomic factors can play important roles when encouraging the use of trade remedy measures. For example, uneven tariff treatment across countries and commodities may encourage industries in countries where tariffs are low to institute AD and CVD actions. Often these types of measures are the only recourse industries have in the event of rising or surging imports. For example, in 2001, an AD case on individually quick-frozen red raspberries from Chile was filed by U.S. growers following a decision by the European Union (EU) to exempt Serbia, an important supplier of raspberries, from the EU duty of 20.8 percent. Following this decision, U.S. growers were concerned that a sudden surge of imports from Chile would be diverted to the U.S. market (USITC 2002b). At the time of the investigation, red raspberries were imported into the United States free of duty under the Generalized System of Preferences (GSP) program.

AD/CVD measures are often used to counter surges of imports from new entrants in the market. For example, cases were filed against the PRC for non-frozen concentrated apple juice and fresh garlic as imports rose rapidly in the years prior to the investigations (USITC 1994; USITC 2000). As tariffs are reduced under bilateral free-trade agreements, or in the future under the next WTO round, some have expressed concern that the gains from tariff liberalization could be reduced if countries resort increasingly to AD/CVD measures. One way to avoid this is for trade negotiators to ensure that tariff liberalization is as broadly based across countries and industries as possible, so that import surges will not result from differences in tariff levels among countries.

One factor working against the increased use of AD/CVD measures, at least in the United States, is the globalization of agricultural industries. A petition in an AD/CVD case must be filed on behalf of an industry—those supporting the petition must account for at least 25 percent of the total production of the domestic product (USITC 2002a). As industries become more global, and both exporters and importers become part of the industry mix, it likely will be harder to find enough interested firms to support a petition. The U.S. trends in exports and imports of agricultural products support this view, as it has been shown that imports have been rising steadily into the United States, reaching around U.S. $44 billion in 2002 (Figure 1.1). To the extent that increasing imports result in a higher level of integration among U.S. producers, exporters, and importers, the ability and interest of domestic industries to file these cases may also decline, all other factors held constant.

The expiration of the Peace Clause in 2003[4] may see an upswing in CVD cases filed for agricultural products (WTO 2003). However, for U.S. producers, this upswing may be directed more at the European Union rather than at NAFTA countries, given the large government assistance programs in the European Union.

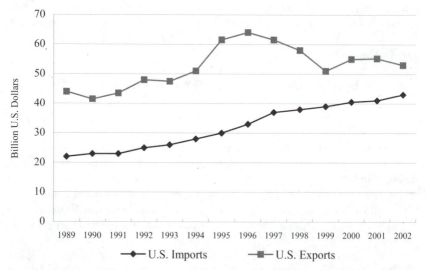

Figure 1.1: Trends in U.S. Exports and Imports of Food and Agriculture Products
Source: USITC (2002a).

CONCLUSIONS

Use of trade remedy measures by U.S. domestic industries constitutes a very small share of U.S. agricultural trade, although these types of trade disputes tend to be visible in the press and trade journals. Among NAFTA countries, aside from long-standing areas of trade dispute such as wheat and lumber, these cases are declining in use between Canada and the United States. Since Canada and the United States are established trading partners, it would be expected that trade disputes between these countries will decline as their respective agricultural industries become globalized and more integrated with each other. However, the use of AD/CVD measures in Mexico, particularly against U.S. products, appears to be on the increase. There is some concern among U.S. industries that Mexico's use of these measures will block the benefits from NAFTA. As these measures are likely on the decline for agricultural products in the United States and Canada, more attention should be focused on the effect of trade remedy measures on U.S. exports.

NOTES

*Supervisory International Trade Analyst and International Trade Analyst, respectively, U.S. International Trade Commission (USITC). The views expressed in this chapter are those of the authors and do not represent those of the USITC or the USITC Commissioners

[1] 66*FR*63672 (December 10, 2001). Programs cited by the U.S. Department of Commerce (USDOC) as countervailable included finance programs for export and purchase of goods by honey producers, and various provincial programs specific to honey.

[2] 68*FR*60641 (October 23, 2003). Canadian programs cited by the USDOC as countervailable include the provision of government-owned and leased railcars and the Government of Canada's guarantee for borrowing by the Canadian Wheat Board.

[3] Since the middle of 2002, the COMPAS-model results have not been included in the staff reports (Armington 1969). In 2002 in a remand to the U.S. International Trade Commission on Certain Circular Seamless Stainless Hollow Products from Japan (Inv. No. 731-TA-859) (USITC 2002c), the domestic industry challenged the rejection by the USITC of the COMPAS results. The USITC voted in the negative on this case, whereas the COMPAS results showed a larger effect on the domestic industry.

[4] Article 13 ("due restraint") of the World Trade Organization (WTO) protects countries using subsidies that comply with the Agreement from being challenged under other WTO agreements. Without this "peace clause," countries would have greater freedom to take action against the subsidies of each other, under the Subsidies and Countervailing Measures Agreement and related provisions (WTO 2003).

REFERENCES

Armington, P.S. (1969). "A Theory of Demand for Products Distinguished by Place of Production." *IMF Staff Papers* 16(1): 159–78.

FR (The Federal Register). (2001). 66*FR*63672, U.S. Department of Commerce, National Archives and Records Administration. Washington, DC: Office of the Federal Register (December 10). Available at: www.access.gpo.gov/su_docs.

_____. (2003). 68*FR*60641, U.S. Department of Commerce, National Archives and Records Administration. Washington, DC: Office of the Federal Register (October 23). Available at: www.access.gpo.gov/su_docs.

GATT (General Agreement on Tariffs and Trade). (1994). The Uruguay Round Agreement. Available at:
http://www.wto.org/english/docs_e/legal_e/legal_e.htm.

Import Administration. (2003). Washington, DC: USDOC. Available at:
http://ia.ita.doc.gov/.

Office of the U.S. Trade Representative. (1994). *Uruguay Round of Multilateral Trade Negotiations General Agreement on Tariffs and Trade.* Washington, DC: Government Printing Office.

Trade Act. (1974). Available at:
http://www.access.gpo.gov/uscode/title19/chapter12_.html.

USDOC (U.S. Department of Commerce, International Trade Administration). (2003a). "Glossary of Terms for Market and Non-Market Economy Cases." Washington, DC: USDOC. Available at: http://ia.ita.doc.gov/glossary.htm.

_____. (2003b). "Fact Sheet: Final Determination of the Antidumping Duty Investigations of Honey from Argentina and the People's Republic of China." Washington, DC: USDOC. Available at: http://www.ita.doc.gov/media/FactSheet/HoneyFin.htm.

_____. (2003c). "New Suspension Agreement of Fresh Tomatoes from Mexico." Washington, DC: USDOC.
Available at: http://www.ia.ita.doc.gov/tomato/new-agreement/new-agreement.html.

USITC (U.S. International Trade Commission). (1994). *Fresh Garlic from China,* Inv. No. 731-TA-683 (Final), USITC Publication 2825. Washington, DC: USITC (November).

_____. (2000). Certain *Non-Frozen Concentrated Apple Juice,* Inv. No. 731-TA- 841 Final, USITC Publication 3303. Washington, DC: USITC (May).

_____. (2001). *Wheat Trading Practice,* Inv. No. 332-429, Publication 3465. Washington, DC: USITC (December).

_____. (2002a). *Antidumping and Countervailing Duty Handbook.* Washington, DC: USITC. Available at: http://www.usitc.gov/wais/reports/arc/w3566.htm.

_____. (2002b). *Individually Quick Frozen Red Raspberries from Chile,* Inv. No. 731-TA-948 (Final), USITC Publication 3524. Washington, DC: USITC (June).

_____. (2002c). *Circular Seamless Stainless Steel Hollow Products From Japan,* Inv. No. 731-TA-859 (Second Remand), USITC Publication 3537. Washington, DC: USITC (August).

_____. (2003). Washington, DC: USITC. Available at: http://itc.central.usitc.gov.88.

WTO (World Trade Organization). (2003). Available at:
http://www.wto.org/english/tratop_e/scm_e/scm_e.htm.

Chapter 2

Trade Remedy Laws and NAFTA's Chapter 12 Agricultural Trade Rulings

Colin A. Carter and Caroline Gunning-Trant

University of California-Davis

INTRODUCTION

In 2001, the World Trade Organization (WTO) initiated a new round of global trade talks with a ministerial conference in Doha, Qatar. At the conference, a Ministerial Declaration was signed on November 14, 2001 establishing the negotiating agenda on agriculture, trade remedy laws, and other issues. Around the world, the meetings were viewed as successful, especially from the perspective of developing countries. One reason for the positive response by developing nations was the agreement by the United States to include trade remedy laws on the WTO within the negotiating agenda. Even though these laws may be in compliance with the WTO, the developing nations view trade remedy laws as hidden protection for the developed world.

In the United States, Congress was not pleased with the outcome of the Doha conference. Just prior to the Doha meetings, the U.S. House of Representatives voted 410 to 4 on a resolution instructing the U.S. Trade Representative, Robert Zoellick, to keep U.S. trade remedy laws from being included in the Ministerial Declaration. Mr. Zoellick did not comply. Clearly, trade remedy laws will be a contentious issue in a new round of trade negotiations.

The trade remedy laws applied by the United States that are at the centre of the controversy are antidumping (AD) and countervailing (CV) duty laws, and include to some extent, import relief (safeguard) laws. The purpose of this chapter is to analyze the use of AD and CV duty trade remedy laws with respect to agriculture in North America. Their use and historical application in agriculture are studied with the intent of clarifying why these laws are so controversial.

The goal of this chapter is to measure the degree of trade diversion and the investigation effect associated with AD and CV duty agricultural cases initiated by the United States.[1] Using U.S. trade data from 1980 to 2000, the existence of trade diversion is demonstrated through both quantitative and econometric analyses. Specific examples of AD duty cases are discussed in order to highlight the degree to which trade diversion offsets the protectionist objectives of trade remedy law.

U.S. TRADE REMEDY LAWS

We present U.S. trade remedy laws and their principal features (Table 2.1). The stated purpose of trade remedy laws is to offset unfair trade that injures domestic producers as a result of either foreign sales that are dumped into the United States at less than fair value (LTFV)[2] or sales that are influenced by foreign government subsidies.[3] Import relief laws, commonly known as safeguards, are intended to provide a period of relief and adjustment for an industry that is being injured seriously by increased competition from imports.

The AD duty statute comes under Section 731 of the *Tariff Act* of 1930, as amended. A related statute is Section 701, which applies to subsidized exports from foreign suppliers. Under Section 701, if a foreign subsidy is found to injure U.S. producers, then a CV duty is applied. In addition, Section 201 of the U.S. *Tariff Act* of 1930 provides for temporary restrictions on imports, such as high tariffs or import quotas that are deemed to be causing injury to a domestic industry (Table 2.1).

The trade remedy laws are collectively known as administered protection. The U.S. Department of Commerce (USDOC) and the U.S. International Trade Commission (USITC) jointly administer AD and CV duty law (Sections 731 and 701). The USDOC first determines whether a commodity is being dumped or subsidized and then the USITC decides whether or not a U.S. industry has been injured as a result of the trade action. The USDOC procedure is much less transparent than the USITC procedure, and normally the USDOC rules in favour of the U.S. industry. Section 201, the safeguard law, is administered jointly by the USITC and by the U.S. President in that the USITC determines whether injury has resulted to the domestic industry and then issues a recommendation to the U.S. President for no relief or for a specific method of relief. The U.S. President then decides whether to heed the recommendation of the USITC, choose an alternative method of relief, or have no method for relief.

Many other countries such as Canada and Mexico have trade remedy laws that are very similar to those in the United States, including AD, CV duty, and safeguard provisions. Traditionally, the United States, the European Union (EU), Australia, and Canada have filed the most AD and CV duty cases against foreign suppliers. More recently, developing countries such as Mexico, Brazil, Argentina, India, Turkey, and South Africa have also filed a number of cases. In fact, in the past few years, developing countries have filed about 50 percent of the total number of AD cases worldwide (Stevenson 2002).

There is an upward trend globally in the filing of trade remedy cases. According to economic literature, the ever-increasing number of trade disputes

Table 2.1: Selected U.S. Trade Remedy Laws

Trade Remedy Law	Statute	USDOC[a] Rules	USITC[b] Rules	Purpose	Remedy
Countervailing duty (CV duty)	Title VII of the *Tariff Act* of 1930, as amended (Section 701)	Countervailable subsidy, direct or indirect, is being provided	Material injury; threat of material injury; or the establishment of an industry is materially retarded by reason of imports or by reason of sales (or likelihood of sales) of that merchandise	To offset any unfair competitive advantage that foreign producers or exporters might have over U.S. producers as a result of subsidization	CV duty equal to the net amount of the countervailable subsidies is imposed upon importation of the subsidized goods into the United States
Antidumping duty (AD duty)	Title VII of the *Tariff Act* of 1930, as amended (Section 731)	Foreign product is being sold (or likely to be sold) at less than fair value	Material injury; threat of material injury; or the establishment of an industry is materially retarded by reason of imports of that merchandise	To offset any unfair competitive advantage that foreign producers or exporters might have over U.S. producers as a result of sales at less than fair value	AD duty equal to the amount by which the price in the foreign market exceeds the U.S. price (i.e., dumping margin) is imposed in addition to any other duty
Import Relief (Safeguard)	Chapter 1 of Title II of the *Trade Act* of 1974, as amended (Sections 201–204)	Not applicable	Serious injury or threat of serious injury substantially caused by reason of imports	To provide a period of relief and adjustment for an industry that is being injured seriously by increased competition from imports (not necessarily unfairly traded imports)	U.S. President has the authority to take action, including the administration of import relief (e.g., imposed tariffs or tariff-rate quotas), to assist a domestic industry that has been seriously injured by imports

[a]U.S. Department of Commerce.
[b]U.S. International Trade Commission.
Source: U.S. House of Representatives (2001).

is due to the liberalization of traditional trade barriers, unsatisfactory safeguard provisions, increasingly weak AD standards, and retaliation. However, many economists generally view AD and CV duty laws as little more than disguised protectionism used to shield domestic industries from foreign competition (Stiglitz 1997).

USE OF TRADE REMEDY LAWS
IN NAFTA AGRICULTURE

The main reason that developing countries have criticized the use of AD and CV duty laws is their frustration with the protectionist use of these laws by developed countries. There is also a perception that these laws have been amended over time to make it easier for domestic industries to receive protection.

The use of trade remedy laws often conflicts with free trade agreements. For example, in 2002 Brazil refused to fully engage itself in discussions on the Free Trade Area of the Americas (FTAA) because of the continued application of AD duties by the United States on Brazilian products such as orange juice. In 2001, the filing of AD cases on Chile's exports of quick frozen red raspberries and spring table grapes to the United States was disruptive to the Chilean industries. It was no surprise that the U.S. grape and raspberry industries filed their cases while the negotiations for the FTAA with Chile were in full swing. More recently, U.S. honey producers received AD protection from competition from Argentina and the People's Republic of China (PRC) as well as CV duty protection from Argentina, which came at an inopportune time for Argentine producers in light of the economic crisis in that country at the time.

During the January 1984 to June 2001 period, 761 AD and CV duty cases were filed in the United States (Young, Wainio, and Meilke 2003), of which approximately 71 (9.3 percent)[4] were agricultural cases. This means that agriculture had a disproportionate share of cases, because agriculture's share of the value of U.S. total imports for that time period was only about 4 percent.[5] U.S. import relief law was used less often; only 30 such total cases were filed from 1980 to 2000, and U.S. agriculture filed 8 of these 30 cases.

During the 1984 to 2001 period, Canada filed 22 agricultural AD and CV duty cases (6.6. percent) out of a total of 334 cases (Young, Wainio, and Meilke 2003), and Mexico filed 23 agricultural AD and CV duty cases (10.5 percent) out of a total of 219 cases (Leycegui and Cornejo 2004). Thus all three North American Free Trade Agreement (NAFTA) countries are extensive users of trade remedy laws in agricultural trade.

The outcomes of American and Canadian agricultural AD and CV duty cases since 1980 are reported in Tables 2.2 and 2.3,[6] with a more detailed break-down available in the Appendix of this chapter. It is clear from the summary statistics in Tables 2.2 and Table 2.3 that AD cases are more popular than are CV duty cases. In the United States, 61 percent of the agricultural cases were AD cases, and in Canada 73 percent were AD cases. Stevenson (2002) offers an

Table 2.2: Outcome of U.S. Agricultural Antidumping (AD) and Countervailing Duty (CV duty) Cases, Filed 1980 to 2000

	AD	CV duty	Total
Affirmative	23	12	35
Negative	9	8	17
Suspended or Terminated	8	5	13
Total agricultural AD and CV duty cases filed	40	25	65

Source: Blonigen (2003) and USITC (2001).

Table 2.3: Outcome of Canadian Agricultural Antidumping (AD) and Countervailing Duty (CV duty) Cases, Filed 1980 to 2000

	AD	CV duty	Total
Affirmative	19	8	27
Negative	5	1	6
Suspended or Terminated	0	0	0
Total agricultural AD and CV duty cases filed	24	9	33

Source: Compiled from CCRA (2002).

explanation as to why AD cases are typically more popular that are CV duty cases. He argues that CV duty cases are more politically sensitive than are AD cases because a foreign government is being investigated in an CV case, while in an AD case only the foreign firm is under investigation. In addition, Stevenson (2002) notes that the methodologies for CV duty calculations are less established than for AD calculations, therefore CV duty cases may be more difficult to win.

We report that 35 of the 65 total U.S. agricultural cases, and 27 of the 33 Canadian cases resulted in an affirmative ruling in favour of the domestic industry (Tables 2.2 and 2.3). Consequently, the success rate of Canadian agricultural cases was 82 percent during the 1980 to 2000 period, compared to the success rate of the United States at 54 percent for the same period. This difference is significant. One likely explanation for the higher success rate in Canada is that the Canada Customs and Revenue Agency, Customs and Excise (CCRA) is better at stopping non-starter cases than is the USDOC of the United States.

The previous economic literature finds that the initial filing of an AD or CV duty case often disrupts trade, regardless of the final legal determination. Research has determined that imports fall about 20 percent even if no tariff is imposed (Prusa 1992; Staiger et al. 1994). This result is interesting, but in previous research the investigation effect was not measured separately for agricultural trade.

AD and CV duty laws are targeted at specific countries. However, non-named third countries may benefit from the use of AD and CV duty law through a phenomenon known as trade diversion. Trade diversion occurs when a trade remedy action diverts trade away from a more efficient supplier targeted by the AD or CV duty action toward a less efficient supplier that is not named in the trade action. Prusa (1997) studies all AD actions in the United States between 1980 and 1988 and finds that trade diversions are significant by-products of AD cases. He arrives at the surprising result that, due to trade diversion, both Canada and Mexico gained (on net) from AD duties of the United States from 1980 to 1988. Prusa (1997) estimates that both Canada and Mexico enjoyed a net gain of more than U.S. $21 billion as a result of AD and CV duties being levied by the United States on other countries. What we try to answer in this chapter is whether or not this finding also applies to agricultural trade within NAFTA.

To begin to understand the impact of U.S. cases on both targeted and non-targeted countries, the statistics in Table 2.4 provide a summary based on the 65 U.S. agricultural AD and CV duty cases filed from 1980 to 2000 (Blonigen 2003; USITC 2003). The column in Table 2.4 labelled t_0 represents the year that any particular investigation was filed. The other columns labelled $t-1$, $t+1$, and so on, represent years immediately before and after the filing year. For each year that a case was initiated, a weighted-average change in the annual value of imports of the named commodity is calculated. The weights are the target commodity's share of the value of U.S. imports of all targeted agricultural commodities with the same (affirmative or negative) ruling in that year. To arrive at a single percentage change in the value of imports, a simple average of the percentage changes for each ruling year is calculated (Table 2.4). For instance, in 1994 the United States initiated two AD cases that resulted in affirmative rulings: one against imports of kiwi fruit from New Zealand and the other against fresh garlic from the PRC. In the case of kiwi fruit, the value of kiwi-fruit imports relative to the sum of the value of kiwi-fruit and garlic imports is used to weight kiwi imports in 1994.

Table 2.4: Weighted Average Percent Change in Value of Imports from Named Versus Non-Named Countries: U.S. Affirmative and Negative Agricultural Antidumping and Countervailing Duty Cases, Filed 1980 to 2000

	$t-2$	$t-1$	t_0	$t+1$	$t+2$
	Weighted Average Percent Change				
Affirmative:					
Named Countries	26.06	26.30	−0.36	8.16	16.46
Non-Named Countries	0.95	15.93	7.76	21.92	8.39
Overall Imports	13.72	24.66	−0.84	6.94	18.45
Negative:					
Named Countries	15.13	20.33	10.21	4.25	3.16
Non-Named Countries	8.68	−0.53	−1.43	18.45	7.95
Overall Imports	9.10	3.80	3.56	10.53	5.22

Source: Import data for U.S. imports post-1989 are estimated from USDA/FAS (2003); Import data for U.S. imports prior to 1989 are estimated from U.S. Census Bureau, Foreign Trade Division (2003).

The statistics in Table 2.4 indicate that for those 35 cases with an affirmative outcome (i.e., in favour of the U.S. domestic industry), the value of targeted imports decreased 0.36 percent in value on average during the year the investigation was initiated t_0 and increased 8.16 percent the following year $t+1$. We also found that targeted imports grew at about 26 percent each year in the two years prior to the launch of the investigation. This rapid rate of growth of imports clearly precipitated the investigation. The value of imports in years $t-1$, t_0, and $t+1$ for non-targeted countries in affirmative cases increased by 15.9 percent, 7.76 percent, and 21.92 percent, respectively. These findings are consistent with the phenomenon of trade diversion.

When the outcome of the cases was negative, growth in the value of targeted imports slowed to 10.21 percent in year t_0 from years $t-2$ and $t-1$. The import slowdown persisted through year $t+1$ and $t+2$. This suggests that trade flows were disrupted even when the ruling was negative. Even when the final ruling was negative, imports from non-named countries decreased by 1.43 percent during the year of investigation. However in years $t+1$ and $t+2$, imports from the non-named countries grew more quickly than they did from the targeted countries. The switch in the source of highest import growth at year t_0 is consistent with the view that there may be an investigation effect even when the ruling is negative.

The results from Table 2.4 are summarized anew in Figures 2.1 and 2.2. Figures 2.1 and 2.2 clearly demonstrate that trade cases with affirmative rulings were initiated after a period of high import growth[7] by both the targeted country as well as by the non-targeted countries. Import growth by countries not named in the investigation increased by 16 percent in the period prior to the case, indicating the existence of significant opportunity in a growing market.

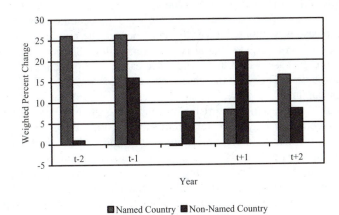

■Named Country ■Non-Named Country

Figure 2.1: Summary of Weighted Percentage Change in U.S. Imports for Antidumping and Countervailing Duty Cases with Affirmative Rulings, 1980 to 2000
Source: U.S. import data post-1989 are estimated from the USDA/FAS (2003); U.S. import data prior to 1989 estimated from the U.S. Census Bureau, Foreign Trade Statistics (2003).

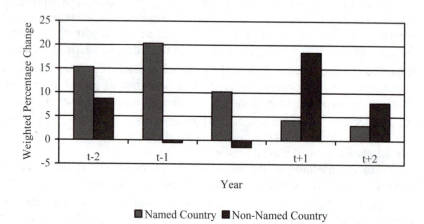

Figure 2.2: Summary of Weighted Percentage Change in U.S. Imports for Antidumping and Countervailing Duty Cases with Negative Rulings, 1980 to 2000
*Source: U.S. import data post-1989 estimated from USDA/FAS (2003) and U.S. imports
prior to 1989 estimated from U.S. Census Bureau, Foreign Trade Statistics (2003).*

The year the case was initiated t_0, import growth by the targeted country (or
countries) was –0.36 percent, while the rest of the world took advantage of the
gap in the market left by the targeted country and continued to export to the
United States at 7.7 percent growth[8] in year t_0 and 22 percent growth in year
$t-1$.

For cases in which the rulings were negative, there was distinct growth in
imports during the period prior to the case being launched (Figure 2.2). The
average annual growth in import value from targeted countries increased 15
percent two years prior to the case and a further 20 percent the year immediately
before the case was initiated. Over the same period, the rate of growth of U.S.
imports from non-targeted countries was lower, with an 8.7 percent growth two
years before the case was initiated and a decrease of 0.5 percent the year before
the investigation. The year the case was launched, imports from the named
countries continued to increase, but at a reduced growth rate of 10 percent.
Perhaps this trend is not surprising given the negative rulings that ensued;
exporting countries may have felt confident that they were not engaging in
unfair trade practices and therefore continued selling to the United States. What
is interesting to note from Figure 2.2 is the significant jump in exports by the
rest of the world in the year following the case, while the value of import growth
by the named countries declined to 4.25 percent. The negative ruling clearly sent
a signal to the rest of the world that prompted a surge in imports from the
non-targeted commodities. The switch in high-growth countries was evident
(Figure 2.2). To the left of t_0, the vertical bars representing targeted countries
were more full than were those representing non-targeted countries. To the right
of t_0, the reverse is true. This finding is consistent with an investigation effect.

ESTIMATION RESULTS FOR AFFIRMATIVE U.S. CASES

We used a modified version of Prusa's (1997) econometric model to estimate the effect on U.S. imports from countries named and from countries not named in agricultural cases subject to affirmative rulings.[9] The effect on overall U.S. imports was also estimated. The model is specified as

$$\ln x_{i,t_j} = \alpha + \beta_0 \ln x_{i,t_{-1}} + \beta_1 \ln(x_{t_{-1}} / x_{i,t_{-2}}) + \beta_2 \ln Duty_i + \beta_3 t_j, j = 0,...,3. \quad (1)$$

The dependent variable x_{i,t_j} denotes the value of imports for case i at time t_j. Recall that t_0 is the year the case was initiated and t_1, t_2, and t_3 represent each of the three years following t_0. Variable t_j is a time-effect dummy variable for each year j. (For consistency with the rest of this chapter, from this point forward we will refer to these time-effect dummies as $t+1$, $t+2$, and $t+3$.) The variable $Duty_i$ denotes the size of the duty in percent. This model was es-timated for the United States, using 1980 to 2000 data for 27 of the 29 affirma-tive cases.[10] The regression results are summarized in Table 2.5.

Imports by the United States from the named country are strongly and positively affected by the value of imports in the year prior to the case being initiated. The estimated duty effect is negative and significant for named countries, indicating a decline in imports as the size of the duty increases. Specifically, given the log-log specification, the estimated parameter on $Duty_i$ may be interpreted as the elasticity. Thus as the duty increases by 10 percent, named imports fall by an estimated 5.6 percent. Given the large range of duty rates, we used an alternative specification that included dummies for the upper and lower quartile of the range of duties.[11] The results indicate that higher duties have a larger but negative effect on imports relative to moderate duties. That is, each 10 percent increase in duties above 60 percent results in a 20 percent decline in the value of named imports. The effect of low duties on imports, however, is not statistically significant. Prusa (1997: 207) maintains that the limited effect of low import duties on imports is "consistent with ... beneficial coordination" between the country initiating the case and the implicated country. As one would expect, the time-effect dummies are large and negative relative to the year the case was initiated indicating a constant decline in the value of imports each year following the initiation of the case.

Using an estimate of the dependent variable taken at the mean of the exogenous variables in the first specification allows us to deduce that U.S. imports from named countries fell from U.S. $40.9 million in year t_0 to that of U.S. $26.7 million in year $t+1$—a decline of 35 percent.[12] In year $t+2$, imports fell an additional U.S. $3.7 million followed by another U.S. $858,000 in year

Table 2.5: The Effect of Affirmative Antidumping and Countervailing Duty Rulings on U.S. Imports

Parameter	Named Countries		Non-Named Countries		Overall Imports	
Constant	2.61 (3.76)*[a]	1.36 (2.17)**	1.37 (2.99)*	1.20 (2.79)*	−1.355 (−1.852)***	−1.82 (−2.99)*
Ln (value in $t-1$)	0.90 (15.16)*	0.92 (16.25)*	0.90 (25.68)*	0.91 (25.04)*	1.14 (21.48)*	1.15 (23.91)*
% chg in value of $t-1$ & $t-2$	−0.26 (−1.01)	−0.259 (-1.11)	0.49 (2.37)*	0.44 (2.09)**	0.24 (2.07)**	0.31 (2.55)*
Size of Duty						
Ln (Duty)	−0.56 (−6.23)*		−0.01 (−0.37)		−0.08 (−2.25)**	
Hi Duty (>60%)[b]		−2.05 (−6.43)*		0.16 (1.15)		−0.25 (−2.02)**
Low Duty (<4.5%)[b]		0.40 (1.46)		0.19 (1.28)		0.05 (0.45)
Years Following the Antidumping Petition (dummies)						
$t+1$	−0.43 (−1.25)	−0.442 (−1.37)	0.16 (1.00)	0.16 (1.01)	−0.02 (−0.15)	−0.02 (−0.15)
$t+2$	−0.57 (−1.69)***	−0.59· (−1.83)***	0.31 (1.91)***	0.31 (1.94)***	0.14 (1.24)	0.14 (1.23)
$t+3$	−0.61 (−1.78)***	−0.58 (−1.78)***	0.32 (1.95)***	0.31 (1.94)***	−0.02 (−0.16)	−0.01 (−0.08)
Adj. R^2	0.77	0.78	0.96	0.96	0.97	0.97
No. of obs.[c]	92	92	51	51	55[b]	55

[a] t-statistics are reported in parentheses below the parameter estimates. *, **, and *** indicate significance at the 1-percent, 5-percent, and 10-percent levels, respectively.
[b] Hi and Low Duty dummies are decided by the upper and lower quartile of the range of duties.
[c] The number of observations in the "Overall Imports" regression is greater than in the "Non-named Countries" regression because there are fewer missing observations arising on account of ln 0 entries.
Source: Authors' Compilations.

$t+3$. Thus from year t_0 to year $t+3$, imports declined by an estimated value of U.S. $9.5 million (−46 percent). It is interesting to note the lasting negative effect of the AD case on imports from the named country extended well into the third year following the initiation of the case.

The value of U.S. imports from non-named countries in the trade dispute is not affected by the size of the duty.[13] However, the positive estimates on the time-effect dummies indicate that U.S. imports from non-named countries in periods $t+2$ and $t+3$ are increasing. Such results are indicative of trade diversion. While imports from the named countries are falling in response to an AD or CV duty case, non-named countries are increasing their exports to the United States. Specifically, there is an estimated increase of 17 percent (i.e., from U.S. $64.3 million to U.S. $75.6 million) between t_0 and $t+1$. Imports from non-named countries increase a further U.S. $11.8 million in $t+2$ and an additional U.S. $1.1 million in $t+3$. Overall, between the time the case is initiated t_0 and year $t+3$, U.S. imports from countries not named in an AD or CV duty case increase by U.S. $24.2 million (+38 percent) versus a decline of U.S. $9.5 million (–46 percent) from the named countries. Thus the values of imports from non-named countries more than offset the decline of imports from named countries, which is a result consistent with the findings of Prusa (1997: 207). Furthermore, the effect of a duty on imports from non-named countries is statistically insignificant. This indicates that non-named countries are responding to the investigation alone rather than they are responding to the imposition of a duty.

In models for both named and non-named imports, it is interesting to note that while the time-effect variable in year $t+1$ has the same sign as years $t+2$ and $t+3$, it is statistically insignificant. This is not a surprising result, given that cases initiated in the early months of year t_0 are often not resolved until year $t+1$, and by the latter half of year $t+1$ imports may have begun to respond to the ruling. In contrast, cases initiated at the end of year t_0 continue to be investigated in year $t+1$ and their exports to the United States continue to decline. Thus, when the value of imports is regressed on imports in year $t+1$, the exact timing of the initiation of these investigations within year t_0 results in no clear trend for dummy variable $t+1$ relative to year t_0. By year $t+2$, however, all cases are resolved and the effect on U.S. imports is consistently lower that in period t_0 for named countries and is consistently higher for non-named countries.

SELECTED EXAMPLES

As explained above, there are two interesting results in the economic literature. First, the mere initiation of an unfair trade investigation has an unsettling effect on targeted country exports, which Prusa (1992) and Staiger et al. (1994) refer to as an investigation effect. Second, trade remedy protection involves substantial trade diversion, so domestic producers are not the only ones who gain (Prusa 1997). Our analysis above suggests that these effects also characterize U.S. agricultural trade cases. However, our findings are still somewhat preliminary, therefore in this section we supplement the results with a discussion of selected cases.

In October 2001, the U.S. government made a preliminary AD ruling that Canadian growers were dumping greenhouse tomatoes into the United States at prices below the Canadian cost of production. As a result of this finding, Canadian tomato sales into the United States were assessed an average tariff of 32 percent. A few weeks later, the legal tables turned as the Canadian government initiated an AD investigation against the U.S. fresh-tomato industry (Barichello 2003). The Canadian counterclaim may not have been a coincidence. It could have been a counter reaction to the steep U.S. duties that were imposed on Canadian greenhouse tomato sales to the United States. By July 2002, both cases were resolved with the identical ruling of no material injury.[14] The impact on imports of greenhouse tomatoes as a result of the investigation differed for the two countries. While U.S. exports of fresh tomatoes to Canada declined 10 percent over the previous year during the period of investigation, Canadian exports of greenhouse tomatoes to the United States actually continued to increase 17 percent over the previous year.[15] Such contrasting effects appear to demonstrate that there was a weak investigation effect associated with the tomato cases.

Three specific recent examples of trade diversion arose as a result of AD cases in the United States that included cases against exports of frozen concentrated apple juice from the PRC in 1999;[16] against exports of preserved mushrooms from Chile, the PRC, India, and Indonesia in 1998;[17] and against exports of garlic from the PRC in 1994 (USITC 2003).[18]

The annual value of U.S. imports of non-frozen concentrated apple juice from the PRC jumped by 212 percent[19] in 1997 from U.S. $8.1 million to that of U.S. $25.4 million (USDA/FAS 2003), with continued but more moderate growth in 1998. This large increase in imports from the PRC displaced imports from Argentina, Chile, and Germany that had been historically the three largest exporters of the product to the U.S. market. Not surprisingly, the large increase in the value of imports from the PRC triggered the U.S. trade action initiated in 1999, causing imports from the PRC to decrease 20 percent in that year. Argentina, Chile, and Germany seized the opportunity provided by the non-frozen concentrated apple juice AD case and increased the combined value of their exports to the United States by 36 percent in the same year. It should be noted that the total value of U.S. imports of non-frozen concentrated apple juice from all countries never declined over the period of investigation but instead increased 12 percent the year the case was initiated and increased a further 24 percent the following year. This result is consistent with Prusa (1997: 207) who determined that "import diversion mitigates most, if not all, of the effect of antidumping actions on the value of imports."

A similar pattern of trade developed for the AD case in which the United States targeted imports of preserved mushrooms from Chile, the PRC, India, and Indonesia in 1998. Between 1993 and 1995, the total value of imports from these four countries increased by 130 percent. Despite a decrease in import value of 24 percent in 1996 and a further 0.6 percent decrease in 1997 from the countries, the value of total imports was still significantly higher (22 percent) than its average through the earlier part of the decade. This prompted the United States to take action against the four countries in 1998, and caused the combined value of imports to decrease nearly 19 percent in that year. This decline provided an opening in the U.S. market that was seized by two other large exporters of preserved mushrooms; Taiwan and Mexico increased their sales of preserved mushrooms to the United States by 44 percent in 1998. Two smaller exporters, the Netherlands and Canada, also increased the value of their exports of preserved mushrooms about 195 percent in the same year. In 1999, imports from the four countries that were targeted continued to decrease by 23 percent while total imports from Taiwan, Mexico, the Netherlands, and Canada increased by 66 percent. Total U.S. imports of preserved mushrooms from all countries actually decreased the year the AD case was initiated, however the following year they increased slightly by 2.4 percent, and further increased 23 percent in 2000. This result supports Prusa's (1997) finding that AD cases do little to curb imports of a given commodity due to trade diversion.

Garlic is another example of a case that gave rise to trade diversion. It was an AD case against Chinese imports of fresh garlic initiated in January 1994, which was resolved the following November. In 1992, two years before the case, 60 percent of U.S. fresh garlic imports came from Mexico, with Argentina and the PRC making up an additional 26 percent. At that time the PRC was already displacing about 40 percent of Argentina's exports to the United States. In 1993, the value of U.S. imports from the PRC increased by 453 percent, overtaking Mexico and suddenly making the PRC the number one garlic supplier to the United States. When the case was initiated in 1994, the value of U.S. imports of garlic from the PRC decreased from U.S. $11.9 million to U.S. $4.1 million—a drop of 65.5 percent. Mexico's imports took a 6 percent drop as well, while Argentina finally regained some ground, and increased the value of its exports to the United States by 33 percent—from U.S. $2.4 million to U.S. $3.2 million. The PRC never regained its market share after the garlic AD case. Thus the value of garlic exports from the PRC to the United States fell to U.S. $250,000 in 1995 while Mexico's exports nearly doubled in value to U.S. $20 million and Argentina's exports increased by an additional 19 percent to U.S. $3.9 million during that same time period.

As an example of a safeguard action, the United States brought a wheat-gluten case against Australia and the European Union in 1997. In June 1998, a safeguard measure was imposed in the form of an import quota that was maintained for three years. Canada and Mexico, among other countries, were excluded from the quota. Only the Canadian exclusion was relevant since none of the other countries were actually exporting wheat gluten to the United States. According to the USITC, the reason given for Canada's exclusion was that Canadian exports of wheat gluten to the United States were stable or decreasing over the period under consideration (i.e., 1993 to 1997), and therefore did not cause injury to the U.S. wheat-gluten industry. In contrast, over the same period, EU exports of wheat gluten to the United States increased by 38 percent.

Table 2.6 shows the value of wheat-gluten imports from the European Union and Canada to the United States from 1998 (the year the quota was imposed)

Table 2.6: U.S. Imports of Wheat Gluten from the European Union, Australia, and Canada

Year	European Union	Australia	Canada	Rest of the World	Total
	U.S. Dollars				
1997	$32,330 (–19%)	$22,302 (–38%)	$8,683 (–19%)	$ 2,693 (–78%)	$66,008 (-27%)
1998	$50,796 (+57%)	$31,423 (41%)	$10,811 (25%)	$ 4,884 (+81%)	$97,914 (+48%)
1999	$24,403 (–54%)	$37,476 (19%)	$19,192 (78%)	$11,073 (+127%)	$92,144 (-6%)
2000	$21,229 (–9%)	$37,133 (–1%)	$18,030 (–6%)	$17,511 (+58%)	$93,903 (+2%)
2001	$31,941 (+50%)	$24,123 (–35%)	$16,752 (–7%)	$ 6,833 (–61%)	$79,649 (-15%)

Source: USDA/FAS (2003).

until 2001. The percentage change from the previous year is reported in brackets underneath the dollar value. In 1998, when the export quota against Australia and the European Union was instituted, Canadian exports increased by 25 percent. The following year they increased a further 78 percent, which is a distinct sign of trade diversion. Trade diversion was also apparent in the increased volume of U.S. wheat gluten imports by the rest of the world. Over the same two-year period, wheat gluten imports from the rest of the world increased by 81 percent and 127 percent, respectively. The bulk of that increase was lead by Poland, the PRC, and Czechoslovakia.

NAFTA'S CHAPTER 19

There has been little research conducted on the impact of NAFTA on the use of AD and CV duty laws. One hypothesis is that as traditional trade barriers (such as tariffs and quotas) are reduced within NAFTA, the use of AD and CV duty cases have risen in order to protect the domestic industries from increased imports. An alternative hypothesis is that Chapter 19 of NAFTA, which entered into force on January 1, 1994, has contributed to greater discipline of the use of AD and CV duty laws, and has served to lower the number of such cases within NAFTA. Chapter 19 established a binational panel (panel) review of final AD and CV duty determinations. The panel replaced the domestic judicial-appeals process previously used to resolve disputes among NAFTA members over the enforcement of unfair trade laws (Jones 2000). Each panel acts as an appellate body, but the appellate body must apply the domestic law of the country in which the original decision was made to the outcome of the issue.

Jones (2000) studies the NAFTA Chapter 19 panel decisions for Canada and the United States from 1989 to 1998. He examines 62 NAFTA panel reviews, 33 of which challenged AD or CV duty decisions in the United States, and 29 that challenged trade remedy decisions in Canada. Jones finds weak evidence that NAFTA's Chapter 19 ruling might have actually changed incentives in the United States and discouraged the filing of AD and CV duty cases against Canada. His results show that Chapter 19 NAFTA panel reviews have tended to criticize U.S. decisions more than they have criticized Canadian decisions. In addition, nine NAFTA panels from 1989 to 1998 altered significantly unfair trade-case outcomes. Jones therefore argues that NAFTA's Chapter 19 might have reduced the likelihood of an affirmative finding of injurious unfair trade.

We show agricultural AD and CV duty cases in the United States that were brought against NAFTA partners and cases against non-NAFTA countries from 1981 to 2000 (Figure 2.3). In our analysis, the data was divided into pre- and post-NAFTA Chapter 19. The first thing we noted was that the total number of AD and CV duty cases decreased between 1981 and 2000. Between 1981 and 1988, there were 38 AD and CV duty cases; between 1989 and 2000 the total number of cases fell to 27.[20] Between 1981 and 1988, 25 percent of the total number of AD cases in the United States was directed at either Canada or Mexico. This proportion decreased to 19 percent between 1989 and 2000, suggesting

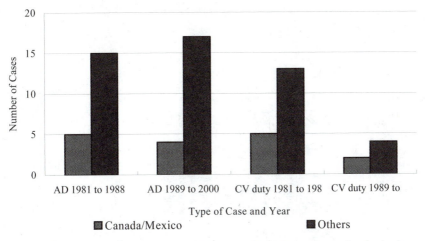

Figure 2.3: U.S. Antidumping and Countervailing Duty Cases in Agriculture: Pre- and Post-NAFTA Chapter 19
Source: USITC (2001).

a NAFTA Chapter 19 effect. There was a slight increase in the share of CV duty cases directed at NAFTA partners over the two time periods, from 27 percent before NAFTA Chapter 19 to 33 percent after it was instituted.

CONCLUSIONS

Since the 1980s, NAFTA members have been extensive users of AD and CV duty trade law in agricultural trade. Many of these cases have involved targeting other NAFTA countries. These actions have not only obstructed agricultural trade but have also encouraged retaliation and increased protectionism in other countries.

We analyzed trade patterns before and after the initiation of AD and CV duty agricultural cases brought by the United States during the 1980 to 2000 period. We found both quantitative and econometric evidence that supported the existence of trade diversion for those cases for which the USITC ruled in the affirmative. Econometric estimation of affirmative cases also supported the presence of an investigation effect, as did the quantitative analysis of negative cases. This is all the more reason to keep trade remedy laws on the negotiating table.

APPENDIX

United States

Affirmative

Initiation Date	Pre-NAFTA Chapter 19				Initiation Date	Post-NAFTA Chapter 19			
	AD Case No.	CV Case No.	Product	Country		AD Case No.	CV Case No.	Product	Country
1981	—	—	—	—	1989	—	701-298	Pork[b]	—
1982	—	701-184	Frozen Conc. O.J.[a]	Brazil	1991	731-454	701-302	Atlantic Salmon	Norway
1984	731-196	—	Red Raspberries	Canada		731-516	—	Kiwi Fruit	New Zealand
1985	731-199	—	Dried Salted Codfish	Canada	1994	731-706	—	Canned Pineapple	Thailand
	—	701-257	Atlantic Groundfish	Canada		731-683	—	Fresh Garlic	China
	731-287	—	In-Shell Pistachios	Iran	1995	731-734	701-365	Pasta	Italy
	—	701-224	Pork[b]	Canada		731-735	701-366	Pasta	Turkey
	—	701-224	Live Swine	Canada	1996	731-752	—	Crawfish Tail Meat	China
1986	731-326	701-326	Orange Juice	Brazil	1997	731-768	—	Atlantic Salmon	Chile
	731-327	701-275	Fresh-Cut Flowers	Canada	1998	731-776	—	Mushrooms[c]	China
	—	701-278	Fresh-Cut Flowers	Netherlands		731-777	—	Mushrooms[c]	Chile
	731-328	701-276	Fresh-Cut Flowers	Chile		731-778	—	Mushrooms[c]	India
	731-329	—	Fresh-Cut Flowers	Colombia		731-779	—	Mushrooms[c]	Indonesia
	731-331	—	Fresh-Cut Flowers	Ecuador	1999	731-841	—	Apple Juice[d]	China
	731-332	—	Fresh-Cut Flowers	Kenya					
	731-333	—	Fresh-Cut Flowers	Mexico					

Negative

Initiation Date	Pre-NAFTA Chapter 19				Initiation Date	Post-NAFTA Chapter 19			
	AD Case No.	CV Case No.	Product	Country		AD Case No.	CV Case No.	Product	Country
1981	—	—	—	—	1989	—	—	—	—
1982	—	701-003	Frozen Potato	Canada	1991	—	—	—	—
1984	731-167	701-214	Lamb	New Zealand	1994	731-684	—	Fresh-Cut Roses	Colombia
		701-210	Table Wine	France		731-685	—	Fresh-Cut Roses	Ecuador

(Continued)

United States *(continued)*

Negative

	Pre-NAFTA Chapter 19					Post-NAFTA Chapter 19			
Initiation Date	AD Case No.	CV Case No.	Product	Country	Initiation Date	AD Case No.	CV Case No.	Product	Country
1985	731-168	701-211	Table Wine	Italy	1995	—	—	—	—
	731-188	—	Lamb	New Zealand	1996	—	—	—	—
	731-283	701-258	Table Wine	West Germany	1997	—	—	—	—
	731-284	701-259	Table Wine	France	1998	—	—	—	—
	731-285	701-260	Table Wine	Italy	1999	—	—	—	—
1986	—	701-277	Fresh-Cut Flowers	Israel					
	731-330	—	Fresh-Cut Flowers	Costa Rica					

Suspended or Terminated

	Pre-NAFTA Chapter 19					Post-NAFTA Chapter 19			
Initiation Date	AD Case No.	CV Case No.	Product	Country	Initiation Date	AD Case No.	CV Case No.	Product	Country
1981	731-043	—	Fresh-Cut Roses	Colombia	1989	—	—	—	—
	—	701-080	Lamb	New Zealand	1991	—	—	—	—
1982	—	—	—	—	1994	731-722	—	Honey	China
1983	—	—	—	—	1995	—	—	—	—
1984	—	701-254	Red Raspberries	Canada	1996	731-747	—	Fresh Tomatoes	Mexico
1985	—	701-021	Fresh-Cut Roses	Netherlands	1997	731-767	—	UHT Milk	Canada
1986	731-334	—	Fresh-Cut Flowers	Peru	1998	731-780	701-374	Butter Cookies	Denmark
						731-809	701-385	Live Cattle	Canada
						731-810	—		
						(731-813)*	—	Live Cattle	Mexico

a Frozen Concentrated Orange Juice.
b Fresh, Chilled or Frozen Pork.
c Preserved.
d Not frozen concentrated.
e Ultra High Temperature.
*New number was assigned to the case during the investigation.
Source: *USITC (1981 to 1999); U.S. Federal Register notices (1980 to 1999); and Blonigen (2002).*

(Continued)

Canada

Affirmative

Pre-NAFTA Chapter 19

Initiation Date	AD Case No.	CV Case No.	Product	Country
1982	—	—	—	—
1983	✓	—	Whole Potatoes	U.S.
	—	✓	C Ham & L Meat[a]	Denmark
	—	✓	C Ham & L Meat	Netherlands
1984	—	—	—	—
1985	✓	—	Whole Potatoes	U.S.
	✓	—	Mnf'd Boneless Beef[a]	Ireland (EEC)
1986	—	✓	Grain Corn	U.S.
	✓	—	Yellow Onions	U.S.
1987	—	—	—	—
1988	✓	—	Sour Tart Cherries	U.S.

Post-NAFTA Chapter 19

Initiation Date	AD Case	CV Case	Product	Country
1991	✓	—	Beer	—
1992	✓	—	Iceberg Head Lettuce	U.S.
1994	✓	—	Red Delicious Apples	U.S.
1995	✓	✓	Refined Sugar	Denmark
	✓	✓	Refined Sugar	Germany
	✓	✓	Refined Sugar	Netherlands
	✓	✓	Refined Sugar	U.K.
	✓	—	Refined Sugar	U.S.
	✓	—	Refined Sugar	Korea
1996	✓	—	Fresh Garlic	China
1997	✓	—	Baby Food and Juice	U.S.
	✓	—	Garlic	China
2000	✓	—	Garlic	Vietnam
	✓	✓	Grain Corn	U.S.

Negative

Pre-NAFTA Chapter 19

Initiation Date	AD Case No.	CV Case No.	Product	Country
1982	✓	✓	Canned Tomatoes	Italy
	✓	—	Canned Tomatoes	Spain
1988	✓	—	Golden Delicious Apples	—

Post-NAFTA Chapter 19

Initiation Date	AD Case No.	CV Case No.	Product	Country
1992	✓	—	Cauliflower (Fresh)	U.S.
	✓	—	Tomato Paste	U.S.

[a]Canned Ham and Luncheon Meat.
Source: Canada Customs and Revenue Agency (2002).

NOTES

[1]Future analysis will incorporate Canada and Mexico.

[2]Sales at less than fair value (LTFV) are defined as having been dumped if the commodity is sold in the United States at a price below the cost of production in the exporting country, if the commodity is sold below the domestic price in the exporting country, or if the commodity is sold below the price in the exporting country's other export markets.

[3]A subsidy is defined as a financial contribution made by a government or any public body, or any form of price support that confers a benefit and results in lower export prices.

[4]There are a number of different ways to count trade remedy cases with the result that summary statistics will vary. For instance, while the United States assigns a case number for each of the countries targeted in any investigation, Canada assigns a case number to each product involved in any investigation, regardless of the number of countries mentioned in the case.

[5]Worldwide, antidumping (AD) cases involving agriculture account for about four percent of all cases filed by all countries (Stevenson 2002).

[6]We did not have a complete data set for Mexico at the time of writing this chapter.

[7]Between 1980 and 2000, annual U.S. agricultural-import value grew on average 4.3 percent (FAOSTAT 2003).

[8]These findings are preliminary because the reported percentage changes are not controlled for other factors such as the magnitude of the duty, the number of countries named in the case, or the import growth without dumping duties. The regression analysis reported in this chapter will attempt to take these issues into consideration in the same manner as in Prusa (1997).

[9]Prusa's (1997) complete model includes a decision variable since duties are often imposed on U.S. imports after the initial USDOC ruling but prior to the final ruling by the USITC. Our model omits this variable since, in the case of agricultural products, only two cases had duties imposed prior to the final ruling. Prusa's (1997) model also includes a dummy variable to account for cases in which more than three countries were named. For agriculture, only two cases met this criterion.

[10]The duties for CV duty cases 701-224 (live swine exports from Canada, initiated 1985) and 701-298 (fresh, chilled, or frozen pork from Canada, initiated in 1989) were in dollars per pound and were not evaluated as *ad valorem* tariffs. Without unit prices, it was not possible to determine the percentage equivalent, therefore these cases were omitted from the data set (USITC 2003).

[11]This alternative specification is used given the large range in duty rates. While the average duty for affirmative cases is 60 percent, the median is 14 percent, suggesting that there are a number of cases with very large duties. These include in-shell pistachios from Iran (1985 at 241 percent), fresh garlic from the People's Republic of China (PRC) (1994 at 376 percent), crawfish tail meat from the PRC (1996 at 202 percent) and
preserved mushrooms from the PRC (1998 at 198 percent) and Chile (1998 at 149 percent). Thus this specification separates analysis for the upper and lower quartiles of the duty rates. The upper quartile contains those cases subject to duties greater than 60 percent; the lower quartile includes cases with duties less than 4.5 percent.

[12]We assume a log-normal distribution of the errors such that

$\ln x_{i,j} \sim N(\mu, \sigma^2)$.

Given this assumption, generating results in dollar values requires the estimated dependent variable to be converted according to the following equation

$$E(x_{i,j}) = e^{\mu + \frac{\sigma^2}{2}}.$$

[13]For cases in which more than one country was named (e.g., preserved mushrooms from Chile, the PRC, India, and Indonesia in 1998), the duty rate used in the regressions for non-named countries was the weighted average duty rate that was applied to the named countries.

[14]On April 10, 2002, the USITC ruled that imports of Canadian greenhouse tomatoes did not injure materially the domestic market and the case was closed. On July 26, 2002, the Canadian International Trade Tribunal (CITT) pronounced the same ruling with regard to imports of U.S. fresh tomatoes.

[15]The percentage change in exports to the United States was calculated over the duration of the trade investigations. For Canada, the investigation lasted from October 2001 to June 2002 and was compared to the same period a year earlier. For the United States, the investigation lasted from March 2001 to April 2002 and was also compared to the same period a year earlier.

[16]Case number 731-841 (USITC 2003).

[17]Case numbers 731-776, 731-777, 731-778, 731-779 (USITC 2003).

[18]Case number 731-683 (USITC 2003).

[19]For the following commodity examples, the percentage changes are all simple averages.

[20]It should be noted, however, that the 1986 AD and CV duty cases against fresh-cut flowers were launched against nine countries, explaining a fourth of the total cases in the pre-Chapter 19 years.

REFERENCES

Barichello, R. (2003). "Antidumping in Agriculture between Canada and the United States: Two Cases of Tomatoes," in *Keeping the Borders Open: Proceedings of the Eighth Policy Disputes Information Workshop,* edited by R.M.A. Loyns, K. Meilke, R.D. Knutson, and A. Yunez-Naude. Winnipeg: Friesen Printers.

Blonigen, B. (2003). "U.S. Antidumping Database and Links." Available at: www.uoregon.edu/~bruceb/adpage.html.

CCRA (Canadian Customs and Revenue Agency, Customs, and Excise). (2002). "Dumping and Subsidy." Available at: www.citt.gc.ca.customs.business/sima/historic-e.html.

Doha Ministerial Declaration. (2001). Available at: www.wto.org/english/thewto_e/minist_e/min01_e/mindecl_e.htm (November 14).

FAOSTAT (Food and Agriculture Organization of the United Nations–Statistics) (2003). "Agricultural Data." Available at: http://apps.fao.org/page/collections?subset=agriculture.

Jones, K. (2000). "Does NAFTA Chapter 19 Make a Difference? Dispute Settlement and the Incentive · Structure of U.S.-Canada Unfair Trade Petitions." *Contemporary Economic Policy* 18(2): 145–58.

Leycegui, B. and M.R. Cornejo. (2004). "Restoring Competition or Granting Protectionism? Trade Remedy Laws in North America," in *Keeping the Borders Open: Proceedings of the Eighth Policy Disputes Information Workshop,* edited by R.M.A. Loyns, K. Meilke, R.D. Knutson, and A. Yunez-Naude. Winnipeg: Friesen Printers.

NAFTA (North America Free Trade Agreement). (1994). "Chapter 19: Review and Dispute Settlement in Antidumping and Countervailing Measures." *SICE Foreign Trade Information System.* Washington, DC: Government Printing Office. Available at: www.sice.oas.org/trade/nafta/chap-19l.asp.

Prusa, T.J. (1992). "Why Are So Many Antidumping Petitions Withdrawn?" *Journal of International Economics* 33(1): 1–20.

_____. (1997). "The Trade Effects of U.S. Antidumping Actions," in *The Effects of U.S. Trade Protection and Promotion Policies,* edited by R.C. Feenstra. Chicago and London: University of Chicago Press (Chapter 7).

Staiger, R.W., F. Wolak, R.E. Litan, M.L. Katz, and L. Waverman. (1994). "Measuring Industry-Specific Protection: Antidumping in the United States." Working Paper, National Bureau of Economic Research, Cambridge, Massachusetts (51–118).

Stevenson, C. (2002). "Global Trade Protection Report 2002." London: Mayer, Brown, Rowe, and Maw (April). Available at: www.mayerbrownrowe.com.

Stiglitz, J.E. (1997). "Dumping on Free Trade: The U.S. Import Trade Laws." *Southern Economic Journal* 64(2): 402–24.

Tariff Act. (1930). Available at: http://www.access.gpo.gov/uscode/title19/chapter4_.html.

U.S. Census Bureau, Foreign Trade Division. (2003). Available at: http://www.census.gov/foreign-trade/www/.

USDA/FAS (U.S. Department of Agriculture, Foreign Agricultural Service). (2003). "U.S. Trade Internet System." Available at: www.fas.usda.gov.

U.S. Federal Registration Notices. (1980 to 1999). "Office of the Federal Register, National Archives and Records Administration." Washington, D.C: Office of the Federal Register. Available at: http://www.gpoaccess.gov/fr/.

U.S. House of Representatives. (2001). 107th Congress, Committee on Ways and Means, *Overview and Compilation of U.S. Trade Statues, 2001 Edition.* Washington DC: U.S. House of Representatives (June).

USITC (U.S. International Trade Commission). (2001). "Commissioner Vote Database." Query results provided by Devry Boughner. Washington, DC: USITC.

_____. (2003). "Antidumping and Countervailing Duty Investigations (Section 701 and 731)." Available at: www.usitc.gov/title7.htm.

WTO Ministerial Declaration. (2001). "WT/MIN(01)/DEC/1." Available at: www.wto.org/english/thewto_e/minist_e/min01_e/mindecl_e.htm (November 14).

Young, L., J. Wainio, and K. Meilke. (2003). "Trade Remedy Actions in NAFTA: Agriculture and Agri-Food Industries," in *Keeping the Borders Open: Proceedings of the Eighth Policy Disputes Information Workshop,* edited by R.M.A. Loyns, K. Meilke, R. D. Knutson, and A. Yunez-Naude. Winnipeg: Friesen Printers.

Chapter 3

The Potential Impacts of Mandatory Country-of-Origin Labelling on U.S. Agriculture

C. Parr Rosson, III and Flynn J. Adcock

Texas A&M University

INTRODUCTION

The *Farm Security and Rural Investment Act* (FSRIA) of 2002 requires mandatory retail country-of-origin labelling on certain fresh and frozen foods by September 30, 2004. However, the 2004 U.S. Appropriations Bill has delayed the implementation of mandatory country-of-origin labelling (MCOOL) for two years. Nonetheless, MCOOL provisions have been supported by various segments of the livestock, beef, pork, fruit, vegetable, and peanut industries.

The U.S. Department of Agriculture, Agricultural Marketing Service (USDA/AMS) is charged with designing and enforcing MCOOL (USDA/AMS 2003). An open comment period has been provided for public input and regulations are being developed. USDA/AMS also hosted a series of twelve listening sessions around the United States to receive input from industries and sectors affected by the law.

It is important to understand the significance of imported meats, fruits, vegetables, and peanuts to U.S. food consumers. U.S. imports of these products were valued at U.S. $19.5 billion in 2002, and represented 2.3 percent of 2001 U.S. food-consumption expenditures. The United States consumed about 12.7 million metric tons (mmt) of beef and 8.7 mmt of pork during 2002. According to the *U.S. Agricultural Trade Update* in 2002, beef imports accounted for about 7.7 percent of U.S. beef consumption and 3.9 percent for pork (USDA/FAS 2003). When beef from imported cattle and swine are added to the calculation, the percentage of imports as a share of consumption increases to approximately 21 percent for beef and 10 percent for pork. Fruit, vegetable, and peanut imports account for 22 percent of fresh- and frozen-fruit consumption, 11 percent of fresh- and frozen-vegetable consumption, and 5 percent of peanut consumption.

Canada exported 1.7 million slaughter cattle to the United States in 2002, and 5.7 million hogs—about two-thirds that required additional feeding, and one-third ready for slaughter (Figure 3.1). Mexico shipped 800,000 head of cattle that were mostly calves to the United States in 2002. These imports represented more than 99 percent of all U.S. cattle and U.S. swine imports in 2002, and illustrate the high degree of economic integration present in the North American livestock industry. Further, U.S. imports of beef from Canada totalled 382,000 metric tons (mt) or about 34 percent of total U.S. beef imports. Imports of pork from Canada totalled 326,000 mt or 89 percent of U.S. pork imports (Figure 3.2). While U.S. imports of beef from Mexico are increasing, this volume was only about 4,000 mt in 2002.

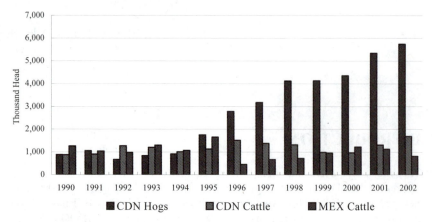

Figure 3.1: U.S. Imports of Livestock from Canada and Mexico
Source: USDA/FAS (2003).

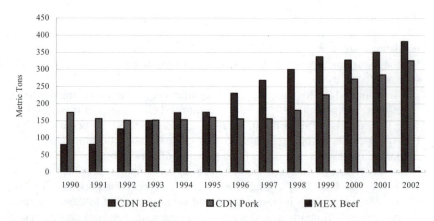

Figure 3.2: U.S. Imports of Meat from Canada and Mexico
Source: USDA/FAS (2003).

Mexico and Canada also supply most of the U.S. fresh- and frozen-vegetable import market and much of the U.S. fruit-import market. The statistics in Figure 3.3 reveal that U.S. imports of vegetables from Mexico totalled 2.4 mmt or 65 percent in 2002, and those from Canada accounted for 876,000 mt or 24 percent of these imports. Mexico's 1.2 mmt of fresh- and frozen-fruit shipments to the United States accounted for 34 percent of U.S. imports, excluding bananas, while the 137,000 mt of fruit imports from Canada accounted for four percent of that same total. The exclusion of bananas is important to note because most of the bananas consumed in the United States are imported, and account for 4.1 mmt (54 percent) of the total of 7.6 mmt of U.S. fruit imports.

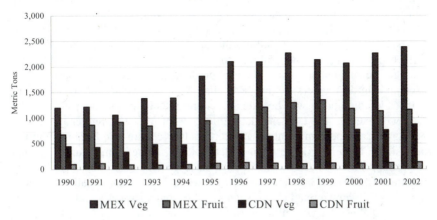

Figure 3.3: U.S. Imports of Fruits and Vegetables from Canada and Mexico
Source: USDA/FAS (2003).

This chapter is divided into three main parts. First, the provisions of country-of-origin labelling will be described. Next, issues surrounding MCOOL will be examined, including foreign-only-labelling issues, consumer views about foreign-only labelling, and labelling costs, and finally, the amount of trade that could be potentially impacted. The final section will explore the potential implications of MCOOL on U.S. and foreign agriculture. It will also explore potential reactions of MCOOL from U.S. trading partners. The results and other information provided in this chapter will improve the understanding of country-of-origin labelling provisions and their potential impacts.

COUNTRY-OF-ORIGIN LABELLING PROVISIONS

Country-of-origin labelling became voluntary on October 11, 2002 and is set to become mandatory for all covered products no later than September 30, 2006. Under MCOOL, retailers are responsible for the accurate labelling of origin for a wide variety of fresh and frozen meats, fruits, vegetables, and peanuts. All covered products are required to carry a MCOOL label, including those produced entirely in the United States.

Commodities covered by MCOOL include fresh-, chilled-, and frozen-muscle cuts of beef, pork, and lamb, including their ground products, fresh and frozen farm-raised fish and wild fish, fresh and frozen fruits and vegetables, and peanuts. To qualify for a "USA" label, the product must have originated and been produced entirely in the United States. Non-U.S. products must have their country-of-origin listed on the label, regardless of how many countries are involved in the production of the product. The labels may be in the form of standard labels, stickers, stamps, or placards on packages, containers, or bins.

There are several major exceptions to the MCOOL provisions. Covered commodities that enter the hotel/restaurant/institutional (HRI) trade are exempt, and include Australian ground beef bound for a McDonald's or Burger King hamburger as well as Mexican tomatoes and peppers headed for restaurant salads. Second, covered commodities that are processed or used as ingredients in further processing are not subject to MCOOL. For instance, cured hams, sausage, peanut butter, tuna fish, and produce to be used in soups will be exempt. Third, retailers selling less than U.S. \$230,000 per year of any perishable commodity will be exempt, as are butcher shops and fish markets. This will exclude most independent grocers from MCOOL provisions. Retail outlets that are meat and seafood markets exclusively are also exempt from the provisions. Therefore, large retail outlets selling covered commodities to grocery shoppers are likely to be the only place country-of-origin labels will be required. USDA/AMS estimates this total to be 31,000 stores nationwide and includes well-known retail chains such as Albertson's, Kroger's, Safeway, Winn Dixie, and WalMart as well as most regional chains. Exports are also exempt from labelling.

Specifically, there are four separate categories of origin for a covered commodity:

- U.S. origin exclusively;
- origin and production entirely outside the United States;
- products of the United States and non-United States that have combined origin; and
- products of blended origin.

Products that are of exclusive U.S. origin may be labelled as "Product of U.S.A.," or simply "U.S.A." Therefore, beef from a calf that is born in Texas, fed in New Mexico, and slaughtered in Colorado qualifies for the U.S. label, as do tomatoes grown in Florida or peanuts grown in Virginia. State promotion programs do not satisfy the labelling requirements, thus Washington apples and Idaho potatoes, for example, will still require a country label.

Products grown and processed entirely outside the United States will be required to have their country of origin listed. Examples of these are onions produced in Mexico, grapes grown in Chile, and beef imported from Canada. Each of these products sold at retail grocery outlets will have to have "Product of Country X"-type labels. The country's name alone will be sufficient.

The previous two categories are fairly clear in the labelling requirement. The next two, mixed-origin and blended products, are slightly more complicated. Mixed-origin products are most commonly found in livestock/meat products. The supply chain in both cattle/beef and hogs/pork traverse national boundaries within North America. Two-way trade between the United States and Canada occurs with both cattle and hogs, and calves are imported each year by the United States from Mexico. This will result in country-of-origin labelling by supply chain. Beef from Mexican-born cattle imported into the United States then fed and slaughtered in the United States may list countries of origin in the following manner: "Born in Mexico, raised and processed in the U.S.A." Likewise, labels of beef from cattle born in the United States, fed in Canada, and slaughtered in the United States may list countries of origin as: "Born in U.S.A., raised in Canada, and processed in the U.S.A."

The final category is for blended products. The same product from different countries packaged in the same container must be labelled by country and listed alphabetically. For instance, frozen bags of broccoli may contain product from the United States only, or may have broccoli from Mexico and/or Chile. The degree of foreign content will depend on harvest times in other countries and relative costs of procurement. At one point during the year, the bag might have a label that says "U.S.A." At other times of the year, the bag might have a label that says "Chile, Mexico, U.S.A.," with other combinations possible during different times of the year. Similar situations can be imagined for other products such as bagged salad lettuce from the United States and Mexico, or ground beef from the United States, Australia, and Canada.

Under MCOOL guidelines, each handler of the product will be responsible for ensuring that the country of origin is listed accurately. Failure to reflect the correct country of origin or combination of countries of origin accurately may result in a fine of up to U.S. $10,000 for the party in violation.

Several misunderstandings regarding the MCOOL provisions have surfaced since MCOOL rules were introduced. One misunderstanding has been the belief by some in the U.S. peanut industry that peanut paste and peanut butter must be covered by the rules. However, since peanut paste and peanut butter are processed products, they are not covered by the regulations. A second misunderstanding has been trace back—the documentation or verification of the origin of a product, and whether or not producers will be required to provide this documentation. The MCOOL provisions state that the U.S. Department of Agriculture (USDA) may require any handler of covered commodities bound for retail sale to maintain a "verifiable record-keeping audit trail" to indicate country of origin, and that any supplier of covered commodities to retailers must provide information to the retailer regarding country of origin of the product. The regulations currently being developed state that "Every person that prepares, stores, handles, or distributes a covered commodity for retail sale must keep records on the country of origin [of that sale] for a period of at least two years" (USDA/AMS 2003). This may include feedlots and ranches. A third misunderstanding relates to the cost of labelling and the subsector of the food industry that will bear the greatest burden for these costs. These and other MCOOL issues prompted the scheduling of twelve listening sessions around the country to educate affected parties and to gain input from the industry.

EMERGING ISSUES IN
COUNTRY-OF-ORIGIN LABELLING

There are many emerging issues related to the implementation and costs of the MCOOL provisions. One basic issue is how intensely consumers desire to know where their fresh meat and produce originates. Survey results indicate that four in five consumers supported MCOOL labelling of fresh produce, however other attributes such as nutrition, appearance, and handling are more important.

A survey (Cogent Research) conducted in April 2003 for the International Food Information Council (2003) shows that 77 percent of U.S. consumers say there is no need for additional information on product labels. Other surveys show apparently divergent results. For instance, a recently published survey indicated that 68 percent of U.S. consumers would pay more for food grown in the United States than they would for food grown in other countries (Wimbereley et al. 2003). However, only 2 percent of respondents in a 2003 *Fresh Trends* survey consider country-of-origin labelling a reason for not purchasing a fresh fruit or vegetable. Therefore, it is unclear if consumers have major concerns about where their food originates, or if they do, just how much they are willing to pay to know country of origin.

A second issue is whether or not foreign-only products will require a country-of-origin label. For instance, the Florida MCOOL law requires country-of-origin labels only for foreign fresh fruits and vegetables, and it was hoped by supporters that this would be the model for MCOOL implementation within the United States. However, this may violate WTO rules regarding equal treatment that indicate, "No rule may be imposed only on imported products." Thus all products must be treated in a like manner. The differences in the application of the WTO rules have major cost implications for U.S. producers in particular.

A third issue relates to the implementation and cost of the MCOOL provisions. USDA/AMS (2003) estimated first-year compliance costs of MCOOL to be U.S. $1.97 billion. The National Pork Producers Council that supported the inclusion of MCOOL into FSRIA, estimated compliance costs to the pork industry alone to be U.S. $1.02 billion per year (Hayes and Meyer 2003). And for this reason they are now opposed to the ultimate implementation of MCOOL provisions.

A fourth issue is the degree to which the present supply chain will be affected by the provisions. Kerr (2003) contends that Mexican and Canadian red meats will have a cost advantage relative to U.S. red meats because they will not be required to implement monitoring and tracing systems that will be necessary for U.S. products. Mexican and Canadian table-ready products will have to be labelled "Product of Mexico" or "Product of Canada" only when leaving the packing plants. Kerr also demonstrates that the current supply chain of mixed-origin products, such as live animals and boxed meats, will be replaced by a more specialized, export-oriented system.

These export-oriented systems will ultimately increase the demand for feeder cattle in Mexico and for fed steers and hogs in Canada that could lead to lower U.S. beef exports to both countries. Two forms of supply chains are likely to develop to service the retail red-meat market in the United States. One will specialize in the production of U.S.-only products in the United States and the other will specialize in the production of foreign consumer-ready products. It is also likely that a new supply chain servicing only the HRI trade will be developed. Specialization in consumer-ready meats will become more profitable in both Canada and Mexico and mixed supply chains may very well disappear.

Impacts of these new-market and supply-chain systems need to be assessed. U.S. packing plants, feedlots, especially those in South Texas and along the U.S.-Mexico border, and cow-calf operations will likely experience disruption to their operations, increased costs, and lower profitability.

It is also likely that higher costs of U.S. beef relative to poultry, and possibly to pork, will result in a lost market share for beef, lower prices for beef producers, and market share and price gains for poultry producers. This may occur at a time when U.S. beef producers are rebuilding cattle herds from the present low levels of inventory, making beef-herd restocking even more costly.

A fifth issue is that there is also the possibility that these provisions may spur retaliation by trading partners, or at the very least, incite challenges within the North American Free Trade Agreement (NAFTA) or the World Trade Organization (WTO) dispute-settlement bodies. It also seems unlikely that Canada or Mexico would impose their own MCOOL systems if substantial costs were to result from verification and record-keeping requirements.

Under the National Treatment rules of the WTO, any import requirements must also apply to U.S. products. This requirement will likely impose significant verification and tracing costs on the U.S. cattle and hog industries. It also appears that requirements to label livestock from Canada and Mexico will reduce exports of live animals to the U.S. market. More exports of beef from Canada should be expected. While Canadian exports may be reduced due to Bovine Spongiform Encephalopathy (BSE) and related health concerns, it is unclear as to when or to what degree the U.S./Canada live cattle and beef trade will achieve more normal patterns.

A sixth issue is that some foreign firms or producer groups may consider MCOOL as an opportunity to differentiate their product, capture a market niche, and receive a price premium. This has occurred in fresh produce without any legislation. Further, much of the fresh produce imported into the U.S. market already has country-of-origin markings or labels on it. U.S. products will be required to verify origin, which will sometimes result in higher costs and loss of competitive advantage to foreign products.

POTENTIAL IMPACTS

The North American livestock, meat, fruit, and vegetable trade is characterized by a high degree of economic and product integration. Intra-NAFTA beef and cattle trade totalled U.S. $2.8 billion in 2002, up 22 percent since 1994 (Table 3.1). While U.S. exports of beef and cattle to Canada were valued at U.S. $268 million, U.S. imports from Canada were U.S. $2.24 billion. These imports were evenly split between slaughter cattle and beef. Intra-NAFTA hog/pork trade was

Table 3.1: 2002 North American Livestock and Meat Trade

	U.S. Imports from Canada	U.S. Exports to Canada	U.S. Imports from Mexico	U.S. Exports to Mexico
Beef Cattle				
(1,000 head)	1,689	134	816	105
(U.S. $ million)	1,148	50	301	75
Beef				
(1,000 metric tons)	382	67	4	206
(U.S. $ million)	1,096	218	16	592
Subtotal: Beef and Cattle				
(U.S. $ million)	2,244	268	317	667
Hogs				
(1,000 head)	5,741	13	n/a	169
(U.S. $ million)	301	2	n/a	30
Pork				
(1,000 metric tons)	326	48	n/a	77
(U.S. $ million)	572	112	n/a	124
Subtotal: Pork and Hogs				
(U.S. $ million)	873	114	n/a	154
Total Value				
(U.S. $ million)	**3,117**	**382**	**317**	**821**

Source: USDA/FAS (2003).

U.S. $1.2 billion in 2002. U.S. exports of beef to Mexico were U.S. $592 million, while the United States imported U.S. $301 million worth of Mexican feeder calves in 2002. These trade patterns reflect the existence of well-integrated mixed-production systems, with Mexico specializing in feeder calves and Canada specializing in slaughter cattle and beef.

Also in 2002, U.S. exports of pork to Canada were U.S. $112 million, while U.S. exports to Mexico were U.S. $124 million. The United States imported U.S. $301 million in live hogs and U.S. $572 million in pork from Canada. This system also reflects a high degree of integration and a mixed supply chain among the three countries, with Canada exporting hogs and pork to the U.S. market and the United States exporting pork to Mexico and Canada.

There are four potential outcomes of MCOOL provisions related to consumer reactions. First, U.S. products may be perceived as having more value or as being safer than foreign goods. In this case, U.S. products will be differentiated from foreign products and will sell at a price premium. Under these conditions, more U.S. product will be available for domestic consumption and exports will fall. Foreign products displaced from the U.S. market will likely find outlets in other countries in the short term. As U.S. producers respond to higher prices by increasing output, U.S. exports could expand.

Second, U.S. consumers may be indifferent to MCOOL provisions. In a market as price sensitive and competitive as the United States, there will not be a premium for U.S. products. No major market shifts will occur, but U.S. producers will incur the additional costs of labelling and therefore will lose market share to foreign items and will experience falling exports. In this case, however, since there will be no price premium, exports may not recover over time.

If foreign products are perceived to have more value and are successfully differentiated from U.S. products, imports may sell at a premium. As U.S. imports increase, it is likely that exports will also increase as U.S. products are displaced, thus somewhat compensating producers for loss of U.S. market share. Long-term effects might include the development of streamlined export-oriented businesses in the United States with economies of scale capable of competing with foreign products.

Third, retail shelf space is at a premium in the U.S. grocery market. It appears likely that some U.S. grocery retailers may reduce the number of suppliers, relying on only those who can supply products that are properly labelled and documented. In the short term, this may mean more reliance on U.S. products. Some retailers may eliminate their foreign supplies altogether, depending upon their analysis of consumer preferences for U.S.-labelled products. If a significant portion of the Canadian beef destined for retail is diverted to HRI or to processing, there is likely be a short-term surplus of this product, which will lead to lower prices for Canadian products and cattle.

Fourth, there could be the development of an export-oriented Mexican beef- and pork-production supply chain to supply the growing Hispanic market along the U.S.-Mexico border. Exceeding 20 million people, this has become one of the fastest growing markets in the United States. Their tastes and preferences favour Mexican products and have resulted in the establishment of several large Mexican-owned grocery outlets in Southern California.

CONCLUSIONS

U.S. imports of meats, fish and shellfish, fruits and vegetables, and peanuts were valued at U.S. $19.5 billion in 2002, which represented about 2.3 percent of the total 2002 U.S. food-consumption expenditure.

Mandatory country-of-origin labelling was scheduled to become effective on September 30, 2004. A two-year delay for implementation of most MCOOL-covered products was included as part of the fiscal year 2004 Appropriations Bill. Once MCOOL is fully implemented, all beef, pork, lamb, fruits, vegetables, fish, and peanuts will be required to display a country-of-origin label at retail. Producers of covered products will be required to keep records to verify product source for two years. Hotels, restaurants, institutions, butcher shops, fish markets, small groceries, processed foods, and products for export are exempt from the required MCOOL labelling. The quantitative impacts of MCOOL are difficult to measure, but several estimates place the costs of implementing legislation and record keeping between U.S. $1.0 billion and U.S. $1.9 billion.

U.S. producers may face higher costs for the sale of their products under MCOOL. Also, implementing MCOOL could result in a loss of competitive advantage relative to Mexico and Canada and relative to chicken, which is not covered by the legislation.

The development of two major beef-cattle supply chains in North America could be one of the results of MCOOL. The Mexican and Canadian systems will be lower cost than the U.S. system if current regulations are implemented.

There is little doubt that Mexican and Canadian cattle will be discounted, disrupting or possibly eliminating the current mixed supply chain of beef produced from cattle raised and fed in Canada but processed in the United States, and cattle raised in Mexico but fed and processed in the United States. It is likely that any retail meats imported from Canada will be produced in export-oriented systems using Canadian cattle and meat-processing facilities. A separate supply chain for foreign-sourced HRI meats may evolve over time.

It may be possible that MCOOL will be challenged in NAFTA or the WTO. If that occurs, the outcome is uncertain, depending on the parts of the law that are challenged. Other forms of retaliation could also occur, such as the imposition of bound tariffs from lower applied rates.

REFERENCES

Fresh Trends. (2003). "What Prevented Shoppers from Purchasing an Intended Item?" *Fresh Trends* 109(54): 12.

Hayes, D. J. and S. R. Meyer. (2003). "Impact of Mandatory Country-of-Origin Labelling on U.S. Pork Exports." National Pork Producers Council, Urbandale, Iowa.

International Food Information Council. (2003). *Americans' Acceptance of Food Biotechnology Matches Growers' Increased Adoption of Biotech Crops.* Survey Conducted by Cogent Research. Washington, DC: International Food Information Council (April).

Kerr, W. A. (2003). "The Free Traders Win the Debates, but the Protectionists Win the Elections: The Curious Case of the MCOOL in the 2002 U.S. Farm Bill." Paper presented at the *Farm Policy Developments and Policy Tensions Under NAFTA, Policy Disputes Information Consortium,* Montreal, Quebec, Canada (April 23–6).

USDA/AMS (U.S. Department of Agriculture, Agricultural Marketing Service). (2003). "Mandatory Country of Origin Labelling of Beef, Lamb, Pork, Fish, Perishable Agricultural Commodities, and Peanuts; Proposed Rule." *Federal Register* 68(210): 61943–91985. Washington, DC: Government Printing Office (October 30). Available at: www.ams.usda.gov/cool/ls0304.txt.

USDA/FAS (U.S. Department of Agriculture, Foreign Agricultural Service). (2003). "U.S. Trade Internet System." Available at: www.fas.usda.gov/ustrade.

Wimbereley, R.C., B. Vander-Mey, B. Wells, and G. Ejimakor. (2003). "The Globalisation of Food and How Americans Feel About It." *Southern Perspectives* 6(2): 1 and 14–6.

Section II:
Legal Considerations

Chapter 4

WTO and NAFTA Dispute Settlement for North American Agricultural Trade

Stephen J. Powell[*]

University of Florida

INTRODUCTION

Dispute settlement under trade agreements has gained such reach that consideration needs to be given to invoking its machinery in a wide variety of international commercial disputes. This chapter explains how these new alternatives to national courts operate with respect to agricultural border disputes and why a litigant might choose one of these new alternatives instead of the courts. The chapter opens with a background on negotiations in the World Trade Organization (WTO) and the North American Free Trade Agreement (NAFTA) to ensure the reader's basic knowledge of the dispute-settlement systems at issue in the discussion to follow.

The template for comparison of the systems will be an actual case that has been addressed by both the WTO and NAFTA dispute-settlement systems. The case involves the imposition of antidumping (AD) duties by Mexico on U.S. imports of High Fructose Corn Syrup (HFCS), a multimillion-dollar U.S. industry whose product is used primarily to sweeten soft drinks. We will not dwell on the substantive findings of the various dispute-settlement panels, but instead use the case to illustrate important differences between the two systems that a litigant might consider, such as how the process is invoked, how a panel is formed, the panel's jurisdiction, what standard of review it will use, how it will treat precedent, what role private counsel will play in the process, the nature of an appeal of a panel decision, and how the decision will be implemented.

There are a number of types of dispute settlement contemplated in NAFTA. Although some of the complex details will be omitted, the chapter will look primarily to the Chapter 19 procedures for resolving disputes involving the trade remedy laws in the United States, Canada, and Mexico.

DISPUTE SETTLEMENT IN THE WORLD TRADE ORGANIZATION (WTO)

The WTO is the repository of the basic international trade rules among its 147 nation-state members. NAFTA is a regional economic integration agreement that builds on the WTO's basic rules to open trade more completely among the three countries (Parties) of North America. The two treaties entered into force in the mid-1990s with powerful systems to resolve trade disputes.

To understand present dispute settlement in the WTO, one needs to picture the winding path taken by its predecessor for the previous 50 years, the General Agreement on Tariffs and Trade (GATT) to reach the stage from which WTO negotiators were able to take a quantum leap. In sum, what began as a diplomacy-driven process of negotiation to resolve disputes has been transformed into nothing short of a rule of law. At their inception, GATT dispute-settlement procedures were straightforward. If a party considered that benefits to which it was entitled under the agreement were being nullified or impaired, the agreement entitled the party to the "sympathetic consideration" of the party alleged to have violated its GATT obligations or otherwise caused the nullification or impairment.[1] If these consultations failed to resolve the dispute, the matter could be referred to the contracting Parties[2] for investigation, to be followed by a recommendation or ruling.[3]

Over time, these investigations progressed from being handled by a working party, to being handled by a panel of experts, to being handled by a separate panel for each case, none of which is identified by the agreement, and each of which is an inexorable step toward greater objectivity in the dispute-resolution process.[4] After receiving the panel's report, the contracting Parties could, if they considered the situation "serious enough," authorize the complaining party to impose countermeasures in the form of suspension of GATT concessions,[5] although they have done so only once, in a complaint by the Netherlands involving U.S. quotas on the importation of dairy products.[6] Modest procedures for the handling of Article XXIII complaints were adopted in 1966.[7]

GATT 1947's very sketchy provisions were fleshed out minimally by a framework understanding of dispute-settlement rules[8] and by the particular provisions of the six new 1979 Tokyo Round codes addressing non-tariff measures (standards, government procurement, subsidies, AD, customs valuation, and import licensing). These provisions again placed the emphasis on stimulating settlement by Parties through an informal, policy-oriented reasoning-together approach, although they made an initial stab at a disciplined process with the setting of loose time limits for panel reports and for compliance with panel recommendations. In hindsight, it is clear that the 60-day targets in the codes for completion of panel proceedings and the "reasonable period" suggested for bringing the offending laws into compliance, harkened back to the clubby 1950s when GATT was made up of twenty-three like-minded countries whose representatives originally negotiated the agreement.[9]

Nonetheless, these improvements failed to ensure successful resolution of the deluge of disputes, both broader and deeper than in earlier times that ushered in the 1980s.[10] The basic remedy of GATT dispute settlement continued to be bringing the offending measure into compliance with GATT or its agreements. The losing party could continue to block adoption of a panel report because adoption required the consensus of the contracting Parties.[11] The codes and the understanding confirmed that countermeasures, in the case of failure of a party to bring its laws into compliance, could include the withdrawal of GATT concessions, that is, increased tariffs on products that were not the subject of the dispute. Under this prescription, countermeasures always had the effect of harming or helping industries that had not been injured by the activity that was the subject of the complaint.

Taken together with the fact that the losing party also had the power to block countermeasures, very few trade disputes were resolved under this political process, which set the stage for improvements in the early stages of the Uruguay Round negotiations launched in 1986.

At the April 1989 mid-term meeting of ministers, the contracting Parties agreed to apply on a trial basis a bold set of initiatives until the expected 1990 end of the Uruguay Round.[12] Automatic establishment of panels and more realistic deadlines were provided in recognition of the intense fact-gathering nature of dispute settlement, as well as the need for considerable legal analysis: a nine-month deadline was set for the panel's report, that had a target date of six months. The GATT Council was to monitor implementation of an adopted report, and the dispute would, until resolved, remain on the Council agenda beginning six months after adoption.

No actual deadline was established for compliance with a panel's recommendations, although peer pressure had become decidedly stronger than in earlier days as Parties, particularly developing countries, came to the view that hard-won GATT benefits were worth substantially less to them if they could not be enforced.

As might have been predicted from these mid-term changes, the dispute-settlement procedures that emerged from the Uruguay Round were easily the most significant advance since GATT was born.[13] Parties subjected their disagreements to truly binding arbitration by the panel process. A panel report must be adopted unless there is consensus to reject the panel report.[14] Because this consensus must include the winner of the dispute, reverse consensus would be exercised only when all agreed to reject an "outlaw" panel decision, one whose adverse impact on other programs would be worse than its favourable effects on the activity under dispute.

Tighter time frames, including those for compliance, are provided. "Urgent" cases (including perishable agricultural products) are to be completed in only three months, while other disputes retain the mid-term target of six months and a deadline of nine months.[15] In a change most resembling the process of court proceedings, there is an appeal of right to a standing Appellate Body.[16] In the event of noncompliance, the winning party has the right to compensation or to retaliation unless there is consensus to reject the countermeasures.[17]

Significantly, the basic remedy remains bringing the offending measure into compliance.[18] Also unchanged from the original GATT, countermeasures constitute the withdrawal of GATT concessions.[19] In essence, although the vestiges of a political process remain, the new dispute settlement in the WTO is mostly a rule-driven, judicially oriented system.

NAFTA BINATIONAL PANEL REVIEW OF ANTIDUMPING AND COUNTERVAILING DUTY DETERMINATIONS

Effective at the beginning of 1995, the United States agreed with its northern and southern neighbours to a unique and still controversial cession of judicial sovereignty. Chapter 19 of the U.S.-Canada Free Trade Agreement (overtaken in 1994 by Chapter 19 of NAFTA when agreement with Mexico was reached), provides an innovative solution to a complex issue: how does one satisfy free-trade-agreement colleagues that unfair trade laws will be applied fairly to their exports that are going to another NAFTA party, while preserving the right of domestic producers to be protected from unfairly traded imports from the most important trading partners of Canada, the United States, and Mexico.

NAFTA's Chapter 19 provides for the review of AD and countervailing (CV) duty determinations involving goods of another NAFTA party by panels composed of private trade-law experts chosen by the two Parties involved in the dispute, instead of providing a traditional review by national courts. Even non-lawyer panellists must have general familiarity with international trade law.[20] This emphasis on legal knowledge is well-placed because the panel's function is to determine whether or not the investigating authority has properly applied its AD or CV duty law based solely on the record created during the administrative process and on the standard of review and the general legal principles that apply in that country's courts.[21] A final determination may be challenged under normal judicial-review procedures only if neither government requests a panel within thirty days after receiving notice of the determination.[22] The government request may be either on its own initiative or at the insistence of a private party that would otherwise have standing under domestic law to bring an action in the courts.[23]

If the panel finds that the investigating authority has incorrectly applied its law, the panel will remand the determination for action not inconsistent with the panel's decision and must establish a time limit for compliance with the remand.[24] Under very limited circumstances, the decision of a panel may be brought before an Extraordinary Challenge Committee (ECC) composed of judges or former judges for an expedited decision.[25] Decisions of the panel are binding on the Parties insofar as the particular matter before the panel is concerned, and the Agreement provides that the governments may not legislate an appeal of a panel decision to the domestic courts.[26]

IMPROVEMENTS MADE BY NAFTA TO THE U.S.-CANADA MODEL

After five years of experience under the U.S.-Canada agreement, the Parties were able to identify modifications to the binational panel system to capture more fully the intent of the system's crafters.

One improvement introduced by NAFTA is a preference for judges, either sitting or retired, from the federal courts of the three Parties. This change emphasizes that a panel's task is to apply existing law as a court would. The panel is not to create a new body of law. This change might also reduce the potential for a conflict of interest by trade practitioners who also represent clients in other trade matters pending before the agencies whose decisions are being challenged.

Another change, the corrective mechanism added by Article 1905 of NAFTA, is substantial. The Parties recognized that some risk attended the melding of Mexico's civil law system, together with its recently enacted AD and CV duty law, with the common law system and the more mature AD and CV duty laws of the other two Parties. The principal protection against a clash of systems was to ensure sufficient change to Mexico's laws that the exporters of all three countries would be in a roughly equivalent position. Essentially, this combination of changes[27] shifts Mexico several steps closer to a common law system for trade remedy laws.

But Article 1905 of NAFTA goes farther: it provides that if a Party's laws prevent a panel from being established, or have the effect of rendering its decisions non-binding, or if these laws fail to provide a meaningful opportunity for judicial review, and a Special Committee agrees that one of these situations exists, the complaining Party may suspend operation of the binational panel system, or suspend equivalent benefits to the other Party. This is a remedy reminiscent of GATT.

As required by NAFTA, panel decisions are implemented by the agencies based directly on the panel's direction, without need for an intervening governmental decision, as befits a forum that substitutes for a court. If the losing party believes the panel has seriously exceeded its powers, it may request reconsideration by an ECC, which is an avenue pursued rarely and never successfully.[28] In the view of some trade practitioners, past ECCs have so limited the availability of this remedy that such a committee can be expected to act only if a panel overtly refuses to apply the clearly relevant standard of review, or if it contains a truly corrupt panellist whose vote mattered.[29]

IMPACT OF NEW ALTERNATIVES
FOR RESOLVING COMMERCIAL DISPUTES

The U.S. General Accounting Office (USGAO) estimates conservatively that U.S. exports have increased by over U.S. $1 billion per year as a direct result of successful U.S. challenges in the WTO. Many millions more have been implicated by disputes won but, to put it delicately, not fully implemented by the losing WTO country. For example, U.S. $530 million in lost sales is being recovered by the United States as the result of the October 2001 settlement of the 30-year Banana War with Europe and U.S. $117 million in lost sales is still pending from Europe's Beef Hormones ban, which was found in 1998 to be inconsistent with the WTO Agreement on the Application of Sanitary and Phytosanitary Measures by the Appellate Body.

Nearly 300 cases have been filed since the WTO came into effect in January 1995. The United States filed fully one-third of these cases to vindicate its commercial interests, mostly against Europe. As expected, given the huge trading volumes between the United States and Europe, most of Europe's WTO challenges have addressed U.S. border measures. These disputes have reached broadly across commercial practice areas, from patent-protection issues in the India Mailbox case or the copyright law interpretation in the *U.S. Music Licensing Act* case, to the novel antitrust arguments advanced in the U.S. case against Japan's Photographic Film distribution system, environmental issues implicated by the Shrimp-Turtle challenge against the United States, systemic global tax policies represented by the U.S. $4 billion per year challenge to the U.S. Foreign Sales Corporation law, health and safety issues treated by panels on Europe's ban of asbestos insulation, and Australia's ban of fresh salmon.

Despite its open market, the United States often is a respondent in WTO dispute settlements. The United States aggressively interprets the limited discretion that remains under WTO agreements to protect domestic industries from the adverse impacts of free trade. Many of these cases have involved agricultural products. In fact, although agricultural commodities constitute about 10 percent of world trade, easily twice that percentage of WTO disputes involve such products and fully 30 percent of the disputes were entertained at the highest level of the WTO dispute process, its Appellate Body, to address agricultural trade disputes.

The picture is equally impressive in the NAFTA dispute-settlement system. From cross-border trucking to groundbreaking investment challenges against NAFTA governments to border conflicts involving wheat, pork, tomatoes, cement, lumber, and corn syrup, the various dispute-settlement mechanisms of this powerful North American trade treaty have determined millions of dollars in business outcomes.

BACKGROUND ON THE U.S.-MEXICO HFCS CASE

While in retrospect the telling one-two punch that occurred in the case of a WTO challenge followed immediately by a NAFTA complaint seems a brilliant tactical move by the United States, the reality is perhaps slightly less dazzling. In January 1998, following a year-long investigation under its AD law, Mexico's Commerce Department found that HFCS exports from the United States were being sold for export below their domestic U.S. price and that this international price discrimination, (i.e., dumping), threatened material injury to Mexico's sugar industry.

To challenge this decision, which had the effect of shutting down a lucrative multimillion dollar market for the U.S. corn industry, consideration will be given to some of the factors the exporters (e.g., Archer Daniels Midland and Cargill) would have considered in choosing a forum other than an *amparo* citizen's suit or a wrongful taxation suit in Mexico's federal courts.

INVOKING THE DISPUTE-SETTLEMENT PROCESS

A WTO challenge can be brought only by a government, consistent with the traditional notion of international dispute resolution as a government-to-government process. In our example, this translates into convincing the U.S. agencies responsible for the area of law in question, the U.S. Department of Commerce (USDOC) and the U.S. International Trade Commission (USITC), of both the merits of legal concerns with Mexico's AD investigation and the errors of raising important issues worth engaging the WTO dispute-settlement process.

The U.S. Trade Representative's (USTR) lawyers also need to be convinced, because they are the official triggers of a dispute-resolution challenge for the United States. This is not as complex as it may sound because these agencies monitor closely their own investigations of U.S. industries being undertaken in other countries. Thus someone already familiar with the case is likely available to meet with industry representatives to get the process rolling. Once the decision to go forward is made, the USTR will send a request for consultations to Mexico through the respective Geneva WTO representatives to open a period of possible negotiated settlement that assesses the merits of each other's positions, and which is generally a cooling-off period.

Many cases are not pursued beyond this stage, but if the WTO member chooses to pursue the challenge, the United States would send its request for the formal establishment of a dispute-settlement panel to the WTO Dispute Settlement Body. Under WTO rules, such a request must be honoured. Dispute Resolution under Chapter 19 of NAFTA, which covers the trade remedy laws (i.e., AD or CV duty cases), actually replaces the national court review of the agency's action if either side of the dispute chooses NAFTA's Chapter 19 dispute-resolution process.

This is an unusual but unique ceding of judicial sovereignty to an international forum, and continues to cause enormous controversy in the United States. For this reason, the industry itself (i.e., the same private Parties who could have triggered a suit in Mexico's courts) can invoke NAFTA Chapter 19 dispute resolution by filing a request for a panel with the NAFTA Secretariat. This does not mean counsel for the corn industry would not consult with the U.S. agencies (certainly that happened here to map out a strategy). It does mean that not only is a challenge filed, but also it means that issues are raised in that challenge that are made by the domestic industry affected and not by the government. The government will be looking at the national interest when deciding what issues should be submitted for decision (i.e., the effect on future U.S. agency practice if a particular issue is resolved against the United States).

In the U.S.-Mexico HFCS case, the government and industry representatives agreed that a WTO case was warranted because of the importance of the issues involved. The U.S. government, however, was unwilling to raise certain issues the sugar industry thought important, so it was agreed that the industry would pursue a separate challenge in NAFTA at the same time.

FORMATION OF THE DISPUTE PANEL

There is both a formal and an informal process for invoking a dispute panel under both WTO and NAFTA. In the WTO, the Secretariat picks three panellists from an "Indicative List" of names advanced by the members, usually current government officials who are most often those involved in implementing the WTO for their countries. Normally, panellists must not be nationals of the disputing Parties and they must not take instruction from their governments.

The disputing WTO members may exchange names informally, and may include trade experts not on the list who are hoped by the submitter to be from a country whose practice suggests they may be amenable to the position the government intends to present. There is no formal process of preemption, although names are eliminated without explanation in a wrenching process that often results in the Parties submitting their preferred panellists to the Secretariat to break the logjam. Most often WTO panels are composed of trade officials from neutral governments and academics whose reputation rises above national politics.

Five panellists are selected for a NAFTA panel and three panellists are selected for the WTO panel. Usually all are selected from a Roster of Panellists created by the three NAFTA governments. Unlike the WTO situation, they will be nationals of one of the three NAFTA countries although normally, but not always, the government of one disputing party chooses three panellists and the government of the other disputing party chooses two panellists. Note that although the private industry invokes the NAFTA process, national governments choose the judges, usually in consultation with industry counsel. In practice, the right to choose the tie-breaking panellist is given to the Party that wins a coin toss.

Unlike the WTO, NAFTA panellists cannot be current government employees, unless they are sitting judges. The prospect of judges serving on panels that replace the jurisdiction of Article III of the U.S. Constitution, like much of Chapter 19, raises issues of constitutional impact. But it does address one of the most difficult issues of choosing panellists who do not have an issue conflict. Most potential panellists are practicing trade lawyers who cannot serve on a WTO panel if they have other cases pending before the agencies with the same or similar issues. Finding qualified panellists often has delayed panel formation long past a treaty deadline, with the result that NAFTA dispute resolution leads rarely to the expeditious resolution of commercial conflicts. Once chosen, the NAFTA panellists choose their own chairperson.

It may be noted in passing that WTO panellists receive substantially greater support from the Secretariat. Thus each panel has its own skilled WTO lawyer and economist to assist its work but NAFTA panellists must, with meagre funds, hire individually their own law clerks. Until recently, WTO panellists were also compensated at a higher rate, although neither system even approaches private legal compensation rates. NAFTA panellists had their salaries doubled in 2001 to CDN $800 per day, which now compares favourably with 600 Swiss Francs for WTO panellists.

In the U.S.-Mexico HFCS case, the industry's request for a panel made in February 1998, one month after Mexico acted, was delayed for a variety of unusual trade reasons. The result was that the NAFTA panel was not even formed until August 2000, which was several months after the first WTO panel, to address the challenge that had already issued its report finding against Mexico. As it happened, this result was quite fortuitous for the United States, as will be explained below. Further delays saw the NAFTA panel's report not issued until August 2001.

LEGAL AND SUBJECT MATTER JURISDICTION OF THE PANELS

WTO panels have the more traditional function of interpreting compliance with the international agreements at issue. That is, they are applying international law to the facts. In the scope of review, the panel's subject-matter jurisdiction in a particular challenge is determined through so-called "terms of reference," which is the nature of the concern set out by the complaining country in its request for establishing a panel. Generally, these requests cite chapter and verse of the international agreements allegedly violated, but details usually remain unknown until briefs are filed later in the proceeding.

On the other hand, NAFTA Chapter 19 panels that are consistent with their role of replacing national judicial review are actually applying the domestic law of the importing country to the facts. They are charged with using the same law and the same general legal principles that would be applied in the courts of the importing nation—the U.S. Court of International Trade in the United States or the counterpart judicial bodies in the other NAFTA countries—depending on what agency's determination is being reviewed. Requests for a Chapter 19 review tend for this reason to look very much like a complaint that would be filed in federal court.

In the U.S.-Mexico HFCS case, the jurisdictional reality of the WTO and NAFTA panels was much closer than the treaty provisions would have predicted. Mexico, as a "monist" country that had incorporated the AD agreement into its federal law, meant that the NAFTA panel necessarily tread exactly the same ground as its WTO counterparts. The NAFTA panel's job did not end there, however, because it also had to rule on compliance by the Mexican agency that had legislative and regulatory gloss put onto the treaty provisions by Mexico's legislative and administrative bodies.

STANDARD OF REVIEW AND PRECEDENT

WTO panels reviewing AD cases apply a special standard of review. For fact-finding, it probably comes closest to the substantial-evidence test, although with a twist that requires the panel to assess whether the agencies were unbiased in their findings. For legal interpretation, the standard closely resembles *Chevron*: a fair degree of deference to the investigating national authority.

Although scholars question whether panels have paid more than lip service to the special standard, WTO panels reviewing other types of challenges have been supplied no written standard for their review other than they must make an objective assessment of the national agency action. Appellate Body reports have effectively grafted a reasonableness test onto the treaty's brief requirement that is not in total deference to the agency, but a panel should not substitute its judgment for that of the national authorities.

As to the sources of law issue, the role of precedent, formal panel decisions, and even appellate decisions bind no one but the Parties before them, and often panels diverge in their interpretations. At the appellate level, given the permanent nature of the Appellate Body, successive appellate decisions tend to track closely prior appellate decisions and, as you would expect, first-level panel decisions rarely stray from a foursquare prior appellate report interpreting a treaty provision.

Because the NAFTA Chapter 19 panels replace national judicial review, the standard of review is the same one that applies in the national courts. This sometimes has the perverse effect of according national agencies three levels of deference: almost complete deference for Canadian cases on the one hand, very little deference for Mexican cases, and deference for the United States cases falls somewhere in between with its substantial evidence standard for factual findings and its "in accordance with law" test for legal conclusions of the agency.

The question of precedent took some time for panels to resolve. It resulted ultimately in NAFTA panels finding that, when they are reviewing U.S. agency determinations, they operate at the same level as the U.S. Court of International Trade. The result is that they are not bound by prior rulings of that court, which is a substantial body of AD law, but they are bound by decisions of the U.S. Court of Appeals for the Federal Circuit to which Court of International Trade decisions are appealed. While the differing standards of review here inspired many pages of discussion virtually of treatise-like length in the NAFTA panel's case in discussing the Mexican standard, it would be difficult to pinpoint any difference in either the analysis or the ultimate result.

Because of the substantial delay in its formation, the NAFTA panel had the benefit not only of the original WTO panel decision finding fault with Mexico's implementation of the AD agreement, but also of the so-called Implementation Panel formed when the U.S. complained that Mexico had failed adequately to bring its measure into compliance with the NAFTA Agreement in spite of Mexico's revision of its AD determination following its first WTO panel loss.

Applying what it termed the "Principle of International Law Comity," the NAFTA panel deferred to the WTO panel's findings and conclusions on virtually all of the pure Antidumping Agreement issues, failing to do so only when it announced that the WTO panel had not considered a particular issue in sufficient detail to justify the NAFTA panel's acceptance of its findings in whole cloth. That left the NAFTA panel with a substantially smaller task of analysis, while simultaneously illustrating an unusual instance of partial merger of the jurisdiction of the two panels.

ROLE OF PRIVATE COUNSEL

A significant legal task is plotting strategy with the government, which means putting together briefs arguing the legal points under both WTO and NAFTA as well as coordinating industry's efforts to convince trade officials of the importance of initiating a WTO case if that forum seems appropriate. But what is private counsel's role after the process is invoked and arguments are being mounted before the panel?

In the WTO, the U.S. Government has guarded zealously its prerogative to have the only U.S. lawyers in the room, and only has recently failed in its effort to apply that same standard to every other country. Many countries cannot afford to employ legal staff sufficient to mount or defend WTO challenges, with the result that they often turn for assistance to private legal experts who are usually from the U.S. trade bar. In 2000, the WTO Appellate Body ruled definitively that these consultants are allowed to actually argue the case before a panel. The Appellate Body theory is that a WTO member has the right to choose who will represent it in its delegation.

In U.S. cases, the affected industry groups, or consumer groups, environmental groups, or other groups interested, play a meaningful role behind the scenes. These affected groups ensure that government counsel is well-prepared before panel hearings being fully de-briefed following such arguments and assisting in drafting written responses to the panel's questions.

In NAFTA Chapter 19 proceedings, as may have been anticipated, private counsel plays the same part it would play in court, which is full and visible representation of their clients. For general NAFTA dispute settlement in the Chapter 20 rulings, a more traditional behind-the-scenes approach is taken. For example, labour-union lawyers were significant hidden players in U.S. legal deliberations when Mexico challenged the U.S. refusal to let Mexican trucks ply their trade on U.S. roadways. Also, in NAFTA Chapter 11 investor-state cases, private counsel provide full representation to their clients before the arbitral panels and the national courts to which arbitral awards may be taken for limited procedural review.

RIGHT OF APPEAL

The Appellate Body process points out a major difference in the two systems. Every WTO panel decision may as of right be sent for review by the standing Appellate Body, often called the Supreme Court of World Trade. One of the founding members and a former chair is a prominent Florida lawyer, James Bacchus of Greenberg Traurig in Orlando. Well over one-half of all panel decisions are appealed, although we may expect that number to decrease as the Appellate Body's reports resolve more and more of the basic issues under WTO Agreements.

Because NAFTA Chapter 19 is a political compromise that permitted Canada to have some role in the review of U.S. trade remedy decisions, it was inconsistent with that goal to allow full appellate review of panel decisions. The drafters created instead an Extraordinary Challenge Committee that could be formed to review panel decisions, but only under the most unusual conditions including corruption of a panellist or an "outlaw" panel decision so outrageous that its very existence threatened the integrity of the binational panel process. No cases yet have met that test, and none ever is likely to do so. This is one of the most frequent criticisms of the appeal process. Because they cannot be second-guessed, it results in original panels having enormous power.

IMPLEMENTATION OF PANEL DECISIONS AND RETALIATION FOR NON-IMPLEMENTATION

There exist important differences in implementation of panel decisions under the WTO and NAFTA systems. It is often said that the centrepiece of the WTO is its binding dispute-settlement system. Unlike the previous Appellate Body system, the losing country cannot block panel reports; instead panel reports are automatically adopted after any appeal is exhausted under the rule of reverse consensus. Thus every voting member, including the country that won the dispute, must agree that the panel report should not be accepted by the WTO.

But the question of whether or not WTO panel decisions truly are binding international obligations is significantly more complex. The losing member retains its sovereign right to ignore the panel decision, in which case it will ultimately face retaliation in the form of withdrawal by the winning country of the tariff or other trade benefits under the WTO Agreements that are comparable to the "nullification or impairment" of benefits worked by the WTO-inconsistent measure.

On the other hand, a formal system of implementation is built into the WTO process. As in our U.S.-Mexico HFCS case, if the winning party is dissatisfied with the efforts taken by the losing party, here in Mexico's revised determination of AD duties the original panel is reconvened to sit as an arbitral panel to decide the level of compensation the United States will be authorized to exact. Thus the panel decision has only indirect impact, but the process will follow through to ensure that some way or another the panel's decision has consequences. This does not guarantee favourable results for the complaining country. U.S. cattle farmers still cannot ship to Europe beef from cattle raised on growth hormones. Europe has not seen a repeal of our Foreign Sales Corporation law.

In the NAFTA Chapter 19 situation, the panel's U.S.-Mexico HFCS decision had direct and binding impact on the Mexican agency that issued the determination in the same way a national judicial decision would apply to the agency. On one level, then, the NAFTA panel decision clearly is more binding as an international legal obligation. On another level, a recalcitrant agency can play havoc with the theory by delay and obfuscation.

The very existence of the post-report arbitration option in the WTO illustrates a significant concern for compliance, which is missing from the NAFTA Chapter 19 process. While the arbitral panel issues authorization for the prevailing WTO member to retaliate in the WTO at a certain level, it still does not guarantee that the responding country will revise its border measure found to have been in violation. It does, however, guarantee at least that noncompliance cannot be pursued without consequences. In fact, not only does the WTO system permit retaliation, it does not let the matter end there; compliance by the losing WTO member remains on the agenda of the Dispute Settlement Body until the panel report is implemented, even if the winning member has already exacted retaliation at the full level of the harm done to its export interests.

Under the NAFTA Chapter 19 process, the only recourse to a Party's recalcitrance or even refusal to implement a panel decision is a new request for a panel decision, and even this step cannot be taken unless the losing agency issues a new determination that can be challenged (i.e., what trade lawyers call the "atom bomb" of Article 1905 of NAFTA). That provision authorizes the dissatisfied government to invoke a separate dispute process to determine whether a Party has failed to implement a panel decision. If the complaining Party succeeds in convincing a special committee that this is the case, its recourse is to suspend operation of the Chapter 19 process with respect to the noncompliant party.

In this respect, the difference between a NAFTA panel and a national court becomes more clear, because panels do not have equitable powers and have no way to enforce their own decisions. The prevailing industry can file a new complaint, and thereby obtain a new panel decision, but the regular and orderly implementation process of the WTO is missing from the NAFTA arsenal.

In the U.S.- Mexico HFCS case, Mexico promptly revised its determination that had been found wanting by the original WTO panel. Its compliance, however, was seen by the NAFTA panel as a transparent exercise in tracking the WTO panel's findings of violations without marginally changing the result, even though the factual and legal premises for the earlier determination had been undermined. This is not to suggest that an adverse panel report should result necessarily in a different outcome in every instance—that is certainly not the law in regard to "reversal" by national courts, and NAFTA Chapter 19 panels are modelled after national judicial processes in the three countries.

CONCLUSIONS

This case study has attempted to trace the historical premises of the two most significant advances in trade-dispute settlement—the WTO and NAFTA Chapter 19 systems—and to demonstrate differences between them that might be important in agricultural border disputes. Successful international litigation strategy requires an understanding by both agricultural lawyers and business officials of these powerful new alternative dispute resolution systems.

LEGAL NOTES

* This chapter follows the guidelines set forth for by legal-citation systems, hence is inconsistent with the references and footnotes in the other chapters of this book.

[1] General Agreement on Tariffs and Trade, opened for signature Oct. 30, 1947, 61 Stat. A3, T.I.A.S. 1700, 55 U.N.T.S. 194, art. XXII(1), reprinted in THE RESULTS OF

THE URUGUAY ROUND OF MULTILATERAL TRADE NEGOTIATIONS: THE LEGAL TEXTS 485 (WTO 1994) [hereinafter GATT 1947].

[2]JOHN H. JACKSON, WORLD TRADE AND THE LAW OF GATT, at xxxix (1969).

[3]GATT 1947, supra note 1, art. XXIII(2).

[4]Compare Chile's complaint against Australia's fertilizer subsidies, GATT, B.I.S.D.at 193 (1952) (working party), with the poultry war between Europe and the United States, GATT, B.I.S.D. (12th Supp.) at 65 (1964) (expert panel), *and* European Communities: Refunds on Exports - Complaint by Brazil, GATT, B.I.S.D. (27th Supp.) at 69 (1981) (individual panel).

[5]GATT 1947, *supra* note 1, art. XXIII(2). If the party whose concessions were withdrawn disapproved of the remedy, its only recourse was to withdraw from the Agreement within a shorter time period than otherwise provided under Article XXXI.

[6]Netherlands Measures of Suspension of Obligations to the United States, GATT, B.I.S.D. (1st Supp.) at 32 (1953).

[7]Procedures Under Article XXIII, GATT B.I.S.D. (14th Supp.) at 18 (1966).

[8]Understanding Regarding Notification, Consultation, Dispute Settlement and Surveillance, GATT B.I.S.D. (26th Supp.) 1980, *reprinted in* THE TEXTS OF THE TOKYO ROUND AGREEMENTS 200 (GATT 1986). Article 7 of the Understanding explicitly reaffirms that the customary practice of GATT in the field of dispute settlement includes the 1966 procedures for the settlement of disputes between developed and less-developed countries.

[9]ROBERT E. HUDEC, ENFORCING INTERNATIONAL TRADE LAW: THE EVOLUTION OF THE MODERN GATT LEGAL SYSTEM 29 (1993). Professor Hudec notes that the cohesiveness of this group was so strong that the first disputes were resolved by a ruling from the chair, usually accepted by consensus without debate. *Id.*

[10]Amelia Porges, *The New Dispute Settlement: From the GATT to the WTO,* 8 LEIDEN J. INT'L L. 115, 117 (1995).

[11]*See generally* HUDEC, *supra* note 9, ch. 7.

[12]Improvement to the GATT Dispute Settlement Rules and Documents, GATT B.I.S.D. (36th Supp.) at 61 (1989).

[13]HUDEC, *supra* note 9, at 194.

[14]Understanding on Rules and Procedures Governing the Settlement of Disputes, art. 16(4), WTO Agreement, Annex 2, 33 I.L.M. 1235 (1994), *reprinted in* THE RESULTS OF THE URUGUAY ROUND OF MULTILATERAL TRADE NEGOTIATIONS: THE LEGAL TEXTS 417 (WTO 1994) [hereinafter Dispute Settlement Understanding].

[15]*Id.* art. 12(8).

[16]*Id.* arts. 16(4), 17.

[17]*Id.* art. 22(6).

[18]*Id.* art. 22(1).

[19]*Id.* art. 22(3).

[20]North American Free Trade Agreement, U.S.-Canada-Mexico, Jan. 1, 1994, annex 1901.2, 32 I.L.M. 289, *reprinted in* H.R. Doc. 103-159 at 1231.

[21]*Id.* art. 1904(2)-(3). *See id. art.* 1911 for definitions of "administrative record," "general legal principles," and "standard of review."

[22]*Id.* art. 1904(10)-(12).

[23]*Id.* art. 1904(5), (7).

[24]*Id.* art. 1904(8).

[25]*Id.* art. 1904(13). The basis for the extraordinary challenge procedure is that: (1) a panel member has a serious conflict of interest; (2) the panel seriously departed from a fundamental procedural rule; or (3) the panel manifestly exceeded its powers, and that such action materially affected the panel's decision and threatens the integrity of the panel process. For procedures, *see id.* annex 1904.13.

[26]*Id.* art. 1904(9), (11).

[27]*Id.* annex 1904.15 (Schedule of Mexico). Through such provisions as disclosure meetings, notices of intended action by SECOFI, access to proprietary business information by counsel under a protective order, detailed reasons for SECOFI decisions, and elimination of the need to seek an administrative appeal before challenging a SECOFI determination before a binational panel, Mexico's law was assured a solid foundation in transparency and due process. One can argue that Mexico's system is more advanced in this respect than that of Canada.

[28]*See* United States - Canada Free Trade Agreement Binational Panel Review, In the matter of: Fresh, Chilled, or Frozen Pork from Canada;ECC-91-1904-01 USA (June 14,1991), United States-Canada Free Trade Agreement Binational Panel Review, In the Matter of: Live Swine from Canada, ECC-93-1904-OIUSA (Apr. 8,1993); Lumber ECC, ECC 94-1904-01USA (Aug. 3, 1994); Article 1904 Extraordinary Challenge Pursuant to the NAFTA, In the Matter of: Gray Portland Cement and Clinker from Mexico, ECC-2000-1904-01USA. These decisions are *available at* the web site of the NAFTA Secretariat,

http://www.nafta-sec-alena.org/DefaultSite/dispute/index_e.aspx?ArticleID=10

[29]Conversations by author with members of trade bar.

Chapter 5

Why Antidumping Law is Good for Agriculture

Mel Annand
University of Saskatchewan

INTRODUCTION

> (W)e will have to leave dumping and countervail measures in
> place as a viable remedy because we haven't addressed the
> underlying problems. … What we would like to see at the
> outset is a reasonable expression of interest on the part of our
> trading partners in the direction of eliminating the underlying
> problems that give rise to dumping and countervailing duty
> actions. (U.S. Under-Secretary of Commerce, Grant Aldonas
> 2002)

Some commentators characterize antidumping (AD) laws as a perpetuation of an economic myth, which imposes substantial costs on firms that engage in commercial transactions, on taxpayers, and on consumers in importing countries. It wastes resources by encouraging rent-seeking behaviour and by requiring the preparation of complex legal arguments by both those bringing a case and the accused that must defend themselves. It allows governments to harass foreign firms. It reduces the credibility of the international trade-law system and its institutions (Kerr 2001).

Further, AD duties can be imposed when a foreign firm engages in price discrimination, which is a normal business practice that is not penalized at the domestic level (Kerr 2001). AD law is therefore criticized by trade lawyers and economists as being an economically inappropriate solution to predatory pricing by firms from another country. The literature is replete with calls for the replacement of AD law with better competition and antitrust law. This will supposedly enhance consumer welfare and reduce rent-seeking behaviour by domestic producers.

The purpose of this chapter is to suggest that the above analysis is superficial and deceptive in the area of agricultural products in the twenty-first century. This chapter also suggests that the analysis of AD law in agriculture should focus on the issue of sales below the cost of production. The chapter does not deal with price discrimination or predatory pricing as such. It does not deal with dumping as a short-run phenomenon. Rather, this chapter deals with sales below the cost of production in agriculture as a long-term structural problem. AD law should be analyzed as a potentially appropriate and useful response to long-term structural dumping of agricultural products in the world market.

AD law is merely a symptomatic treatment of a larger economic ill caused by subsidies in agriculture. The real illness in international trade in agricultural products is overproduction generated by domestic subsidies. This results in depressed and declining real prices for agricultural products. It causes countries to create trade barriers to maintain high prices in domestic markets, while the countries export their surplus production. Real treatment of the cause of overproduction reduces the need for the aspirin-like solutions of AD actions. Real action to deal with the domestic-subsidy cause of overproduction would perhaps ultimately allow economists to persuade politicians to give up AD remedies in favour of new competition law. Until we have real reform of domestic-subsidy law, we should embrace AD law as a good thing for agriculture.

At the root of the domestic-subsidy problem is the fact of changing comparative advantage in agricultural production. An industry with real comparative advantage will not need subsidies to survive and thrive. But the fact is that the comparative advantage of U.S. agriculture is declining in many areas (e.g., soybeans and corn). The same is true in other developed countries as well. This chapter will not examine the causes in detail, but the causes include high input costs for land and chemicals. The result is that the relative cost of U.S. production is increasing compared to some other areas of the world.

What has been the U.S. reaction to this loss of comparative advantage in the face of a declining real price for corn? Certainly, it has not reduced production. Rather, it has subsidized the corn producers. This domestic support has allowed corn producers to stay in business, although they may not have retained much of the subsidy in terms of real income. But the inevitable result has been to maintain or increase corn production over what it otherwise would have been without producer subsidies. The consequent result is that corn is now sold in the U.S. domestic market and in foreign markets at below the cost of production.

A sale below the cost of production is dumping. Foreign consumers are happy, but foreign producers and their governments are not happy. They have strategic reasons: producers are put out of business, economic spin-offs and development are drawn into the United States, and tax revenues are lost or foregone. Predictably, U.S. agricultural goods, including corn, will be challenged under Canadian AD trade law. The recent Canadian corn case is an example. It will be used to demonstrate how the Canadian law works.

First, I will describe some of the features of Canada's *Special Import Measures Act* (SIMA) that will provide an example of how AD legislation works in Canadian law. Second, I will describe some of the details of the World Trade Organization (WTO) Antidumping Agreement and how it affects domestic law, which will also show how Canadian AD law is WTO compliant. Third, I will describe the extent of U.S. dumping of agricultural products, including corn. Fourth, I will describe the Canadian AD cases dealing with grain corn, which will show how persistent sales of agricultural products below the cost of production will result in negative AD action. Fifth, I will describe briefly the increased use of AD actions around the world and how this is significant for agriculture. Finally, I will conclude with a section detailing why AD law is a good thing for agriculture.

THE SPECIAL IMPORT MEASURES ACT (SIMA)

SIMA sets out the Canadian domestic law for AD-duty actions (SIMA 1995). SIMA is intended to provide some protection to Canadian producers, including agricultural producers, from the dumping of goods into Canada.

It should be noted that there are no special rules in SIMA for dealing with agricultural products. The criteria used for resolving AD disputes are the same for agricultural products as they are for manufactured products. However, the Canadian legal system has not had difficulty applying the AD rules to agricultural products. Despite the cyclical nature of some agricultural production, the legal tools that are available through SIMA allow the Canadian government to deal effectively with the question of dumping in agricultural products. There appears to be no need to specifically amend the SIMA rules in order to properly deal with questions of dumping of agricultural products.

The *Special Import Measures Act*, implemented in 1985 by the Canadian government, brings together the instruments and processes relating to contingency projectionist matters. This legislation gathered together and brought up-to-date these elements of Canadian trade legislation. Canada had first introduced AD legislation in 1904. At that early date, Canada realized that its proximity to the United States and the large difference in the size of the two economies made the possibility of dumped imports from the United States a very present danger to Canadian producers. It was quite possible for U.S. producers to sell goods at dumped prices in quantities that were insignificant in terms of volume of production and sales in the United States, but which were extremely large in size relative to Canadian production and sales. This difference in market size made dumping goods in Canada a very attractive business proposition for U.S. exporters, and it still does.

CALCULATING THE MARGIN OF DUMPING

The main point of interest in SIMA is that it contains a definition of dumping that includes sales below the cost of production (SIMA 1995). Dumping of goods can be found if the export price of goods in a country is less than the price it is in that country's domestic market. Dumping can also be found if the export price of a good in a country is less than that same country's total cost of production for that good. The domestic selling price of a foreign producer or that producer's total cost of production is referred to as the "normal value" of the goods. Thus, goods are dumped if their normal value exceeds their export price. The margin of dumping in either of these cases is the amount by which the normal value of the goods exceeds the export price.

The key issue in dumping is the value of the normal value of the goods. The normal value can be determined in the following ways:

- the domestic sales price of the goods;
- third-country sales price of the goods; or
- the constructed value of the goods, which is the aggregate of the costs of production, an amount for selling, administrative and other costs, and a reasonable amount for profit. (SIMA 1995)

It is the constructed value of the goods that is of the most interest in this chapter, since it can be used when the domestic price of the goods in the exporting country is not profitable. The authority for using the constructed value of goods as their normal value is:

> Subject to Section 20, where the normal value of any goods cannot be determined under section 15 by reason that there was not, in the opinion of the Commissioner, such a number of sales of like goods that comply with all the terms and conditions referred to in that section or that are applicable by virtue of subsection 16(1) as to permit a proper comparison with the sale of the goods to the importer, the normal value of the goods shall be determined, at the option of the Commissioner in any case or class of cases, as:

> (b) the aggregate of:
>
> > i   the cost of production of the goods;
> > ii a reasonable amount for administrative, selling, and all other costs; and
> > iii a reasonable amount for profits. (SIMA 1995: Section 19)

THE WTO ANTIDUMPING RULES

The WTO rules on dumping started with Article VI of the General Agreement on Tariffs and Trades (GATT) in 1947. This provision was intended to limit the use of AD measures by subjecting them to specific rules. Article VI does not make rules about dumping, but rather makes rules regulating national laws about antidumping. The WTO is concerned about the protectionist nature of AD law and thus attempts to limit the use of AD law by setting standards of openness and procedural uniformity. Of interest for this chapter is the basic formula set out in Article VI:1 for determining the margin of dumping. It provides:

a product is to be considered as being introduced into the commerce of an importing country at less than its normal value, if the price of the product exported from one country to another:

(a) **is less than the comparable price, in the ordinary course of trade**, for the like product when destined for consumption in the exporting country, or,

(b) **in the absence of such domestic price, is less than either**

> i the highest comparable price for the like product for export to any third country in the ordinary course of trade, or
>
> ii **the cost of production of the product in the country of origin plus a reasonable addition for selling cost and profit** (emphasis added). (GATT 1947)

The Uruguay Round of GATT 1994 resulted in the new Agreement on the Implementation of Article VI (generally referred to as the Antidumping Agreement).

The Antidumping Agreement adds precision to normal-value determinations in four key areas.[1] First, unprofitable sales in the domestic market can be disregarded, and the use of constructed costs is permitted only if unprofitable sales have been made for an extended period of time in substantial quantities. Second, cost data are to be based on records kept by the exporter, provided that the records are in accordance with generally accepted accounting principles in the exporting country. Third, authorities are required to use the historical method of cost allocation by the exporter, with appropriate adjustments to be made for certain non-recurring items such as capital cost allowance and development costs. Fourth, selling, administrative, and any other costs and the amounts for profits are to be based on actual data pertaining to production and sales in the ordinary course of trade, with prescriptions for determining these costs and profit levels.

Article 2.2.1 of the Antidumping Agreement provides the details of when domestic sales below the cost of production may be treated as not being in the ordinary course of trade, and therefore may be ignored in the determination of normal value dumping actions:

> Sales of the like product in the domestic market of the exporting country or sales to a third country at prices below per unit (fixed and variable) costs of production plus administrative, selling and general costs may be treated as not being in the ordinary course of trade by reason of price and may be disregarded in determining normal value only if the authorities determine that such sales are made within an extended period of time in substantial quantities and are at prices which do not provide for the recovery of all costs within a reasonable period of time. If prices, which are below per unit costs at the time of sale, are above weighted average per unit costs for the period

of investigation, such prices shall be considered to provide for recovery of costs within a reasonable period of time. (GATT 1994: Article 2.2.1)

This provision contemplates significant long-term sales below the cost of production as being subject to AD duties.

The concept of using a constructed cost to determine if dumping exists is clearly enshrined in international trade law. As long as national laws comply with Article VI of GATT 1994 and the Antidumping Agreement, countries can use the constructed-cost approach to deal with dumped goods. SIMA provisions appear to comply with these requirements. The next section describes how this approach has been used to examine some U.S. exports of agricultural products.

U.S. DUMPING IN WORLD AGRICULTURAL MARKETS

A recent report from the Institute for Agriculture and Trade Policy (IATP) identifies the huge extent to which the United States exports agricultural products at prices below the cost of production (Ritchie, Murphy, and Lake 2003). The IATP report provides detailed cost-of-production calculations from the U.S. Department of Agriculture (USDA) and the Organization for Economic Co-Operation and Development (OECD) for five crops, and compares them to export prices to determine the margin of dumping. The results for corn show dumping margins of 30 percent to 33 percent for 1999 through 2001. The full details of the dumping margins for corn are shown in Table 5.1 (details of the table calculations are contained in the Appendix of this chapter).

The IATP report also provides similar calculations of the dumping margins for wheat, soybeans, rice, and cotton. The dumping margins for each of these commodities is similar to that of corn. The report shows that the dumping of these commodities by the United States is a long-term part of the structure of U.S. agriculture, with 1997 through 2001 showing the highest margins of U.S. dumping. Oxfam International (2002) shows similar numbers for the European Union. The dumping margins are shockingly high for 2001: wheat at 44 percent; soybeans at 29 percent; corn at 33 percent; cotton at 57 percent; and rice at 22 percent. This report quantifies the extent of U.S. dumping on world agricultural markets. The IATP report also examines the detrimental effect this dumping has on agriculture industries, particularly in developing countries. The depression of agricultural prices from the dumping of agricultural commodities prevents farmers from earning a living. Farmers in developing countries are driven out of the export market by lower-priced competition. This drives farmers off the land and destroys the local physical and social infrastructure of a country. A

Table 5.1: U.S. Percentage of Export Dumping, Maize

Year	Gov't Support Costs	Farmer Production Costs	Transportation and Handling Costs	Full Cost	Export Price	Export Dumping
	PSE		U.S dollars per bushel			Percent
1990	0.08	2.49	0.54	3.11	2.79	10
1991	0.09	2.65	0.54	3.27	2.75	16
1992	0.07	2.26	0.54	2.86	2.66	7
1993	0.08	2.90	0.54	3.51	2.62	25
1994	0.07	2.25	0.54	2.85	2.74	4
1995	0.10	2.88	0.54	3.51	3.13	11
1996	0.08	2.70	0.54	3.31	4.17	−26
1997	0.07	2.77	0.54	3.37	2.98	12
1998	0.06	2.64	0.54	3.24	2.58	20
1999	0.06	2.68	0.54	3.27	2.29	30
2000	0.06	2.72	0.54	3.31	2.24	32
2001	0.06	2.81	0.54	3.41	2.28	33

Source: Richie, Murphy, and Lake (2003).

similar result is now being observed in developed countries such as Canada. The amazing thing is that the depression of agricultural prices from excess production is happening in the United States as well.

The IATP report is troubling because the calculations do not include the much larger sums that the U.S. government spends on direct-income support. The direct-income support paid by governments is significant because it is what allows farmers to remain in business while they sell their products for prices below the cost of production. Without this support, farmers could soon stop producing an oversupply of products from which they lose money. Economic resources could be shifted to other uses and supply would diminish. With the present level of direct-income support in the United States, however, farmers will continue to produce and dump their main crops into international markets.

An OECD report in 2001 confirms that the WTO Agreement on Agriculture did not reduce the amount of support that OECD countries had given to agriculture (OECD 2001). The report shows that the key Producer Support Estimate (PSE) still represents 40 percent of the gross farm receipts in OECD countries as it did in 1999. (This is the same 40 percent as was determined in the WTO base period of 1986 through 1988.) The total PSE dollar amount actually increased from U.S. $246 billion for the 1986 through 1988 period to U.S. $270 billion in 1999. Countries simply have shifted their support from regulated USDA, Agricultural Marketing Service (USDA/AMS) programs to WTO-exempt programs. This leaves importing countries with no WTO-compatible remedy except for AD law. The IATP report recognizes this might be the easiest approach for importing countries to protect their own economies from dumped agricultural goods.

The OECD study recognizes that the theoretical distinction, created by the WTO between trade-distorting and non-trade-distorting subsidies, is of little practical value when creating trade based on true comparative advantage. Countries have simply moved their support from one category to another. Economists generally are beginning to recognize the failure of the artificial "boxes" of domestic support to eliminate trade distortions. This should result in the development of more rigorous WTO discipline in the area of domestic support for agriculture. Much work needs to be done to address questions of economic structure and, perhaps some day, to prevent dumping in agriculture.

So lawyers and economists should save their breath and their ink on AD law. They will contribute more to real economic benefit if they deal with the trade-distorting effects of rampant domestic support and the resulting dumping below cost. Thus the next section shows how Canada has attempted to deal with the dumping of U.S. corn.

THE GRAIN-CORN CASES

The Grain-Corn Case No. 1

The first grain-corn case between Canada and the United States occurred in 1986. The case dealt with an allegation of subsidizing (not of dumping) by the United States, so it lacks cost-of-production analysis. It started with a complaint by the Ontario Corn Producers Association alleging injurious subsidization of corn exports by the United States. The Department of National Revenue, which is the predecessor of the Canada Customs and Revenue Agency, Customs, and Excise (CCRA), investigated and made a determination that imports of grain corn from the United States were benefiting from a subsidy of U.S. $0.849 per bushel (Department of National Revenue 1987). In March of 1987, the Canadian International Trade Tribunal (CITT) made a finding of injury to the Canadian production of grain corn and a duty was imposed of U.S. $0.849 per bushel (CITT 1987).

An interesting aspect of this case is that it involved the first application of the public interest provisions of SIMA. The CITT heard representations from many corn users that they would be adversely impacted by the duty. As a result, the CITT recommended to the Canadian Minister of Finance that, in the public interest, the duty be limited to CDN $0.30 per bushel. The Minister of Finance heard further submissions, and, in February of 1988 he reduced the duty to CDN $0.46 per bushel. In typical Canadian style, this political solution satisfied no one. Economists complained that the national economic efficiency was not promoted. Domestic producers still perceived injury, but likely received as much government protection through this process as was possible realistically.

This case is significant because it represents the protectionist response of Canadian farmers to the diverging farm economies in Canada and the United States. Canada's domestic support for the corn farmers had been falling behind the massive subsidies being granted to U.S. corn farmers, so the impact on Ontario corn producers of subsidized U.S. corn has been significant. The Ontario producers have been well organized and active when protecting their own interests. The result has been the imposition of duty by Canada that has lasted for five years. However, the structural long-term differences between the two farm economies have not disappeared. In fact, they have become larger. The result has been further action taken by Canadian farmers to protect farmers from the dumping of U.S. corn.

The Grain-Corn Case No. 2

Canada Customs and Revenue Agency, Customs, and Excise (CCRA) Preliminary Determination

The next grain-corn case arose in June of 2000 when the Manitoba Corn Growers Association, Inc. (MCGA) alleged injurious dumping and subsidizing of grain-corn exports from the United States. On August 9, 2000, the Antidumping and Countervailing Directorate of the CCRA began an investigation into the allegation. The investigation began with a Statement of Reasons by the CCRA as to why the investigation was undertaken (CCRA 2000). This Statement of Reasons summarized the legal requirements that have been satisfied by the complainant at that stage including:

Evidence of Dumping
Dumping occurs when the normal value of the goods exceeds the export price of the goods shipped to Canada. The MCGA provided evidence of a U.S. domestic selling price of less than U.S. $2.00 per bushel for the 1998 to 2000 time period. The MCGA also provided evidence of a constructed normal value based on published USDA, Economic Research Service (USDA/ ERS) information.

The CCRA held that domestic selling prices in the United States were alleged to not represent profitable prices and therefore could not be used to estimate a normal value for the imported corn. Rather, the CCRA used the USDA/ERS data, revised it somewhat, including an amount for profit, and used a constructed normal value to determine dumping.

To determine the actual export price of the U.S. corn, the CCRA relied on actual customs documentation from corn imported by Canada from the United States. It relied on this information because the customs documentation was based on declared selling prices.

When the CCRA compared the U.S. normal value and the U.S. export prices, it found that 54 percent of the U.S. grain-corn imports appeared to have been dumped. The margins of dumping ranged from 26 percent to 53 percent, expressed as a percentage of normal value. The overall average margin of dumping was estimated at 40 percent.

The CCRA went on to find that there was also evidence of subsidization by the United States through a number of government programs. The CCRA concluded that at least the nonrecourse marketing-assistance loans and loan-deficiency payments provided subsidies to the U.S. corn growers. The CCRA found those subsidy payments amounted to benefits of U.S. $0.14 per bushel in 1998 (8 percent), U.S. $0.22 in 1999 (13 percent), and U.S. $0.21 in 2000 (12.5 percent). The CCRA was therefore satisfied that a subsidy investigation was warranted.

Evidence of Injury

The CCRA proceeded to find injury to Manitoba corn producers through price suppression, lost sales, reduced income, impaired lines of credit, and lost incentive to expand production in a growing market.

Although the ultimate determination of injury is left to the CITT by SIMA, the CCRA has to be satisfied that there is reasonable evidence supporting the existence of injury to a regional industry. In this case, the Commissioner of the CCRA was satisfied that Manitoba corn producers had been injured. The first condition for an injury finding is that there must be a concentration of dumped imports into the regional market—that being Western Canada. Three tests that show concentration of dumped imports are: (1) the Density Test, which shows that there are more imports in the market than there is Canadian production; (2) the Distribution Test, which shows that there is proportionally more corn imported into the Western market than there is into the Eastern market; and (3) the Ratio Test, which shows that the Western Canadian market accounts for only 7.5 percent of the total Canadian market, but experiences roughly one-third of the total U.S. imports of corn into Canada in the subject years.

The second condition for injury to a regional market requires that the dumped imports injure all or almost all of the producers within the regional market. Since MCGA represented from 89 percent to 97 percent of the Western Canadian grain-corn production, and since the complaint demonstrating injury was filed on behalf of all of the MGCA members, the CCRA found that this condition was satisfied.

Based on these findings, the CCRA concluded there was evidence that the subject goods had been dumped and that there was a reasonable indication that dumping was causing material injury to the grain-corn industry in Western Canada.

Canadian International Trade Tribunal (CITT)
Preliminary Injury Inquiry

The next stage in the process is for the CITT to make a preliminary inquiry under Subsection 34(2) of SIMA, into whether or not the evidence discloses a reasonable indication that the dumping and subsidizing of grain corn has caused injury to the domestic industry. The CITT conducted its inquiry and released its decision on October 10, 2000 (CITT 2000). The decision upheld the CCRA preliminary finding of dumping, subsidization, and injury. The CITT noted that the case involved a regional market within the meaning of Article 4.1(ii) of the Agreement on Implementation of Article VI of GATT, 1994, and Article 16.2 of the Agreement on Subsidies and Countervailing Measures. The CITT noted that the regional market cases are extraordinary cases in which an investigation may be initiated even though the complainant does not represent a major portion of the total domestic injury.

The Final Determination of the Canada Customs and Revenue Agency, Customs, and Excise (CCRA)

The CCRA final determination was released on February 5, 2001, upholding the earlier determination of the dumping and the subsidization of U.S. grain corn in Canada. It is interesting to note that exporters and producers of grain corn from the United States did not provide additional information during the final determination phase of the investigation. The CCRA was therefore left with insufficient information to determine normal values based on export selling prices. When considering the normal value of corn, the CCRA in its determination stated:

> A normal value is usually based on profitable sales in the exporter's home market, or, in the absence of profitable sales, on the basis of all costs of the goods plus an amount for profit. As none of the submissions provided sufficient information, it was necessary to estimate normal values based on the facts available. (CCRA 2001)

In its final determination, the CCRA used a constructed normal value pursuant to Section 29 (1) of SIMA. In the constructed normal value, CCRA used a profit amount of 2.4 percent. Total costs, which included profit, resulted in a normal value of U.S. $2.39 per bushel in 1998 and a normal value of U.S. $2.46 per bushel in 1999.

To complete the dumping calculation, the CCRA used the same average selling price from Canadian Customs records that was used in the preliminary determination. CCRA reviewed 89 percent of the actual goods shipped to Western Canada during the dumping period. In the final determination, the CCRA found that 94 percent of the corn had been dumped and that margins ranging from 0.2 percent to 75 percent had been found. The average margin of dumping was 27 percent, or U.S. $0.67 per bushel. The CCRA was satisfied that this margin of dumping was not insignificant.

The CCRA also proceeded with a subsidy investigation, concluding that there was a subsidy of U.S. $0.35 per bushel of grain corn in the United States in 1998 and U.S. $0.63 per bushel in 1999. These subsidy amounts represented approximately 35 percent of the weighted average export price of the goods in 1999, and the CCRA found that this was a significant amount of subsidy.

Canadian International Trade Tribunal (CITT) Final Injury Inquiry

The last step for the imposition of the AD duty was the final determination by the CITT on the question of injury. The CITT found no injury on a narrow legal test related to the regional market (CITT 2001). In the final injury hearing, the CITT heard from a number of parties opposed to an injury finding. These parties included livestock-producer groups, livestock-feed manufacturers, grain dealers and importers, distillers, and other provincial agricultural organizations representing corn importers or corn users. The main issue became whether the U.S. dumping or subsidizing of grain corn caused or threatened to cause material injury to the Canadian domestic producers of all or almost all of the production of like goods in that regional market.

A key finding by the CITT is that production for on-farm use constitutes domestic production and that such producers are part of the domestic regional industry. Therefore the CITT examined whether or not the dumped U.S. grain corn was injuring the Canadian producers who produced grain corn for on-farm use. The CITT found that on-farm users were indifferent to market prices and had lower-than-average costs of production. Therefore the CITT accepted that dumped or subsidized U.S. grain corn had not injured Canadian on-farm users. The CITT then found that the on-farm use of corn exceeded 30 percent of total domestic production. Since most or all of the on-farm production had not been injured, it followed for the CITT that the U.S. dumped or subsidized grain corn had not injured a substantial proportion of corn growers. When this proportion of the market was added to other commercial production segments that did not appear to have been materially injured, the CITT found that the minimum injury threshold of 90 percent of producers in a regional market had not been satisfied.

Result

The direct result of the Grain Corn No. 2 case was that no duty was imposed. This result came from the narrow regional market "test" requiring more than 90 percent of producers to be injured. The result does not change the fact that the CITT found dumping and subsidy in corn. The real significance of the decision is that, for the second time, the CITT found significant levels of U.S. subsidized corn coming into Canada. In this case, the CITT also found dumping below the cost of production. These findings reflect the long-term reality that U.S. corn is competitive in the Canadian market only if it is sold below the U.S. cost of production.

THE INCREASED USE OF ANTIDUMPING IN AGRICULTURE

Several authors have documented the growth of AD actions in recent years (Prusa 2001). These authors identified a small group of traditional users of AD legislation, including Canada and the United States, which have had AD legislation since the 1970s and have used the legislation regularly. However, there is a new group of countries that have recently adopted and become active users of AD legislation. These countries include Mexico, Argentina, Brazil, and South Africa.

These new users of AD legislation have been attracted by AD's unique combination of WTO consistency and ease of use. Countries can use AD duties to levy sector-specific duties without blatant violation of tariff bindings or of market-access commitments.

Countries will also learn quickly that they can use AD legislation to counteract both domestic and export subsidies in agriculture. A trend is likely developing in the use of AD measures by countries seeking to protect their own agricultural industries from U.S.-dumped and EU-dumped products. Examining the reports made to the WTO concerning AD activity could identify this trend.

AD measures have been called the weapon of choice for protection in the new millennium. There will no doubt be much discussion in future WTO round of trade negotiations in agriculture about the use of AD duties. The United States may seek to reform AD law through the WTO to restrict AD use by other countries. However, it will be very difficult for the major agricultural exporting countries such as Canada and the United States to restrict the use of AD duties by other countries unless they are prepared to limit their own use of the law.

WHY ANTIDUMPING IS A GOOD THING IN AGRICULTURE

General Theory Supporting Antidumping Law

AD and countervailing (CV) duty laws have long been recognized as a necessary part of a successful international free-trade regime (Bhagwati 1988). If an international free-trade regime is to be based on economic comparative advantage, then rules must prevent the use of subsidies to create an artificial comparative advantage on the one hand and protection on the other. Therefore, part of the international order must be to prevent dumping as dumping is a trade technique that is used to secure and maintain an inappropriate share of world markets.

The WTO trading system includes rules to regulate the use of national AD laws. The WTO rules can be seen as having three functions:

- the anti-protectionist function;
- the liberalizing function; and
- the interface function. (Denton 1989)

The anti-protectionist function of the WTO rules reflects the concern that nations would use their AD laws in a protectionist fashion. WTO rules restrict the possibility that AD duties will replace tariff barriers as a method of limiting imports.

The liberalizing function of WTO rules arises from the suggestion that the prevention of dumping is an important component of liberalizing free trade. Strong national AD laws prevent dumping, therefore the WTO rules serve to legitimize and standardize beneficial national AD laws that promote liberalized free trade.

The interface function is the main topic of interest for the purposes of this chapter. The interface function suggests that World Trade Organization AD principles allow economies with significant structural differences to interact and trade (Jackson 1989). The fact that different economies have different structures and different economic distortions creates trade tensions between the two economies. These tensions result in protectionist sentiments, which are given expression in national AD rules. The fact that the international trading community, through the WTO, implicitly sanctions the national AD rules helps to justify the rules and smooth out the structural differences between the two economies. The interface justification of AD rules does not solve the problem of structural differences. However, the interface function does justify the use of AD laws to reduce the friction between two structurally different systems. It is a corollary to the interface argument that the political function of AD laws to satisfy producer groups is at least as important as the economic function of maximizing national welfare (Wright 1989).

The interface argument is important in the context of the dumping of U.S. agriculture products on the world market at prices below cost. Structural differences in the U.S. agricultural industry have resulted in the United States becoming a relatively high-cost producer of agricultural goods. U.S. producers have not kept pace with the rest of the world when reducing their costs of production of agricultural goods. However, they have been sheltered from the effects of becoming high-cost producers by the creation of an institutional framework of domestic support by the U.S. government. Specifically, the maintenance and growth of WTO Green Box subsidies to U.S. farmers has allowed U.S. farmers to remain in business despite the fact that they sell their products at less than the cost of production. These institutional supports for U.S. agribusiness have now become part of the structure of agriculture in the United States.

How will foreign agricultural producers react to this phenomenon? To the extent possible, foreign agricultural producers will use national AD laws to protect their own production from these WTO Green Box subsidies. Foreign producers, including those in Canada, will use their AD laws to keep out subsidized U.S. products such as corn. These actions will show evidence of dumping by using the constructed-cost approach in the calculation of a dumping margin. Until the United States takes steps to deal with its own structural distortions in the agricultural-products market, AD rules will be a means by which the two economies will interact without major confrontations. At the very least, agricultural-producer groups in Canada will use AD laws as an important means of political expression on the national scene.

Economic Theory and Antidumping Law

It is contrary to widespread economic belief that welfare benefits across the whole economy may outweigh the welfare costs of antidumping on a sectoral basis. Economists have perceived the idea that there is a trade off between sectoral costs and whole economy benefits, but it is not a popular view. For example, it is stated that:

> … the World Trading Order ought to reflect the essence of the principle of free trade for all—for example, by permitting the appropriate use of countervailing duties and antidumping actions to maintain fair, competitive trade. (Bhagwati 1988: 35)

There are other examples of the trade off between trade liberalization and antidumping, including Boltuck (1992) and Moore and Suranovic (1994). This literature is explored by Miranda, Torres, and Ruiz (1998).[2]

It is a traditional view among economists that dumping has positive effects on the welfare of the importing nation. In this view, AD law would be justifiable if it were intended to offset only a predatory pricing strategy by the exporter. However, this is a narrow approach to the issue, which is not shared by all economists. For example, it is pointed out that:

> ... short-run dumping, whatever its objective, may result in serious injury to or even the total elimination of the domestic industry. The gain to the consumer from a short period of abnormally low prices may not be nearly great enough to offset the damage to the domestic industry, included the capital invested therein. (Viner 1966: 140)

Viner was primarily concerned about short-run dumping, but he recognized that dumping could amount to the export of recessions when predatory export pricing takes place during part of the business cycle (Viner 1966). What must be answered now is the extent of damage incurred to the domestic industry, particularly the capital invested in it, if dumping is allowed in the long run. The agriculture industry has significant sunk costs, partly due to factor specificity. What will be the result for this capital investment if the domestic industry is destroyed in the long run? These are topics that should be considered and investigated when arriving at a conclusion about the appropriateness of AD law in long-run dumping situations such as those that exist in agriculture. Baldwin examines these long-run implications and points out:

> However, in the case of long-run price-discriminatory dumping by a foreign monopolist in a competitive market, later economists showed that an AD duty had ambiguous national welfare effects: the producer surplus and tariff revenue gains might or might not offset the consumer surplus losses. As might be expected, more recent analyses of AD duties in response to long run dumping in oligopolistic markets also yield ambiguous welfare outcomes. (Baldwin 1988: 315)

The key element to consider in this literature is the question of the time frame of the dumping. The predatory pricing issues are usually considered in the context of short-run dumping. However, dumping that results from long-term structural domestic support of an industry may raise other considerations. There is a need to move beyond short-run considerations and examine long-run considerations. In this area, it may not even be sufficient to examine long run price-discriminatory dumping. Price discrimination is not a necessary precondition for dumping. If dumping is happening in the sense of sales below cost of production, this can be a long-run phenomenon if it is supported by domestic subsidies. Presently, AD legislation is the only trade tool available to deal with this phenomenon. It should not be dismissed immediately as inappropriate economically. In such circumstances, an AD duty may yield positive welfare outcomes for the domestic market and for the domestic economy as a whole.

The concept is not well developed that AD law would include the problem of long-run sales below the cost of production (WTO 2003). Below-cost sales are traditionally excluded from AD calculations because they are considered to be short-run phenomenon and are not indicative of a true price in the exporter's home market. The WTO Antidumping Agreement recognizes that long-term sales below the cost of production should not be used to determine the normal value of goods for AD purposes. Rather, if domestic prices are shown to be below the cost of production for a long period of time, those prices can be disregarded, and the higher constructed-cost price can be used for duty determination.[3] There are three requirements to be met in the WTO Antidumping Agreement before below-cost sales will be disregarded. The three criteria are:

- sales in substantial quantities;
- sales within an extended period of time; and
- sales at prices that do not permit the recovery of all costs within a reasonable period of time. (WTO 2003)

The most significant of these three criteria is the third criterion. For example, in the case of grain corn, the CCRA determined that prices in the U.S. grain-corn market did not permit the recovery of all costs within a reasonable time. This criterion is satisfied when the price in the U.S. market at the time of the sale is below the average production cost for the entire investigation. The CCRA determined that the U.S. home market corn price should not be used to determine the dumping margin since it did not allow U.S. corn producers to recover all costs within a reasonable period of time. On this basis, the CCRA excluded the U.S. home-market corn cost when calculating the dumping margin. This left it open to the CCRA to use the constructed cost-of-production calculation from published cost data.

Thus, the idea that there is no dumping when the U.S. home-market price of agricultural goods is the same as the export price can be dismissed. If the home-market price results in a price below the cost of production, then foreign countries are entitled under the WTO Antidumping Agreement, to construct the full production cost in order to determine the margin of dumping.

Miranda, Torres, and Ruiz (1998) note that economic literature provides an example in which AD laws can be supported by a welfare analysis in the case of oligopolistic trade (Bian and Gaudet 1997). Considering the oligopolistic nature of much trade in agricultural products, this literature might also provide an explanation or justification for the current use of AD laws in agriculture. In the case of corn, over 80 percent of U.S. corn is exported by three firms: Cargill, Archer Daniels Midland (ADM), and Zen Noh. This oligopoly can have a significant impact on trade flows and prices. If their business is to sell corn and they can buy it in the United States at below the cost of production, they have a natural incentive to sell it wherever they can around the world at dumped prices.

As noted above, there is a suggestion in the economic literature that economies evolving from a controlled to a more liberal trading regime tend to increase their use of AD measures. In the area of agricultural trade, this should be examined from the perspective of whether increased domestic-support payments have increased the use of AD measures by trading partners or by competitors. It is recognized that the benefits of trade liberalization would be lost to some extent if AD measures were to bring back tariff protection to its previous level. But this should not be assumed. It should be examined empirically. It may be possible to prove that antidumping is costly on a sectoral basis. However, economists should also examine the welfare effects of AD measures on an entire economy, such as the Canadian economy in the case of corn. It may be that the benefits to the whole economy outweigh adverse impacts on welfare from the sectoral application of AD duties.

Just as AD duties have allowed developing countries to move toward a more liberalized trading regime, AD duties may also allow developed countries to justify a reduction in domestic support, particularly in agriculture industries. If we can reform AD law to better deal with a question of dumping, which results from structural long-term support for an industry, AD duties will have a place in the future development of free-trade law.

Why Not Countervail or Safeguard Measures?

Why Not Countervailing Duties?

This chapter suggests that AD duties are legally available trade weapons as a response to domestic subsidies for agriculture. The use of AD duties for this purpose does not fit the traditional economic analysis, which sees CV duties as the appropriate response to domestic subsidies. AD duties might therefore be seen as legal loopholes that may upset the international legal regime regulating agricultural subsidies through the WTO. Will such a legal use of an AD duty be allowed by the WTO?

First, the Uruguay Round Agreement on Agriculture (URAA) should be considered (GATT 1994). Article 4 of this agreement contains the member commitments on market access, including tariffication and tariff bindings and reductions. However, Article 4.2 allows members to maintain or resort to measures that were not of the kind that were required to be converted into ordinary customs duties. In other words, if measures are not ratified as tariffs, they are still allowed. This applies to AD duties. A note to Article 4.2 of the URAA shows that members can keep a measure allowed under other general, nonagriculture-specific provisions of GATT 1994. This reference allows members to resort to AD duties under Article VI of GATT 1994, even for agricultural products. The provisions of GATT 1994 Article VI and the WTO Agreement on the Implementation of Article VI are detailed above. They show that AD duties can be legally levied on sales below the cost of production.

The due restraint clause in Article 13 of GATT 1994 protects domestic-support measures and export subsidies from CV duties only during the nine-year implementation period that expired in 2003. Article 13 contains no restriction on the use of AD duties. The conclusion should be that the URAA does not restrict the use of AD duties.

Article VI of GATT 1994 does not define what an AD duty is. It is referred to only as an amount to offset or prevent dumping, which is recognized as a sale at less than a normal value and defines a CV duty to mean:

> A special duty levied for the purpose of offsetting any bounty
> or subsidy bestowed, directly, or indirectly, upon the manufacture,
> production or export of any merchandise. (GATT 1994)

This definition is repeated and confirmed by the WTO in Note 36 to Article 10 of the Agreement on Subsidies and Countervailing Measures (ASCM) (ASCM 2004).

Thus it seems that a CV duty must be aimed at a specific measure of domestic support or export subsidy in the exporting country. An AD duty carries no such requirement, and is dependent only on the price in the importing market and on the cost of production. The AD duty carries none of the political baggage associated with a CV duty claim. This is one of the reasons that an AD duty is becoming a weapon of choice in trade disputes.

So an AD duty may be used to circumvent the restrictions and legal limitations contained in the ASCM (2004). Since an AD duty is not taking action against a subsidy, there is no need to comply with the strict requirements of the ASCM. GATT 1994 Article VI, and the WTO Agreement on the Implementation of Article VI should be the only agreements that impose WTO restrictions in an AD case.

Why Not "Safeguard" Measures?

WTO rules presently allow countries to use "safeguard" measures to provide temporary protection against surges in imports. It is suggested that these are the appropriate measures to be used to deal with dumping. This argument should be rejected as an appropriate way to deal with the long-term implications of growing imports of subsidized agricultural products. First, safeguard measures are only temporary protection measures that are designed to be implemented as protection against short-term import surges. Second, these safeguard measures require compensation to be paid, which would be totally inappropriate in the case of long-term dumping by an exporter (*The Economist* 1998).

Miranda, Torres, and Ruiz (1998) also deal with the suggestion that the most appropriate contingent trade remedy is a safeguard measure rather than an AD measure. They suggest that it is not necessarily true that safeguard measures are less trade distorting than AD measures and point out that the selectivity of the application of AD measures may moderate the overall market effect when compared with broader safeguard measures. Further, despite the fact that safeguard measures require a higher "serious" injury standard, it may be that dumping cases can also satisfy the higher injury standard. Therefore, they conclude that it is not possible to assume in the abstract that a safeguard measure will always have a lower trade impact than will an AD measure.

CONCLUSIONS

AD law is a good thing for agriculture. It is good because it is a legal and effective response to the dumping of agricultural surpluses generated by trade distorting, but still legal, domestic subsidies in agriculture. When other trade remedies like tariffs and CV duties are now limited by international law, a legal response to sales below the cost of production is possible. AD duties may protect some Canadian industries from being destroyed by long run dumping. These duties may also be good for the United States if confrontation by its trading partners causes the United States to recognize the extent and impact of dumping of its agricultural products.

Further, trade and industrial policy issues cannot be separated in Canada. We are made extremely mindful of this reality by the results of the Canada Dairy case (Furtan, Romain, and Mussell 2005). The intrusive and unexpected results of the WTO decision in that case will have a significant impact on Canadian dairy farmers, particularly in the politically sensitive regions of Ontario and Quebec. Many parts of the WTO agreements have had large and detrimental effects to Canadian agriculture. It is politically unlikely that the Canadian government will take steps to restrict the use of AD legislation to further harm Canadian agriculture. In fact, it is much more likely that the Canadian government will use AD legislation to stand up for and protect agricultural interests in the next few years. Anything less would seem like the total abandonment of Canadian agriculture at the altar of international free trade.

On a larger scale, the reduction in legislative restraints on free trade, such as AD laws, rests much more in U.S. law than in Canadian law. As long as U.S. producers have access to U.S. laws to harass and intimidate Canadian producers over exports to the United States, such as grain and lumber, Canadian agricultural producers will have no stomach for their politicians unilaterally making further trade law concessions to the United States. If the United States is not prepared to provide more concrete assurances that Canada will have access to the U.S. market for its agricultural products, U.S. producers can expect the same kind of treatment in its attempts to send agricultural products to Canada.

Finally, economic considerations demand that Canada maintain robust AD laws to protect the national welfare. As long as the U.S. system allows producers to sell below the cost of production in the long run, Canada must be ready to respond. The survival of our agriculture industry may depend on it. Viewed from that perspective, AD law is a good thing for Canadian agriculture.

APPENDIX

Total economic costs are full ownership costs (cash and noncash) for operating the business. They include variable-cash and fixed-cash expenses (except interest payments); capital replacement; input costs of land; unpaid labour; and capital invested in production inputs and machinery. Total economic costs are divided by the yield to calculate the total cost of production of corn (Table A5.1).

Table A5.2 shows the government-paid cost of production, which is represented by "Producer Support Estimate (PSE), Payments Based on Input Use." The figure is an indicator of the annual monetary value of gross transfers

Table A5.1: Farmer Cost of Production

Year	Total Economic Cost of Production	Yield	Cost of Production
	U.S. $/acre	Bushels/planted acre	U.S. $/bushel
1990	292.52	117.50	2.49
1991	292.55	110.38	2.65
1992	302.33	133.82	2.26
1993	287.10	99.15	2.90
1994	321.47	143.15	2.25
1995	333.42	115.85	2.88
1996	350.53	130.00	2.70
1997	360.29	130.00	2.77
1998	359.46	136.00	2.64
1999	361.30	135.00	2.68
2000	374.84	138.00	2.72
2001	390.59	139.00	2.81

Source: USDA/ERS (1989 to 2001).

Table A5.2: Government Cost of Production

Year	Payments Based on Input Use	Production	PSE[a] Per Bushel	Production
	Million U.S. $	1,000 bushels	U.S. $/bushel	1,000 tons
1990	655.1	7,934,022	0.08	201,534.8
1991	641.4	7,475,019	0.09	189,875.5
1992	626.7	9,477,023	0.07	240,729.1
1993	514.8	6,336,016	0.08	160,943.3
1994	688.7	10,050,544	0.07	255,297.3
1995	709.1	7,400,070	0.10	187,971.7
1996	700.8	9,232,579	0.08	234,519.9
1997	623.1	9,206,856	0.07	233,866.5
1998	581.4	9,759,024	0.06	247,892.3
1999	563.6	9,431,026	0.06	239,560.7
2000	605.7	9,968,025	0.06	253,201.2
2001	617.2	9,546,024	0.06	242,481.8

[a]Producer support estimate.
Source: OECD (2003).

from taxpayers to agricultural producers arising from policy measures based on the use of a specific input or a specific group of inputs or factors of production.

These payments are divided by total production, converted from tons to bushels using 1 metric ton = 39.368 bushels, in order to calculate the cost of production paid by the U.S. government.

"Payments Based on Input Use" is an indicator of the annual monetary value of gross transfers from taxpayers to U.S. agricultural producers arising from policy measures based on the use of a specific inputs or a specific group of input or factors of production. This figure is conditional on the on-farm use of specific fixed or variable inputs, which includes explicit and implicit payments affecting specific variable input costs. Policies included are: Agricultural Credit Program or Agricultural Credit Insurance Program; Energy Payments; Irrigation Payments; Grazing Payments, Feed Assistance, or Emergency Feed Assistance Program; Forage Assistance Program; and Disaster Reserve Assistance Program; Extension Service; Agricultural Cooperative Service; Outreach for Socially Disadvantaged Farms; Grazing Land Conservation Initiative; Pet and Disease Control; Emergency Conservation Program; and the Farmland Protection Program.

Table A5.3 gives the export price for U.S. maize, valued free on board at Gulf Ports and Table A5.4 shows the calculation of the transportation costs. The market year average price received by farmers in Iowa is subtracted from the export price at the Gulf. It should be noted that, since this value was not calculated prior to 1991, the 1990 price is a U.S. average price received by farmers. Since this method provides only a rough estimation of this cost, the transportation and handling costs were averaged over the 12 years to create a transportation marker for the export-dumping calculation.

Table A5.3: Export Prices: U.S. Maize

Year	Export Price	Year	Export Price
	U.S. $/bushel		U.S. $/bushel
1990	2.79	1996	4.17
1991	2.75	1997	2.98
1992	2.66	1998	2.58
1993	2.62	1999	2.29
1994	2.74	2000	2.24
1995	3.13	2001	2.28

Source: USDA/ERS (1992 to 2002a).

Table A5.4: Transportation and Handling Costs

Year	Export Price (U.S.$/bu)	Market Year Avg. Prices (Iowa)	Transportation and Handling Costs (U.S.$/bu)	Full Cost (U.S.$/bu)	Transport Percent of Full Cost	Avg. Transport Cost (U.S.$/bu.)
1990	2.79	2.28	0.51	3.08	17	0.54
1991	2.75	2.30	0.45	3.19	14	
1992	2.66	2.00	0.66	2.99	22	
1993	2.62	2.44	0.18	3.16	6	
1994	2.74	2.22	0.52	2.83	18	
1995	3.13	3.20	(0.07)	2.90	-2	
1996	4.17	2.60	1.57	4.34	36	
1997	2.98	2.33	0.65	3.49	19	
1998	2.58	1.86	0.72	3.42	21	
1999	2.29	1.72	0.57	3.31	17	
2000	2.24	1.75	0.49	3.27	15	
2001	2.28	2.10	0.18	3.05	6	

Source: USDA/NASS (1994 to 2002) and USDA/ERS (1992 to 2002b).

NOTES

[1]Agreement on the Implementation of Article VI, Article 2.2.

[2]J. Miranda, R. Torres and M. Ruiz (1987 to 1998) conclude that it is possible to contemplate antidumping as a trade-policy instrument making unilateral liberalization feasible and/or sustainable. However, he points out that evidence must be gathered in specific cases to determine whether or not this justification for AD law does exist.

[3]Support for this approach to a full expression of average total cost of production is found in the last WTO Appellate Milk Body Report in Canada-Milk, in which the full average total cost of production is used to determine the existence of a subsidy. It therefore appears to be the theoretical basis for calculating the cost at which a good is introduced into international commerce. From an economist's point of view, it is interesting that the WTO appears to require firms to sell above full average costs, rather than at marginal costs, despite the accepted economic wisdom that it makes sense to sell at marginal cost in certain circumstances.

REFERENCES

ASCM (Agreement on Subsidies and Countervailing Measures). (2004). Available at: http://www.wto.org/english/docs_e/legal_e/24-scm.pdf.

Baldwin, R.E. (1988). "Imposing Multilateral Discipline on Administered Protection," in *The WTO as an International Organization*, edited by Anne O. Krueger. Chicago: The University of Chicago Press.

Bhagwati, J. (1988). *Protectionism*. Cambridge: The MIT Press (33–7).

Bian, J. and G. Gaudet. (1997). "Antidumping Laws and Oligopolistic Trade." *Journal of Economic Integration* 12(1): 62–86.

Boltuck, R.D. (1992). "Remarks made at the IDB/ECLAC Project Fifth Colloquium: Support to Process of Hemispheric Trade Liberalization." *The Negotiating Agenda and Perspectives*. Washington, DC (September 28).

CCRA (Commissioner of Customs and Revenue—Grain). (2000). "Corn, Preliminary Determination, Statement of Reasons." Ottawa: CCRA. Available at: www.ccra-adrc.gc.ca/customs/business/sima.

_____. (2001). "Final Determination - Grain Corn Statement of Reasons." Ottawa: CCRA. Available at: http://www.ccra-adrc.gc.ca/customs/business/sima/anti-dumping/ad1242f-e.html.

CITT (Canadian International Trade Tribunal). (1987). "Findings Concerning Dumped or Subsidized Imports of Grain Corn from the United States." Ottawa: CITT. Available at: http://www.citt.gc.ca/index_e.asp.

_____. (2000). "Grain Corn, Preliminary Injury Inquiry, Statement of Reasons." Ottawa: CITT (October 25). Available at: http://www.citt.gc.ca/index_e.asp.

_____. (2001). *Grain Corn, Finding and Statement of Reasons*. Ottawa: CITT (March 22). Available at: www.citt.gc.ca.

Corr, C. (1997). "Trade Protection in the New Millennium: The Ascendancy of Antidumping Measures." *Northwestern Law: Journal of International Law & Business* 18(1): 49.

Denton, R. (1989). "[Why] Should Nations Utilize Antidumping Measures?" *Michigan Journal of International Law* (11): 224.

Department of National Revenue (Department of National Revenue, Customs and Excise). (1987). *Grain Corn, Final Determination, Statement of Reasons.* Ottawa: Department of National Revenue (February 2).

Furtan, W. H., R. Romain, and A. Mussell. (2004). See Chapter 7, this volume.

GATT (General Agreement on Tariffs and Trade). (1947). Available at: http://www.wto.org/english/tratop_e/gatt_e.gatt_e.htm.

_____. (1994). "The Uruguay Round Agreement." Available at: http://www.wto.org/english/docs_e/legal_e/legal_e.htm.

Horlick, G.N. and Shea, E.C. (1995). "The World Trade Organization Antidumping Agreement." *Journal of World Trade* 29(1): 7.

Jackson, J. (1980). "United States Policy Regarding Disruptive Imports from State Trading Countries or Government-Owned Enterprises," in *Interface One: Proceedings on the Application of U.S. Antidumping and Countervailing Laws to Imports from State-Controlled Economies or State-Owned Enterprises,* edited by D. Wallace, G. Spina, R. Rawson, and B. McGill. Chicago: University of Chicago Press (1–21).

_____. (1989). *The World Trading System.* Chicago: University of Chicago Press.

Kerr, W.A. (2001). "Dumping – One of Those Economic Myths." *Estey Centre Journal of International Law and Trade Policy* 2(2): 211.

Miranda, J., R. Torres, and M. Ruiz. (1998). "The International Use of Antidumping: 1987–1997." *Journal of World Trade* 32(5): 5–71.

Moore, M.O. and S.M. Suranovic. (1994). "Welfare Effects of Introducing Antidumping Procedures in a Trade-Liberalizing Country." *Journal of Economic Integration* 9(2).

OECD (Organization for Economic Co-Operation and Development). (2001). "The Uruguay Round Agreement on Agriculture: An Evaluation of its Implementation in OECD Countries." Available at: http://www.sourceoecd.org/content/html/index.htm.

_____. (2003). *Producer Support Estimate by Commodity.* Paris: OECD. Available at: http://www.sourceoecd.org/content/html/index.htm.

Oxfam International. (2002). *Rigged Rules and Double Standards: Trade, Globalization, and the Fight Against Poverty.* Oxford, UK: Oxfam International.

Prusa, T. (2001). "On the Spread and Impact of Antidumping." *Canadian Journal of Economics* 34(3): 591–611.

Ritchie, M., S. Murphy, and M. Lake. (2003). *United States Dumping on World Agricultural Markets.* Report to the Institute for Agriculture and Trade Policy. Minneapolis: IATP. Available at: www.iatp.org.

SIMA (*Special Import Measures Act*). (1995). *Special Import Measures Act, Section 19.* Ottawa: Government of Canada. Available at: http://laws.justice.gc.ca/en/S-15/

The Economist. (1998). "The Surge in Antidumping Cases." 175(1).

Thomas, J., G. Tereposky, and K. Fujihara. (1995). "Canadian Antidumping and Countervailing Duty Law and Procedure," in *Trading Punches: Trade Remedy Law and Disputes under NAFTA* 83, edited by B. Leycegui, W.B.P. Robson, and S. Stein. Washington: National Planning Association (1–23).

USDA/ERS (U.S. Department of Agriculture, Economic Research Service). (1989 to 2001). "U.S. Corn Production Costs and Returns." Available at: http://www.ers.usda.gov/data/costsandreturns/testpick.htm.

_____. (1992 to 2002a). *Agricultural Outlook.* Washington DC: USDA/ERS. Available at: http://www.ers.usda.gov/data/costsandreturns/testpick.htm.

_____. (1992 to 2002b). *Agricultural Outlook.* Washington DC: USDA/ERS. Available at: http://www.ers.usda.gov/data/costsandreturns/testpick.htm.

USDA/NASS (U.S. Department of Agriculture, National Agricultural Statistics Service). (1994 to 2002). "Agricultural Statistics." Washington DC: USDA/NASS. Available at: (http://www.usda.gov/nass/pubs/agstats.htm).

Viner, J. (1966). *Dumping: A Problem in International Trade*. New York: Augustus M. Kelley Publishers (140).

Wright, R. (1989). "Validity of Antidumping Remedies - Some Thoughts," in *Antidumping Law and Practice: A Comparative Study*, edited by J. Jackson and E. Vernulst. Ann Arbor: University of Michigan Press (418–24).

Chapter 6

Welfare Implications of
the Byrd Amendment

Troy G. Schmitz and James L. Seale, Jr.
Arizona State University
University of Florida

INTRODUCTION

The *Continued Dumping and Subsidy Offset Act* (CDSOA) of 2000 (WTO 2002) allows producers who successfully petition the U.S. government to impose antidumping (AD) or countervailing (CV) tariffs on competing imports to personally keep the proceeds of those tariffs. This so-called Byrd Amendment has already provided benefits to a variety of producers and processors in the United States, including more than U.S. $7 million to Louisiana crayfish producers and processors and U.S. $65 million to U.S. candle makers. These benefits originated from AD duties imposed on U.S. imports of Chinese products (King 2002). One U.S. candle company, Candle-Lite, received U.S. $38 million in fiscal year 2002, while a ball-bearings company, Torrington, received U.S. $37 million in 2002 (U.S. Customs Service 2003). The Byrd Amendment also has financial implications for steel, rubber, pencil, pineapple, and pasta markets (King 2002). In fiscal year 2002 alone, the U.S. government wrote checks totalling nearly U.S. $320 million to companies that could prove they were involved in AD or CV duty cases that eventually led to imposed tariffs (U.S. Department of the Treasury 2002).

The so-called Byrd Amendment effectively allows U.S. producers and processors to collect the resulting import-tariff revenue that would otherwise accrue to the U.S. government. Furthermore, even though CDSOA was passed in 2000, there is a grandfather clause that allows U.S. producer and processor groups to collect tariff revenues from certain AD duties and CV duties that were implemented prior to the CDSOA. The CDSOA has serious present and future welfare implications in terms of transfers of Ricardian rent among consumers, producers, and taxpayers. It also provides an even greater incentive for a proliferation of future AD lawsuits.

We begin by providing a general discussion of CDSOA. We also provide empirical evidence regarding AD and CV tariffs placed on specific products. We then draw on trade theory to develop an optimal AD tariff that maximizes the sum of producer surplus and tariff revenue. This optimal AD tariff represents the first-best situation for producers who lobby successfully for AD and CV tariffs against competing products from other countries under the CDSOA. Once the optimal AD tariff is derived, the welfare associated with it is compared to the optimal-revenue tariff that maximizes tariff revenue only. The welfare associated with the derived AD tariff is also compared to the optimal-welfare tariff that maximizes the sum of producer surplus, consumer surplus, and tariff revenue.[1]

THE BYRD AMENDMENT

The *Continued Dumping and Subsidy Offset Act* of 2000, also called the CDSOA or Byrd Amendment, was enacted on October 28, 2000 as Title X of the 2001 *Agriculture, Rural Development, Food and Drug Appropriations Act* ("Act"), Public Law 106-387.[2] The CDSOA modified Title VII of the *Tariff Act* of 1930 by instructing U.S. Customs to put all collected AD and CV tariffs into special accounts, one for each case, and to pay out these collected revenues directly to companies that successfully petition the U.S. Government for these monies (U.S. Department of the Treasury 2002). (Previously, the collected tariff revenues accrued to the general U.S. Treasury.) In order for a company to be eligible for payouts, it must prove that it successfully litigated an AD or CV duty case against a specific industry in a specific country. If a company is eligible, it shares all past and future collected AD and CV duties with the other original litigating companies. Companies that did not participate in the original AD or CV duty case do not receive any of the collected funds (eBearing.com 2000).

The CDSOA went into effect in 2001 and was controversial from its inception. President Clinton signed the "Act" but asked Congress to revisit and repeal the CDSOA before adjournment. Congress, however, neither revisited nor repealed the "Act". Within agricultural industries that receive protection from imports under U.S. AD and/or CV duty laws, ineligible companies for CDSOA payouts complain that eligible companies receive an unfair advantage derived from these subsidies. Small companies complain that their industry is harmed by unfair imports, but they do not have the money to hire expensive lawyers to litigate AD and/or CV cases. The budget report of the U.S. Treasury Department states that the CDSOA allows 'double dipping' because eligible companies not only receive protection from imports through increased import prices due to AD and/or CV tariffs, but now they also receive corporate subsidies from the collected AD and/or CV revenues (Thomas 2003).

U.S. trading partners have also reacted vigorously against the CDSOA. Eleven World Trade Organization (WTO) Member countries asked the WTO to form a panel to investigate the CDSOA with respect to U.S. obligations under the WTO Antidumping Agreement and the WTO Subsidies Agreement. The

WTO formed a panel on September 10, 2001. On September 16, 2002, that WTO panel ruled against the United States on the CDSOA payments and recommended that the CDSOA be repealed (U.S. Department of State 2003). On October 18, 2002, the United States appealed the ruling to the WTO Appellate Body. On January 16, 2003, the Appellate Body confirmed that the CDSOA was incompatible with WTO rules (Lamy 2003).

President Bush's budget for fiscal year 2004 also called for a repeal of the CDSOA. In spite of this repeal and the ruling of the WTO as of February 4, 2003, sixty-seven U.S. senators had signed a letter to the U.S. President requesting that he resist the WTO action and maintain the CDSOA. With such strong support in the U.S. Senate for the CDSOA, it is still not clear that the law will be repealed.

In fiscal year 2001, which was the first year of U.S. government CDSOA payouts, 900 claimants received U.S. $230 million dollars (Table 6.1). For the second year of payouts in 2002, more than 1,200 claimants received approximately U.S. $330 million. Although most of the payouts went to non-food companies, food companies received more than U.S. $22 million in 2001 and nearly U.S. $20 million in 2002. In 2001, there were 9 food-industry AD cases and

Table 6.1: *Continued Dumping and Subsidy Offset Act,* **Fiscal Years 2001 and 2002 Disbursements for Food Products**

Case Number	Case Name	FY[a] 2001	FY[a] 2002
		1,000 U.S. $	
A-570-848	Crawfish tail meat/PRC[b]	0	7,469
A-475-818	Pasta/Italy	17,533	4,674
C-475-819	Pasta/Italy	2,480	2,528
A-533-813	Preserved mushrooms/India	171	2,155
A-351-605	Frozen concentrated orange juice/Brazil	0	1,175
A-570-831	Fresh garlic/PRC	25	536
A-549-813	Canned pineapple/Thailand	1,792	531
A-560-802	Preserved mushrooms/Indonesia	83	443
A-337-803	Fresh Atlantic salmon/Chile	0	173
A-403-801	Fresh and chilled Atlantic salmon/Norway	46	59
C-403-802	Fresh and chilled Atlantic salmon/Norway	18	29
A-570-851	Preserved mushrooms/PRC	0	20
C-408-046	Sugar/European Union	8	17
C-489-806	Pasta/Turkey	7	9
A-489-805	Pasta/Turkey	11	4
A-570-855	Non-frozen apple juice concentrate/PRC	0	1
A-301-602	Fresh-cut flowers/Columbia	33	0
	Food Total	22,209	19,824
	Grand Total for all Products	231,202	329,871

[a] Fiscal Year.
[b] People's Republic of China.
Source: U.S. Customs Service (2003).

4 food-industry CV duty cases for which companies received tariff revenues under the CDSOA. In 2002, food-industry AD cases in which companies received payouts increased to 12 while food-industry CV duty cases remained at 4.

In some cases, the same company that received payouts under an AD duty case also received payouts under a CV duty case. As an example, eligible U.S. pasta firms shared U.S. $17.5 million and U.S. $4.7 million under AD case A-475-818 in 2001 and 2002, respectively. They also shared U.S. $2.5 million under CV duty case C-475-810 in both 2001 and 2002. In the Maui Pineapple AD case (A-540-843), Maui Pineapple received the entire portion of the U.S. $1.8 million in 2001 and U.S. $0.5 million in 2002 that originated from duties collected on canned-pineapple imports from Thailand.

Table 6.2: *Continued Dumping and Subsidy Offset Act,* **Disbursements for Crawfish Tail Meat from People's Republic of China, Fiscal Year 2002**

Claimant	Claim Filed	Amount Paid	Allocation
	1,000 U.S. $	1,000 U.S. $	Percentage
Atchafalaya Crawfish Processors	3,758	793	10.6
Seafood International Distributors	3,347	707	9.5
Catahoula Crawfish	2,937	620	8.3
Prairie Cajun Wholesale Seafood Dist.	2,449	517	6.9
Bayou Land Seafood	1,990	420	5.6
Crawfish Enterprises, Inc. (CPA)[a]	1,892	399	5.3
C.J.'s Seafood & Purged Crawfish	1,773	374	5.0
Riceland Crawfish	1,517	320	4.3
Cajun Seafood Distributors	1,511	319	4.3
Acadiana Fishermen's Co-Op	1,508	318	4.3
Bonanza Crawfish Farm	1,482	313	4.2
Randol's Seafood & Restaurant (CPA)[a]	1,445	305	4.1
L.T. West	1,126	238	3.2
Sylvester's Processors	1,036	219	2.9
Carl's Seafood	1,037	219	2.9
Choplin Seafood	999	211	2.8
Blanchard Seafood, Inc (CPA)[a]	990	209	2.8
Louisiana Seafood	947	200	2.7
Harvey's Seafood	783	165	2.2
Louisiana Premium Seafoods	771	163	2.2
Bellard's Poultry & Crawfish	502	106	1.4
Phillips Seafood	450	95	1.3
A&S Crawfish	330	70	0.9
Becnel's Meat & Seafood	324	68	0.9
Teche Valley Seafood	225	48	0.6
Arnaudville Seaford	171	36	0.5
Lawtell Crawfish Processors	80	17	0.2
Total for Case #A-570-848	35,380	7,469	100.0

[a] Crawfish Processors Alliance.
Source: U. S. Customs Service (2003).

In fiscal year 2002, crayfish firms received in total the largest food-industry CDSOA payouts (Table 6.2). Of the 27 eligible firms, Atchafalaya Crawfish Processors received payouts of U.S. $800,000. Four companies received payouts in excess of U.S. $500,000 and another 17 firms received payouts of more than U.S. $100,000. On average, the 27 crayfish firms received U.S. $300,000 in fiscal year 2002. In total, CDSOA payouts (Table 6.2, Column 3) amounted to 21 percent of the total production and operating costs (Table 6.2, Column 4) of these firms. In fiscal year 2002, three citrus processors received U.S. $1.18 million in CDSOA payouts. Citrus World received 67 percent of the payouts for a total of U.S. $800,000 (Table 6.3).

Table 6.3: *Continued Dumping and Subsidy Offset Act,* **Disbursements for Frozen Concentrated Orange Juice from Brazil, Fiscal Year 2002**

Claimant	Claim Filed	Amount Paid	Allocation
	1,000 U.S. $		Percentage
Citrus World	277,335	784	66.7
A. Duda & Sons *dba* Citrus Belle	75,817	214	18.2
LD Citrus, Inc.	62,553	177	15.0
Total for Case #A-351-605	414,705	1,175	100.0

Source: U.S. Customs Service (2003).

DERIVATION OF OPTIMAL TARIFFS

In order to derive and compare the optimal-AD tariff, the optimal-revenue tariff, and the optimal-welfare tariff, we consider the following system of equations that represent the supply, demand, and excess demand curves for a particular product in the United States along with the excess supply curve for the foreign market (i.e., the rest of the world). To make the solution tractable, we assume that each of these equations is linear and that U.S. and foreign markets are competitive. This system can be viewed as a linear approximation to the actual underlying behavioural relationships

$$
\begin{aligned}
P_D &= a + bQ_D \\
P_S &= \alpha + \beta Q_S \\
P_{ED} &= c + dI \\
P_{ES} &= \gamma + \delta I
\end{aligned}
\tag{1}
$$

in which P is the price, Q_s is the quantity supplied by the United States, I represents U.S. imports from the foreign market, and Q_D is the quantity demanded, which equals the quantity supplied Q_S plus imports I. If we introduce a specific tariff T, then T drives a wedge between the excess demand and excess supply curves. In partial equilibrium, the following relationship must hold

$$P_{ED} - P_{ES} = T. \tag{2}$$

Inserting the relationships for P_{ED} and P_{ES} and solving for imports I yields

$$I = \frac{T + \gamma - c}{(d - \delta)}. \tag{3}$$

The equilibrium U.S. price is derived by inserting Equation (3) into the excess demand curve P_{ED} that yields

$$P = c + \frac{d(T + \gamma - c)}{(d - \delta)}. \tag{4}$$

Finally, the U.S. quantity supplied in equilibrium is derived by inserting Equation (4) into the demand curve of Equation (1)

$$Q = \frac{(c - \alpha)(d - \delta) + d(T + \gamma - c)}{\beta(d - \delta)}. \tag{5}$$

Equation (3), Equation (4), and Equation (5) give the equilibrium quantity imported, the U.S. price, and the quantity supplied as functions of the specific tariff T and the parameters of the various supply and demand equations. These relationships can be used to find the equilibrium tariff under various tariff regimes.

As a base of reference, we first derive the optimal-revenue tariff in terms of the parameters of the various supply and demand equations. We then derive the optimal AD tariff, rewrite it as a function of the underlying optimal-revenue tariff, convert the parameters to point elasticities, and compare the two tariffs. Finally, we make inferences with respect to the optimal-welfare tariff.

First, consider the optimal-revenue tariff. The objective of the optimal-revenue tariff is to maximize tariff revenue with respect to the tariff. However, since tariff revenue is simply equal to the specific tariff T multiplied by equilibrium imports I, this problem can be written mathematically as

$$MAX_T \left\{ TR = \frac{T(T + \gamma - c)}{(d - \delta)} \right\}, \tag{6}$$

which makes use of Equation (3). The optimal-revenue tariff T_{ORT} is found by taking the derivative of Equation (6) with respect to the specific tariff T, setting it equal to zero, and solving for T. The derivative of Equation (6) with respect to T is

$$\frac{\partial TR}{\partial T} = \frac{2T + (\gamma - c)}{(d - \delta)} = 0. \tag{7}$$

After simplification, the optimal-revenue tariff becomes

$$T_{ORT} = \frac{(c - \gamma)}{2}. \tag{8}$$

Hence the optimal-revenue tariff is always exactly one-half of the distance between the intercept of the excess demand curve and the excess supply curve.

Now, consider the optimal AD tariff defined as the tariff that maximizes the sum of producer surplus and tariff revenue. The tariff revenue TR is the same as in Equation (6). Producer surplus for U.S. producers (as defined by Just, Hueth, and Schmitz 1982) is equal to the area above the supply curve, and bounded by the domestic price. Since the supply curve is linear, producer surplus is

$$PS = \frac{1}{2} Q_s (P - \alpha). \tag{9}$$

However, the quantity supplied $Q_{S'}$ can be written in terms of P, α, and β using Equation (1), so that producer surplus can be rewritten as

$$PS = \frac{(P - \alpha)^2}{2\beta}. \tag{10}$$

The optimal AD tariff is derived by making use of Equation (4) to get the price in terms of the specific tariff T, and maximizing the sum of producer surplus and tariff revenue. This can be written as

$$MAX_T \; TR + PS = \frac{T(T + \gamma - c)}{(d - \delta)} + \frac{1}{2\beta}\left[(c - \alpha) + \frac{d(T + \gamma - c)}{(d - \delta)}\right]^2. \tag{11}$$

Taking the derivative of Equation (11) with respect to T and setting it equal to zero yields

$$\frac{\partial (TR + PS)}{\partial T} = \frac{2T + (\gamma - c)}{(d - \delta)} + \frac{d(c - \alpha)}{\beta(d - \delta)} + \frac{d^2(T + \gamma - c)}{\beta(d - \delta)^2} = 0. \tag{12}$$

Solving for Equation (12) with respect to T and simplifying yields

$$T_{ANT} = \frac{-d(c - \alpha)(d - \delta) + \beta(c - \gamma)(d - \delta) + d^2(c - \gamma)}{2\beta(d - \delta) + d^2}. \tag{13}$$

In order to simplify this relationship further, the above parameters can be converted into their elasticity equivalents using the technique developed by Schmitz and Schmitz (2003). Assuming that the point elasticity for each of the four curves is taken at the price, domestic quantity, and import levels that would exist under free trade, each of the parameters can be written in terms of elasticities and corresponding values that would exist under free trade using the following relationships

$$
\begin{aligned}
& a = P_W\left(1 - \frac{1}{\varepsilon_D}\right), && b = \frac{P_W}{\varepsilon_D\left(Q_W + I_W\right)} \\
& \alpha = P_W\left(1 - \frac{1}{\varepsilon_S}\right), && \beta = \frac{P_W}{\varepsilon_S Q_W} \\
& c = P_W\left(1 - \frac{1}{\varepsilon_{ED}}\right), && d = \frac{P_W}{\varepsilon_{ED} I_W} \\
& \gamma = P_W\left(1 - \frac{1}{\varepsilon_{ES}}\right), && \delta = \frac{P_W}{\varepsilon_{ES} I_W}
\end{aligned}
\tag{14}
$$

in which P_W, Q_W, and I_W are the equilibrium price, quantity, and imports, respectively, that would exist under free trade and $\varepsilon_D, \varepsilon_S, \varepsilon_{ED}$, and ε_{ES} are the elasticities of demand, supply, excess demand, and excess supply, respectively.

If we further substitute Equation (14) into Equation (13) and perform several rounds of simplifications, the optimal AD tariff can be expressed as

$$
T_{ANT} = \frac{P_W\left(v-1\right)w\left[1+\varphi\left(1-v\right)\right]}{\varepsilon_{ED}\left[1+2w\varphi\left(1-v\right)\right]},
\tag{15}
$$

in which v is the ratio of the excess demand elasticity with respect to the excess supply elasticity, w is the ratio of the excess demand elasticity with respect to the domestic supply elasticity, and φ is the ratio of imports that would exist under free trade I_W with respect to the domestic quantity that would exist under free trade Q_W.

In order to compare the optimal AD tariff in Equation (15) with the optimal-revenue tariff in Equation (8), we substitute the relationships in Equation (14) into Equation (8) and simplify to get

$$
T_{ORT} = \frac{P_W\left(v-1\right)}{2\varepsilon_{ED}}.
\tag{16}
$$

To obtain the optimal AD tariff in terms of the optimal-revenue tariff, take the relationship of Equation (16) and insert it into Equation (15) to get

$$T_{ANT} = T_{ORT} \frac{2w + 2w\varphi(1-v)}{1 + 2w\varphi(1-v)} = mT_{ORT}, \tag{17}$$

in which m represents the percentage mark up of the optimal AD tariff over the optimal-revenue tariff. The top and the bottom of the mark-up rule m have a common right-hand term that contains v, w, and φ. This common right-hand term is always negative because v and w are always negative as long as the domestic and excess supply curves are upward sloping and the domestic demand and excess demand curves are downward sloping. Furthermore, φ is a share parameter that is always positive.

After accounting for the common right-hand term, the only remaining terms to compare are $2w$ in the numerator with number one in the denominator. However, since w is the ratio of the excess demand elasticity to the domestic supply elasticity, the absolute value of w is always greater than one, because the absolute value of the elasticity of the excess demand curve must always be larger than the elasticity of the domestic supply curve, by construction. Hence the absolute value of the numerator of Equation (17) is always larger than the absolute value of the denominator. Hence, m is always greater than one, which implies that the optimal AD tariff is always larger than the optimal revenue tariff.

The relationship established in Equation (17) raises the possibility that the optimal AD tariff could be prohibitive. In fact, the optimal AD tariff would be prohibitive if $m = 2$. To see this, note that the prohibitive tariff level is equal to the difference between the intercept of the excess demand and excess supply curves $(c - \gamma)$. However, since the optimal revenue tariff is $T_{ORT} = (c - \gamma)/2$ (from Equation 8) and since the optimal AD tariff equals m multiplied by T_{ORT}, it must be the case that the optimal AD tariff in Equation (17) is prohibitive whenever $m = 2$.

To summarize, the optimal AD tariff is larger than the optimal-revenue tariff by a factor of m in Equation (17) and is prohibitive if $m = 2$. Using the above results, we can also compare the optimal AD tariff that maximizes the sum of tariff revenue and producer surplus to the optimal-welfare tariff that maximizes the sum of tariff revenue, producer surplus, and consumer surplus. It is well known that the optimal-welfare tariff is always smaller than the optimal-revenue tariff (Schmitz and Schmitz 1994). Hence through transitivity, the optimal AD tariff must also be larger than the optimal-welfare tariff.

The above arguments are further illustrated in Figure 6.1, in which S and D in the left-hand panel represent the supply and demand curves, and ES and ED in the right-hand panel represent the excess supply and excess demand curves. First, consider the optimal AD tariff. The optimal AD tariff is the tariff that maximizes the sum of tariff revenue and producer surplus. In Figure 6.1, the optimal AD tariff is represented by $p_1 - \pi_1$, in which p_1 is the domestic price under the optimal AD tariff and π_1 is the resulting equilibrium world price

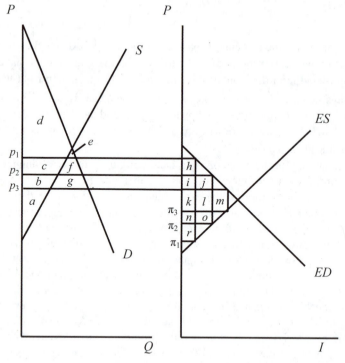

Figure 6.1: Optimal Antidumping, Revenue, and Welfare Tariffs

under the optimal AD tariff. Tariff revenue under the optimal AD tariff is given by area *hiknr* and producer surplus under the optimal AD tariff equals area *abc*. Thus total producer welfare equals area *hiknr + abc*.

The optimal-revenue tariff in Figure 6.1 is $p_2 - \pi_2$, in which p_2 is the domestic price under the optimal-revenue tariff, and π_2 is the resulting equilibrium world price. Tariff revenue under the optimal-revenue tariff area *ijklno* is always larger than the tariff revenue under the optimal AD tariff, but producer surplus *ab* is always lower under the optimal-revenue tariff. Furthermore, since the sum of tariff revenue and producer surplus is maximized under the AD tariff, it must be the case that *chr > jlo*.

Now consider the optimal-welfare tariff represented by $p_3 - \pi_3$, in which p_3 is the domestic price, and π_3 is the resulting equilibrium world price. The tariff revenue under the optimal-welfare tariff area *klm* could be larger or smaller than the tariff revenue under the optimal AD tariff area *hiknr*. Producer surplus under the optimal-welfare tariff area *a* is always lower than under the optimal AD tariff. However total welfare (the sum of consumer surplus, producer surplus, and tariff revenue) under the optimal-welfare tariff area *abcdefg + klm,* is always larger than total welfare under the optimal AD tariff area *abcde + hiknr.*

CONCLUSIONS AND FURTHER DISCUSSION

The *Continued Dumping and Subsidy Offset Act* of 2000 (also known as the Byrd amendment) allows producers to petition the U.S. Government in order to collect the proceeds that the U.S. Government received from AD or CV tariffs on imports. We analyzed the economic implications of the Byrd Amendment by deriving an optimal AD tariff for U.S. producers who received AD or CV tariffs. This optimal AD tariff is, in turn, compared to the optimal-revenue and optimal-welfare tariffs. We showed that the optimal AD tariff is always larger than either the optimal-revenue or the optimal-welfare tariffs and could become prohibitive under certain conditions.

We also compared tariff revenue and producer welfare under the optimal AD tariff, the optimal-revenue tariff, and the optimal-welfare tariff. We showed that tariff revenue is always largest under the optimal-revenue tariff, but we also showed that producer surplus is always largest under the optimal AD tariff. Tariff revenue under an optimal AD tariff may be larger or smaller than under the optimal-welfare tariff. Although producer welfare is always lowest under an optimal-welfare tariff, total surplus (consumer and producer surpluses plus tariff revenue) is always largest under an optimal-welfare tariff.

NOTES

[1]The optimal-revenue tariff and optimal-welfare tariff are well-known results from trade theory. A detailed discussion of each tariff instrument can be found in Just, Hueth, and Schmitz (1982) or Schmitz and Schmitz (1994).
[2]Senator DeWine (Ohio) was the original author of the CDSOA but it was Senator Byrd (West Virginia) who added the CDSOA to the Agriculture Spending Bill of 2000. Available at: http://www.ebearing.com/legislation/2000act.htm.

REFERENCES

Agriculture, Rural Development, Food and Drug Appropriations Act. (2001). Available at: http://www4.nationalacademies.org/ocga/publaw.nsf/0/31874c069f7 af44b8525698c005acf8e?OpenDocument.
CDSOA (*Continued Dumping and Subsidy Offset Act*). (2000). Available at: http://www.ustr.gov/enforcement/2002-01-21-exec-dumping.PDF.
eBearing.com. (2000). *Continued Dumping and Subsidy Offset Act* of 2000 (CDSOA): the Byrd Amendment. Available at: http://www.ebearing.com/legislation/2000act.htm.
Just, R.E., D.L. Hueth, and A. Schmitz. (1982). *Applied Welfare Economics and Public Policy.* Ingle Cliffs: Prentice-Hall, Inc.

King, Jr., N. (2002). "Trade Imbalance: New Dumping Law Lines the Pockets of Manufacturers." *The Wall Street Journal*. Dow Jones & Company, New York, New York. (December 5: 1).

Lamy, P. (2003). "WTO Appellate Body Condemns the 'Byrd Amendment'—The US Must Now Repeal It." *Delegation of the European Commission to the United States*. Geneva: WTO. Available at: http://www.eurunion.org/news/press/2003/2003003.htm.

Schmitz, A. and T.G. Schmitz. (1994). "Tariffs and Trade." Chapter 6 in the *Encyclopaedia of Agricultural Sciences*, Vol. 4. San Diego: Academic Press, Inc.

Schmitz, T.G. and A. Schmitz. (2003). "Food Supply Management and Tariffication: A Game Theoretic Approach." *Journal of Agriculture and Food Industrial Organization* 1(1): 1–19.

Tariff Act. (1930). Available at: http://www.access.gpo.gov/uscode/title19/chapter4_.html.

Thomas, B. (2003). "Bush Budget Slashes Byrd Amendment, Alters Byrd Bill." *The Intelligence Wheeling News Register*. Available at: http://www.news-register.net/news/story/025202003_new03.asp. (February 5).

U.S. Customs Services (U.S. Customs Services, U.S. Department of Homeland Security). (2003). "CDSOA FY2001 and FY2002 Disbursements, Final." Available at: http://www.customs.ustreas.gov/xp/cgov/import/add_cvd/.

U.S. Department of State (U.S. Department of State, Office of International Information Programs). (2003). "USTR Seeks to Comply with WTO Ruling on Byrd Amendment: Underlying Antidumping Laws not Affected, USTR Emphasizes." Available at: http://usinfo.state.gov/topical/econ/wto/03011601.htm (January 16).

U.S. Department of the Treasury (U.S. Department of the Treasury, Customs Service). (2002). "Distribution of Continued Dumping and Subsidy Offset to Affected Domestic Procedures; Notice." *Federal Registry* 67, No. 128 (Wednesday, July 3). Washington DC: Government Printing Office. Available at: http://frwebgate.access.gpo.gov/cgi-in/getdoc.cgi?dbname=2002_register&docid=02-16693-filed.pdf.

WTO (World Trade Organization). (2002). *United States - Continued Dumping and Subsidy Offset Act of 2000*. Second Panel Hearing: Oral Statement by Australia. WT/DS217 and WT/DS234. Geneva: WTO.

Section III:
Canada-U.S. Trade Dispute Case Studies

Chapter 7

The WTO Ruling on Canadian Dairy Exports

W. Hartley Furtan, Robert F. Romain, and Al Mussell

University of Saskatchewan
Université Laval
George Morris Centre

INTRODUCTION

In 1994, the General Agreement on Tariffs and Trade (GATT) through its Agreement on Agriculture placed limits on the quantity of Canadian dairy exports. The Canadian domestic dairy market is protected from foreign competition through the use of restrictive trade practices, including very high tariffs on imported dairy products. In addition to high import tariffs, there exists a production quota that restricts the amount of milk produced within Canada. Canadian dairy producers receive a price higher than the world price for their raw milk because of Canadian import tariffs and domestic-production quotas.

The dairy industry is one of the most highly protected sectors of Canadian agriculture (Schmitz, Furtan, and Baylis 2002). As a result of this protection, Canada exports only a small quantity of dairy products and most of these dairy products go to the United States. Protection takes the form of high tariffs on imports in combination with domestic-production quotas that occur partly as the result of rent-seeking activities by the provincial dairy boards. In the negotiations that preceded the 1994 GATT agreement, the Canadian dairy producers lobbied the Canadian Federal government to maintain both the supply-management system and tariff protection from dairy imports. As a result of this high level of protectionism, Canada has a limited ability to export dairy products.

In 1999, the United States and New Zealand initiated a complaint with the World Trade Organization (WTO) claiming that the Canadian dairy industry benefited from the high domestic price of raw milk (WTO 2002). The United States and New Zealand (the appellants) claimed that the protected Canadian dairy market enabled the exportation of its products because farmers used income earned in the domestic market to subsidize processors who exported milk products. The appellants also claimed that the enabling of the exportation of dairy products resulted from a cross-subsidization of revenue between the Canadian domestic-dairy market and its export market. In essence, Canadian dairy exports were benefiting from an export subsidy. The WTO agreed with the appellants.

In the 1994 GATT Agreement on Agriculture, Canada was allowed to export dairy products even though its dairy producers received an export subsidy.[1] The quantities of dairy exports allowed under the GATT Agreement on Agriculture are presented in Table 7.1 (Mussell 2002). Since 1995, however,

Table 7.1: WTO Subsidized Export Commitments

Subsidized Export	Year	Committed Quantity	Actual Quantity	Actual/ Committed
		Metric Tons	Metric Tons	Percent
Butter	1995/96	9,464	13,956	147.5
	1996/97	8,271	10,987	132.8
	1997/98	7,079	10,894	153.9
	1998/99	5,886	4,327	73.5
	1999/00	4,693	1,803	38.4
	2000/01	3,500	808	23.1
	2001/02	3,500	1,501	42.9
Cheese	1995/96	12,448	13,751	110.5
	1996/97	11,773	20,409	173.4
	1997/98	11,099	27,397	246.8
	1998/99	10,424	26,027	249.7
	1999/00	9,750	20,480	210.1
	2000/01	9,076	17,945	197.7
	2001/02	9,076	14,445	159.2
SMP	1995/96	54,910	35,252	64.2
	1996/97	52,919	24,888	47.0
	1997/98	50,927	29,886	58.7
	1998/99	48,936	40,728	83.2
	1999/00	46,944	39,061	83.2
	2000/01	44,953	41,197	91.6
	2001/02	44,953	52,294	116.3
Other Milk	1995/96	36,990	37,573	101.6
Products	1996/97	35,649	62,146	174.3
	1997/98	34,307	71,023	207.0
	1898/99	32,966	46,630	141.4
	1999/00*	31,624	57,058	180.4
	2000/01*	30,282	63,794	210.7
	2001/02*	30,282	60,721	200.5

Source: Mussel (2002).

Canada has exported amounts of dairy products that have exceeded the prescribed limits of the GATT Agreement on Agriculture, especially those for the higher valued dairy products like cheese.

The two GATT articles under contention, Article 10(a) and Article 9.1(c), are used by the United States and New Zealand to challenge Canadian dairy exports. Article 10(a) deals with the burden of evidence and will not be discussed in this chapter. Article 9.1(c), however, concerns "Payments Financed by Virtue of Government Action" and is the link between government payments and the creation of export subsidies. In this chapter, our attention is focused on the implications of Article 9.1(c).

Canadian milk processors are able to purchase milk from Canadian dairy producers at the world price through the Canadian Dairy Commission (CDC), process the milk, and export the milk products, provided none of the milk products enter the Canadian domestic milk market. This milk is called commercial-export milk (CEM) and is produced above the existing domestic dairy-production quota. The Canadians argue that there is no link between the milk produced under this quota and the milk produced for export. Because farmers voluntarily enter the CEM contracts, the marginal costs must equal the purchase price of the milk and must cover the average variable costs of the producer. In 1999, New Zealand and the United States argued that the Canadian dairy producers were cross-subsidizing revenue between the fluid and CEM types of milk. Therefore, once Canadian exports exceeded the GATT limits, Canada was in violation of the GATT Agreement on Agriculture. In essence, the appellants argued that the export price for CEM dairy products must cover the average total cost of production, which it does not. The GATT panel agreed with the appellants.

In this chapter, we explain how the production-quota (supply-management) system works in Canada. We then model how CEM is produced and why the appellants argued that the Canadian dairy industry benefits from an export subsidy. Finally, we discuss what options Canada has to reform its dairy system to bring it in line with the 1994 GATT Agreement on Agriculture.

CANADIAN DAIRY SUPPLY MANAGEMENT

Canadian dairy production is regulated through production quotas, administered pricing schemes, and import tariffs (Baylis and Furtan 2003). Specifically, the supply-management system restricts production and allows producers to price discriminate based on the end use of the milk. Because these regulations create sizeable economic rents for producers, dairy farmers continuously lobby the government to maintain these programs. On the other side of the issue, Canadian consumer and dairy-processor groups lobby the government for the elimination of these policies.[2]

The total fluid (fresh) milk-production quota is set at the provincial level and is based on current provincial population levels, thus the distribution of the share of the national fluid-milk-production quota is not subject to bargaining.[3] The Canadian Dairy Commission (which represents dairy producers) in consultation with the Canadian Milk Supply Management Committee

(CMSMC) (which represents producers, processors, and consumers) set the national quantity of industrial milk used by processors to make milk products, including ice cream and cheese. The total industrial-milk quota is divided among all the provinces and is based on the production of industrial milk within each province based on its price at the time of the creation of the 1973 Milk Supply Management Agreement (CDC 1975). Based on this allocation policy, the bulk of industrial milk is produced in Quebec and Ontario. The quota is then allocated among individual producers by the producer's provincial marketing board. The minimum farm price of milk is set by the CMSMC to cover the average cost of production of the producer after the CDC has consulted with representatives from the dairy industry and with representatives of the consumer groups.

In addition to restricting the total amount of milk produced, the supply-management system facilitates price discrimination by allocating quantities of milk to the fluid-milk market and to the processed dairy-products market. Were it not for this allocation system, milk producers would sell milk for use as fluid or industrial milk at the same price, albeit at higher-than-competitive prices due to the quota. Because the demand for fluid milk is less elastic than is the demand for milk in processed products, the Canadian supply-management system restricts the share of milk for fluid use, thereby raising the price for fluid milk and lowering the price for milk used to produce processed-milk products. The gain to farmers from raising the price for fluid milk more than offsets the loss from lowering the price for processed milk. Even though this reallocation of milk tends to lower the price of milk for processing, the quota—which raises both fluid- and processing-milk prices—causes the final price for processing milk to exceed its competitive world price. Figure 7.1 presents the Quebec farm-gate prices of milk and milk quotas from 1996 to 2002. Note that the Quebec prices for all types of milk substantially exceeded the world price during that time.

The import tariff is yet another dairy-production-regulating technique. GATT 1994 altered the distribution of rents between domestic producers and importers and also increased the quantity of dairy imports allowable, which implies that domestic producers had a smaller market. Prior to the Uruguay Round of GATT 1994, under Article 11.2(c) of GATT 1947 (GATT 1947), Canada used quantitative border restrictions to block dairy imports. The quantitative border restriction allows dairy imports into Canada, but this occurs only when necessary to maintain a stable domestic-consumer price in Canada. That is, if there were a domestic shortage of milk products in Canada and the price of these products rose sharply, imports would be allowed into Canada to bring the price of Canadian milk back to the level it was previous to the price rise. The Canadian dairy market is illustrated in Figure 7.2. The domestic demand curve is D, the domestic supply curve is S, and the world price is P^w. If there were free trade in which the domestic dairy price would equal its world price, Canada would then produce quantity Q^S and would import quantity $Q^d - Q^s$.

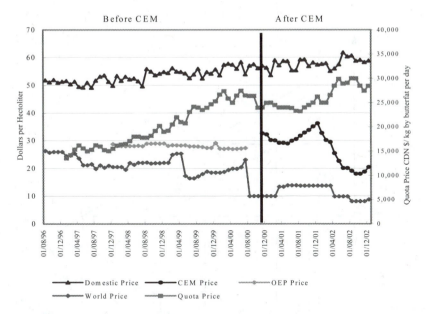

Figure 7.1: Quota Prices and Producer Prices by Quebec Markets, August 1996 to November 2002
Source: GREPA 1998.

Prior to GATT 1994, the CMSMC chose a quantity-price pair $Q^c P^c$ in which few, if any, imports were permitted. By reducing or eliminating imports and increasing price, the supply-management system created rents for domestic producers. If the CMSMC were to set quantity and price at $Q^c P^c$, farmer producer surplus would exceed that from free trade by area $A + D$. The Canadian government, through the CDC which administers the supply-management system for the CMSMC, permits just enough imports to keep the domestic dairy price from rising above P^c. Thus if the CMSMC were to err and set domestic production too low, say Q^m in Figure 7.2 so that domestic price would exceed P^c in the absence of imports, the government would permit imports of $Q^c - Q^m$. Importers would buy the product at the world price P^w and would sell it in the domestic market at P^c. Thus the value of the import quota would be $\left(P^c - P^w \right)\left(Q^c - Q^m \right)$, which is area $\left(C + D \right)$ in Figure 7.2, and farmer rents from supply management would fall to area A.

GATT 1994 required that all import quotas be replaced by a system of tariff-rate quotas (TRQs). Under a TRQ system, a small quantity of imports,

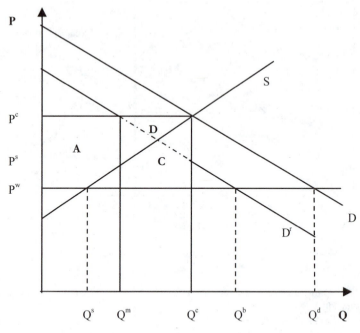

Figure 7.2: Supply Management Before and After GATT 1994

in quota, or Minimum Access Commitment (MAC) imports enter the country virtually tariff free.[4] (In 1995, MAC was set at 3 percent of the 1986 to 1988 average domestic consumption; by the year 2000 it was set at 5 percent.) All subsequent imports in excess of the quota, hence over-quota imports, enter at a higher tariff rate. For Canadian dairy, the over-quota tariffs were prohibitive, with tariffs in excess of 250 percent.

Suppose that MAC dairy imports equal $Q^d - Q^b$, and domestic producers face a residual demand curve D^r (Figure 7.2). If the domestic production quota is set at Q^m, Canadian consumers will face a price of P^c. Thus, the expansion of the MAC in the Uruguay Round of GATT 1994 caused a shift of area D from producers to importers, so importers received area $D + C$, but only area D was transferred from producers.[5]

EXPORTING UNDER SUPPLY MANAGEMENT

Canadian milk processors source milk from producers, process it into milk products, and sell it into the domestic and foreign market. Thus Canadian producers are able to differentiate between the domestic and foreign market for milk products (Turvey, Weersink, and Martin 2003). The processed milk sold into the domestic market must be purchased within the production quota shown as Q^0 in Figure 7.3. The demand curve D represents the demand for only the milk produced domestically. The foreign demand for processed Canadian milk, which is not shown in Figure 7.3, can be supplemented with milk purchased under the CEM scheme at the world price. Some of the milk produced under quota can then be processed and exported, however processed CEM milk products can be exported only, they *cannot* be sold into the domestic market.[6]

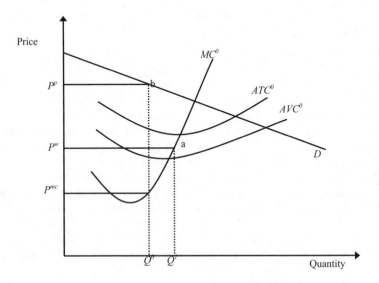

Figure 7.3: Dairy Exports within the Supply-Management System

In Figure 7.3, the Canadian demand curve for milk products is D. The Canadian export demand curve for milk products is P^w, and is perfectly elastic because Canada is a small exporter of milk products within the world market. The average total cost of producing milk in Canada is shown as ATC^0, the average variable cost is AVC^0, and the marginal cost is MC^0.

If the domestic production quota of milk is set at quantity Q^0, the marginal cost of milk will be P^{mc}, the profit-maximizing price charged to processors for milk sold into the domestic market will be P^p, and the value of the quota will be equal to area $P^p P^{mc} ab$. If the world milk price is P^w and intersects the marginal cost curve MC^0 above the average variable cost curve AVC^0, Canadian producers will expand production milk from Q^0 to Q^1. The additional milk production $Q^1 - Q^0$ will be CEM milk, which is milk produced outside the quota system at the world price. This milk will then be processed by Canadian processors and will be exported in the form of processed dairy products. Canadian dairy producers could maximize profits by reducing the quantity of milk sold into the domestic market and increasing exports until the marginal revenue from the processed milk sales will be equated in the two markets. So long as the world price P^w intersects the marginal cost curve MC^0 at a quantity greater than Q^0 and is above the average variable cost curve AVC^0, Canadian producers will find it profitable to export milk products in the CEM form.

The world price of milk P^w does not cover the average total cost of milk production ATC^0 in Canada (Figure 7.3). Depending on how the fixed costs for milk production are calculated, P^w may not cover the average variable costs AVC^0 of milk production. The appellants argued to GATT that the Canadian Dairy Commission placed some of the variable costs from milk production into the fixed-cost category, which reduced the average variable cost of milk production in Canada. If this argument is correct, CEM could be receiving a subsidy from milk that is produced under quota within Canada's supply-management system. The Canadian government argued that the world price P^w was in fact above the minimum of the average total cost ATC^0 for some Canadian dairy producers. If this is the case, Canadian milk producers will be covering the full cost of CEM production and no subsidy will be required (Figure 7.3).

The question, which follows directly from the above discussion, is what is the appropriate cost of production of dairy in Canada? Much of the debate at the GATT talks during the 1999 to 2001 period was over this very point. Currently in Canada, the cost of the quota is not included in the cost-of-production formula, whereas the appellants argued it must be included. If the value of the quota is fully incorporated into the cost curve, only a normal profit will remain if the price of milk were to equal the ATC^0.

THE CHALLENGE OF EXPORT SUBSIDIES

In 1999, the United States and New Zealand argued that the Canadian CEM produced for export only violated the 1994 GATT Agreement on Agriculture, Article 9.1(c), which lists the conditions for exporting agricultural commodities when there are "Payments Financed by Virtue of Government Action." The appellants pointed out that Canadian government payments were made on exported CEM dairy products, and that these payments were made by virtue of government action.

The phrase, "Payments Financed by Virtue of Governmental Action," refers to the link between the domestic dairy market, CEM sales, and Canadian governmental action. It was the view of the appellants in 1999 that the sole purpose of processors being exempt from purchasing milk at the domestic price was to make the CEM a lower cost so it would be competitive in the export market. In addition, CEM must be pre-committed by the farmers and processors before it can be produced. The pre-commitment demonstrates the link between the management of the two milk-pricing schemes by the CDC. The appellants argued that, without government intervention, some CEM would go into the domestic market, which would reduce the domestic price of raw milk. The Canadian government argued against both of these points and stated that the arrangement for CEM was strictly between the farmer and the processor.

Further, the appellants claimed that the term "payments" referred to the export subsidy made to dairy products produced and exported from CEM. A key consideration is that the payments do not need to be made by the government. In fact, GATT ruled that the farmers made the payments to the processors. In essence, the farmers provided the subsidy by pooling the high-priced domestic milk with the lower priced CEM (i.e., the farmer cross-subsidized the price of milk between the two markets).

A second part of the issue is related to how farmers could make such a payment. Because of government action to protect the Canadian milk market, the appellants argued that the domestic milk price was sufficient to subsidize the price of CEM. The Canadian cost of production that is used to set the domestic milk price is an industry average not unlike an Olympic-average price, which is the average price calculated over 5 years with the highest and lowest prices removed from the calculation. Because farmers sign CEM contracts on an individual basis, the Canadians argued that the payments needed to be determined farm by farm to calculate the correct export subsidy. The appellants argued that because the cost-of-production formula based on an average cost as reported by the Canadian dairy industry is used to formulate domestic-milk prices, it is the correct cost-of-production price to use when calculating the export subsidy.

Another point of contention was how Canada calculated the domestic cost of milk production. The appellants made the claim that the cost of production should include the cost of marketing, transportation, and administration; the cost of the production quota; the imputed cost of family labour and management; and a return to equity. All of these costs are not included in the Canadian cost-of-production formula. The Canadian position was that the payments should not include the above costs.

If all costs (including quota costs) were included in the formula that determined the price of milk, both the marginal cost MC^0 and average total cost of milk ATC^0, would need to be equal at the market-clearing price. If this is the case, only normal profit will remain. This will remove all the benefit of the supply-managed system to the producers because it is the *difference* between price and cost that gives the production quota its value.

Finally, there is the issue of cross-subsidization that the Canadian government claimed was beyond the mandate of the GATT panel. GATT ruled initially that domestic-milk quota holders could cross-subsidize milk produced for the domestic market and the milk produced for CEM. This allows producers to engage in less remunerative CEM sales, while at least covering their marginal costs of production. Thus it appears GATT accepted the principle that cross-subsidization does occur between the price of domestic milk and CEM.

POLICY IMPLICATIONS AND CONCLUSIONS

Canada agreed to abide by the GATT ruling and reduced its exports of processed dairy products. The first question faced by Canadian dairy producers is who would cut back on production? Approximately 0.5 percent of the CEM was contracted by producers without domestic quota. It would be difficult for these producers to do anything but to go completely out of business. The existing producers could provide them with some quota; however this could be problematic because the existing producers would then need to cut back on their quota.

If 0.5 percent of producers without domestic quota could cover all of their costs at the world price, why should they be forced to exit the industry? Are they not the most efficient producers? Some industry observers suggest that this small group of new producers will initiate change within the Canadian dairy system.

Processors will experience a loss in profits. Processors will also have to reduce the volume of milk processed. One would expect that Canadian processors who are able to export their CEM dairy products into world markets at the world milk price would lose market share. Given that Canadian processors are small by North American standards, the prospect of reducing production will not be well received. If Canada maintains its current dairy program, growth in the processing industry will be limited to the domestic market. How does Canada deal with this issue when one of the many planks of the new Canadian farm policy, "The Agricultural Policy Framework," is attempting to expand sales of value-added products?

One way to partially ease the concern over the export market is for the processors to export high-valued products. There are no constraints on exports from milk produced within the quota, so long as the products are sold in the domestic market at the same price as they are sold in the export market. It may be possible to move some processed products into different classes of milk and change the pricing strategy. This innovation needs to be explored and its effect on total revenue needs to be determined.

There are two implications of this GATT ruling that may be the most far-reaching. First, agencies or groups other than the government can make export-subsidy payments. To see the extent of this issue, suppose we have a government-mandated marketing board that has no production controls but is able to price discriminate on the export market. The final price the farmers will receive from the marketing board will be a pooled price, in which the high and low prices will be averaged. The final price is then a weighted-average price. Are farmers subsidizing the marketing board by virtue of a payment earned in the high-priced market to enable the marketing board to sell into the low-priced market? If this is the case, all marketing boards that export and price pool will be deemed to be using export subsidizes.

Second, GATT ruled that export prices must cover all costs of production inclusive of fixed costs if there is to be no subsidy. Generally, economists argue that prices should be equated to marginal cost. If all costs are included, programs such as decoupled U.S. farm programs that inflate land prices could be seen as GATT Amber Box programs. This is a major change in how subsidizes will be viewed in the future.

Canada does not have to abandon the supply-managed system to fully participate in the export market, but GATT restrictions are clearly placed on dairy exports and on dairy-product exports. Given that the majority of existing dairy producers have a production quota and quota rents, they are unlikely to agree to the abandonment of the supply-management scheme. In the past, Canada has tried a number of methods to price pool and to avoid GATT restrictions. Unfortunately for the Canadian dairy producer, these avenues appear to be closed.

NOTES

[1] The milk used for export must be produced within the production quota (GATT 1994).

[2] A former representative of the Canadian Association of Consumers (CAC) stated in an interview that the CAC actively lobbies and supports research on supply-management issues. Data were not available for either the consumer- or processor-lobby expenditures.

[3] A dairy producer cannot sell milk without a production quota. The production quota of a dairy farm is a license that gives the owner the right to produce the specified quantity. These quotas are tradable only between producers within a single province.

[4] For example, the tariff on in-quota cheese imports is 3.5 cents per kilogram, which is less than one-half of one percent of most retail cheese prices.

[5] The Canadian federal government offers the import quotas (for a nominal lump-sum fee) to firms in proportion to their previous imports. Historically, these importers were firms such as Safeway rather than producers or processors.

[6] Milk produced under quota can be exported under the special milk classes 5(a), 5(b), and 5(c).

REFERENCES

Baylis, K. R. and W. H. Furtan. (2003). "Free Riding on Federalism: Trade Protection and the Canadian Dairy Industry." *Canadian Public Policy* 29(2):145–67.

CDC (Canadian Dairy Commission). (1975 to 2002). *Annual Report.* Ottawa: CDC.

GATT (General Agreement on Tariffs and Trade). (1947). Available at: http://www.jurisint.org/pub/06/en/doc/05.htm.

_____. (1994). *The Results of the Uruguay Round of Multilateral Trade Negotiations, Agreement on Agriculture.* Geneva: GATT Secretariat.

GREPA (Groupe de Recherche en Économique et Politique Agricole). (1998). *Les Faits saillants laitiers Québecois, 12th edition.* Faculté des sciences de l'agriculure et de l'ailmentation, Université Laval. Québec: Université Laval.

Mussell, A. (2002). *The WTO Dairy Export Decision: What Next For Growth in the Canadian Dairy Sector?* Guelph: George Morris Centre (January).

Schmitz, A., H. de Gorter, and T. G. Schmitz. (1996). "Consequences of Tariffication," in *Regulation and Protectionism under GATT: Case Studies in North America*, edited by A. Schmitz, G. Coffin, and K. Rosaasen. Boulder: Westview Press, Inc.

Schmitz, A., W. H. Furtan, and K. R. Baylis. (2002). *Agricultural Policy, Agribusiness, and Rent-Seeking Behaviour.* Toronto: University of Toronto Press.

Turvey, C., A. Weersink, and C. Martin. (2003). "The Value of Dairy Quota under a Commercial Export Milk Program." *Canadian Journal of Agricultural Economics* 51(1): 69–84.

WTO (World Trade Organization). (2002). *Canada Measures Affecting the Importation of Milk and the Exportation of Dairy Products.* Second Recourse to Article 21.5 of the /DSU/ by New Zealand and the United States, AB-2002-6. Geneva: WTO.

Chapter 8

The WTO Case on Canadian Dairy Export Subsidies: Implications for Two-Tiered Pricing

Carol Goodloe
*U.S. Department of Agriculture**

INTRODUCTION

The United States and New Zealand challenge of Canada's dairy-export subsidies was the first World Trade Organization (WTO) case on the agricultural export subsidy provisions of the Uruguay Round Agreement on Agriculture (URAA). The case broke new ground in the area of two-tiered price regimes and export subsidies. After five years, two Compliance Panel reports, and three Appellate Body (AB) reports, the WTO reached a sound decision that Canada's two-tiered pricing system was an export subsidy. But a key aspect of the finding, the use of costs of production in assessing two-tiered pricing systems, added an unanticipated, and perhaps unnecessary, twist to the case. This chapter reviews the findings of the final two AB reports, focusing on the choice of a benchmark, and discusses some of the implications of the rulings for two-tiered export-pricing systems.

BACKGROUND ON THE WTO PROCESS

Prior to the URAA, Canada maintained a dairy system based on high internal prices to support income, production quotas to regulate output, border measures to limit imports, and export subsidies to remove the resulting surpluses. Following the implementation of the URAA, Canada maintained its system of production quotas and converted border measures on dairy imports to high tariffs. But Canada eliminated the system of producer levies on over-quota milk that had been used to finance export subsidies, and extended the system of classified pricing based on end use to milk used for exports and for import-competing products.

Canada shifted from a system of penalties that discouraged over-quota production to one that allowed producers to voluntarily provide milk outside the quota to export processors at a discounted price (Mussell 2003; Waino 2001). This new export element of Canada's classified pricing became the subject of a lengthy WTO dispute-settlement process.

After losing the original 1999 WTO panel and subsequent appeal, Canada established a new export system to implement the AB rulings. Under the new regulations, milk could be marketed either on the domestic market subject to a quota, or as Class 4(m)[1] animal feed for any amount above the quota. Milk could also be pre-committed for sale outside the quota system and could be sold to processors for export as commercial export milk (CEM). Prices for CEM were negotiated between processors and individual producers. CEM was subject to health regulations but was excluded from quota and levy requirements; it was not marketed through the provincial marketing boards, and the proceeds from sales were not subject to national or regional pooling schemes. Nevertheless, the United States and New Zealand challenged the new system as continuing to provide export subsidies, and requested the formation of a WTO Compliance Panel in early 2001.

Similar to the first Compliance Panel and AB ruling, at issue was whether products made from CEM constituted an export subsidy and should count toward Canada's WTO export-subsidy commitments. The primary legal issue continued to be whether or not the provision of CEM (i.e., discounted milk) to processors constitutes "payments on the export of milk that are financed by virtue of government action." [2]

The WTO Compliance Panel ruled in July 2001 that CEM constituted an export subsidy. Canada appealed that decision. On December 3, 2001, a second AB delivered a surprising ruling. The AB overturned the Compliance Panel's decision that CEM was an export subsidy because the AB did not have sufficient evidence to determine whether or not Canada's system constituted an export subsidy. The AB further stated that evidence should be based on a new standard or benchmark and they established the average total cost of production (ATCP). Once the AB said it could not rule on the subsidy issue because it did not have the data, it also said it could not rule whether or not a subsidy had been financed by virtue of government action.

A second Compliance Panel was established and ruled in July 2002 that CEM was an export subsidy. Canada appealed that decision, but a third AB report in December 2002 upheld the ruling by the WTO Compliance Panel because CEM was sold at prices below the ATCP, payments were provided, and such payments were financed by virtue of government action.

WHAT CONSTITUTES A PAYMENT: THE SEARCH FOR A BENCHMARK

In the first WTO Compliance Panel, much of the discussion revolved around the issue of a benchmark against which to judge whether a payment on an export had occurred; that is, against what standard should the CEM price be compared?

The URAA provided no definition or guidance on this question, especially since this case concerned a payment-in-kind. Canada argued that no benchmark was needed because CEM was sold on a fully commercial basis. The United States argued that a payment occurred because the price for export milk was below the price for domestic milk. As a third party, the European Union (EU) argued that CEM should be compared to a world market price because the domestic market was not available to exporters. Since world market prices and CEM prices were effectively the same thing, this view supported Canada's position.

The first Compliance Panel used the domestic milk price as the benchmark to determine whether or not a payment had been made. The second AB agreed there needed to be a standard or benchmark in order to determine if a payment had occurred, but rejected both domestic administered prices and world market prices as benchmarks stating, "that the standard must be objective and based on the value of the milk to the producer" (WTO 2001). Thus, the compelling issue became how to define or measure the proper value of CEM milk. Determining the proper value of something is a question that has bedevilled philosophers and economists for centuries. But the AB had to address the issue in a practical way.

The AB reasoned that the value of milk to the producer should be the amount the producer must recoup in the long term to avoid incurring economic losses, including opportunity costs, and concluded an appropriate basis for determining the value was the ATCP. The AB noted that costs of production could be measured as either an average or marginal cost of production, and acknowledged different interpretations of what constitutes ATCP, based on data already submitted by the United States, New Zealand, and Canada. The AB noted that production requires an investment in fixed assets, such as land, machinery, and facilities, as well as variable costs, such as labour and animal feed. The AB concluded that the ATCP was the appropriate benchmark and should include all fixed and variable costs for producing all milk.

THE COST OF PRODUCTION CONUNDRUM

There are many ways to slice the cost-of-production pie, assuming reliable data are even available to do so. Countries that collect data or conduct surveys often use different concepts or measures, making comparisons across countries very difficult. The specific data collected may be a function of what concept is being measured. For example in agriculture, most annual planting decisions are based on covering operating or cash costs but longer-term decisions must consider ownership and economic costs. The effects of domestic subsidies or border measures on costs are generally not taken into account. Average or mean costs may be biased depending on the distribution of costs. The AB did not consider any of these issues when making its decision about a proper benchmark.

The United States and New Zealand, the Parties to the dispute, had different views over what should be included in the costs of production (Table 8.1). They presented data based on the Canadian Dairy Commission (CDC) cost surveys that included fixed and variable costs. Canada used the same CDC data; costs

Table 8.1: Canadian Dairy Commission Cost Surveys: CDN $ per Hectare Litre

Year	U.S/CDC[a]	Canada[b]	Commercial Export Market Price
2000	57.27	18.53–46.60	29.00
2001	58.12	18.53–46.60	31.72

[a] The United States presented total cost-of-production data from CDC data.
[b] Canada used the same CDC data as the United States, but used only variable costs.
Source: WTO (2001)and WTO (2002).

of production should include only cash costs and should not include imputed values for land and labour or quota costs. (Earlier in the process Canada had argued for a cost-of-production standard to avoid the damaging comparison to the domestic milk price.) Depending on the source of data and what is included, especially how non-cash costs are valued, estimates of costs of production can vary significantly. Ultimately, Canada's arguments did not prevail.

The reasoning based on ATCP is further complicated when examining how two-tiered pricing schemes function. Two-tiered pricing schemes often involve a high domestic price maintained by border measures and may involve production quotas. The high domestic price covers a producer's ATCP. But even in a supply-managed system like Canada has, there may be producers who have excess capacity to produce milk beyond their quota. As long as the lower export price covers their marginal costs, these producers have an incentive to expand output at the export price. In that case, the proper value of the milk to the producer would be equal to its marginal cost and not to its average cost. Otherwise, the producer would not sell the milk into the CEM market.

Supply management and costs of production present a complicated mix of issues that the AB did not fully explore. Even if one believes that the marginal cost would have been a more appropriate standard based on the economics of two-tiered schemes, supply-management systems further complicate the concept and the measurement of marginal cost. Various studies have attempted to determine rent-free or marginal cost curves for the Canadian dairy industry (Barichello 1999). Had the AB steered in this direction, establishing a benchmark based on marginal cost would have been exceedingly difficult. In addition, a ruling that marginal cost was the appropriate benchmark could have been the green light for two-tiered pricing systems.

PAYMENT FINANCED BY VIRTUE OF GOVERNMENT ACTION

This standard or benchmark used to define whether a payment exists was also crucial when determining whether or not the payment "was financed by Virtue of Government Action." The WTO Compliance Panels and the AB wrestled with the legal aspects of this linkage in different ways throughout the process. For example, the second AB overturned the reasoning behind the Compliance Panel's findings that processors would not have access to low-cost milk but for government action. In this case, the AB focused on the Compliance Panel's argument that Canadian producers are "obligated or forced" to sell over-quota milk into the CEM market. The AB correctly noted that producers are not forced to sell CEM milk. Only those who can cover their marginal costs and earn additional revenue can choose to sell into the CEM market.

The economics of the two-tiered pricing system clearly established the linkage between domestic and export markets. If producers were unable to cover their total costs from sales in the domestic market, the export price alone would have to cover the ATCPs, or else a producer would go out of business. In this case, Canadian producers clearly would not be able to cover their ATCPs from export sales alone. Therefore, as concluded in the final AB report, the provision of export milk is financed by government action. The AB defined government action as being the entire government-controlled supply-management system, including the process of setting production quotas and support prices for milk.

RELATIONSHIP BETWEEN COST OF PRODUCTION AND WTO SUBSIDY DISCIPLINES

When wrestling with how to establish a benchmark for the proper value of milk, the AB argued that using ATCP as a benchmark maintains the integrity of the separate WTO disciplines on domestic support and export subsidies. The AB noted that even WTO-consistent domestic support may "spill over" to benefit export production because no distinction is made during the production process whether the output is destined for the domestic or for the export market. The report cautions against treating such domestic support as an export subsidy.

This distinction seems less relevant in the case of Canada's supply management system, where CEM is segregated from quota milk for the domestic market. However, quota milk can spill over into the export market (i.e., through milk Classes 5(a), 5(b), and 5(c)[3] for import substitution products) but CEM, by law, cannot enter the domestic market and must be exported. One can understand the concern better in the case of a commodity that benefits from WTO-consistent domestic support and is also exported with a specific export subsidy.

U.S. milk benefits from a dairy price-support program. For example, if cheese made from price-supported milk is exported commercially, no export subsidy will be involved even though the milk is subsidized. If that cheese is exported with an export subsidy under the U.S. Dairy Export Incentive Program (DEIP), the DEIP bonus will roughly equal the difference between the domestic and the world price. Costs of production are irrelevant.

The AB report claims that if one accepts the argument that CEM sales at any price below the domestic price constitutes a "payment," then the distinction between domestic and export subsidies becomes blurred, and the basis for comparison between domestic and export subsidies loses its distinction (WTO 2001). However, these concerns appear to be addressed by the URAA definitions of domestic and export subsidies, including the WTO requirements that an export subsidy be contingent on export. In addition, another definition of export subsidy (surplus disposal) found in Article 9.1(b) of the URAA uses domestic price as the benchmark. The AB raised a valid concern about the relation of domestic and export subsidies, but the cost-of-production standard may not be the best way to address them.

SUBSIDIZED INPUTS FOR EXPORT PROCESSING

The second search for a benchmark by the AB led them to the related issue of subsidized inputs for export processing. The AB stated that using a world market price, as a benchmark was unacceptable because CEM could still be competitive with world-priced milk if CEM benefited from domestic subsidies. The report noted that if the benchmark is a world market price, WTO members will be able to subsidize the price of the input to processors at a level that equals or marginally exceeds world market prices. By this process, WTO members could easily defeat the export subsidy commitments (WTO 2001).

The AB identified a legitimate issue and there are examples of this kind of practice, including Canada's Milk Class 4(m) and Classes 5(a), 5(b), and 5(c), if these products are exported. Prior to the 2002 U.S. Farm Bill, additional U.S. peanuts were available to processors at a price far below the price of quota peanuts. Additional peanuts had to be crushed and could not be used in the domestic edible market. Oil and meal made from lower-priced peanuts were exported. (The peanut program was completely changed in the 2002 U.S. Farm Bill, with the distinction between quota and additional peanuts gone.) A variation on the theme is the EU "Inward Processing Relief," whereby manufacturers of processed foods import raw agricultural products at zero duty, provided that the finished product is exported without subsidy. The zero-duty import can be acquired at a lower cost than the comparable domestic product and has been used to avoid WTO limits on export subsidies for some processed products (USDA/ERS 1998).

The cost-of-production benchmark that established price discounts as payments in kind may be relevant for identifying such indirect export subsidies, but the "contingent on export" would remain a crucial test in asserting programs such as Canada's classified milk pricing under 5(a), 5(b), and 5(c) as export subsidies.

HOW TO RUN A WTO-LEGAL TWO-TIER SYSTEM

Can there be such a thing as a WTO-legal two-tier price system under which exports are not subsidized? The AB report says yes, subject to two tests. First, any product that is exported under a two-tier system at a price above the ATCP will not be subsidized. Second, a product could be exported at a price below the total average cost of production so long as it was not financed by virtue of government action. A test might be a Canadian dairy producer who sets up a shop with no production quota or other government support and simply produces milk for the CEM market. One could reasonably argue that these products do not benefit from export subsidies. Canada claimed there were about 100 such producers out of 19,000, but the final AB did not think it needed to make a finding on these producers.[4]

The economics of two-tiered systems suggests a product would be exported rarely at a price equal to or greater than the ATCP. To be able to maintain a two-tier pricing system, a producer must have the ability to restrict output, which can be done only through government intervention. An extreme example would be a completely unregulated private producer who has some market power in the home market and economies of scale, and who is also able to price discriminate between the domestic and foreign markets (Baylis 2001). But a firm that could export at a price that covered total average costs of production could still be guilty of dumping if the export price were below the domestic home price.

CONCLUSIONS

The WTO dispute-settlement process reached a sound decision when identifying Canada's two-tiered pricing system for dairy as an export subsidy and should have the positive effect of curtailing attempts to create similar schemes. But the manner in which the decision was reached—the choice of ATCP as the crucial benchmark—unnecessarily complicated the findings. Costs of production (i.e., as evidenced by its use in dumping laws) present many difficulties, both in concept and measurement. Marginal cost would have been a more economically appropriate standard, but would have effectively sanctioned a two-tiered pricing scheme for milk exports. And, as is often the case for agricultural products, and especially perishables, sales of unsubsidized products are made at prices below the full costs of production because of seasonal market conditions. For all these reasons, a benchmark of the domestic price, as used in the original Compliance Panel report, would have been appropriate and rendered the same finding on two-tiered pricing and export subsidies.

NOTES

[*]The views expressed here are those of the author and do not represent the official views of the U.S. Department of Agriculture. The author greatly appreciates the comments of Art Coffing, Suchada Langley, and John Wainio, but any errors of fact or interpretation are solely those of the author.

[1]Class 4(m) is defined as "marginal markets," such as milk destined for use in animal feed.

[2]The relevant text of the URAA is Article 9.1(c): "...payments on the export of an agricultural product that are financed by virtue of government action, whether or not a charge on the public account is involved, including payments that are financed from the proceeds of a levy imposed on the agricultural product concerned or on an agricultural product from which the exported product is derived."

[3]Under the classified pricing system, Class 5(a) milk refers to industrial milk used to produce cheese ingredients for further processing, Class 5(b) milk refers to industrial milk used for all other dairy products, and Class 5(c) milk refers to industrial milk

used in the confectionary sector. These further processed products can be sold either domestically or they can be exported.

[4]Canada has evidently abolished the CEM system to come into compliance with the Dispute Settlement Body of the WTO.

REFERENCES

Barichello, R. (1999). "The Canadian Dairy Industry: Prospects for Future Trade." *Canadian Journal of Agricultural Economics* 47(5): 45–51.

Baylis, K. (2001). On appointment to the Council of Economic Advisors, personal communication, December.

Mielke, K., R. Sarker, and D. Le Roy. (1996). "Analyzing the Potential for Increased Trade in Dairy Products: A Canadian Perspective." *Understanding Canada/United States Dairy Disputes*. Proceedings of "The Second Canada/U.S. Agricultural and Food Policy Systems Information Workshop," University of Guelph, Ontario (December).

Mussell, A. (2003). *The WTO Dairy Decision: What Next for Growth in the Canadian Dairy Industry?* Ottawa: The George Morris Centre (January 21).

USDA/ERS (U.S. Department of Agriculture/Economic Research Service). (1998). *Agriculture in the WTO*. WRS-98-4. Washington DC: USDA/ERS (December).

Wainio, J. (2001). "Canada's Subsidized Dairy Exports: The Issue of WTO Compliance." *Agricultural Outlook*. Washington DC: USDA/ERS (August).

WTO (World Trade Organization). (2001). *Canada-Measures Affecting the Importation of Milk and the Exportation of Dairy Products*. Recourse to Article 21.5 of the DSU by New Zealand and the United States, Report AB-2001-6 of the Appellate Body, WT/DS103/AB/RW, WT/113/AB/RW. Geneva: WTO (December 3). Available at: www.wto.org.

_____. (2002). *Canada Measures Affecting the Importation of Milk and the Exportation of Dairy Products*. Second Recourse to Article 21.5 of the DSU by New Zealand and the United States, Report AB-2002-6 of the Appellate Body, WT/DS103/AB/RW, WT/113/AB/RW. Geneva: WTO (December 2). Available at: www.wto.org.

Chapter 9

Contested Trade
in Logs and Lumber

Peter Berck
University of Califonia at Berkeley

INTRODUCTION

The United States and Canada have been at loggerheads over softwood lumber and the log trade for over two decades. The low stumpage (standing timber) paid for logging on Crown Lands in Canada as well as the ban on log exports are the principal targets of the U.S. countervailing (CV) duties. Both countries have long banned the export of raw logs to reap the benefits of local milling. While the tariff aspects of the lumber dispute have received considerable attention, the basic issues surrounding the log-export ban are less well investigated.

It is not possible to consider U.S. claims against British Columbia (B.C.) without indulging in a major exercise in hypocrisy. The essence of the U.S. claims has been that the B.C. market for stumpage is less than competitive in its use of administrative pricing, and that British Columbia has restricted the export of logs. These are alleged by the United States to be a B.C. logging-industry subsidy that causes harm to U.S. lumber producers. Of course, the case for U.S. harm to B.C. producers is much easier to make because U.S. subsidies to the timber sector are simply legendary. As this chapter will show, the responsiveness of U.S. forests to economic signals relative to B.C. forests leaves a great deal to be desired. In this chapter, we analyze the log-export ban by studying its effect on two interrelated markets—the market for logs as well as the market for finished lumber. We develop a formal model that illuminates cases in which these markets are unaffected by the export ban. We also examine the market responsiveness of both Canada- and U.S.-administered forests and conclude that the Canadian method better approximates a competitive market outcome than does the U.S. Pacific Northwestern (USPNW) method.

LUMBER WARS

The over two-decade-long dispute between Canada and the United States regarding the trade of softwood lumber began in 1982. An alliance of U.S. lumber companies, called the Coalition for Fair Lumber Imports (CFLI), alleged that Canadian companies enjoyed subsidies in terms of extremely low stumpage rates they pay to log on Canada's Crown Lands. They also held that the Canadian ban on the export of logs depressed log prices in the provinces. Hence it constituted a CV subsidy to the Canadian lumber industry. That conflict, commonly referred to as Lumber I, resulted in the U.S. Department of Commerce (USDOC) ruling in 1983 that the Canadian stumpage programs were not countervailable because they were not restricted to a specific industry.

In 1986, however, following changes in U.S. trade laws that assisted U.S. lumber companies to assert subsidy charges, the USDOC reversed its earlier findings and maintained that Canadian stumpage programs did amount to a subsidy. This set of proceedings is referred to as Lumber II. It concluded in December 1986 with a memorandum of understanding (MOU) requiring the Canadian government to impose a 15 percent export duty on lumber that they exported to the United States.

In December 1991, the Canadian government unilaterally terminated MOU because it was seen increasingly as an infringement of national sovereignty. This prompted the USDOC to impose a CV duty of 6.51 percent in May of 1992. Canada appealed the determination, and binational panels established under the North America Free Trade Agreement (NAFTA) ultimately decided the case. The USDOC finally reversed its finding, and Lumber III ended with the revocation of the CV duty in August 1994.

The latest episode, Lumber IV, began on April 2, 2001. Since 1996, Canadian lumber exports from the provinces of British Columbia, Alberta, Ontario, and Quebec into the United States have been regulated by the Voluntary Export Restraint (VER) contained within the Softwood Lumber Agreement (SLA) between the Government of Canada and the Government of the United States of America. It allowed Canadian producers to export up to 14.7 billion board feet (bbf) of softwood lumber without export fee and imposed high export fees on volumes that exceeded that limit. The SLA expired on March 31, 2001 and was immediately followed by the resumption of U.S. trade action against Canada regarding the export of Canadian lumber and logs.

The SLA sought CV duties of 39.9 percent on imported Canadian lumber to counter the effects of provincial stumpage rates and raw-log-export restrictions. In addition, they asked for an antidumping (AD) penalty of from 28 percent to 38 percent. They further asked for a critical-circumstance ruling from the USDOC, which implied that any imposed duties would apply retroactively from the date of the initiation of the trade action.

The preliminary CV duty determination by the USDOC on August 9, 2001 imposed provisional 19.31 percent cash deposit or bond on Canadian softwood lumber. The USDOC also ruled that critical circumstances existed and, therefore, applied the CV duties retroactively from May 17, 2001 until December 5, 2001. On May 16, 2001, the U.S. International Trade Commission

(USITC) made a preliminary determination that the subsidies posed a threat of injury to U.S. companies. A year later, on May 2, 2002, the USITC made their final determination that U.S. producers are threatened only with material injury. Consequently, it ordered the U.S. Customs to refund the bonds and cash deposits posted by Canadian softwood lumber companies prior to May 16, 2002.

On April 25, 2002, the final determination by the USDOC in the CV and AD cases was that Canadian producers enjoyed a subsidy rate of 18.7 percent. So the USDOC imposed a combined AD duty and CV duty of 27.22 percent.

The dispute was presented to the World Trade Organization (WTO), and a WTO panel issued an interim report on July 26, 2002, ruling on a number of issues. In a finding in favour of Canada, it ruled that the cross-border benchmark methodology used by the USDOC to arrive at the CV duty was illegal under the WTO Subsidies and Countervailing Measures (SCM) Agreement. But, on the matter of whether standing timber is a good, it rejected Canada's claim that it is an *in situ* natural resource and should not be considered as a provision of a good or a service by the government as required by the SCM Agreement.

The most important ruling of the WTO was the position that it took against the use of cross-border benchmarks. The Canadians argued that, even if stumpage rates were found to be a financial contribution to the Canadian lumber companies, the USDOC should not determine the size of the benefit by using cross-border benchmarks. The United States argued that, because some Canadian companies purchased stumpage in the United States, those prices were part of the Canadian market. The WTO agreed with Canada and rejected the U.S. claim.

ORIGINAL SIN: HOW THE GOVERNMENT DISPOSES OF FOREST LAND

Any examination of the Canadian-American West Coast lumber trade needs to begin with a discussion of the subsidies offered by the two countries. The original subsidy was the granting of the rights to cut timber in the two countries. In the United States, the forested public domain was disposed of through railroad land grants and through the *Timber and Stone Act* (1878). In both cases, fee title was given to the private sector for very little money. The U.S. Department of Agriculture, Forest Service (USDA/FS) and the Bureau of Land Management (BLM) sold large amounts of the remaining timber from government-owned land. The USDA/FS sells timber by auction, the purchaser having the right and obligation to remove the stumpage in a set number of years. (Prior to the 1980s, contracts were five years in length; shorter contracts were more normal in later years.) In fact, in the early 1980s, when it was not in the interests of the industry to adhere to the terms of the contract, Congress forgave the obligation. Thus, one cannot view the U.S. system as a market system because the consequences of bad decisions are not incumbent upon the agents. The USDA/FS has a number of programs that are meant to subsidize the forest industry, including cost sharing for pest control. Most fundamentally, the USDA/FS is not run for profit. According to the Congressional Research Service in 1994, 77 of the 120 national forests lost money over a five-year period with one-half losing money in every year (Gorte 1994). In a competitive model, these forests, including the Klamath and Wallowa-Whitman forests in Oregon, would not have undertaken operations resulting in continuing losses. The USDA/FS very definitely supplied timber well beyond economic amounts by cross-subsidizing profitable forests with unprofitable ones and by direct subventions for the U.S. treasury. Unfortunately, the data are not so organized as to give an easy estimate of the implied supply curve if the USDA/FS were forced to operate each unit at a net profit, but the decrease in output would surely have been substantial.[1] Until recently, the United States certainly overproduced timber from its own lands.

The method by which the USDA/FS sells timber, which is the method that the USDOC urges upon British Columbia, is auction (USDOC 2003). The system begins with a forest plan and a mandate for a yearly cut, often not consistent with the forest plans but imposed by Congress. The mandated cut is assigned to a forest, which then prepares sales for bidding. Part of the preparation is an estimate of the value of the sale that is based on a conversion return that is on the low side intentionally. This estimate serves as the reservation price (Berck and Bible 1982). The bidders are free to examine the proposed sale; they bid. The high bidder wins the sale. It is not uncommon for the sales to go unclaimed or for them to go at the reservation price when the economy is in or near a recession. The process is cumbersome, expensive, and time consuming, but all available evidence is that it does recover the value of the timber.[2]

Despite the administrative and political nature of the timber process, the timing of sales and, more importantly, the timing of harvest in the United States was much more market driven than were the policy documents, which emphasized even flow and community stability. Burton and Berck (1996) find there was no causation from the USDA/FS policy variable of timber sold to timber cut while the quantity cut was heavily dependent on macroeconomic factors. Next, we re-examine this sensitivity to economic conditions.

The American industry can thus be characterized as subsidized either through cheap land, through intentional operating subsidies for pest management, or through less-intentional subsidies in below-cost forest sales. However, the U.S. industry responds basically to macroeconomic factors through the business cycle, and the price of the timber is determined at auction.

The timber industry in British Columbia is characterized by volume tenures on Crown lands, which make up 90 percent to 95 percent of the land base (Royal Commission on Forest Resources 1976). The Crown gives timber companies the right to cut a set volume of timber somewhere on Crown lands each year. The long-term tenures are renewable indefinitely. The Crown identifies the lands to be cut via a seven-day letter to the firm. The letter identifies the land and the price. The price is set by a conversion-return mechanism. From the price in the presumably competitive log market in Vancouver, B.C., the government subtracts transport and logging costs to get the price to be paid by the timber firm. The firm has no realistic choice other than to accept the terms offered, as the volume tenure requires taking the timber or losing one's rights. At first blush, the volume sold would seem to be governed by a planning process not unlike the U.S. process with the final yearly determination of volume made by the Chief Forester. One would think that the B.C. system would be characterized by a rather steady flow of timber at a price guaranteed to profit the cutting firm.

While the United States does not use volume tenures for USDA/FS sales, the mechanism of granting a nearly perpetual usufruct is common in U.S. resource policy. Grazing rights in the Western United States have been granted historically to ranchers and, despite considerable public outcry, grazing rights remain with these ranchers today. The rights are uniformly priced so the ranchers underpay the market by amounts that increase as one goes northward where there is better range (LaFrance and Watts 1994). Water development is also effectively perpetual. The Central Valley Project, for instance, sells water to farmers at a price that purports to represent the operations and maintenance costs of the project. The interest on the capital costs of the project is intended as a gift to irrigators. In fact, the project accounts for the electricity used to pump the water in the project at much less than market value, which conveys an additional subsidy to the farmers (Leveen and Goldman 1978). The rights to project water are only marginally transferable. Although the contracts were of finite duration, they, like the volume tenures in British Columbia, are effective forever. Continuing the parallel, as environmental conditions have required lower water flows, the holders of the permits have succeeded in related Federal Court action and, through Congress, have succeeded in getting much of their property rights made whole. Volume tenures in British Columbia, the subject of three serious U.S.-Canada trade disputes, are no more and probably are less distorting of market pricing than U.S. policies are for water, grazing, and forestry. A comparison of the two systems also reveals that the B.C. system appears to have less business-cycle flexibility while the U.S. system transfers more of the value of the forests to the private sector.

CLINTON FOREST PLAN

Though the dispute over lumber predates the Clinton Forest Plan (1993), the unanticipated regulatory-based decreases in USDA/FS harvests in the early 1990s left the USPNW region with far more milling capacity than it had timber supply. The USPNW region derived a large fraction of its timber supply from old growth. Environmentalists prized these stands and were empowered by the *Endangered Species Act* (1973) and *Forest and Rangeland Renewable Resource Planning Act* (1974) to intervene in the determination to cut these stands. The Spotted Owl was listed as endangered in June 1990, though it had substantial impact on forest planning before that date (Jaffe et al. 1995). In truth, the USPNW region old-growth economy would have run out of timber in the early twenty-first century without further regulation, at least at the rate of cutting in the mid-1980s, but political forces decreased cutting from 15.7 bbf to 8.0 bbf between 1986 and 2000. The level of cutting has never come back, though the Bush administration wishes to revive the industry. Figure 9.1 shows the decrease of timber harvest by the states of the USPNW region and by British Columbia from 1960 to 2000.

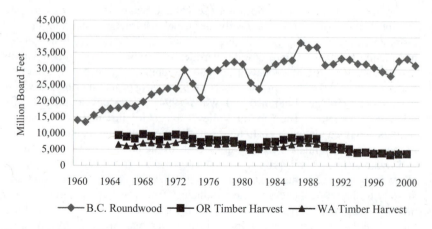

Figure 9.1: Timber Harvest in Oregon, Washington, and British Columbia
Source: USDA/FS (2003).

The decrease in cutting led to an increase in U.S. unemployment and emigration. It was politically expedient to find ways to import logs to the United States for the remaining mills to cut, hence the political need to pressure British Columbia into revoking its ban on the export of logs.

JOBS AND LOGS

To encourage a local milling industry, both Canada and the United States have long banned the export of raw logs. In the United States, restrictions that prevent the sale or export of timber from government-owned land dates back to 1897 when the U.S. Congress organized the national forest system. This ban was relaxed in 1926, and the export of local surplus was allowed. Between 1973 and 1990, a ban on log exports from Western federal lands was enacted annually.[3] In 1990 the *Forest Resource Conservation and Shortage Relief Act* (1990) made the ban permanent.

The development logic of forcing at least first-stage processing in the region of harvest is that there is far more processing employment than there is harvesting employment. Keeping processing local maximizes the jobs per board foot harvested—a common goal of governments. Of course, if the ban on exports is effective, it must lower the sum of consumer surplus and profits less transportation costs over the consuming and producing regions. Unlike the VER on automobiles, textiles, and other manufactured goods that are well described in the literature, achieving a greater price on what is exported does not compensate for a country's restriction of log exports. The simple reason for the difference is that all log exports are banned. The more complicated reason is that the market for logs and lumber are both closely approximated as competitive whereas the market for cars is oligopsonistic.

While there has been a great deal of empirical research published on the tariff aspects of the long-running U.S.-Canada lumber disputes, the basic issues surrounding the log-export ban are less well illuminated. The log-export ban became the reason for a CV tariff in May of 1992. The major piece of evidence used to support the allegation that American producers were disadvantaged was a working paper by Margolick and Uhler (1992). In that paper, a supply-and-demand model of the B.C. forest-products market was used to show that allowing log exports from Canada to the United States would increase the price of logs; hence it would also increase the price of stumpage. The surprising finding of Margolick and Uhler (1992) was empirical: An increase in the stumpage price leads to more stumpage harvested despite the volume-tenure scheme. However, the analysis they present examines only one of two interrelated markets.

In order to analyze the effects of a ban on the export of a raw material, one must analyze at least the raw-material market and the processed market (in the case of logs, the log and lumber markets). The purpose of a raw-material export ban is precisely to achieve an increase in processed-material exports.[4] Thus, the importing country will have its lumber supply augmented by imports and will have its lumber supply decreased by lack of imported raw material. There are cases in which the quantity of lumber in the importing country and the price of lumber are unaffected by the export ban. The purpose of this section is to illuminate those cases and, more generally, to provide expressions for the effect of decreased log exports on the price and quantity of lumber on logs.

FORMAL MODEL OF THE B.C.-JAPAN TRADE

To approach realism, a model of the timber trade needs to include lumber as well as logs. Japan was the largest buyer of American logs, and it is safe to assume (despite the American desire for B.C. logs) that it would have been a major purchaser of B.C. logs as well. To a first approximation, it is possible that the quantity of logs remaining in British Columbia for meeting Canadian and American demand will be the same, or nearly the same, after the log-import ban is lifted. With the same amount of logs available for the domestic market (or a larger amount if the logs are now more highly valued), the quantity of lumber shipped by British Columbia to its customers will remain the same. Since it is the quantity of lumber that determines price, North American competitors to British Columbia will neither see their market share nor their realized price change. Under these circumstances, there would be no damage whatsoever from a log-export ban.

Let L be lumber and G be logs, both scaled in board-feet mill tally (i.e., the logs are scaled based upon their lumber yield). There are two countries: Japan J and the domestic country C. For simplicity, J produces no logs but may mill logs into lumber.

Any logs imported into Japan are converted to lumber for domestic use, so the price of lumber in Japan is found from the demand curve, which is a function of the imported quantities of the two commodities $P_L^J = D^J \left(G^J + L^J \right)$. The price in Canada for lumber depends on how many of the total number of logs G are retained in Canada for milling purposes and how much of the lumber is retained for sale $P_L^C = D^C \left(G - G^J - L^J \right)$. The marginal cost of milling logs into lumber in country k is $C^K \left(G^k \right)$, and the marginal costs of transporting lumber is T. One could include a tariff in T. All marginal cost curves are assumed to be increasing.

Let us now assume that, with or without a log-export ban, lumber will always be traded from Canada to Japan. This assumption matches the historical record. Trade of lumber requires that the lumber price in Japan equal the lumber price in Canada plus export costs

$$D^J \left(G^J + L^J \right) = D^C \left(L^C \right) + T. \tag{1}$$

Now the total quantity of logs G equals those exported, those milled and kept, and those milled and exported, so $L^J = G - L^C - G^J$

$$D^J \left(G - L^C \right) = D^C \left(L^C \right) + T. \tag{2}$$

In the special case in which G is constant (zero elasticity of logs supplied), the price of lumber in both countries is invariant to the number of logs exported.[5] What does change with log exports is the location of the milling operations. With an additional export of logs, the marginal cost of milling in Japan increases and the marginal cost of milling in Canada decreases. The rents to stumpage in Canada are the lumber price (unchanged) less the marginal cost of milling, so exports raise the rents to the owners of stumpage rights. This suggests that an increase in log exports leads to more harvest of timber, which means more logs and lower lumber prices (see below).

The equation for supply is that the supply price equals the lumber price less the marginal cost of milling

$$S \left(L^C + L^J + G^J \right) - \left[D^C \left(L^C \right) - C \left(L^C + L^J \right) \right] = 0. \tag{3}$$

Totally differentiating Equation (1) and Equation (3), we get

$$D^{J'} \cdot dL^J - D^{C'} \cdot dL^C = -D^{J'} \cdot dG^J \tag{4}$$

$$\left(S' + C' \right) dL^J + \left(S' - D^{C'} + C' \right) dL^C = -S' dG^J. \tag{5}$$

Thus

$$\frac{dL^J}{dG^J} = \frac{-\left[D^{J'} \left(S' - D^{c'} + C' \right) + S' D^{c'} \right]}{D^{J'} \left(S' - D^{c'} + C' \right) + D^{c'} \left(S' + C' \right)}, \tag{6}$$

and

$$\frac{dL^c}{dG^J} = \frac{D^{J'}C'}{D^{J'}\left(S'-D^{c'}+C'\right)+D^{C'}\left(S'+C'\right)}.$$ (7)

The denominator in Equation (6) and Equation (7) is negative. The numerator of Equation (6) is positive and less than the denominator, so $0 \geq dL^J/dG^J \geq -1$. A unit increase in log exports decreases lumber exports to Japan by less than one unit, so the total volume of lumber for sale in Japan increases and the price of lumber everywhere falls. Equation (7) shows that the quantity of lumber remaining in Canada increases by less than one unit for each additional log unit exported, which is consistent with the lower price of lumber in both countries. Adding together Equation (6) and Equation (7) gives the change in total milling done in Canada, and it is

$$\frac{dL^C+dL^J}{dG^J} = \frac{-\left[D^{J'}\left(S'-D^C\right)+S'D^{C'}\right]}{D^{J'}\left(S'-D^{C'}+C'\right)+D^{C'}\left(S'+C'\right)},$$ (8)

which is again negative and less than one in absolute value. Thus, the quantity of timber milled in Canada decreases but the total quantity of stumpage produced increases, since it is log exports plus the two types of milling. Log exports increase by one, and milling for the two markets decreases by less than one. Since the quantity of stumpage goes up, the price of lumber less the marginal costs of milling must also have risen and the rents to stumpage rise.

The importance of this result to the U.S.-Canada trade is that a repeal of the log-export ban likely results in an increased log trade between Canada and Japan. The increase in log trade results in more lumber for sale in Japan, leading to lower prices. Since lumber is traded, there are lower lumber prices in North America as well. The lower lumber prices hurt American producers.

The other peculiarity of the B.C. rule is that alleged sales of stumpage at less than free-market value are easier to analyze. It reduces the government incentive to supply stumpage, leading to fewer raw materials in North America and to higher prices for lumber. How this *harms* American producers is very difficult to see though the effect of the claim of harm—worked through the political magic of the USITC—wondrously enhances American prices in a way that only a monopolist could dream of.

Insofar as this is the correct story—that the log-export ban prevents Japan, which has many anticompetitive mechanisms in place to thwart trade in lumber, from buying more logs—the log-export ban helps U.S. producers because it restricts the supply of B.C. stumpage and raises the overall price of lumber. Of course, American mills that would otherwise process B.C. logs do lose from such a ban and, given the transport costs for logs, it is unclear how many such mills there are.

TRANSPORT COSTS

Given the huge decrease in stumpage production in the USPNW in the 1990s, sawmills in the area wanted to import logs, making the log-export ban particularly irritating. With considerable excess capacity, the Washington mills would likely have bid sufficiently high for B.C. mills to transport at least some of those logs to the Washington waterside mills. While the short-run answer to log flow between British Columbia and Washington certainly has a lot to do with the marginal cost of milling, the long-run location of the industry is likely determined by transportation economics.

Most lumber is milled very near where it is felled, and it is usually assumed that economic forces make this universally so. In that case, Vancouver, B.C., with its plethora of very efficient sawmills would, as a natural consequence of economic forces, mill all the lumber from the B.C. coast. In fact, British Columbia has long maintained log-export restrictions that drive a significant wedge between Pacific Rim log-market prices and the Vancouver, B.C. log-market prices to keep logs in British Columbia. If economics would naturally do the job, why do we need the regulations?

Logs are bulky, relatively low in value, irregular in shape, and difficult to handle safely. Lumber is much higher in value, square, and easily dealt with in pallets but in need of protection from the elements and still not cheap to handle. One determinant of the minimum-cost way of handling lumber is the number of times the product or its raw material needs to be handled. The typical course for timber harvested in British Columbia is that the round wood is placed on a barge for delivery to Vancouver. It is then off-loaded, milled, loaded onto a ship, off-loaded onto a dock, reloaded onto a truck, and delivered somewhere in Japan. Without a ban on log exports, the round wood would be off-loaded to a dockside mill in Japan, milled, and loaded onto a truck. Direct delivery of logs involves less handling than does the delivery of lumber, and the cost per mile (not per handling) of water transport is quite cheap.

For a time, a California Redwood producer delivered logs into Ensenada, Mexico, milled them there, and re-imported the lumber into Southern California. This scheme used cheap water transport, unencumbered by the *Jones Act* (1920), and also took advantage of the dry Mexican climate to help cure the lumber.

It is by no means obvious that the least-cost way of delivering lumber to Japan is to make the lumber in British Columbia and ship it.[6] In the case of the United States, the economics would depend upon such things as the relative cost of using the Canadian and American railways for Midwest delivery and the ability to use third-party-flagged shipping for delivery on the West Coast.

In the case of internal B.C. production, the economics of shipment are also unclear. Where there are data on the cost of log shipment by truck, the data reveal a very high per-mile cost. However, the cost is more per hour than it is per mile. The first miles out of the woods are very slow and costly while the miles driven on the blacktop are much less costly. Mills are very specific to the size and type of lumber they cut efficiently. These two facts together open the possibility of sorting logs by intended mill and then driving the logs to the mill that will have the highest return. Sierra Pacific Industries in California does this rather than just trying to minimize hauling distance. In order to figure out how many logs from the interior of British Columbia would naturally come to the United States, one would need to account for the quality of the roads connecting the harvest sites and mills, and the optimization of the mills for size and species. Certainly, some logs would be more profitably cut in U.S. mills near the border but few would make it any great distance into the United States. Unemployment in logging in Southern Washington would stay the same with or without this type of trade, yet the trade could be quite substantial and could be two-way trade.

One other concern with log trading is that forest insects shelter under the bark of trees, so the log trade will spread the insects across the Northern Hemisphere. Japan has accepted this risk for a long time, and Washington is at no risk from B.C. insects since B.C. insect species are already present in Washington. Local milling no longer serves a phytosanitary purpose for the B.C. trading partners.

The conclusion from this is that the transport economics for stumpage and timber are not obvious and certainly are not amenable to a theoretical or simple empirical answer. This is the sort of messy coordination problem best solved by markets and worst solved by governments and their economists.

TIMBER SUPPLY IN AN ADMINISTRATIVE WORLD

Timber supply from government-owned land in both British Columbia and the United States is governed by administrative procedure. Stated objectives include community stability, production of forest products, employment, and even government revenue. The political economy of government provision gives both environmental groups and producers a hand at trying to determine the outcome of the process.

In British Columbia, the Chief Forester is responsible for setting an allowable cut. There is a process to do this that spans years. In the United States, Congress sets an allowable sales quantity that the USDA/FS is then obliged to fulfill. However, it must do so within the confines of forest plans that are only revised each decade. In neither case is the system fleet of foot and quickly responsive to changes in the market for timber.

In the United States, the response to market conditions on federal sales occurs because the sales are for multiple years and the contractor chooses the year to harvest the product. With the shortening of the sale period in the 1980s to less than five years, this effect should be less pronounced. In British Columbia, the volume-tenure system does not allow flexibility across years for cutting.

The ultimate level of cutting, quite apart from the allocation of cut to different years in the business cycle, is determined by politics and by environmental and physical concerns. The influence of economics is most strongly felt in the determination of which stands are economic to harvest, or, in planning parlance, in the land base for harvesting. The higher the prices the more that can be spent to extract timber and the more stands that can be potentially cut. While the stands that are marginal will not be planned for cutting in the near future, the legislated need for non-declining flow in the United States and the desire for community stability in British Columbia lead to an immediate price effect. If more can be cut later, then non-declining flow leads to plans that allow more to be cut now.[7] It is through this type of planning exercise that stumpage price has an effect on the long-run quantity of stumpage supplied. Failure to charge the full stumpage price has the effect of depressing the supply from the public agency through the planning mechanism, since it makes uneconomic, stands that should be harvestable.

The United States, in a spectacular show of disregard for the market, operates about one-half of its national forests in a below-cost mode. The stumpage fees collected do not cover the cost of sales administration. Thus the United States, through its below-cost sales, increases its supply of stumpage beyond what is economic while British Columbia, through its failure to collect market rates for stumpage, depresses its supply of stumpage.

EMPIRICAL EVIDENCE

If British Columbia, Washington, or Oregon were really run in an administrative manner that considers mostly long-run forest-condition consequences, then the price elasticity of demand should be with a long lag, long enough to account for the time it takes to re-plan a forest, and the supply elasticity with respect to aggregate demand should be near zero. A planned forest is not responsive to market forces. One underlying assumption of the CFLI view of the B.C. system is that it is less-responsive than is the U.S. system to changes in economic conditions that affect demand.

Margolick and Uhler (1992) present evidence that the B.C. system is price responsive. Indeed, it is because of this price responsiveness that there is the deadweight loss to the measures, such as the log-export ban and below-market timber sales. Without the price responsiveness of stumpage, the only effect B.C. policy has is to deny the Crown its revenue. Models of the U.S. forest sector, such as the timber assessment market models (TAMM), incorporate price responsiveness, and it seems to be well agreed that the totality of the U.S. system does respond to price.

Indeed, the estimation of price responsiveness of the forest sector is not as easy as the Margolick and Uhler (1992) equations or TAMM equations make it seem. Price spikes occur because of the differences in anticipated demand relative to actual demand, and because getting timber to market is not a short process (Berck 1999).

Response to changes in aggregate demand, measured either as gross domestic product (GDP) or as housing starts, can be found from a simple reduced-form equation. The reduced form of a proper forestry model includes current stock (here it is proxied by time) and aggregate demand as explanatory variables. In order to account for possible lags in adjustment to demand conditions, a lagged-dependent variable has been included in the regression. The B.C. regression uses the GDP of both the United States and Japan, as these countries are the major buyers of B.C. lumber products. Data were available from 1960 to 2002 and are further described in Table 9.1.

Table 9.1: Variables and Sources

Name	Definition
LAGBCV	Natural log of BC roundwood production, lagged one year in million meters cubed
LNJAG	Natural log of GDP of Japan
LNUSG	Natural log of GDP of United States
TIME	Time trend
CLINTON	Dummy variable 1 after 1988
LAGORV	Natural log of Oregon timber harvest, lagged (board feet)
LNHS	Natural log of U.S. housing starts
LAHS	Lag of natural log of U.S. housing starts
LAGWA	Lagged natural log of Washington timber harvest (board feet)

Source: Author's Compilation.

Table 9.2 has the regression results. The R^2 of 0.92 shows that this simple regression captures nearly all the variance in the output of the stumpage sector (round wood includes both logs and bolts). The coefficients on aggregate demand, time, and the dummy for the post-Clinton Forest Plan period are all significant. The lagged-dependent variable is not different significantly from zero. There was no appreciable residual autocorrelation. The variables are in log terms, so assuming a steady state, the long-run elasticities are given by the coefficient divided by 1 minus the coefficient on the lagged term. The B.C. regression shows that a 1 percent increase in Japanese GDP leads to about a 0.5 percent increase in output; a 1 percent increase in the GDP of the United States leads to more than a 1 percent increase in output. The response of B.C. forestry to aggregate demand is quite large and is not consistent with a view that the output in British Columbia is dependent on policy and independent of economic conditions. Indeed, there is a finding in Burton and Berck (1996) for the United States: economics, and only economics, drives the U.S. timber harvest. The same environmental forces that caused dramatically decreased cuts in the United States in the 1990s also affected British Columbia, but much less severely as shown by the positive but small coefficient on the Clinton Forest Plan dummy.

Table 9.2: Regression of B.C. Roundwood Output

Variable Name[a]	Estimated Coefficient	Standard Error	*t*-ratio 35 df[b]
LAGBCV	0.19544	0.1493	1.309
LNJAG	0.40785	0.1436	2.841
LNUSG	0.98054	0.5299	1.851
TIME	−3.04E-02	1.64E-02	−1.855
CLINTON	−0.13932	5.74E-02	−2.426
CONSTANT	28.851	17.92	1.61

[a] Please refer to Table 9.1.
[b] $R^2 = .92$.

Source: Author's Computation.

Table 9.3: Regression of Oregon Timber Harvest

Variable Name[a]	Estimated Coefficient	Standard Error	*t*-ratio 17 df[b]
LAGORV	0.74308	0.195	3.81
LNHS	0.41	7.71E-02	5.319
LAHS	−0.24629	0.1147	−2.148
TIME	−1.79E-03	3.68E-03	−0.4877
CONSTANT	4.6473	8.253	0.5631

[a] Please refer to Table 9.1.
[b] $R^2 = .77$.
Source: Author's Computation.

Neither Washington nor Oregon has anything close to the public ownership of forests of British Columbia. Oregon has a much higher percent of USDA/FS forests than has Washington. Starting in the very late 1980s, the determinants of harvest in both states shifted from the demand to the supply side. Oregon, with its large (3.7 bbf private and 4.3 bbf USDA/FS + BLM) public harvests experienced a dramatic decline of over 90 percent in BLM and USDA/FS harvests from 1989 to 2000. As a result, regressions for Oregon are run only for the period before the Clinton Forest Plan. The data readily available begin in 1965 and are in million board feet for output. Housing starts is the aggregate demand variable that provides the best explanation for the Oregon data, because regressions using either the American or Japanese GDP have low explanatory power. Tables 9.3, 9.4, and 9.5 present these results for the 1965 to 1988 period.

The regressions for Washington were both run in the form used for the Oregon and B.C. regressions. The post 1988 period is too short for regression analysis but is dominated by a decreasing time trend, a clear result of the withdrawal of public timber.

Table 9.4: Washington Timber Harvest

Variable Name[a]	Estimated Coefficient	Standard Error	*t*-ratio 26 df[b]
LAGWA	0.43663	0.1601	2.727
LNJAG	1.3739	0.6723	2.044
LAJAG	−0.92322	0.612	−1.509
LNUSG	2.0144	1.089	1.85
LAUSG	−1.287	0.7629	−1.687
LAHS	−8.57E-03	0.1022	−0.8387E-
TIME	−4.12E-02	4.28E-02	−0.9639
CLINTON	−0.1241	5.09E-02	−2.437
CONSTANT	52.336	47.69	1.097

[a] Please refer to Table 9.1.
[b] $R^2 = .90$.
Source: Author's Computation.

Table 9.5: Regression of Washington Timber Harvest

Variable Name[a]	Estimated Coefficient	Standard Error	*t*-ratio 26 df[b]
LAGWA	0.41294	0.2435	1.696
LNHS	0.29333	8.67E-02	3.384
LAHS	−6.40E-03	0.126	−5.08E-02
TIME	−3.45E-03	3.10E-03	−1.114
CONSTANT	9.8575	7.207	1.368

[a] Please refer to Table 9.1.
[b] $R^2 = .66$.
Source: Author's Computation.

The regression for Oregon has a large and significant lag term, suggesting a slow adjustment process. Housing starts and lagged housing starts are both significant and opposite in sign. The long-run effect is the sum of the housing-start coefficients divided by one less the lag term and is about two-thirds. This is less than the B.C. responsiveness. The coefficient on time is small and not significant. This would be true if the public sector's actual output were politically driven and nearly stock independent, which seems plausible over this period.

For the Washington regression using housing starts, the lagged term is less prominent and lagged housing starts are insignificant. In the long run, the response to housing starts in Washington is not much different than those in Oregon. The response just comes sooner. In this sense it is more like the B.C. results. Using the full period, the long-run elasticity with respect to the Japanese GDP is 0.8; with respect to the American GDP, it is 1.3. This is very similar to the B.C. results.

CONCLUSION

The conclusion one should draw from this exercise are that the B.C. system responds more like the private sector (e.g., Washington) than the public sector (e.g., Oregon). The anomalous response is a result of the U.S. public sector and not of British Columbia.

NOTES

[1] Below-cost forest sales were first discovered by Barlow et al. (1980).
[2] Allegations of collusion on a large scale have not been proven in the Western United States. However, a more concentrated industry, such as the B.C. industry, might be more amenable to collusion.
[3] Available at: http://www.openmarkets.org/openmarkets/issues/background.shtml.
[4] There are cases in which the ban encourages domestic consumption at below world market price. That is clearly not the case in lumber and logs.

[5]If per-unit transport costs do change with the volume of lumber shipped and with the quantity of stumpage held constant, then the quantity of lumber retained in Canada changes with a change in exports according to the following formula

$$dL^C/dG^J = T'/(D^{J'} + D^C - T').$$

Again, the key element in this formulation is that, if the marginal transport costs for lumber are constant, then the quantity of lumber retained in Canada (and sold to the United States) is independent of the number of logs exported.

[6]Kalt (1999) took the position that export of logs from British Columbia made no economic sense and was driven only by trade barriers erected by the Japanese.

[7]The allowable cut effect can be more pernicious (Schweitzer, Sassaman, and Schallau 1972).

REFERENCES

Barlow, T., G. Helfand, T. Orr, and T.B. Stoel. (1980). *Giving Away the National Forests: An Analysis of U.S. Forest Service Timber Sales Below Cost.* Washington, DC: Natural Resources Defense Council, Inc.

Berck, P. (1999). "Estimation in a Long-run Short-run Model," in *Modern Time Series Analysis in Forest Products Markets* edited by J. Abildtrup, F. Helles, P. Holten-Andersen, J. F. Larsen, and B. J. Thorsen (117–26). Dordrect: Kluwer Academic Publishers.

Berck, P. and T. Bible. (1982). "Futures Markets and the Reservation Price of Stumpage." Paper presented at the meeting of the Western Forest Economists, Wemme, Oregon (May).

Burton, D. and P. Berck. (1996). "Statistical Causation and National Forest Policy." *Forest Science* 42(1): 86–92.

Clinton Forest Plan. (1993). *The Forest Plan for a Sustainable Economy and a Sustainable Environment.* Washington, DC: The White House Press Office.

Endangered Species Act. (1973). Available at: http://endangered.fws.gov/esasum.html.

Forest and Rangeland Renewable Resource Planning Act. (1974). Available at: http://www.fs.fed.us/emc/nfma/includes/range74.pdf.

Forest Resource Conservation and Shortage Relief Act. (1990). Available at: http://ipl.unm.edu/cwl/fedbook/frcsra.html.

Gorte, R.W. (1994). *Below Cost Sales: Overview.* Washington, DC: Congressional Research Service (December 20: 19).

Jaffe, A., S. Peterson, P. Portney, and R. Stavins. (1995). "Environmental Regulation and the Competitiveness of U.S. Manufacturing: What Does the Evidence Tell Us?" *Journal of Economic Literature* 33(1): 132–63.

Jones Act. (1920). Available at: http://www.shipguide.com/jones-act/toc.html.

Kalt, J. (1999). "Economic Analysis of Canadian Log Export Policy." Exhibit B to Government of Canada et al., *Memorandum Concerning the Non-Counteravailability of Canadian Log Export Regulations, in the Matter of Certain Softwood Lumber Products from Canada* (INV. C-122-816), International Trade Administration, U.S. Department of Commerce, Washington, DC.

LaFrance, J.T. and M.J. Watts. (1994). "Public Grazing in the West and Rangeland Reform 94." *American Journal of Agricultural Economics* 77(3): 447–61.

Leveen, E.P. and G.E. Goldman. (1978). "Reclamation Policy and the Water Subsidy: An Analysis of Emerging Policy Choices." *American Journal of Agricultural Economics* 60(5): 929–34.

Margolick, M. and R.S. Uhler. (1992). "The Economic Impact on British Columbia of Removing Log Export Restrictions," in *Emerging Issues in Forest Policy* (273–96), edited by P.N. Nemetz. Vancouver: UBC Press.

Royal Commission on Forest Resources. (1976). *Timber Rights and Forest Policy in British Columbia*. Report of the Royal Commission on Forest Resources, P.H. Pearse, Commissioner. Victoria: Royal Commission on Forest Resources.

Schweitzer, D.L., R.W. Sassaman, and C.H. Schallau. (1972). "Allowable Cut Effect: Some Physical and Economic Implications." *Journal of Forestry* 70(7): 415–18.

Timber and Stone Act. (1878). Available at:
www.college.hmco.com/history/readerscomp/rcah/html/ah_071800_publiclandpo.htm

USDA/FS (U.S. Department of Agriculture/Forestry Service). (2003). Available at:
http://www.fs.fed.us/.

USDOC (U.S. Department of Commerce). (2003). "Proposed Analytical Framework for Changed Circumstances Reviews of the Outstanding Countervailing Duty Order on Imports of Softwood Lumber from Canada." (January 7). Available at:
http://www.usembassycanada.gov/content/can_usa/softwood_lumber_framework.pdf.

Chapter 10

Political Economy of the Canada-U.S. Softwood Lumber Trade Dispute

Janaki R.R. Alavalapati and Shiv Mehrotra
University of Florida

INTRODUCTION

This chapter reviews the economics and politics behind the Canada-U.S. Softwood Lumber Trade Dispute. Drawing on previous studies, we trace the history of the trade dispute, discuss the reasons fuelling the dispute, provide a rationale for the unusual alliances among stakeholders of the dispute, and present the economic impacts of the dispute on producers and consumers. Finally, we offer some conclusions about the future of the dispute.

Although the United States is the largest producer of forest products in the world, it is a net importer. The domestic production of softwood lumber accounts for only about 60 percent of U.S. consumption and the rest is met with imports. On the other hand, Canada is the largest exporter of forest products in the world. Forest-product exports make a substantial contribution to the Canadian economy. In 2001, for example, forest-product exports accounted for almost 10 percent of national merchandise exports and generated a trade surplus of CDN \$36.4 billion (about 57 percent of Canada's total trade surplus) (Dufour 2002). Approximately 80 percent of these forest-product exports find their home in the United States. Softwood lumber exports alone amount to over U.S. \$7 billion. Lumber imports from Canada account for more than 90 percent of total U.S. lumber imports. Since the United States is the largest buyer of Canadian forest products and Canada is the largest seller of forest products to the U.S. market, one can expect that both countries exercise market power in the softwood lumber trade. The following discussion of the history of the Canada-U.S. softwood lumber dispute, however, suggests that the United States has been more successful when exercising market power than has Canada.

HISTORY OF THE DISPUTE

The Canada-U.S. softwood lumber dispute dates back over two hundred years, when the first tariff on Canadian lumber imports was adopted through legislation passed by the first U.S. Congress in 1789 (Reed 2001). Since then the issue of duties and tariffs on Canadian lumber imports has become a recurrent feature with the U.S. government. Following World War II, the sudden surge in domestic demand for construction lumber in the United States and the creation of the General Agreement on Trade and Tariffs (GATT) resulted in the reduction and eventual elimination of U.S. tariffs on Canadian lumber imports. Not surprisingly, between the late 1940s and 1960 the share of Canadian lumber imports in the U.S. market rose from 5 percent to 13 percent. This rise in Canadian lumber imports concerned U.S. lumber producers and prompted them to seek political intervention to restrict Canadian lumber imports. However, the U.S. Tariff Commission in 1962 concluded that the fundamental reason for the increase in Canadian lumber imports was a shortage of domestic supply and associated increase in the domestic price, especially in the northern U.S. markets.

Countervail I

In the early 1980s, several factors influenced U.S. lumber producers to intensify their efforts to limit Canadian lumber imports. The onset of a recession in the U.S. economy and the creation of the U.S. International Trade Commission (USITC) that replaced the U.S. Tariff Commission and the International Trade Administration (ITA) within the U.S. Department of Commerce (USDOC) (created to deal with international trade issues), prompted U.S. lumber producers to pursue actions through both political and governmental institutions. U.S. lumber producers, primarily from the U.S. Pacific Northwest (USPNW) region, led by the Coalition for Fair Canadian Lumber Imports, presently know as Coalition for Fair Lumber Imports (CFLI), claimed injury from the unfair subsidization of Canadian lumber imports. In particular, they alleged that Canadian producers receive an unfair advantage in the form of lower stumpage prices that are fixed administratively and not fixed through a competitive bidding process. Lobbyists in the U.S. Congress asked the USDOC to investigate and see if the Canadian timber licensing system constituted a subsidy that would warrant imposing a countervail (CV) duty on Canadian lumber imports. On the other hand, with support from the International Wood Workers of America (lumber workers in Canada and the United States), the National Lumber and Material Dealers Association (softwood lumber wholesalers), and the Manufactured Housing Institute (home builders) as well as the neutral position of the National Lumber Manufacturers Association (softwood lumber producers), Canadian lumber producers lobbied their government to oppose the CV duty petition. In 1983, the USDOC concluded that there was no evidence that Canadian producers were being subsidized.

Countervail II

In response to the conclusion by the USDOC that there was no evidence of subsidies to Canadian producers, U.S. lumber producers changed their focus, seeking congressional support for tariff regulations on Canadian lumber imports. By mid-1985, five different bills dealing with Canadian lumber imports were under deliberation. In February of 1986, thirty-nine U.S. senators criticized the administration for failing to adequately address the issue of alleged subsidies associated with Canadian lumber imports. In April of 1986, the Reagan administration changed its neutral position on the Canada-U.S. lumber trade to one advocating the imposition of tariffs. This favourable political atmosphere stimulated the CFLI to file another CV petition in May of 1986, asking the U.S. Government to impose a 27 percent duty on lumber imported from Canada. In response to this petition, the ITA made a preliminary ruling that the Canadian stumpage system constitutes a subsidy and suggested a 15 percent duty on Canadian lumber imports. Before the issuance of a final ruling, however, negotiations between the two governments led to a Memorandum of Understanding (MOU) whereby the Canadian government imposed a 15 percent tax on lumber exports to the United States beginning in 1987. Both governments thought the MOU was set up in their favour. The Canadian government felt that an export tax would increase the price of lumber in the U.S. market and thus would increase profits to Canadian lumber exporters while simultaneously raising tax revenues. On the other hand, the United States believed the MOU would restrict Canadian lumber imports and thus would create a favourable atmosphere to U.S. producers. Furthermore, the Canadian Prime Minister, Brian Mulroney, did not want to derail or delay the execution of the North American Free Trade Agreement (NAFTA) between the United States and Canada by launching another legal/institutional resolution process. Also, Canadian lumber producers were confident that the MOU would become obsolete once NAFTA was in place.

Countervail III

Even after NAFTA was in place beginning January of 1989, the MOU remained binding. Canadian lumber producers started to intensify efforts to drop the MOU, and in late 1991 the Canadian government dropped it. In response, the USDOC imposed a 6.2 percent provisional duty and initiated another CV case alleging subsidies stemming from stumpage fees and log-export restraints. In May 1992, the USITC and USDOC ruled in support of the subsidy allegations, but Canada challenged the ruling under GATT and NAFTA. After a series of deliberations under NAFTA's binational dispute-settlement procedure, the CV duty was dropped and the U.S. $800 million duty collected was refunded to Canada. When further threats of duties arose in 1995, Canada, who was concerned by escalating transaction costs of contesting U.S. actions, negotiated the Canada-U.S. Softwood Lumber Agreement (SLA). The SLA was in place from 1996 to 2001 and constrained annual lumber exports by Canada to the United States from four Canadian provinces, British Columbia, Alberta, Ontario, and Quebec (in 1995, these four provinces accounted for about 85 percent of all softwood lumber exports to the United States). Under the SLA, the first 14.7 billion board feet of softwood lumber from the above four provinces entered the United States duty free. Any exports above this quantity were taxed at a rate of U.S. $50 per thousand board feet for the first 650 million board feet and U.S. $100 per thousand board feet beyond that amount with an adjustment for inflation. The SLA expired on March 31, 2001, and lumber producers in the United States started to rekindle the dispute. The U.S. President blamed Canadian timber pricing for unemployment in the U.S. forest sector and even for global warming. In April of 2002, the USDOC determined a CV duty of 18.79 percent and an AD duty rate of 8.43 percent along with several company-specific rates. The Canadians have since challenged these duties in the WTO, and political negotiations are in progress for another settlement.

FACTORS INFLUENCING THE TRADE DISPUTE

Differences in Forestland Ownership and Tenure Systems

Public ownership is dominant in Canadian forestry (90 percent), while private ownership (73 percent) dominates U.S. forestry. Furthermore, the number of nonindustrial private forestland owners in Canada is 425,000, while the corresponding number in the United States is 10 million. Canadian forestry is largely characterized by tenure arrangements, under which companies assume management responsibilities in exchange for access to timber on public lands (Nelson and Vertinsky 2003). These agreements can be long-, medium-, or short-term and can be area based or volume based. Long- and medium-term agreements are usually renewable, so long as companies are in compliance with stipulated regulations and build and operate a major timber processing facility. Short-term agreements, which are mostly volume-based permits, are non-renewable and do not require the setting up of timber-processing facilities (Canadian Institute of Forestry 2002). The United States alleges that long- and medium-term timber concessions will serve as subsidies to Canadian timber producers, since they do not have to make upfront payments except to set up timber-processing facilities. Canada contends that in the absence of long-term or secure concessions, it is difficult to attract investment into forestry operations.

Differences in the Timber-Pricing System

In the United States, timber on public lands is sold by auction in the open market and timber on private lands is sold in a typical market setting. In Canada, timber on public lands is sold or transferred to a private company at a stumpage price set by the provincial government (Canadian Institute of Forestry 2002). These stumpage prices, which are calculated as residual values by subtracting production costs from final-product prices, are supposed to reflect market conditions and forest-management responsibilities that companies face. Under perfect market conditions, stumpage prices determined under both residual and auction methods yield the same value (Nelson and Vertinsky 2003). However, the United States contends that prices set administratively are likely to be lower than those determined at open auction.

Trade-Related Factors

The United States asserts that Canadian restrictions on log exports, similar to those that exist for timber on public lands in the United States, would indirectly subsidize Canadian timber producers in the form of lower timber prices within Canada (Nelson and Vertinsky 2003). A recent change in U.S. trade law, the Byrd Amendment, envisages that if injury is confirmed after the investigation of a trade dispute, and a duty is imposed, the money collected as duty will be distributed to the companies that filed the petition (Canadian Institute of Forestry 2002). This has provided an added incentive for U.S. lumber producers to register complaints against Canadian softwood-lumber imports. On the exchange-rate front, the U.S. dollar has remained strong against the Canadian dollar since the late 1990s (*Wood Markets* 2003) and this has permitted Canadian lumber producers to increase export volumes.

Environmental Factors

Some argue that environmental standards in Canada are lower than those in the United States, thus Canadian forest-management practices are less environmentally friendly. Since the 1990s, concerns over the loss of old-growth forests and the loss of biodiversity have resulted in a substantial decrease in timber harvests in the U.S. national forests and the USPNW in particular. Conversely, Canadian forestry has not yet experienced this type of timber-harvest restriction to a significant degree. Although there is no scientific evidence suggesting that Canadian environmental standards are lower, lumber producers in the United States have a different perception. This environmental argument has proven very effective for U.S. timber producers when mustering the support of numerous environmental organizations in both the United States and Canada.

ECONOMICS OF THE DISPUTE

How trade restrictions will impact output, exports, and prices is illustrated in Figure 10.1. The analysis also sheds light on the ongoing bilateral trade dispute relating to softwood lumber (Alavalapati, Das, and Wilkerson 2003). In the absence of trade, Q_c is the quantity produced/consumed at a market price P_c in Canada while Q_u is the quantity produced/consumed at a market price P_u in the United States. In the presence of free trade, the excess supply ES from Canada and excess demand ED from the United States result in a bilateral price P_w. As

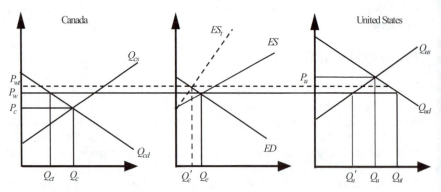

Figure 10.1: A Conceptual Framework of Canada-U.S. Lumber Trade

a result, Canadian exports Q_e quantity to the United States and consumes only Q_{ct}. On the other hand, U.S. consumption increases from Q_u to Q_{ut} and domestic production drops from Q_u to Q_u' because of imports from Canada.

In the presence of a tariff on Canadian imports, the excess supply curve shifts upwardly, thereby resulting in a new bilateral price P_{wt}. As can be seen in Figure 10.1, this new price decreases Canadian exports from Q_e to Q_e' and expands production in the United States. This is the reason why U.S. producers lobby intensively for a tariff on Canadian softwood lumber.

Several studies have been conducted to assess the economic impacts of various agreements reached over the dispute. Wear and Lee (1993) find that the MOU reached between the United States and Canada in 1986 resulted in a U.S. $2.6 billion gain to U.S. producers and a U.S. $3.8 billion loss to U.S. consumers. Zhang (2001) notes that between 1996 and 2001 the SLA had increased U.S. lumber prices by U.S. $59 per million board feet, raised profits to American producers by U.S. $7.7 billion, and decreased consumer surplus by U.S. $12.6 billion. In a more recent study, van Kooten (2002) finds that the SLA resulted in a CDN $109 million per year benefit to Canadian consumers and a U.S. $22 million and CDN $544 million benefit annually to producers in the United States and Canada, respectively. Adams (2003) finds that the gross revenues of U.S. lumber producers and private timber sellers escalate at the expense of increased expenditures by U.S. lumber consumers in response to a tariff on Canadian lumber imports. All these gains have come at the expense of American consumers.

The impact of the lumber dispute may not be restricted to the forest sectors of Canada and the United States. They may spill over to other sectors of the national economies and other timber-trading nations in the world. Alavalapati, Adamowicz, and White (1999) simulate the impact of a 1 percent increase in the tax on Canada, the United States, and other regions of the world using a general equilibrium analysis. They find that forest-product production drops in Canada while it increases in the corresponding sectors of the United States and other regions of the world. Also, they show that there was an increase in the output of other sectors in Canada, and a decrease in the corresponding sectors of other regions. For example, the output of agricultural and other resource sectors in Canada decreased while the output of corresponding sectors in the United States increased in response to the tax. Although forest firms in the United States benefit from trade restrictions, Alavalapati, Adamowicz, and White (1999) find a decrease in overall U.S. welfare and an increase in overall Canadian welfare in response to a 1 percent tax on Canadian lumber and wood-product exports. They also find that the production of wood products increases in South America, Europe, and Southeast Asian countries as a result of this tax. Taking all of these countries into account in response to a 1 percent increase in tax, Global welfare is shown to drop by U.S. $5.78 million.

RENT SEEKING AND UNUSUAL ALLIANCES

While U.S. lumber producers were the principal complainants in the United States vs. Canada lumber imports dispute, several new parties have been drawn into the dispute. Involvement of these parties can be attributed largely to rent-seeking behaviour. Rent-seeking behaviour can be defined as the use of productive resources to convince the government to introduce distortions into the economy in such a way as to advance the economic interests of the rent seeker (Peterson 2001). From a rent-seeking perspective, this dispute provides a convenient forum for various special-interest groups to pursue the economic interests of their members. Members of the CFLI, for example, can realize net gains by investing resources to lobby the government to impose tariffs or some other restrictions on Canadian lumber imports as opposed to using resources to improve their competitiveness through increasing productivity. Although tariffs will reduce the welfare to the majority of constituents, it is difficult for policy-makers to resist the pressure for trade restrictions from interest groups that are capable of mobilizing resources and votes for those who support their agenda (Peterson 2001).

As the dispute is not a priority in peoples' daily lives, special-interest groups have an added incentive to pursue rent-seeking behaviour and policy-makers are more likely to endorse that behaviour. The Canadian government is trying its best to draw support from the U.S. public for their side of the story by working with the American Consumers for Affordable Homes, lumber dealers, and retailers. For many people, the problem is that benefits from imposing tariffs or other restrictions on Canadian lumber prices are public goods. Individuals know that once a public good is in place, individuals cannot be excluded from enjoying that good even if they did not contribute to its production. Also, in a large society, they know that it is hard for others to notice their behaviour. Therefore, individuals tend to enjoy a free ride. On the other hand, special-interest groups, such as the CFLI and other timber producers, realize that there are rewards to their participation. Their peers are watching their actions and inactions, so they cannot afford not to participate in the lobbying process.

Alavalapati, Adamowicz, and White (1999) point out that rent-seeking behaviour increases the welfare of supporting groups at the expense of the general public and thus violates Pareto optimality. This may contribute to increased income inequality, if the CFLI and other supporting groups with resources to conduct lobbying efforts are more wealthy than the U.S. consumers who end up paying higher prices for lumber. It is important to note that some interest groups seek to influence policy outcomes for noneconomic reasons. For example, many environmental and conservation organizations, such as the Natural Resource Defence Council, B.C. Sierra Legal Defence Fund, and the World Resource Institute, are endorsing the arguments of the CFLI. These groups do not have economic interests but want to decrease timber harvests in Canadian old-growth forests.

CONCLUSIONS

Several solutions have been suggested to settle the dispute over lumber between Canada and the United States (Berck 2005):

Canadian provinces could adopt a competitive bidding system to award timber concessions
Although this transition may address the CFLI's allegation of stumpage subsidization, special-interest groups in Canada (tenure holders and the logging industry) are unlikely to accept this change. There is a perception among Canadian provinces that the current system is very effective attracting private investment that ensures sustainable forestry. Furthermore, government officials and timber producers in Canada believe that U.S. companies will simply find other ways to countervail softwood exports even if a competitive bidding system is followed.

The United States and Canada can allow free trade in raw softwood logs
This proposal will address the issue of subsidies as they allow U.S. producers to have access to Canadian raw materials. But subsidization is not consistent with the growing perception and argument for creating value-added industries and jobs. There are restrictions in the United States about the export of logs produced from public forests. Therefore, we believe it is not practically feasible to settle the dispute.

Canada can adopt a voluntary restraint on exports in a cooperative arrangement with U.S. producers
Since competitive methods have failed to resolve the dispute, a cooperative arrangement that benefits both parties has been proposed. Voluntary restraints on exports raise lumber prices in U.S. markets, benefiting both the American and Canadian producers. The Canadian producers suffer a loss of market share, which is compensated by the higher revenues from sales and the lowering of volatility in trade due to the dispute. This proposal will work only if there are no alternative suppliers in the market. The price impacts will not be significant if other suppliers can capture market share.

Berck (2005) examines the market responsiveness of both Canada- and U.S.-administered forests and concludes that the Canadian method better approximates a competitive market outcome than does the USPNW method.

This finding, however, may not change the perceptions of U.S. lumber producers. The fact of the matter is that Canada has a lot of harvestable timber and the United States provides a key market. In the absence of effective and enforceable legal and institutional mechanisms, U.S. lumber producers will continue to practice rent-seeking behaviour by lobbying the administration. Helping Canadian lumber producers to seek alternative market sources may provide a long-term solution to this problem and the Canadian government should pursue this strategy more seriously. In the recent past, the Canadian government has sponsored many teams to explore markets for its forest products in Japan, China, and other countries across the world.

REFERENCES

Adams, D. (2003). "Market and resource impacts of a Canadian lumber tariff." *Journal of Forestry* (March): 48–52.

Alavalapati, J.R.R., W.L. Adamowicz, and W. White. (1999). "Random variables in forest policy: A systematic sensitivity analysis using CGE models." *Journal of Forest Economics* 5(2): 321–35.

Alavalapati, J.R.R., G.G. Das, and C. Wilkerson. (2003). "Emerging issues of Globalization: Implications for Forest Use in the U.S. and Canada," in *Two Paths Through the Forest: The Sustainability Challenge in Canada and the United States* (251–70), edited by B. Shindler, B. Steel, T. Beckley, and C. Finley. Corvallis: Oregon University Press.

Berck, P. (2005). "Contested Trade in Logs and Lumber." See Chapter 9, this volume.

Canadian Institute of Forestry. (2002). "The Canada-United States softwood lumber dispute." Information Paper. Ottawa: Canadian Institute of Forestry.

Dufour, D. (2002). "The Lumber Industry: Crucial Contribution to Canada's Prosperity." *Statistics Canada*. Catalogue No. 31F0027. Ottawa: Statistics Canada.

Nelson, H. and I. Vertinsky. (2003). The Canada-U.S. Softwood Lumber Disputes." Paper presented at the Conference entitled *U.S.-Canada Trade: Investment and Related Issues*, Bloomington, Indiana (April 11–2).

Peterson, E.W. (2001). *The Political Economy of Agricultural, Natural Resource, and Environmental Policy Analysis*. Ames: Iowa State Press.

Reed, L. (2001). "Two Centuries of the Softwood Lumber War Between Canada and the United States." Paper presented to the Free Trade Lumber Council. Montreal, Quebec. Available at: http://ftlc.org/.

van Kooten, G.C. (2002). "Economic analysis of the Canada United States Softwood Lumber Dispute: Playing the quota game." *Forest Science* 48(4): 712–21.

Wear, D. and K. Lee. (1993). "U.S. policy and Canadian Lumber: Effects of the 1986 Memorandum of Understanding." *Forest Science* 39(4): 799–815.

Wood Markets. (2003). "Global Currencies: Strong U.S. Dollar Creates Winners at America's Expense." *Wood Markets* 8(3): 1. Available at: http://www.woodmarkets.com/WMQ.htm.

Zhang, D. (2001). "Welfare impacts of the 1996 United States-Canada softwood lumber (trade) agreement." *Canadian Journal of Forest Research* 31: 1958–67.

This adds an element of curiosity to what otherwise seems to be just another pair of cases in a long list of such dumping cases that seem to crop up regularly in the post-Uruguay Round period. It is the purpose of this chapter to give an overview of what happened in each of these two cases, and to examine them more closely to see if there are any lessons of broader interest. One question that arises is whether these dumping cases are legitimate or just thinly veiled attempts at protectionism. Other questions are whether or not dumping actions make sense within the agricultural sector in which significant market power at the commodity level is not prevalent, and whether or not current regulations should be applied at all to cases within the agricultural sector. We will try to shed some light on each of these questions.

LEGAL BACKGROUND FOR ANTIDUMPING CASES

Drawing on the 1994 updating of Article VI of GATT, dumping is defined as a situation "by which products of one country are introduced into the commerce of another country at less than the normal value of the products in the exporting country." This kind of action "is to be condemned if dumping causes or threatens material injury or materially retards the establishment of a domestic industry" (GATT 1994).

Article VI of GATT goes on to define what importing at less than normal value is, and that to offset or prevent dumping, an AD duty may be levied at a level of less than or equal to the margin of dumping, which is the difference between the exported and the normal value of the product. To impose an AD duty, it must be determined that "the effect of the dumping ... is such as to cause or threaten material injury to an established domestic industry or is such as to retard materially the establishment of a domestic industry" (GATT 1994).

Importing at less than its normal value occurs under three alternative situations. These are defined as being:

... if the price of the product exported from one country to another:

- is less than the comparable price, in the ordinary course of trade, for the like product when destined for consumption in the exporting country; or
- in the absence of such domestic price, is less than either the highest comparable price of the like product for export to any third country in the ordinary course of trade; or
- the cost of production of the product in the country of origin plus a reasonable addition for selling costs and profit. (GATT 1994)

Of these three situations, one commonly observes within agriculture-related AD cases that it is the cost of production that is the focus of debate, and not the import price that is used to indicate whether dumping is occurring.

Little guidance on what exactly constitutes material injury is given in Article VI of GATT, but in the Uruguay Round Agreements Act (URAA), there is a special Agreement on the Implementation of Article VI of GATT 1994 that, among other things, spells out in Article III in more detail the procedures by which injury occurs. This quite lengthy article emphasizes the importance of the volume of imports, price undercutting, price depression, and the importance of separating the price effects of imports compared to other economic factors that may be relevant in price determination. In other words, some emphasis is given to showing convincingly, not just allegedly, a causal relationship between increased imports and the resulting price declines that injure domestic firms (GATT 1994).

These are the legal guidelines given to countries investigating dumping complaints that are lodged, but each country sets up its own operating procedures. Following these guidelines, the investigations have two components, proving first that dumping has occurred and then proving that this dumping has provoked injury.

THE U.S. CASE AGAINST GREENHOUSE TOMATOES FROM CANADA

There were six main issues in the U.S. case against greenhouse tomatoes from Canada:

- How is the product and industry under consideration defined (i.e., what is "like product")?
- What is the export price?
- What is the normal value?
- What is the exporter's cost of production?
- What is the margin of dumping?
- Does the importation of Canadian greenhouse tomatoes inflict injury on the U.S. industry?

It is important to determine product definition to understand the industry and markets being compared. The export price, normal value, and cost of production are also needed to determine if dumping is occurring. These latter three issues are also used to help determine the margin of dumping. Finally, once the existence of dumping is detected, injury must also be proven for an AD duty to be charged.

Like Product

The main issue for like-product definition is whether the investigation should be limited to greenhouse tomatoes or whether it should encompass all fresh tomatoes, including field tomatoes. In this case, the USDOC ruled that the investigation would focus on greenhouse tomatoes, which is a distinct domestic product. They arrived at this conclusion by examining evidence on the production processes involved such as costs, pricing, and marketing. Also, they examined physical characteristics like skin thickness, water content, colour, texture, and taste. They did not, however, use the notion of consumer demand or empirical evidence when considering the substitutability of fresh and greenhouse tomatoes.

During the injury investigation, it is important to determine if attention should be given to all fresh tomatoes or just to greenhouse tomatoes. It would seem that the use of consumer-demand theory would be a more appropriate methodology that could be used to make the distinction between the different types of tomatoes. Specifically, one could estimate the own- and cross-elasticity of demand and use them to determine the extent to which a specified increase in sales of imported greenhouse tomatoes would cause the price of greenhouse tomatoes to drop in the exporting country. If field and greenhouse tomatoes were close substitutes, an increased volume of imported greenhouse tomatoes would have little effect on the greenhouse-industry price, because field tomatoes dominate total consumption. In this case, there would be little injury to domestic greenhouse-tomato growers arising from imports. Conversely, the volume of imports could have enough of an effect on the domestic greenhouse-tomato price that increased imports would injure domestic greenhouse-tomato growers.

Export Price

The next major issue is the export price. The objective is to ascertain the price at which the offending imports were sold into the United States. Data regarding terminal market prices (adjusted for transportation costs and customs duties), inland freight within the United States, and standard commissions obtained from the U.S. Department of Agriculture (USDA) were used to arrive at the ex-factory or free on board (f.o.b.) prices. Subsequently, USDOC officials obtained data directly from the exporting firms alleged to be dumping and followed a procedure similar to that used to examine USDA data in order to determine the f.o.b. price in Canada. These calculations were undertaken for each of the following categories of greenhouse tomatoes: common round (beefsteak); cherry; plum or pear; and cluster or on-the-vine tomatoes. In this case, 20 tariff-line products were involved.

Normal Value

"Normal value" is the price in the exporter's domestic market at which the product in question is sold during the course of normal trade. Normal value can be determined only if sales into the Canadian domestic market are sufficient to allow its calculation. Published data from Agriculture and Agri-Food Canada (AAFC 2003) were used as the starting point to determine normal value. More detailed data regarding actual selling prices obtained from exporters involved in the case were also analyzed.

The complainants in this case (certain U.S. greenhouse-industry firms) had reason to believe that the within-Canada sales of greenhouse tomatoes were made at prices below the cost of production of those tomatoes. Therefore, they requested that the USDOC conduct a sales-below-cost investigation. This is a fairly standard procedure that is used to determine if a significant share of domestic sales is being made at prices below the cost of production. If so, the previously constructed "normal value" is of no use, because one would be comparing the export price in the United States against an artificially low domestic price in Canada. In these situations, sales within Canada at prices below the cost of production are not included in the calculation of normal value.

Cost-of-Production Analysis

The USDOC undertook a countrywide analysis following the legislative guidelines laid out for such calculations. Cost-of-production analysis includes cost of materials and fabrication, selling, general administrative, interest, and packing expenses. Capital costs are included and an amount for profit is added. These costs were obtained from the exporting companies concerned, with numerous interactions between the companies and the USDOC investigators in the preparation of the final determination. A cost for each type of tomato was arrived at for each Canadian greenhouse-tomato-exporting firm by determining a weighted average of all contributing farms.

Antidumping Margin Calculations

The final step in the determination of dumping and of a dumping margin is to compare the constructed export prices to the normal values, adjusted using the cost of production data and deleting domestic sales made at prices below cost, as noted above. This was done for each greenhouse exporter, using a weighted average across all tomato products being exported. There was a USDOC preliminary determination of these margins on October 2, 2001, in which the margins ranged from 0 percent to 50.75 percent. The Final Determination on February 19, 2002 confirmed that dumping was occurring, but the rates ranged by exporter from less than 2 percent (*de minimis* margins, treated as if they were zero) to 18 percent, with an average of 16 percent. These final-determination rates were imposed on all greenhouse tomatoes with exporter-specific rates. They were, however, subject to the final determination of injury by the USITC.

Injury Determination

This part of the process is undertaken by the USITC, which completed its preliminary determination in May 2001. The first element of the injury examination is the subject of "like product." The issues involved here are raised in the like-product section of this chapter. In the preliminary determination, it was concluded that greenhouse tomatoes alone were the like product. But the conclusion was mixed and this question must be re-examined in the final phase of the investigation. It was acknowledged that the two tomato types are substitutes in demand in a variety of situations. Given the much larger field-tomato market, if the two products are relatively close substitutes, the greenhouse-tomato price would be determined largely by the field-tomato price. In that case, the impact of import volumes of greenhouse tomatoes would have a much more modest effect on tomato prices and modest levels of injury would arise.

In determining injury, the USITC concluded, "there is reasonable indication that the domestic greenhouse-tomato industry is materially injured by reason of subject imports from Canada." However, the evidence given was sufficiently mixed that it acknowledged this would have to be examined in more detail in the final determination.

Some of the evidence brought forward was the following. The market for greenhouse tomatoes has grown steadily since 1998, while the demand for field tomatoes has remained stable at a higher level of consumption. The production of U.S. greenhouse tomatoes has also expanded over this period at the same rate as consumption has expanded, therefore the market share of U.S. production has remained constant.

The volume of Canadian imports has grown more rapidly than has its domestic consumption. The Canadian market share has grown from 34 percent to 44 percent, which has caused non-Canadian greenhouse-tomato imports to decline equivalently. Canadian export expansion in this market has been at the expense of Mexican and European export contraction.

Price Effects

As is appropriate, considerable attention was paid to the price-formation process of greenhouse tomatoes. At the outset, it was noted that the domestic industry is highly concentrated. With the product being perishable and with no inventories, the ability of individual market participants to affect market-wide prices is constrained. This is confirmed by the fact that most of these tomatoes are sold on the spot market or under one-week sales contracts. Of particular relevance to this inquiry, is whether Canadian imports have depressed the price in this market or if they have prevented prices from increasing. Price patterns on individual sales show a mixed pattern of underselling and overselling, but increasingly they undersold domestic product in the last year, 2000, in 61 percent of the cases to retailers, which is the dominant channel of sales. Average unit values of prices to domestic producers fell from 1998 to 1999 but rose again from 1999 to 2000. The USITC notes that the supply and price of field tomatoes appears to influence the price of greenhouse tomatoes, and the seasonal pattern conforms to field-tomato seasonality, which predates greenhouse-tomato production. Finally, it was observed that the U.S. tomato prices in 2000, although higher than those in 1999, were lower than they were in 1998. It was also observed that this price distinction was more pronounced for those tomato-product types for which the Canadian product was also available.

For the purpose of its preliminary determination, the USITC found that there was "sufficient information to conclude that the subject imports had significant price-depressing and price-suppressing effects on prices of the domestic like product" (i.e., greenhouse tomatoes). The USITC also acknowledged that in the final investigation, it would explore further the effects of Canadian imports as well as field tomatoes and non-subject imports on the price of U.S. greenhouse tomatoes.

In its summary-injury assessment, the USITC noted that production was growing, net sales were increasing, and hours worked by and wages paid to production and related workers were also increasing. But by many financial indicators, the U.S. domestic-greenhouse industry was in some difficulty because profit margins were flat or declining over the three years. Due to the price-depressing effects of the Canadian imports and the U.S. industry's poor financial condition, the USITC concluded that there was a reasonable indication that the U.S. tomato industry was injured materially by reason of these Canadian imports.

THE CANADIAN CASE AGAINST FRESH TOMATOES FROM THE UNITED STATES

On September 28, 2001, a collection of greenhouse-tomato growers in Canada, the Canadian Tomato Trade Alliance (CTTA), filed a complaint that alleged dumping by U.S. fresh-tomato growers. On November 9, 2001, the CCRA initiated a dumping investigation into this case and filed a Statement of Reasons to outline the initial analysis. At the completion of this investigation, the CCRA issued a preliminary determination of dumping in March of 2002. Simultaneously, the Canadian International Trade Tribunal (CITT) conducted a preliminary inquiry to determine if dumping caused or threatened to cause material injury to the Canadian industry. These investigations revealed evidence of dumping and injury, and a provisional duty was applied that was equal to the estimated margin of dumping.

Like Goods

Under Canadian AD legislation, like goods have "the same physical characteristics (same genus and species), are substitutes, follow the same distribution network and fulfill the same customer needs." On this basis, fresh tomatoes produced by the Canadian industry, largely greenhouse tomatoes,[1] were found to be "like the subject goods" (U.S. fresh-tomatoes), which are almost always field tomatoes. However, fresh tomatoes for the fresh market were distinguished as being different from fresh tomatoes used for processing. It should be noted that in the Canadian case, the determination of like goods or like product is different than it is in the U.S. case against Canadian greenhouse tomatoes, despite the use of similar criteria as to what constitutes like goods.

Export Price

The export price in Canada is considered to be "generally the lesser of the importer's purchase price or the exporter's selling price to Canada, less all costs, charges, and expenses resulting from the exportation of the goods." The CTTA estimated these prices in its complaint drawing on terminal-market prices published by Agriculture Canada. These were compared to the actual declared selling prices on customs documentation by the CCRA and it was found that the CTTA prices if anything were higher. This would make dumping less likely (i.e., a more conservative estimate), so the CTTA prices were accepted by the CCRA as reasonable.

Normal Value: Domestic Price

Similar to the United States AD legislation and procedures described above, Canadian AD procedures base "normal values" on the domestic selling price of goods in the country of export, or on the total unit cost of the goods plus an amount for profit. In this case, the CTTA chose not to use U.S. domestic selling prices for estimating normal value because the CTTA alleged that there are substantial quantities of tomatoes sold domestically at prices below production costs in the United States. This is not unusual in sales of agricultural products in both Canada and the United States, and the CTTA was able to find newspaper articles to support their claim that U.S. field tomatoes were being sold below cost for the majority of the year.

Normal Value: Cost of Production

When normal values are derived from the costs of production, normal value is defined to include the costs of producing the goods, plus a reasonable amount for administrative, selling, all other costs (presumably including capital costs), and profit. Because there are two main field-tomato producing areas of the United States, (California and Florida account for more than 70 percent of U.S. field tomatoes), the CTTA produced two sets of production costs, one for each region. For California, a University of California study of tomato costs was used as the base for cash costs, and a consultant developed a cost model that added noncash overhead costs that included capital costs (Cook 2001). In addition, local distribution and freight costs were added, as were administrative, marketing, and selling costs. For Florida, a University of Florida, Food and Resource Economics Department study was used as the base, adjusted to include local distribution, freight, administrative, marketing, and selling costs. No component for profit was added. These estimates, for California in 1998 and for Florida in 1999, were brought up to the year 2000 by the CTTA when they indexed them using the U.S. Farm Input Price Index. The CCRA verified the cost estimates with the USITC and the California Tomato Commission and found the CTTA estimates to be in line with other data. Thus the CTTA's estimated normal values were accepted by the CCRA.

Margin of Dumping

On the basis of the CCRA-accepted CTTA data comparing normal values with export prices, the CCRA concluded that there was reasonable evidence that dumping of field tomatoes did occur in the period from October 1, 2000 to September 30, 2001, the period under consideration. Further, the estimated dumping margins ranged from 14 percent to 76 percent as a percentage of normal value.

Injury

The issue of injury was first addressed by the CTTA, the complainants, who argued that Canadian incomes had been reduced as a result of price suppression by imports from the United States. They estimate the loss of revenue due to this dumping at U.S. $20 million annually. The CITT argue that the lowered prices, in addition to reducing incomes, reduced incentives to expand and upgrade operations, which raised the risk of lowered capital investment, employment, and market share. The United States claimed that Canadian greenhouse growers are price takers, and that the U.S. price is determined primarily by the Canadian selling price of U.S. tomatoes. The argument that Canadian tomato growers are basically price takers is in contrast to the arguments made by U.S. complainants in the U.S. AD case against Canadian greenhouse tomatoes.

The issue of injury was taken up further by the CITT, which issued its preliminary determination of injury on January 8, 2002. As in the U.S. case, the issues of "like goods" and "domestic industry" were the first to be addressed. The criteria are similar to those used by the USITC, except that demand-side factors that include substitutability and pricing appear to get more attention by the CITT. With briefs submitted from both the Canadian greenhouse growers and the U.S. field-tomato growers, the CITT concluded that the similarities among greenhouse tomatoes in both countries outweighed the differences. Therefore, the "subject goods" were judged to be in a class referred to as fresh tomatoes and tomatoes grown domestically for fresh consumption were judged to be "like goods" to the subject goods and were referred to as imported fresh tomatoes. On the "domestic industry" question, Canadian greenhouse-tomato growers were judged to represent more than 85 percent of their domestic fresh-market-tomato production (CITT 2002).

On the question of injury, the CITT examined the evidence submitted by the CTTA, which revealed persistent dumping of U.S. tomatoes that depressed Canadian greenhouse-tomato prices. Many letters from Canadian greenhouse-tomato producers supported this argument. The CITT did not collect independent data on these matters, but found from the evidence presented that there was a reasonable indication that the Canadian tomato industry had been injured by the dumping of the subject goods by the United States.

THE ECONOMICS OF ANTIDUMPING IN TOMATOES

There is a long history in the economics literature of dissatisfaction with AD measures and procedures. It has long been argued that AD provisions serve only protectionists, particularly the interests of firms desiring protection against normal and fair competition from foreign firms. Much of what is argued to be dumping is garden-variety price discrimination, which is neither illegal in domestic commerce nor rare.

Another argument is that if dumping occurs, it benefits consumers by offering them a cheaper source of the commodity in question. Measures that prevent consumers from obtaining a cheaper source would typically not be in a country's overall interest, unless of course the measures represented only temporary gains followed by higher prices, which would occur from predatory pricing.

The only substantial concern that AD measures address is the exertion of market power by a firm wishing to injure its competitor sufficiently by undercutting its prices, driving the competitor out of business, then later raising prices. This is the practice known as predatory pricing. In this context, AD measures might be considered as an international application of antitrust or competition policy. If this aspect of antidumping were given importance, there would be within the regulations some effort to address the extent of market power of the dumping firm, yet such provisions are not in place. There have been attempts to modify AD procedures so they would more closely mimic antitrust or competition policies (Krishna 1966). However, efforts such as these to limit the applicability of AD measures have usually run into strong political opposition from firms that see AD measures as helpful sources of protection when an industry is under some competitive stress.

Many would argue that the abuse of AD measures by firms and industries seeking another means of achieving protective duties against imports is a major weakness in the existing trade rules. Consequently, it has been on the agenda of the Doha Round of WTO negotiations to find ways to reform the existing Article and the national regulations that fall under the original GATT Article VI (1994) and the WTO Agreement on Implementation of GATT Article VI.

However, I wish to focus more on the economics of the agriculture industry in general and the tomato industry in particular, and on the validity of these AD actions from an economic perspective. I argue that proving dumping and injury is particularly easy in the agricultural sector due to some of its inherent economic characteristics, when combined with the kind of AD procedures we see so clearly applied in both tomato cases. We will begin with the determination of dumping and the normal-value calculation, with reference to domestic prices and to costs of production. We will then turn to injury determination, in which my comments will focus on the evidence needed for injury.

All it takes for a dumping margin to be determined is for there to be some price discrimination between the domestic market and the export market. Especially for smaller countries selling into larger ones, it is not unusual to find there is more competition in export markets than in the domestic market. For reasons of either active price discrimination or price taking in export markets but with an element of market power at home, any profit-maximizing firm will price higher domestically than in the more competitive, more elastic demand export market. By itself, this will meet the test of dumping. As more product differentiation is established, one can expect increased consumer interest fuelled by the increased identity-preservation (IP) costs, particularly in horticultural products.

In virtually all agriculture commodities, especially in the horticulture sector, the trend in real producer prices is downward. What is going on is no mystery to economists. In the agricultural sector there is a long history of improvements in technology resulting in increased productivity of farm commodities. This means two things: (1) firms that are slow when adopting the improved methods are going to face cost-price squeezes and some will be driven out of the industry by poor financial performance. These situations will bias upward the likelihood of disclosing losses in the industry; and (2) with the necessary lags in getting up-to-date cost data there will be a stronger likelihood of finding costs exceeding revenues, even for the firms that are current in their technology. In a slight variation on this last point, farmers will be making decisions on which market to serve and what prices to charge based on marginal costs, yet the calculated cost of production data is explicitly average cost.

In addition, there are cycles in agricultural commodity prices that frequently extend beyond the two or three years used in AD analyses, and in the lower parts of the cycle, it is a foregone conclusion that the farm prices will be below the costs of production.

Thus it is not surprising to find that export prices may be below costs of production for an agricultural commodity. What makes the results on AD investigations even more meaningless in terms of the economics of the industry is that firms can be found to be "selling at a loss" in both their export markets and their domestic markets. What kind of economic sense does this make? Obviously the time period is too short or the cost data are inappropriate to give a long-run picture of the future of the industry.

For similar reasons, these characteristics of the agricultural sector make it pre-disposed to a finding of material injury as well. First, on like-product questions, what is really important is the price-determination process of the domestic product in the allegedly injured industry. What effect in the medium to longer term on the price of that product is likely to arise from an increase in the "dumped" imports? This requires attention to demand-side characteristics and to the substitutability of the import and domestic product in the consumption decisions of the consumers. Supply-side characteristics are secondary.

Tomato Industry Data

The greenhouse-tomato industry is a market in which demand is growing at 13 percent per year. Production within the United States is growing at approximately 12.3 percent, and capacity is growing at about 12.6 percent. This means that the U.S. market share is being maintained, despite expanding Canadian imports. However, industry volume growth rates of 12 percent per year are considered unusually rapid growth rates in any context, and investment in the industry is increasing equivalently. This does not suggest injury.

There are several salient characteristics of pricing within the tomato industry. First, with the institutional arrangements for pricing and the industry structure, the Canadian tomato industry does not look like it is exerting significant power on the markets. This is especially true when you look at the strong influence of the price of fresh field tomatoes over the greenhouse price. Thus there is evidence of neither predatory pricing nor the structural elements that would generate predatory pricing.

Second, Canadian tomato produce within the U.S. greenhouse tomato market accounts for one-third of all U.S. greenhouse tomatoes, which by itself would give Canada a modest degree of market power. However, in the context of substitution with fresh tomatoes, Canadian imports account for only about 5 percent of the market. The ability for Canada to affect U.S. tomato prices overall under these conditions is very small indeed.

Third, real prices in the U.S. market are falling, as they are in virtually all farm commodities. Taking USDA annual prices for fresh tomatoes from 1989 to 2000 for the United States as a whole (USDA/NASS 1994 to 2003), deflating the prices by the Consumer Price Index, and regressing the real price series against a time variable, the trend rate of decline is –3.3 percent. This is a relatively rapid rate of decline in real prices, although not unusual for the horticultural industry. These data serve to underline the impact of declining real prices. Injury as defined for dumping investigations would be relatively easy to show under such conditions, at least for a general state of injury, assuming one can argue that the imports played a significant role in causing material injury.

From this quick review of the apparent economics of the U.S. tomato industry, it does not appear that the industry is being injured in aggregate, and it certainly does not look like financial distress that may exist with some U.S. firms is due to Canadian imports.

There is a healthy U.S. tomato industry growing and exporting field tomatoes, albeit with more competition from the Canadian greenhouse-tomato sector (Cook 2001). But there is substantial technical change occurring with relatively rapid declines in real prices, and it is likely this situation will lead Canadian investigators, following their own legal procedures, to find that U.S. dumping of tomatoes is also occurring in Canada. These panel investigations may also find injury, but again, the injury is not due to an economic definition of dumping. Injury being imposed on Canadian tomato growers will be due to the normal market forces of improving technology and of declining real prices, which are conditions faced by all participants in all segments of the fresh-tomato market.

FINAL RESOLUTION OF THESE CASES

In the face of the preliminary details about these two tomato cases and the view expressed in the previous section of how dumping cases in the agricultural sector are more likely to meet the conditions for dumping and injury, we now turn to the ultimate resolution of these two cases.

A Discussion of the U.S. Case against Canadian Tomatoes

In April 2002, the USITC completed its final investigation into the case on greenhouse tomatoes from Canada. Although the USDOC had earlier established that greenhouse tomatoes had been dumped into the U.S. market (sold at less than fair value), the USITC determined that "an industry in the United States is not materially injured or threatened with material injury by reason of imports of greenhouse tomatoes from Canada" (USITC 2002:1). This decision was not unanimous; one commissioner held the dissenting view.

A critical part of this decision was the determination of domestic-like product and industry. In this case the USITC found "that differences between greenhouse and field tomatoes generally represent variations in the quality of the tomato rather than distinctions that represent clear dividing lines."

(USITC 2002: 4). This judgment follows three previous USITC tomato cases in which no distinction was made across all forms and varieties of fresh tomatoes. Furthermore, this conclusion was shown to be consistent with end use of the tomatoes, physical characteristics, distribution channels, and consumer perceptions. The USITC also determined that there is a single domestic industry that includes all fresh tomatoes, and that it includes all producers of fresh tomatoes.

The USITC states that the facts regarding material injury are consistent with the characterization that Canadian tomato growers are "price takers" (USITC 2002: 18). The volume of Canadian greenhouse-tomato imports was judged to be insignificant, absolutely or relatively, with reference to the U.S. market. Over the period of growth in Canadian greenhouse-tomato exports in the latter 1990s, the share of the U.S. market accounted for by U.S. tomato production generally increased. Prices tended to be driven by the volume of all fresh tomatoes, not by Canadian greenhouse tomatoes alone. Indeed, the Canadian product tended to sell at prices above the U.S. competition. When looking at only U.S. greenhouse-tomato growers, financial difficulties were due to short-term (one to two year) industry price movements, the financial difficulties were not due to the impact of Canadian imports. Finally, there was judged to be no threat of material injury justified for future cases of Canadian greenhouse-tomato imports in the United States.

A Discussion of the Canadian Case against U.S. Tomatoes

In the Canadian case on the dumping of U.S. fresh-tomato imports into Canada, the result was very similar. Although there was a determination by the CCRA on dumping (selling at less than fair value) in March 2002, the CITT and the USITC concluded that "the dumping of the aforementioned goods has not caused material injury or retardation and is not threatening to cause material injury to the domestic industry" (CITT 2002: 1).

A unique aspect to this finding is that the Canadian tomato-industry complainants, the CTTA, just prior to the public hearing in June 2002, decided that it did not wish to further advance its case. Therefore, it was requested that the CITT terminate proceedings on the dumping investigation.

POTENTIAL AREAS FOR REFORM

It should be clear from the foregoing that changes to the existing AD agreement rules and country legislation are highly desirable, given that this existing AD agreement is not going to go away. There are several measures that could be taken to reform the AD agreement and its country-specific implementing legislation.

There are a number of general areas in which changes have been proposed (Neufeld 2001) including the importance of considering the economic impact of AD actions and the benefits to domestic producers from implementing AD actions. In other words, a public-interest clause should be considered as part of assessing the economy-wide impact of applying AD measures. It has also been suggested that numerous technical details should be included to increase clarity and to remove ambiguities. Finally, one could impose higher legal costs on applicants for cases in which the final decision is made against the complainants.

It is open to question whether AD legislation should define dumping in a way that includes standard price discrimination without limiting dumping to those cases in which predatory pricing is occurring. This widely used practice of firms exerting market power is fully acceptable in domestic policy, yet, as AD rules now stand, price discrimination across international borders qualifies as dumping. Price discrimination, however, is a necessary but not a sufficient condition for predatory pricing.

Even if one wishes to follow current practice and accept the broad definition of dumping that includes normal-price discrimination, one thing is clear: if a firm is not price discriminating, its sales should not fall under the definition of dumping. To keep such situations out of dumping investigations would require that some test for price discrimination be added to existing rules. This is particularly important for cases within the agricultural sector in which price discrimination at the commodity level is not so common. This would mean that investigations of dumping should be undertaken at the individual firm level in which dumping decisions could be made, not at the aggregate country level in which dumping decisions are not made.

Arguably the most egregious AD cases arise in agriculture when producers in both countries are price takers, yet dumping can be found to occur in either country in those periods when prices are below that country's costs of production. A problematic case occurs when firms in both importing and exporting countries are being injured due to generally low prices in the industry concerned during some time period. The injury this causes must be distinguished from injury due to dumping. Greater efforts to distinguish such cases must be made, especially for agricultural cases in which such circumstances are common.

Another test added to those undertaken to determine dumping should be that there be clear evidence that the dumping firm possesses market power. If the exporting firm itself does not have significant market power, it cannot be following predatory pricing practices, cannot be affecting the market price, and cannot be injuring firms in the importing country.

Finally, with respect to injury determination, one must link the actions of exporters in a causative manner to decreases in prices and injury to domestic firms. This also is particularly important within the agricultural sector, as the U.S.-Canada tomato cases make it clear.

CONCLUSIONS

AD regulations and actions are controversial elements of current trade policy. The economic arguments against dumping have been going on for the best part of the last century, and these tomato cases illustrate the weak economic foundations of those regulations once again. However, these economic foundations are even weaker in the agricultural sector than they are in the manufacturing sector.

Both tomato-dumping cases we have reviewed follow established legal structure and procedures. However, due to the combination of the dumping tests, dumping procedures, and certain characteristics of the agricultural sector in both the U.S. and Canadian cases, the decisions had a high probability of resulting in dumping decisions and duties. The conditions within the agricultural sector that pre-dispose it to dumping decisions are a combination of price cycles and negative real-price trends, plus the more general phenomenon of price discrimination that is not unique to agriculture.

Neither of these two tomato cases represents behaviour that an economist would call dumping. There is no monopoly power involved and no evidence of predatory pricing. In both cases, the exporting firms alleged to be causing the dumping are selling the same commodity in their own markets but they are found to be selling these products below their production cost in those markets. How can it be that a large number of firms in both countries, with apparently plenty of competition and market growth for their product, are hurting them-selves by selling below the cost of production in both markets? There is no economic logic to such behaviour. Selling below the cost of production is some-times unavoidable in a period of low prices for a price-taking firm. It is not a choice for such firms and it is not dumping by reasonable definition.

What makes the current dumping regulations laughable is the fact that both cases are indistinguishable from normal competition in international markets in which there are firms that may have acquired some competitive advantage or increased efficiency, and there are firms that are acting to exploit those advantages in competitive markets. For example, improved technology or favourable exchange-rate movements that increase exports should not be determined to cause material injury. There is no injury occurring caused by exports from the other country. The only injury some of these firms are experiencing is material injury due to declining real prices that are putting pressures on the finances of these firms, which is a situation we find in most parts of agriculture. However, the end result of these AD provisions, which are so well illustrated by these two cases and not unique to one country or another, is the increased potential for extra duties being imposed, a retreat from freer trade, and a reversion to more protection in the agricultural sector. The situation identified in the Canada-U.S. tomato dumping cases cries out for major reform of the AD agreement and the necessary implementing legislation in individual countries along the lines we have suggested.

NOTES

*I would like to thank Bryant Fairley and Mark Kurschner for their helpful comments in the preparation of this chapter. I also wish to acknowledge the excellent research assistance I have received from David Coney. However, none of these individuals is responsible for the interpretations and conclusions in this chapter, which are entirely those of the author.

[1] Looking at the fresh-tomato production within Canada, the market has shifted substantially toward greenhouse production in the last five years. In 1996, in terms of tonnage, field tomatoes accounted for 65 percent of all fresh tomatoes (the remainder, 35 percent, was greenhouse tomatoes). In 2000, greenhouse tomatoes accounted for 88 percent of this market volume. Processing-tomato production is still much larger

within Canada. For comparison, the tonnage of field tomatoes for processing in 2000 was 2.4 times as large as total fresh-tomato production in Canada in that year.

REFERENCES

AAFC (Agriculture and Agri-Food Canada). (2003). Available at:
    http://www.agr.gc.ca/index_e.phtml.
Cook, R. (2001). "Emerging Hothouse Industry Poses Challenges for California's Fresh Tomato Industry." Giannini Foundation of Agricultural Economics Update, University of California, Davis (January).
CITT (Canadian International Trade Tribunal). (2002). *Fresh Tomatoes, Originating in or Exported from the United States of America, Excluding Tomatoes for Processing.* Inquiry No. NQ-2001-004. Ottawa: CITT (June 26).
GATT (General Agreement on Tariffs and Trade). (1994). Available at:
    http://www.ciesin.org/TG/PI/TRADE/gatt.html.
Kerr, W.A. (2001)."Dumping: One of Those Economic Myths." *Estey Centre Journal of International Law and Trade Policy* 2(2): 211–20.
Krishna, R. (2003). "Some Aspects of Antidumping in Law and Practice." Available at:
    www.worldbank.org/html/doc/Publications/wps1800series/wps1823/wps1823.pdf.
Neufeld, I.N. (2001). *Antidumping and Countervailing Procedures—Use or Abuse? Implications for Developing Countries.* Policy Issues in International Trade and Commodities Study Series No. 9, United Nations Conference on Trade and Development, New York and Geneva.
Uruguay Round Agreements Act of GATT. (1996). Available at:
    http://www.uspto.gov/web/offices/com/doc/uruguay/.
USDA/NASS (U.S. Department of Agriculture/National Agricultural Statistics Service). (1994 to 2003). "Vegetables for Fresh Markets: Marketing Year Average Prices by State and United States." Annual Price Summary, Agricultural Statistics Board. Washington, DC: USDA/NASS. Available at: http://www.usda.gov/nass/.
USITC (U.S. International Trade Commission). (2002). *Greenhouse Tomatoes from Canada (Investigation No. 731-TA-925 Final): Determination and Views of the Commission.* USITC Publication No. 3499. Washington DC: USITC (April).

Chapter 12

Asymmetric Canada-U.S. Bilateral Trade in Grains and Trade Remedy Actions

Won W. Koo and Ihn H. Uhm
North Dakota State University
Canadian International Trade Tribunal

INTRODUCTION

As two of the world's largest exporters of wheat and barley, the United States and Canada compete with each other in major foreign markets (International Grains Council 1996 to 2002). They share a common interest when reducing government interference within world agricultural markets and when encouraging freer world trade. This does not preclude the United States and Canada from having disagreements over agricultural trade that arise from the differences in agricultural policies and marketing systems between the two countries.

The Canada-U.S. Free Trade Agreement (CUSTA)[1] became effective in 1989 and has been fully implemented for bilateral trade between the United States and Canada. The North America Free Trade Agreement (NAFTA)[2] became effective in 1994 between Canada, the United States, and Mexico, and when the agreement is fully implemented, it will create the largest single market in the world comprised of about 400 million consumers with trade valued at more than U.S. $300 billion annually. Although the economies of the three NAFTA partners are highly interdependent, the degree of interdependence has been asymmetric because Mexico and Canada depend more on the United States than the United States depends on Mexico and Canada. Prior to the implementation of NAFTA in 1994, 75 percent of Canadian exports and 88 percent of Mexican exports were destined for the United States. On the other hand, only 22 percent of U.S. exports were shipped to Canada and 7 percent of U.S. exports were shipped to Mexico. This trade imbalance arose mainly because of differences in economic conditions, differences in the relative sizes of the economies, and differences in the social structures among these countries.

In terms of economic conditions and social structure, Mexico differs significantly from the United States and Canada, its trading partners. The United States has the highest per-capita gross domestic product (GDP) at U.S. $35,400, followed by Canada at U.S. $22,700 (Table 12.1). Per-capita GDP in Mexico is about one-sixth of that in the United States. However, the farm population in Mexico is approximately 23 percent of its total population, while the farm population in the United States and Canada is less than 2.5 percent of each country's population. Per-capita farmland in Mexico (0.6 acres) is smaller than in the United States (1.8 acres) and Canada (3.9 acres), but the United States is about 9 times larger than Canada in terms of population and about 3 times larger than Mexico.

Table 12.1: Characteristics of the Participating Countries, 2001

	United States	Canada	Mexico
Population (Million)	285.9	31.0	100.4
Per Capita GDP[a] (1,000 U.S. Dollars)	35.4	22.7	6.0
Population in Agriculture (Percent)	2.2	2.5	23.0
Land (Million Acres)	465.0	122.0	57.3
Per Capita Land (Acres)	1.6	3.9	0.6
Average Age (Years)	35.5	36.9	23.3
Education (Years in School)	15.2	14.8	11.5

[a] Gross Domestic Product.
Source: International Monetary Fund (2001).

NAFTA will generate more inter-industry trade than intra-industry trade between the United States and Mexico mainly because of the dissimilarity in resource endowments. However, there will be more intra-industry trade between the United States and Canada than inter-industry trade because of the similarity of their resource endowments. Mexico exports mostly labour-intensive goods to the United States, while the United States exports technology and capital-intensive goods to Mexico. Trade between Canada and the United States, however, consists mostly of wheat and livestock products and/or cattle that are exported to each other. Under an intra-industry trade environment, trade disputes between the United States and Canada could be more likely to increase, compared to a similar situation under an inter-industry trade environment.

CUSTA has resulted in an increase in trade volume between the United States and Canada. For agricultural commodities and products, the increase has been greater for Canadian exports to the United States than it has been for U.S. exports to Canada. Average volumes of Canadian exports of wheat and barley to the United States were much greater than the average U.S. exports to Canada for the 1990 to 2002 period (Table 12.2). In addition, Canadian exports to the United States increased faster than did U.S. exports to Canada. U.S. imports of

Table 12.2: Bilateral Trade of Selected Agricultural Commodities between the United States and Canada

	1989	1999	2002	Average
	Million Bushels			
U.S. Imports from Canada				
HRS	4.4	52.8	39.0	37.3
Durum	8.0	23.7	21.8	14.7
Barley	11.6	28.9	21.9	31.4
U.S. Exports to Canada				
HRS	0.0	0.2	0.3	0.8
Durum	0.0	0.4	0.2	0.1
Barley	0.0	1.8	5.9	1.2

Source: USDA/FAS (2002).

Canadian western red spring (CWRS) wheat, for example, increased from 4.4 million bushels in 1989 to more than 52.8 million bushels in 1999 but decreased to 39 million bushels in 2002. However, U.S. exports of hard red spring (HRS) wheat to Canada averaged only about 0.8 million bushels annually during the same period. Trade of durum wheat between Canada and the United States was similar to that for HRS wheat. An import surge of durum wheat from Canada to the United States in 1993 led to the negotiation of a temporary one-year agreement between Canada and the United States that limited Canadian wheat exports to the United States.[3]

U.S. barley imports from Canada also grew rapidly from 11.6 million bushels in 1989 to nearly 28.9 million bushels in 1999 and decreased to 21.9 million bushels in 2002 (Table 12.2). Canadian imports accounted for more than 10 percent of U.S. domestic consumption for the 1990 to 2001 period. During the same period, U.S. barley exports to Canada were less than 1.2 million bushels. However, when analyzing trade disputes between the two countries, it is important to note that at times the Prairie region of Canada imported sizeable quantities of corn from the U.S. for cattle feeding (Schmitz and Furtan 2003). In 2002, for example, the value of Canadian corn imports from the United States far exceeded the value of U.S. barley imports from Canada.

Because of the rapid increase of Canadian exports of agricultural commodities to the United States in the post-CUSTA era, concerned grain producers in Minnesota, Montana, and North Dakota sought the government's protection through trade remedy laws. At times, in addition to legal means, producers in these states engaged in the blockade of Canadian grain and livestock shipments to the United States. Furthermore, the South Dakota governor announced new inspection requirements for all trucks carrying Canadian grain and livestock into South Dakota beginning September 16, 1998 (ROU 1999).[4] Governors of North Dakota, Montana, and Idaho followed the South Dakota measures and announced a stepped-up effort to inspect Canadian trucks as they crossed the border into these states.[5] On December 2, 1998, in the aftermath of a series of trade disputes, the United States and Canada announced a record of understanding (ROU) in agricultural trade to ease the tension between the two countries.[6] However, ROU has not been successful totally.

In this chapter, we will examine the market conditions conducive to trade flows and to the causes of trade disputes between the United States and Canada with respect to wheat and barley. To this end, we will analyze U.S. trade disputes with Canada over wheat under U.S. trade remedy laws. We will discuss new developments for conflict resolution between the two countries and then present our concluding remarks.

CONTRIBUTING FACTORS FOR ASYMMETRIC BILATERAL TRADE FLOWS AND TRADE DISPUTES

Bilateral trade flows of wheat and barley between the United States and Canada under CUSTA have been influenced by differences in resource endowments, marketing systems, availability of marketable surpluses, differences in crop quality, and differences of farm policies between the two countries. These differences have resulted in several trade disputes between the two countries for the last 15 years.

The size of the domestic markets for HRS wheat, durum wheat, and barley in Canada is much smaller than the size of the U.S. domestic markets for these commodities. However, the quantities of wheat and barley produced in Canada are larger than those quantities produced in the United States (International Grains Council 1996 to 2002). As a result, Canada has substantial marketable surpluses of grain and is therefore more dependent on export markets than is the United States. On average, Canada exports in the neighbourhood of 10 percent of its spring wheat production and 15 percent of its durum wheat production to the United States. Under CUSTA, the U.S. market has become attractive to Canadian producers mainly because it is Canada's closest and largest market.

The Canadian Wheat Board (CWB) markets all Canadian wheat and barley produced in Canada. The CWB pays Canadian producers an initial price when the grain is delivered to them and returns any revenue surplus to producers as a final payment after all exports have been distributed for the year (Simonot 1997). In the United States, however, grain-trading firms market U.S. grain. U.S. wheat and barley compete with CWB grain in the world and U.S. markets. Some Canadian producers of wheat and barley who are in close proximity to the United States view that the Canadian producers' lack of direct access to the U.S. market is due mainly to the CWB's control of Canadian grain. These producers feel that the CWB marketing policy works against their own best interests. On the other hand, some groups in the United States argue that the CWB distorts trade flows (Ingco and Ng 1998). The CWB has monopsony power when purchasing wheat and barley from producers, and at the same time it is a single-desk sales agency that has the exclusive right to make Canadian marketing decisions regarding wheat and barley prices and quantities. Thus, the U.S. government argues that the CWB is able to practice price discrimination in order to maximize profits in world markets,[7] which causes an unfair advantage over private firms in the United States. However, the WTO, under Article XVII:1, allows a state-trading enterprise to charge different prices between markets provided it is done for commercial reasons based on market conditions in export markets. The U.S. government also argues that the CWB does not provide sufficient information regarding its general operation. This is especially true regarding purchase-price and sales-price information for agricultural commodities.[8] Schmitz and Koo (1996) argue that the CWB has an advantage over its U.S. competitors.

The Canadian rail subsidy (the Crow) was an indirect subsidy provided by the Canadian government under the 1983 *Western Grain Transportation Act* (WGTA) to farmers for the shipment of designated grains from their producing region to their export ports.[9] Under the WGTA, U.S. grain producers argued that Canadian grains were more competitive in offshore markets. Canada, however, eliminated the controversial Crow subsidy of the WGTA in 1995. Contrary to the expectations of U.S. grain producers, the elimination of the rail subsidy induced larger inflows of grain into the United States. The elimination of the WGTA has ultimately made the U.S. market more attractive for Canadian producers because transportation costs from the Canadian Prairies to the United States are lower than are those from the Canadian Prairies to most offshore markets (Johnson and Wilson 1995; Mao, Koo, and Krause 1996).

The exchange rate between the American and Canadian currencies also plays an important role in the bilateral trade of agricultural commodities and products. Since the U.S. economy has been stronger than the Canadian economy since 1985, the U.S. dollar has appreciated against the Canadian dollar. U.S. dollar appreciation makes U.S. agricultural commodities more expensive in the Canadian market and conversely makes Canadian agricultural commodities less expensive in the U.S. market.[10] Exchange-rate movements have significant short-run and long-run influences on bilateral trade between the United States and Canada (Kim, Cho, and Koo 2002).

Another important contributing factor affecting trade flows of grain between the United States and Canada is the difference of the quality of grain delivered to downstream industries such as millers and pasta manufacturers.[11] This is especially true for HRS wheat, durum wheat, and barley traded between the two countries. U.S. millers demand high-quality durum wheat. In the past, whenever the United States could not produce enough high-quality durum wheat to meet the domestic demand because of weather conditions and diseases during the growing season, U.S. millers have imported high-quality durum wheat from Canada. Similarly, Canadian malting barley is desired by U.S. maltsters because of its favourable attributes in producing beer. Canadian feed barley, on the other hand, competes with other carbohydrate materials such as corn and sorghum as a livestock feedstuff.

TRADE BARRIERS OF GRAINS IN THE PRE- AND POST-CUSTA/NAFTA ERA

Prior to the CUSTA and NAFTA agreements, there were barriers in place (e.g., tariffs and non-tariff barriers) for the trading of small grains (including durum wheat) between the United States and Canada. Tariffs imposed by the United States prior to 1989 were U.S. $7.70 per ton for wheat, U.S. $2.30 per ton for malting barley, and U.S. $3.40 per ton for other barley; and those imposed by Canada were CDN $4.40 per ton for wheat and CDN $2.30 per ton for all barley. Under CUSTA, tariffs on wheat and barley were placed on a schedule of elimination in 10 equal segments and were eliminated completely by January 1, 1998. In Canada, imports of wheat from the United States were subject to import licenses administered by the CWB[12] but these were removed in 1990 after the adoption of CUSTA. In 1991, however, Canada instituted a legal regime under which American wheat destined for processing in Canada must be accompanied by an end-use certificate (EUC) permitted under CUSTA, Article 705(1). Canadian processors importing U.S. wheat must request an EUC from the Canadian Grain Commission. Subsequently, the U.S. government also instituted an EUC requirement for all Canadian wheat entering the United States, effective February 27, 1995.[13]

U.S. TRADE REMEDY LAWS AND TRADE DISPUTES ON WHEAT

The recent history of grain-trade disputes between Canada and the United States reveals that U.S. producers have attempted to stop or to reduce the flow of Canadian wheat and/or barley into the U.S. market to enhance U.S. grain producers' incomes, using numerous facets of U.S. trade statutes and other means such as border blockades. A number of U.S. trade statutes are available to protect domestic producers of like goods from unfair trading practices by foreign exporters. These include antidumping (AD) duties (Subtitle B of Title VII of the *Tariff Act* of 1930, as amended) and countervailing (CV) duties (Subtitle A of title VII of the *Tariff Act* of 1930, as amended) (Table 12.3).

The AD and CV duty laws are two important trade remedy laws. Although these two laws are aimed at different forms of unfair trade, they have many procedural and substantive similarities. Dumping generally refers to a form of international price discrimination, whereby goods are sold in one export market at prices lower than the price at which comparable goods are sold in the home market of the exporter, or in its other export markets.[14] The purpose of the CV duty law, on the other hand, is to offset any unfair competitive advantage that foreign manufacturers (or exporters) might enjoy over U.S. domestic producers as a result of foreign CV subsidies.[15]

Table 12.3: U.S. Trade Statutes and Required Injury Test for Relief

Trade Statutes in the United States	Primary Purpose of the Statute	Investigating Agencies	Required Legal Test for Relief[a]
***Agricultural Adjustment Act* (AAA)** (Section 22 of the AAA of 1933, as amended)[b]	To ensure that imports of agricultural products do not undermine domestic farm programs	USITC[c] for determination of material interference USDA is a designated interested party	Required "material interference test" vis-à-vis a farm commodity programs administered by USDA[d]
Antidumping Dumped imports (Title VII of the *Tariff Act* of 1930, as amended)	To protect domestic industries from injurious effects of dumping	USDOC/ITA[e] for determination of dumping; USITC for determination of injury	Required "material injury test" caused by the subject imports
Conditions of Competition (*Tariff Act* of 1930, as amended, Section 332)	To investigate the conditions affecting competition and the U.S. industries competitiveness	USITC USDOC/ITA	Not applicable
Countervailing Duty Subsidized imports (Subtitle *A* of title VII of the *Tariff Act* of 1930, as amended)	To protect domestic industries from subsidization by foreign government	USDOC/ITA for determination of subsidization; USITC for determination of injury	Required "material injury test" caused by the subject imports
Enforcement Action Unfair trade (Section 301 of the *Trade Act* of 1974, as amended)	To enforce U.S. rights gained under international trade agreement	USTR[f]	Not applicable
Import Relief (Safeguard Actions) (Section 201 of the *Trade Act* of 1974, as amended)	To deal with the temporary adverse effects of fair import competition	USITC for determination of injury	Required "serious injury test" caused by the subject imports[g]

[a] E.g., material injury test.
[b] 7 U.S.C. (United States Code) 624. Section 22 authority (the Agricultural Adjustment Act of 1933, as amended) is available now only for imports from countries to which the United States does not apply the WTO Agreement.
[c] U.S. International Trade Commission.
[d] U.S. Department of Agriculture.
[e] U.S. Department of Commerce/International Trade Administration.
[f] U.S. Trade Representative.
[g] It is generally accepted that serious injury test requires somewhat higher legal standard than that of the material injury threshold.
Source: U.S. House of Representatives (1997).

In addition to AD and CV duty provisions, import relief (safeguard) under Section 201 of the *Trade Act* of 1974, as amended by Section 1401 of the *Omnibus Trade and Competitiveness Act* of 1988, and Sections 301 to 304 of the *Uruguay Round Agreements Act*, set forth the authority and procedures for the U.S. President to take action. These actions may include import relief in the form of tariffs, quotas, or tariff-rate quotas (TRQs), which will facilitate efforts by a domestic industry that has been seriously injured by these imports, to make a positive adjustment to this import competition (Table 12.3).[16]

Section 22 of the *Agricultural Adjustment Act* of 1933 (AAA), as amended, also provides:

> ... relief through the U.S. President, if he agrees whenever the U.S. Secretary of Agriculture has reason to believe that any article or articles are being or are practically certain to be imported into the United States under such conditions and in such quantities as to render or tend to render ineffective, or materially interfere with any program or operation undertaken under this title or the *Soil Conservation and Domestic Allotment Act*, as amended. (AAA 1933: Section 22)

The U.S. Secretary of Agriculture shall so advise the U.S. President and, if the U.S. President agrees that there is reason for such relief, the U.S. President "shall cause an immediate investigation to be made by the U.S. International Trade Commission (USITC), which shall give precedence to investigations under this section to determine such facts" (U.S. House of Representatives 1997).

Section *332* of the *Tariff Act* of 1930, as amended, also provides the authority that:

> ... the USITC investigate and report to the U.S. President and his Congress on the administrative, fiscal and industrial effects of the customs laws of the United States. The USITC shall have power to investigate the tariff relations between the United States and foreign countries, commercial treaties, preferential provisions, economic alliances, the effect of export bounties and preferential transportation rates, the volume of imports compared with domestic production and consumption, and conditions, causes, and effects relating to competition of foreign industries with those of the United States, including dumping and the cost of production. (U.S. House of Representatives 1997)

Finally, Section 301 of the *Trade Act* of 1974, as amended:

> ... provides the authority and procedures to enforce U.S. rights under international trade agreements and to respond to certain unfair foreign practices. If the U.S. Trade Representative (USTR) determines that a foreign act, policy, or practice violates or is inconsistent with a trade agreement, or is

unjustifiable and burdens or restricts U.S. commerce, then action by the USTR to enforce the trade agreement rights or to obtain the elimination of the act, policy, or practice is mandatory, subject to the specific direction, if any, of the President.[17] (U.S. House of Representatives 1997)

Given these trade statutes available to the U.S. grain producers, the first legal challenge with respect to the bilateral asymmetric wheat-trade flows in the post-CUSTA era began in 1989 when North Dakota durum wheat producers complained that the Canadian freight subsidies provided under the WGTA constituted an export subsidy, in violation of CUSTA Article 701.2. The USTR examined the allegation and concluded that "subsidies under the WGTA would not appear to be classified as export subsidies," which implied that Canada had not violated Article 701.2, because the freight subsidy under the WGTA applied to all shipments to Thunder Bay, whether destined for export or domestic use. Subsequently, the Canadian government in 1995 eliminated the controversial WGTA.

The second legal challenge was initiated on October 26, 1989 by the U.S. Congress, instructing the USITC, under the provisions of Section 332 of the *Tariff Act* of 1930, as amended, to examine the "condition of competition" of durum wheat between the American and Canadian industries.[18] In accordance with Section 332(g) of the *Tariff Act* of 1930, as amended, the USITC instituted investigation No. 332-285, *Durum Wheat: Conditions of Competition Between the U.S. and Canadian Industries* (USITC 1990). The U.S. Senate Committee on Finance requested the USITC to report the results of its investigation by June 22, 1990. The USITC, pursuant to the request by the U.S. Congress, reported on that date the results of its investigation to the House Committee on Ways and Means and the Senate Committee on Finance (USITC 1990). The USITC rejected the U.S. wheat industry's allegation that the CWB had been dumping durum wheat into the U.S. market (i.e., selling below acquisition price).

Subsequently, based on complaints filed by grain producers in North Dakota and Montana, the U.S. Congress requested that the U.S. Government Accounting Office (USGAO)[19] conduct a study analyzing the responsiveness of durum prices to market forces. The results of the USGOA study, presented during a Congressional field hearing in Bismarck, North Dakota on December 1989, indicated that prices of durum wheat from 1973 to 1988 had generally followed the movement of market forces such as the stocks-to-use ratios (i.e., price level bears a strong inverse relationship to stocks on hand at the end of the year).[20] A binational panel hearing, held in 1992 pursuant to Article 701(3) of CUSTA, unanimously ruled that there was no compelling evidence that the CWB was selling wheat below its acquisition cost into the U.S. market.

Having failed to reduce Canadian exports of wheat (including durum) into the U.S. market by use of the mentioned U.S. trade statutes and CUSTA Articles, in 1993 the U.S. wheat industry pressured the Clinton Administration to take further legal action through the Executive Branch under the provisions of Section 22, the AAA, as amended.[21] As directed by the U.S. President, the USITC instituted investigation No. 22-54, on November 17, 1993, under Section 22(a) of the AAA.

By a majority rule, the USITC determined that wheat, wheat flour, and semolina were being imported into the United States under such conditions and in such quantities as to "materially interfere" with the price-support programs conducted by the U.S. Department of Agriculture for wheat.[22] The USITC's report to the U.S. President indicates that the USITC had seriously considered five economic analyses, *inter alia*, containing empirical evidence submitted by the participants of the investigation as well as by the USITC staff in its deliberations (USITC 1994).[23] The USITC report to the U.S. President led to a negotiated settlement, which is known as the Wheat Peace Agreement, for the 1994/95 crop year.[24] In market response to the agreement, the U.S. domestic price of durum wheat rose from U.S. $4.67 per bushel in 1994 to U.S. $5.75 per bushel in 1995. However, the durum price fell to U.S. $3.95 per bushel in 1997.[25]

In September 2000, the North Dakota Wheat Commission filed a petition under Section 301 of the *Trade Act* of 1974 requesting an investigation of the wheat-marketing practices used by the CWB. The USTR undertook a 16-month investigation and requested the USITC to examine the competitive practices of the CWB in the U.S. market and overseas. In February 2002, the USTR released the findings of their investigation that found that the CWB used special monopoly rights and privileges that disadvantaged U.S. farmers and were unfair to trade. The USTR determined that the CWB has, in effect, been taking sales from U.S. farmers. As a result of these findings, the USTR decided to attempt to level the playing field aggressively for U.S. farmers by stating that they would examine the possibility of filing U.S. CV duty and AD petitions with the U.S. Department of Commerce (USDOC) and the USITC.[26]

The USITC instituted AD and CV duty investigations effective September 13, 2002, following receipt of a petition filed with the USITC and USDOC by the North Dakota Wheat Commission (HRS wheat), Bismarck, ND; the Durum Growers Trade Action Committee (durum wheat), Bismarck, ND; and the U.S. Durum Growers Association (durum wheat), Bismarck, ND. The other principal parties to these investigations were the CWB (a respondent interested party that opposed the petition) and the North American Millers' Association (an association of purchasers of both the imported and domestically produced wheat, which also opposed the petition).

On October 23, 2002, the USDOC announced its decision to initiate AD duty and CV duty investigations on imports of durum and HRS wheat from Canada. On May 8, 2003, the USDOC published in the *Federal Register* the preliminary determinations in its AD duty investigations of durum wheat and HRS wheat from Canada. The USDOC found that durum wheat and HRS wheat from Canada were sold in the United States below normal value during the period of investigation (July 1, 2001 through June 30, 2002). The final weighted-average dumping margins for durum wheat and HRS wheat are 8.26 percent and 8.87 percent, respectively (USDOC 2003a).[27]

In addition, the USDOC has made final determinations that CV subsidies are being provided to certain producers and exporters of certain durum wheat and HRS wheat from Canada. The period for which the USDOC is measuring subsidies is August 1, 2001 to July 31, 2002. The USDOC determined that the total estimated net subsidy rate for the CWB and "all others" to be 5.29 percent for durum wheat and 5.29 percent for HRS wheat (USDOC 2003b).[28]

On the basis of the record developed in the subject investigations, the USITC determined that, pursuant to Section 705(b) and 735(b) of the *Tariff Act* of 1930 under (United States Code) U.S.C. 19 § 1673D(B), the U.S. HRS wheat industry is injured materially by reason of imports from Canada of HRS wheat that have been found by the USDOC to be subsidized by the Government of Canada and sold in the United States at less than fair value. Interestingly, the USITC determined that the U.S. durum wheat industry was not injured materially or threatened by imports of durum wheat from Canada, even though the USDOC argued that durum wheat was being sold in the United States at less than fair value (USDOC 2003b).[29]

When determining material injury, the statute directs the USITC in the context of U.S. production operation to consider the volume of imports, the effect of the imports on prices for the domestic-like product, and the impact on domestic producers of the domestic-like product. The statute defines material injury as "harm which is not inconsequential, immaterial, or unimportant."[30] When assessing whether the domestic industry is injured materially by imports, the statute directs the USITC to consider all relevant economic factors that bear on the state U.S. industry.[31] All relevant factors are considered "within the context of the business cycle and conditions of competition that are distinctive to the affected industry."[32]

The USITC's positive material-injury determination for subject HRS wheat imports from Canada underscores the lack of a clear quantitative definition and the application of the concept of material injury. The U.S. trade remedy law defines material injury as "harm which is not inconsequential, immaterial, or unimportant." The question remains over how much harm constitutes material injury (Featherstone and Uhm 2002).

Trade disputes between the two countries did not end with the above findings by the USITC. The World Trade Organization (WTO), under pressure from the United States, is investigating unfair trading practices by the CWB. In addition, Canada launched an appeal in 2003 under NAFTA over the imposition of tariffs by the U.S. on HRS wheat imports.

A SETTLEMENT THROUGH NEGOTIATIONS

Even with several negotiations over the wheat trade between the United States and Canada, trade disputes continue between the two countries. On December 2, 1998, in the aftermath of a series of legal actions, hostile words, and border blockades, the United States and Canada announced a ROU on bilateral agricultural trade that includes the Canada-U.S. Action Plan to improve and expand agricultural trade relations between the two countries.[33] The primary purpose of the ROU is to ease the tension between the United States and Canada that results from trade in grain and livestock. The highlights of the ROU between the two governments are as follows:

- The action plan is designed to improve U.S. farmer access to primary elevators in Western Canada, while preserving the integrity of the Canadian grain-quality-control system. In this regard, 4 grain companies have suggested that a total of 27 elevators within 60 miles of the border receive U.S. grains. The program complements existing arrangements that facilitate the direct movement of U.S. wheat and barley to Canadian feedlots, feed mills, and flour mills, effective January 1, 1999;

- Growers in the United States are able to ship wheat under a "Master Phytosanitary Certificate" without the requirement of having each individual shipment tested. Wheat must originate from an approved grower in a state that is eligible under the program and at least one sample per grower, per crop, must be tested officially and found free of Karnal bunt spores. The program was implemented for both North Dakota and Montana on January 1, 1999;

- The Canadian Food Inspection Agency has developed an alternative certification program that permits shipments of wheat, barley, rye and/or triticale, excluding seed, to transit through Canada based on a certificate of origin in lieu of a phytosanitary certificate with mandatory sampling and testing. This allows U.S. grain to be shipped on the Canadian rail system to final destinations in the United States beginning January 1, 1999 for producers from Montana, Minnesota, and North Dakota; and

- Other grain-related measures include phased-in changes in phytosanitary regulations for U.S. grain shipments to Canada and efforts to harmonize pesticide regulations. In addition, Canada and the United States agreed to meet quarterly, or more frequently on request, to consult on global grain production and marketing to strengthen cooperation and trust on issues of mutual interest.

Although this Canada-U.S. action plan has provided opportunities for U.S. growers to ship their grains to Canada and to use the Canadian rail system to ship grain to destinations in the United States, the plan did not fully satisfy grain producers in the United States because the major issue is not U.S. access to the Canadian market. Grain producers' major concerns are the rapidly increasing volumes of Canadian exports of wheat and barley that are shipped into the United States and their impact on local grain prices and farm incomes, particularly in the Northern Plains region. The root of the problem remains unaddressed as far as grain producers in the United States are concerned.

CONCLUSIONS

CUSTA created one of the largest single markets in the world. The overall effects of the CUSTA agreement have generally been very positive on both sides of the border as the two-way trade in 2004 is nearly 2.5 times the level of that before CUSTA. However, there have been several trade disputes concerning agricultural commodities during the post-CUSTA era. The disputes seem likely to continue as long as the surge in Canadian exports remains unabated.

Trade disputes between the United States and Canada were reviewed in this chapter. We also identified interwoven multiple factors that influence bilateral trade, which include the persistent differences in the grain-marketing and delivery systems, farm-subsidy programs, trade policies between Canada and the United States, and the relative value of the Canadian dollar. The trade disputes between Canada and the United States are extremely complex and undoubtedly will require the wisdom of Solomon to resolve. Some economists argue that the gradual harmonization of trade policies, farm-subsidy programs, and marketing institutions may reduce trade disputes between the two countries in the future. Some economists, however, are sceptical of such a view based on the fact that the elimination of the Canadian WGTA harmonized the grain-freight rate structures between the two countries, but did not lead to a significant reduction in Canadian exports to the United States. To the contrary, the elimination of the century-long freight-rate subsidy in Canada (the Crow) encouraged Canadian grain producers to divert grain shipments from the world market to the United States. Simultaneous harmonization of trade policies, farm subsidies, and marketing institutions could be more effective at reducing trade disputes between the two countries than can partial harmonization.

As long as U.S. imports of wheat from Canada are much larger than U.S. exports to Canada and the increased imports cause material injuries to the United States, limited trade disputes could continue. Thus policy harmonization between the two countries is far from a reality. To diffuse the threat of future trade disputes, a Canada-U.S. joint research team should be established to deal with the matter through better understanding of bilateral trade for agricultural commodities and/or products, especially wheat and barley, between Canada and the United States.

NOTES

[1]The Canada-U.S. Trade Agreement (CUSTA) created a free-trade area comprised of Canada and the United States. Objectives of CUSTA are to eliminate barriers to trade in goods and services between the two countries; facilitate conditions of fair competition within the free-trade area; liberalize significantly conditions for investment within the free-trade area; establish effective procedures for the joint administration of this agreement and the resolution of disputes; and lay the foundation for further bilateral and multilateral cooperation to expand and enhance the benefits of this agreement. CUSTA established rules for determining where trade of a commodity originated and established rules as to whether or not that trade was entitled to CUSTA tariffs. Tariffs were to have been eliminated on all goods by January 1, 1998 (External Affairs and International Trade Canada 1987).

[2]The North American Free Trade Agreement (NAFTA) created a free-trade area that encompasses Canada, Mexico, and the United States. The basic format of NAFTA closely follows that of CUSTA. A number of provisions of NAFTA have been designed to rectify difficulties experienced under CUSTA (External Affairs and International Trade Canada 1993; Lipsey, Schwanen, and Wonnacott 1994).

[3]The agreement was effective for only one year from September 12, 1994 to September 11, 1995 (USTR 1994).

[4]Trucks carrying Canadian grain must supply proof that the grain is free from Karnal Bunt and wild oats. In addition, the grain should be free of dimetridazole, ipronidazol, nitroimidazoles, fluoroquinolones, glycopeptides, and sulfamethazine, which are six chemicals used in the production of grain.

[5]The press release by the Office of the Governor, State of North Dakota on September 15, 1998, the press release by the Office of the Governor, State of Montana on September 18, 1998, and the press release by the Office of the Governor, State of Idaho on September 18, 1998 (ROU 1999). In addition, North Dakota proposed a law that would restrict the entry of Canadian products under the guise of technical requirements. The proposed new law would prohibit a wide range of Canadian agricultural products from entering North Dakota without the necessary scientific justification required by NAFTA and by domestic U.S. regulations. The Canadian government protested vigorously to defend the rights of Canadian exporters of agricultural goods. In this regard, Canada requested NAFTA consultations on the North Dakota trade barrier (Department of Foreign Affairs and International Trade 1999).

[6]The Record of Understanding (ROU) between the governments of Canada and the United States of America regarding areas of agricultural trade (Agriculture and Agri-Food Canada 2003).

[7]The CWB is a state-trading agency that is the sole legal exporter for wheat and barley grown in Canada. The Canadians argue the CWB is a "cooperative," while others argue that it is a state agency. Its obligatory relationship with the wheat-grain farmer sets it apart from the usual concept of a cooperative. The CWB operates both as a monopoly and as a monopsony within the boundaries of Canada. Internationally, the CWB and the large U.S. grain-marketing firms may be considered as oligopolies within the North American wheat market.

[8]Agricultural economists in Canada argue that American grain-exporting firms (e.g., Cargill, Inc.) do not reveal their export prices either. The Canadian economists further argue that it is a moot point as to whether or not Canadian producers have benefited from price discrimination.

[9]The *Western Grain Transportation Act* was enacted in 1983 in an attempt to modernize the century-old statutory rail freight rate known as the Crows Nest Pass Agreement or the Crow Rate. Under the WGTA, the Canadian government provided rail companies with annual payments of up to CDN $658 million with an adjustment for inflation to cover the transportation costs of eligible grain shipments to selected shipping terminals at Western Canadian and Eastern Canadian ports. Under the WGTA, shipping costs from the Canadian Prairies to offshore markets were lower than were the shipping costs were from U.S.-producing regions to the same offshore markets. It is argued by U.S. grain producers that Canada enjoyed a competitive advantage over the United States when shipping grains to these markets. Under CUSTA, however, Canada's WGTA was eliminated for grain shipped through west coast ports for U.S. consumption (Koo and Uhm 1984).

[10]For example, assume that Canadian wheat priced at CDN $5.00 per bushel is sold at U.S. $3.57 per bushel in the U.S. market at an exchange rate of CDN $1.40 per U.S. $1.00. If the U.S. dollar appreciates from CDN $1.40 per bushel to CDN $1.50 per bushel, the price of Canadian wheat decreases from U.S. $3.57 per bushel to U.S. $3.33 per bushel in the U.S. market. On the other hand, U.S. wheat priced at U.S. $3.57 per bushel will be CDN $4.90 per bushel in Canada at an exchange rate of CDN $1.40 per U.S. $1.00 and will be CDN $5.25 per bushel at an exchange rate of CDN $1.50 per U.S. $1.00. Since most transactions occur in terms of U.S. dollars in the world market, an appreciation of the U.S. dollar against the Canadian dollar makes grains worth more at the Canadian farm gate and encourages overall exports. There are numerous empirical studies that confirm this hypothesis (Coleman and Meilke 1988).

[11]The quality variables of concern to the millers in the United States have grown from basic visual grade specifications to include the following: vitreousness and protein (the quality of gluten); crop years used in blending; moisture content; mold and mildew; dockage/cleanliness; falling number, which is a measure of sprouting damage; sedimentation; mixograph tests; and colour. It should be noted that while the colour of bread wheat does not carry to the end product, the colour of durum wheat does, thereby determining the colour of the pasta end product. According to U.S. milling industry sources, mills are not willing to purchase on the basis of U.S. grade alone. The U.S. system of post-harvest grain handling and distribution permits the blending of different grades of grain; the Canadian grain-handling system does not. Millers purchasing grain from Canada will receive the average of a grade, with cleanliness and uniformity assured. The difference between the two sources has led to a perception that U.S. grain is of lower quality than is Canadian grain when comparing similar grades (USITC 1990).

[12]This requirement allowed the CWB to operate the "two-price wheat policy." The CWB has an explicit policy to sell to domestic millers at a price equal to or less than the landed price of equivalent U.S. grain. Interest groups in the United States argue that, as a result of CWB policy on wheat, imports into Canada from the United States have been limited to very small volumes and have been restricted at times when there has been a shortage of specific qualities of Canadian wheat.

[13]The use of end-use certificates (EUCs) on commodities applies only when Canada applies them to American products (Section 321(f) of the *NAFTA Implementation Act* 1993).

[14]Section 731 of the *Tariff Act* of 1930, as amended, provides that an AD duty shall be imposed, in addition to any other duty, if two conditions are met. First, the U. S. Department of Commerce (USDOC) must determine that "a class or kind of foreign merchandise is being, or is likely to be, sold in the United States at less than its fair value." Second, the USITC must determine that "an industry in the United States is materially injured, or is threatened with material injury, or the establishment of an industry in the United States is materially retarded, by reason of imports of that merchandise."

[15]Subtitle A of title VII of the *Tariff Act* of 1930, as added by the *Trade Agreements Act* of 1979 and amended by the *Trade and Tariff Act* of 1984, the *Omnibus Trade and Competitiveness Act* of 1988, and the *Uruguay Round Agreements Act* of 1994, provides that a CV duty shall be imposed, in addition to any other duty, equal to the amount of net CV subsidy if the following two conditions are met. First, the USDOC must determine that a CV subsidy is being provided, directly or indirectly, "with respect to the manufacture, production, or export of a class or kind of merchandise imported, or sold into the United States," and also must determine the amount of the net CV subsidy. Second, the USITC must determine that "an industry in the U.S. is materially injured, or is threatened with material injury, or the establishment of an industry in the United States is materially retarded by reason of imports of that merchandise or by reason of sales of that merchandise for importation" (U.S. House of Representatives 1997).

[16]Chapter 1 of Title II (Sections 201 through 204) of the *Trade Act* of 1974, as amended by Section 1401 of the *Omnibus Trade and Competitiveness Act* of 1988, provides for a so-called "escape clause" or "safeguard" mechanism for import relief. This mechanism, which has been amended over the years, has provided authority for the U.S. President to withdraw or modify concessions and impose duties or other restrictions for a limited period of time on imports of any article that causes or threatens serious injury to the domestic industry producing a like or directly competitive article, following an investigation and determination by the USITC. An escape clause (safeguard) provision modelled after language in the 1947 executive

order was included in Article XIX of the original General Agreement on Tariffs and Trade (GATT). As a result of the GATT Uruguay Round of Multilateral Trade Negotiations, which resulted in the agreement establishing the WTO, GATT 1994 has replaced GATT 1947. However, in a departure from GATT 1947, Article XIX, which authorized retaliation by members adversely affected by the measure when appropriate compensation was not forthcoming, the Uruguay Round Agreement (GATT 1994) provides that a member country may not exercise its right to take retaliatory action during the first 3 years that a safeguard measure is in effect, provided that the safeguard measure resulted from an absolute increase in imports and otherwise conforms to the Agreement (U.S. House of Representatives 1997).

[17]Chapter 1 of Title III (Sections 301 to 310) of the *Trade Act* of 1974, as amended, provides the authority and procedures to enforce U.S. rights under international trade agreements and to respond to certain unfair foreign practices. Section 301 was amended under title IX of the *Trade Agreements Act* of 1979 in two principle respects: (1) to include specific authority to enforce U.S. rights and to respond to actions   by foreign countries inconsistent with or otherwise denying U.S. benefits under trade agreements; and (2) to place specific time limits on the procedures for investigating and taking action on petitions. Further, modifications were made by the *Uruguay Round Agreements Act* to Sections 301 to 310 and 182 of the *Trade Act* of 1974 to confirm to the time limits under the WTO Understanding on Rules and Procedures Governing the Settlement of Disputes (dispute-settlement understanding) and to clarify and strengthen the scope and application of these domestic authorities (U.S. House of Representatives 1997).

[18]On November 15, 1989, the USITC received a letter from the Committee on Finance, U.S. Senate, containing an identical request.

[19]The U.S. General Accounting Office (USGAO) undertook an audit of CWB pricing practices. However, it is generally viewed in the United States that the USGAO was not able to complete the study mainly because the CWB refused to provide the information required for this USGAO investigation.

[20]Canadian exporters viewed these investigations as indirect probes of alleged dumping.

[21]The USITC received a letter from the President Clinton stating that he had been advised by the U.S. Secretary of Agriculture:

> ... that there is reason to believe that wheat, wheat flour, and semolina are being imported into the United States under such conditions and in such quantities as to render or tend to render ineffective, or materially interfere with, the price support payment and production adjustment program for wheat conducted by the U.S. Department of Agriculture. (USITC 1994)

[22]Material interference is defined by the USITC in past cases as "more than slight interference but less than major interference." When determining whether material interference is occurring or would occur, the USITC has examined factors such as: (1) the available supply of imports, including import levels, changes in import volumes, world production, and world stocks of the imported products; (2) pricing data, including the relationship between import prices, U.S. prices, and the support price; (3) information relating to domestic supply and demand; (4) data relating to the government programs, including Commodity Credit Corporation (CCC) outlays, CCC surpluses, and changes in the cost to the government of running a program. Three Commissioners (Rohr, Newquist, and Bragg) determined that the subject goods are imported into the United States under such conditions and in such quantities as to interfere materially with the price support programs conducted by the USDA for wheat. However, three other Commissioners (including Chairman Watson, Vice

Chairman Nuzum, and USITC Commissioner Crawford) determined that (1) wheat, wheat flour, and semolina are not being imported under such conditions and in such quantities as to render, or tend to render, ineffective the USDA wheat program; and that (2) the evidence of the recent impact of increased wheat imports could support the U.S. President finding either material interference or nonmaterial interference. When the vote by the six commissioners is tied, it is considered an affirmative determination.

[23]During the investigation, the USITC received four economic submissions from parties to the proceeding: (1) a study by Sumner, Alston, and Gray (SAG) on behalf of the CWB; (2) a study by the Law and Economic Consulting Group (LECG), U.S. Department of Agriculture (USDA); (3) a study by Abel, Draft and Earley on behalf of the Millers National Federation, the National Pasta Association; and (4) a study by the National Grain Trade Council. (The most detailed is the one submitted on behalf of the CWB by SAG.) The SAG submission presents a partial equilibrium simulation model of the world market consisting of the United States, Canada, and the "rest of the world." The SAG submission suggested that the Canadian wheat-export supply had very small effects on U.S. wheat prices and on U.S. wheat program costs. The USITC report indicates that the SAG analysis contained an extensive discussion of the parameters underlying a model of the effects of imports on a market. The common-ground comparison of the results of economic models presented by the SAG, USDA, and USITC empirical models indicate that a one percent rise in domestic supply (including imports) generated a 0.424 percent decline in domestic price. The USDA price response is a much larger, at -1.47 percent, while SAG response is far less, at -0.15 percent. The USITC report stated further "on the basis of this discussion, SAG parameters are chosen such that the effects of Canadian wheat on the U.S. market are small" (USITC 1994).

[24] The Agreement was effective only one crop year from September 12, 1994 to September 11, 1995 (Alston, Gray, and Sumner 1994).

[25] A chronology of the Canada/U.S. wheat-trade disputes and the CWB can be found in Schmitz and Furtan (2000: Chapter 7). However, their analysis does not discuss disputes beginning in 2000.

[26] In an April 19 press release the USTR stated that:

> ...the USTR decided not to impose a tariff rate quota (TRQ) at that time since such an action would violate our NAFTA and World Trade Organization (WTO) commitments, could result in Canadian retaliation against U.S. agriculture, and would not achieve a durable solution or a permanent change to the market distortions caused by the monopoly of the Canadian Wheat Board. (USTR 2002)

[27]In accordance with Section 733(d)(2) of the *Agricultural Adjustment Act* (AAA), the USDOC directed the U.S. Bureau of Customs and Border Protection (USBCBP) to continue to suspend liquidation of all imports of subject merchandise from Canada that are entered or withdrawn from warehouse for consumption on or after May 8, 2003, the date of publication of the Preliminary Determinations in the U.S. *Federal Register* (USDOC 2003a).

[28]Pursuant to section 705(c)(1)(B)(ii) of the AAA, the USDOC instructed the USBCBP to suspend liquidation of all entries of durum wheat and HRS wheat from Canada which were entered or withdrawn from warehouse, for consumption on or after March 10, 2003, the date of the publication of the Preliminary Determinations in the *Federal Register*. If the USITC determines that material injury, or threat of material injury, does not exist, these proceedings will be terminated and all estimated duties deposited

or securities posted due to the suspension of liquidation will be refunded or cancelled (USDOC 2003b).

[29]It should be noted that the decision was not unanimous. Chairman Okun and Commissioner Koplan dissenting. Commissioner Charlotte R. Lane not participating.

[30]19 U.S.C. § 1677(7)(A) (USDOC 2003c).

[31]19 U.S.C. § 1677(7)(C)(iii) (USDOC 2003c).

[32]19 U.S.C. § 1677(7)(C)(iii) (USDOC 2003c).

[33]The ROU is the result of negotiations in the fall of 1998 between the United States and Canada on a number of trade issues. Many of these issues fall into the category of technical barriers to trade for grains, livestock and meats, and horticultural products. (ROU 1999: Annexes 6–9).

REFERENCES

Abel, M.E. (1995). *A Comparison of the U.S. and Canadian Marketing Systems for Wheat and Barley: Transparency, Differential Pricing, and Monopolistic Behaviour.* Study prepared for the Canada/ U.S. Joint Commission on Grains, New Orleans (February 22–3).

Agriculture and Agri-Food Canada. (2003). Available at: www.agr.ca/cb/trade.

Agricultural Adjustment Act. (1933). Available at: http://www.access.gpo.gov/uscode/title7/chapter35_.html.

Alston, J.M., R. Gray, and D. Sumner. (1994). "The Wheat War of 1994." *Canadian Journal of Agricultural Economics* 42: 231–51.

Canada/U.S. Joint Commission on Grains. (1995). *Canada/U.S. Joint Commission Final Report.* Vol. 1-II. Washington, DC.

Canadian Grain Act. (1983). *Form 1 of Schedule XV.* Ottawa: Government of Canada.

Canada West Foundation. (1999). *Ten Years After: Cross-Border Export/Import Trends since the Canada-U.S. Free trade Agreement.* Calgary: University of Calgary Press.

Coleman and Mielke. (1988). "The Influence of Exchange Rates on the Red Meat Trade Between Canada and the United States." *Canadian Journal of Agricultural Economics* 36: 401–24.

Department of Foreign Affairs and International Trade. (1999). Available at: http://webapps.dfait-maeci.gc.ca/minpub/default.asp?language=E.

External Affairs and International Trade Canada. (1987). *The Canada-U.S. Free Trade Agreement.* Ottawa: External Affairs Canada.

_____. (1993). *NAFTA What's it all about?* Catalogue No. E-74-56/1993E. Ottawa: Government of Canada.

Featherstone, D. and I.H. Uhm. (2002). "Trade Disputes: The Antidumping and Countervailing Duty Laws and the Role of Quantitative Economic Analysis," in *Agricultural Trade under CUSTA* (300–22), edited by Won W. Koo and William W. Wilson. New York: Nova Science Publishers Inc.

FR (The Federal Register). (1994 to 2003). *Issues on antidumping cases by the Department of Commerce (USDOC), International Trade Administration, and the U.S. International Trade Commission (USITC).* National Archives and Records Administration, Office of the Federal Register. Available at: www.access.gpo.gov/su_docs/aces/aces140.html.

Furtan, W. H. (1995). *Transparency and Differential Pricing: An Analysis of Canadian and American Grain Handling Systems.* Study prepared for the Canada/U.S. Joint Commission on Grains, New Orleans (February 22–3).

GATT (General Agreement on Tariffs and Trade). (1947). Available at: http://www.ciesin.org/TG/PI/TRADE/gatt.html.

_____. (1994). Available at: http://www.ciesin.org/TG/PI/TRADE/gatt.html.

Gray, R. and B. Gardner. (1995). *The Impact of Canadian and U.S. Farm Policies on Grain Production and Trade*. Study prepared for the Canada/U.S. Joint Commission on Grains, New Orleans (February 22–23).

Ingco and Ng. (1998). *Distortionary Effects of State Trading in Agriculture: Issues for the Next Round of Multinational Negotiations*. Study prepared for The World Bank by the Development Research Group. Washington, DC: The World Bank.

International Grains Council. (1996 to 2002). *International Grain Statistics*. London: International Grain Council.

International Monetary Fund. (2001). *International Financial Statistics*. Available at: http://www.imf.org/.

Johnson, D. and W. Wilson. (1995). "Canadian Rail Subsidies and Continental Barley Flows: A Spatial Analysis." *Logistic and Transportation Review* 31: 31–46.

Kim, M., G. Cho, and W.W. Koo. (2002). *Does Exchange Rate Matter to Agricultural Bilateral Trade Between the United States and Canada?* Agribusiness and Applied Economics Report No. 466, Center for Agricultural Policy and Trade Studies, Department of Agribusiness and Applied Economics, North Dakota State University, Fargo.

Koo, W.W. (1998). *Bilateral Trade of Durum Wheat and Barley Under CUSTA and Implications for Farm Price and Income*. Agricultural Economics Report No. 385, Department of Agricultural Economics, North Dakota State University, Fargo.

Koo, W.W. and I.H. Uhm. (1984). "United States and Canadian Rail Freight-Rate Structures: A Comparative Analysis." *Canadian Journal of Agricultural Economics* 32: 301–26.

Lipsey, R.G., D. Schwanen, and R.J. Wonnacott. (1994). *The NAFTA: What's In? What's Out? What's Next?* Policy Study 21. Toronto: Howe Institute.

Mao, W., W.W. Koo, and M. Krause. (1996). *World Feed Barley Trade Under Alternative Trade Policy Scenarios*. Agricultural Economic Report No. 350, Department of Agricultural Economics, North Dakota State University, Fargo.

NAFTA (North American Free Trade Agreement). *Implementation Act*. (1993). Available at: http://nodis3.gsfc.nasa.gov/displayEO.cfm?id=EO_12889.

Omnibus Trade and Competitiveness Act. (1988). Available at: http://www.nibs.org/Metric/Omnibus.pdf.

ROU (Record of Understanding: Canada and the United States). (1999). Available at: http://www.fas.usda.gov/itp/canada/canadrou.pdf.

Schmitz, A. and H. Furtan. (2000). *The Canadian Wheat Board: Marketing in the New Millennium*. Regina: Canadian Plains Research Centre.

_____. (2003). "The Impact on Canada-U.S. Agricultural Trade of the 2002/03 U.S. Farm Bill." Paper presented at the North American Economic and Financial Integration Conference, Bloomington, Indiana (April 11–12).

Schmitz, T.G. and W.W. Koo. (1996). *An Economic Analysis of International Feed and Malting Barley Markets: An Econometric Spatial Oligopolistic Approach*. Agricultural Economics Report No. 357, Department of Agricultural Economics, North Dakota State University, Fargo.

Simonot. (1997). *The Economics of State Trading in Wheat*. Masters' Thesis, Department of Agricultural Economics, University of Saskatchewan, Saskatoon.

Trade Act. (1974). Available at: http://www.access.gpo.gov/uscode/title19/chapter12_.html.

Trade Agreements Act. (1979). Available at: http://www.access.gpo.gov/uscode/index.html.

Trade and Tariff Act. (1984). Available at: http://www.dbtrade.com/legal_sources/crs_summary_tt_1984.htm.

Uruguay Round Agreements Act. (1994). Available at:

http://www.uspto.gov/web/offices/com/doc/uruguay/.

USDA/FAS (U.S. Department of Agriculture/Foreign Agricultural Service). (1989 to 2002). Available at: http://www.fas.usda.gov/.

USDOC (U.S. Department of Commerce). (1996 to 2002). *Highlight of U.S. Exports and Imports*. Washington, DC.

_____. (2003a). "Notice of Preliminary Determinations of Sales at Less Than Fair Value: Certain Durum Wheat and Hard Red Spring Wheat from Canada," 67 *Federal Registrar* 24707 (May 8).

_____. (2003b). "Notice of Final Affirmative Countervailing Duty Determinations: Certain Durum Wheat and Hard Red Spring Wheat from Canada." 68 *Federal Register* 172 (September 5).

_____. (2003c). Available at: http://www.commerce.gov/.

U.S. House of Representatives (Committee on Ways and Means). (1997). *Overview and Compilation of U.S. Trade Statutes*. Washington, DC: U.S. Government Printing Office.

USITC (U.S. International Trade Commission). (1990). *Durum Wheat: Conditions of Competition Between the U.S. and Canadian Industries*. USITC Publication 2274, Washington, DC.

_____. (1994). *Wheat, Wheat Flour, and Semolina*. Investigation No. 22-54, Publication 2794, Washington, DC.

_____. (2003). *Durum and Hard Red Spring Wheat from Canada*. Investigation Nos. 701-TA-430A and 430B and 731-TA-1019A and 1019B (Final), Publication 3639, Washington DC.

U.S. Tariff Act. (1930). Available at:
http://www.access.gpo.gov/uscode/title19/chapter4_.html.

USTR (U.S. Trade Representatives). (1994 to 2002). Available at: http://www.ustr.gov/.

WGTA (Western Grain Transportation Act). (1983). Available at:
http://laws.justice.gc.ca/en/W-8/.

Chapter 13

Canada-U.S. Beef Dumping and Countervailing Disputes

Michael Wohlgenant and Andrew Schmitz

North Carolina State University
University of Florida

INTRODUCTION

In January 1999, the Rancher-Cattlemen Action Legal Foundation (R-CALF) filed a petition with the United States International Trade Commission (USITC) alleging that Canada was dumping live cattle onto the U.S. market. The USITC ruled that U.S. cattle producers might have been materially injured by the Canadian live-cattle imports. In June 1999, the U.S. Department of Commerce (USDOC) issued a preliminary ruling that a countervailing (CV) duty of 5.57 percent be placed on the value of live cattle imported from Canada. Subsequent to a public hearing in October 1999, the USITC announced its final determination on November 17, 1999 in a 5 to 1 opinion that live cattle from Canada were not causing, or threatening to cause, material injury to the U.S. cattle industry. Hence the antidumping (AD) duty on live-cattle imports from Canada was removed (R-CALF 2003).

In the late 1990s, R-CALF also filed a CV complaint against the Canadian cattle industry contending that Canadian cattle were being fed cheap barley by their producers because of the alleged inefficiencies in the marketing of barley by the Canadian Wheat Board (CWB). In response, the USDOC launched a CV duty investigation into the exports of live cattle from Canada. Like the AD case above, the United States ruled in Canada's favour in the CV duty case.

The purpose of this chapter is to review the economic basis for the U.S. governmental decisions in favour of Canada in both the dumping and CV cases and to evaluate the economic rationale for these decisions. Particular attention will focus on the relevant economic criteria for establishing material injury in the context of the Canada-U.S. cattle industry. This chapter also reviews the CV case presenting the economic arguments as to why there was no justification for the United States to impose CV duties on Canadian feed barley exported to the United States.

THE R-CALF DUMPING CASE

The U.S. International Trade Commission Decision

When determining whether material injury has occurred, the USITC must first define the domestic-like product and industry. Section 771(4)(A) of the *Tariff Act* of 1930 (USITC 2003) is used to define the relevant industry as "producers as a whole of a domestic-like product, or those producers whose collective output of a domestic-like product constitutes a major proportion of the total domestic production of the product." A domestic-like product is defined as "a product, which is like, or in the absence of like, most similar in characteristics and uses with, the article subject to an investigation…" (USITC 2003). After considerable deliberation on the live-cattle investigation, the USITC determined that there is a single product, live cattle, with three primary developmental stages that exist prior to slaughter: (1) calf stage, (2) stocker/yearling stage, and (3) feeder stage. The ultimate end-use of cattle is perceived to be beef, so cattle and beef are considered part of the same product. Likewise, the definition of domestic industry, as put forth by the USITC, includes cow-calf operators, stocker/yearling operators, and feedlot operators (USITC 1999).

The USITC is also required to consider the volume of imports, their effect on prices for the domestic-like product, and their effect on domestic producers of the domestic-like product when determining whether material injury has occurred. Material injury is defined as "harm that is not inconsequential, immaterial or unimportant" (USITC 2003). Based on the evaluation of these factors, in 1999 the USITC, determined that the domestic industry producing live cattle was neither materially injured nor was it threatened with material injury as a result of imports from Canada (USITC 1999).

The USITC placed particular emphasis on conditions of competitiveness, volume of imports, and price effects of imports when arriving at their determination. The USITC found that when the dumping allegedly occurred, the U.S. "cattle cycle" competitively was near the end of its liquidation phase and that the cattle cycle was neither different nor worse than were previous cattle cycles. The USITC also determined that U.S. cow-calf operations are the least concentrated with some 800,000 family-owned operations. Based on this consideration and the fact that cattle prices are determined in a national market, the USITC decided that cattle producers are price takers. In addition, due to the close geographic proximity and relatively open borders between the United States and Canada, the USITC determined cattle and beef markets in the two countries as highly integrated. Finally, the beef market itself is subject to competitiveness. There is competition between different cuts and grades of beef, between these cuts and manufactured grades of beef (e.g., ground beef), and between beef and other meats and foods (USITC 1999).

The most important consideration to the USITC was that live-cattle imports from Canada were a small and a decreasing share of the U.S. cattle market over the period of investigation. The market share by weight of cattle in Canada was 4.2 percent in 1996, 3.8 percent in 1997, and 3.7 percent in 1998. The market share by number of head in Canada was 3.8 percent in 1996, 3.5 percent in 1997, and 3.4 percent in 1998, and decreased further to 2.8 percent in 1999. A major reason that the U.S. import share declined over time was because of the expansion of slaughter capacity in Canada between 1996 and 1999 that increased by 25 percent.[1]

Nearly 80 percent of the U.S. imports entered secondary markets (Washington, Utah, Pennsylvania) rather than entering the primary feeder-belt states of Texas, Kansas, Nebraska, Colorado, and Iowa. The USITC determined that the changing geographic distribution of U.S. beef imports diminished rather than enhanced the economic impact of imports.

When considering the price effects of Canadian beef exports to the United States, the USITC is required to determine if there has been significant price underselling of the imported merchandise compared to the price of domestic-like products of the United States, and if the effects of imports of such merchandise otherwise depress prices significantly or prevent price increases that otherwise would have occurred. The USITC determined that live-cattle imports from Canada had not affected U.S. cattle prices to a significant degree and that price underselling in Canada, while present, was not significant but could be explained by factors related to differences in availability, quality, yield, and grade of beef (USITC 1999).

In summary, the USITC did not find that the U.S. cattle industry was materially injured by Canadian live-cattle imports under the period of their investigation, from 1996 to 1999. Live-cattle imports from Canada had a significant price effect on the U.S. cattle industry. As noted in the conclusion by the USITC, the U.S. cattle industry experienced weak performance and financial stress over that time period, but its condition was not materially affected by live-cattle imports. U.S. import volumes of live cattle from Canada were small and declining.

Economic Modelling of the Impact of Live-Cattle Imports

Wohlgenant (1989) was retained by respondents in the live-cattle dispute discussed above, to conduct an independent analysis of the effect of Canadian imports on the U.S. domestic-cattle market. This section of our chapter presents the findings from Wohlgenant's analysis.

As a share of the U.S. cattle market, Canadian imports ranged from 3 percent to 4 percent of total U.S. beef consumption during the 1996 to 1999 period of the investigation by the USITC. This small import share coupled with significant price responsiveness in demand for live cattle are the main reasons why it is reasonable to believe that increased Canadian imports could not have had a significant effect on the price of U.S.-produced cattle at that time.

Real inflation-adjusted prices of cattle in both Canada and the United States declined from 1996 to 1998. There are a number of factors contributing to this decline in prices, including lower feed costs, lower pork and poultry prices, a depressed export market for beef due to the Asian financial crisis, and increased supplies of both Canadian and U.S. cattle marketed due to the liquidation phase of their cattle cycles.

It is necessary to quantify how much imports would have increased in response to the alleged dumping margin of 5.57 percent posited by the USDOC in their preliminary ruling. The following calculation takes into account how price-responsive U.S. consumers are to a change in the price of cattle, how substitutable Canadian imports are for U.S.-produced cattle, and how price responsive cattle producers are to changes in prices.

A widely accepted approach to the estimation of the effect of shock, such as the increase in supply of Canadian cattle imports to a market, is the supply-demand framework in which prices and quantities of imported and domestically produced cattle are determined by the intersection of supply and demand for cattle. Because Canada is a surplus producer of cattle, it exports the difference between what is produced and what is consumed in Canada. This amount exported obviously represents imports to someone else, so we can view this quantity as the amount demanded by the United States for Canadian live cattle. This amount exported is indicated by the quantity Q_m in Figure 13.1a where the supply curve S_m intersects the demand curve D_m.

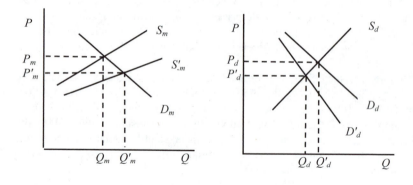

(a) U.S. Market for Canadian Cattle   (b) Domestic U.S. Market for Cattle

Figure 13.1: Markets for Canadian and U.S. Cattle
Source: Authors' calculations.

Suppose that the supply of cattle imports to the United States from Canada increases either because of an increase in the Canadian production of cattle, a decrease in the Canadian demand for cattle, or because of alleged dumping. This effect is shown by a shift downward in the Canadian supply of cattle to the United States from S_m to S'_m. As a result of this increase in supply of cattle from Canada, the new quantity of imports becomes Q'_m. The increase in imports resulting from the supply increase is $Q'_m - Q_m$. As this diagram illustrates, the effect of this increase in supply of imports to the United States also causes the price paid for imported cattle to decline from P_m to P'_m. How this change in imports is transmitted to the market for U.S.-produced cattle is explained with the aid of Figure 13.1b.

Because processors are able to buy Canadian cattle at a lower price, they will purchase more Canadian cattle and fewer U.S. cattle, which will cause the demand for U.S. cattle to decline from D_d to D'_d (Figure 13.1b). Given the supply curve S_d for U.S.-produced cattle, the price of U.S. cattle must fall from P_d to P'_d to remain competitive with Canadian cattle.

The model outlined above is different than models that are based on the assumption of homogeneous goods. In the homogeneous-goods model, there is a single price for both imported and domestic products. In the case of live cattle, it is important to model the two products as if each is distinct. This is because cattle coming from Canada could have a higher proportion ready for slaughter (which was the case over the period of investigation), and because of differences in breeding and feeding that cause differences in the quality of cattle slaughtered. Both the U.S. and Canadian cattle industries are characterized by considerable heterogeneity of breeds. In fact, even the same producer may have many different breeds as well as mixed breeds represented in the same herd.

The model used to quantify the impact of imports on the U.S. cattle market consists of demand and supply equations for Canadian imports as well as for U.S.-produced cattle. Demand for cattle from Canada and the United States is not assumed to be perfectly substitutable for the reasons indicated above, but the degree of substitutability is accounted for in an Armington-type model, similar to the COMPAS model of the USITC (Chapter 13 Appendix).

The key parameters of the model are:

- the share of imports in total domestic consumption S_m;
- the elasticity of substitution between Canadian live cattle and U.S produced cattle σ;
- the price elasticity of derived demand for cattle η;
- the price elasticity of supply of U.S. produced beef ε_d; and
- the price elasticity of supply of Canadian imports ε_m.

For all simulations, the import share is assumed to be 0.04. Using quantity and unit import values from the U.S. Department of Agriculture (USDA) and USDOC data from 1989 to 1998, the elasticity of substitution estimated using the Armington (1969) model is 2. Based on two widely cited studies by Wohlgenant (1989) and Marsh (1992), η is assumed to equal –0.7. The U.S. supply elasticity is assumed to be 0.1 (Marsh 1994). Finally, assuming similar demand and supply elasticities for Canada as in the United States and assuming 40 percent of Canada's supply is exported to the United States, the excess supply elasticity (supply elasticity of imports) is estimated to be 1.3.

With these parameter values, the effect of a 5.57 percent dumping margin is found to increase the supply of imports by 7.2 percent (5.57 x 1.3). This causes the quantity of imports to increase by 4.3 percent and the price of imports to decrease by 2.3 percent. As processors substitute away from U.S. cattle to Canadian cattle, demand for U.S. cattle falls by about 0.1 percent (the cross-price elasticity of demand for U.S. cattle with respect to import is 0.05, therefore 2.3 x 0.05 = .1). With this decrease in demand, the price of U.S.-produced cattle then falls by a mere .14 percent. Notice that the percentage decline in the U.S price is less than the percentage decline in the Canadian price. While a lower Canadian price could give the appearance of underselling through dumping, such an effect is consistent with less-than-perfect substitutability between Canadian and U.S. cattle.

The results in Table 13.1 show various effects on U.S. cattle prices when parameter values are changed. The range of values considered provides upper and lower bounds to the estimated price effects. Even in the extreme case in which we assume Canadian- and U.S.-produced cattle are highly substitutable $\sigma = 5$ and the price elasticity of demand for all cattle is –0.4, the price decline is still only 0.28 percent. Overall, we expect the price effects to be very modest because of the small import share. Because a small import share translates into a minimal increase in total U.S. cattle supply, the effect on cattle price must be miniscule so long as there is even a moderate degree of price responsiveness of U.S. consumers to changes in cattle prices. Therefore, few Canadian imports could not have had a substantial material impact on the U.S. cattle market.

Table 13.1: Changes in Canadian Live Cattle Imports on the U.S. Cattle Market

Percent Change in U.S. Cattle Prices	Elasticity of Substitution	Elasticity of Derived Demand	Elasticity of U.S. Supply
–0.14	2	–0.7	0.1
–0.21	2	–0.4	0.1
–0.24	5	–0.7	0.1
–0.28	5	–0.4	0.1
–0.22	5	–0.7	0
–0.26	5	–0.4	0

Source: Wohlgenant (1989) calculations.

The foregoing analysis actually overstates the effect of imports on the over-all U.S. beef market. In particular, the market change depicted in Figure 13.1 assumes that there has been a net increase in cattle production. If in fact the increases in live-cattle imports are exactly offset by a reduction in beef exports to the United States, the price effect will be even smaller. If this is the case, and assuming the baseline parameter values (Figure 13.1a), cattle supplied to the Canadian market will decline by 4.8 percent. This 4.8 percent reduction in supply would lead to a 3.3 percent price increase in the Canadian market. Assuming an elasticity of price transmission between the farm and retail price of 0.5, the Canadian beef price will increase by 1.65 percent. If the cross-elasticity of demand for U.S. beef with respect to Canadian beef is 0.05 (i.e., the same value estimated for the cross-elasticity between U.S. live cattle and Canadian live cattle), demand for U.S. beef will increase 0.08 percent. If the demand for cattle increases by the same percentage (which would occur if the processing sector exhibited constant returns to scale), the price effect will be 0.07 percent.

Subtracting this from the price effect of –0.14 suggests that, in this instance, the net price effect of increased imports will be only –0.07. Therefore, the net price effect of increasing live-cattle imports from Canada will be considerably smaller if supplies from Canada are simply diverted away from their domestic market to the U.S. market.

THE R-CALF COUNTERVAILING DUTY CASE

Live beef-cattle exports to the United States from Canada rose sharply between 1989 and 1998 (Figure 13.2). The R-CALF arguments concerned the matter of the control of barley exports by the CWB and the influence of the CWB on the prices of feed barley in Western Canada. Because of the CWB, R-CALF contended that barley prices from 1989 to 2001 were lower than would have been the case in a free market.

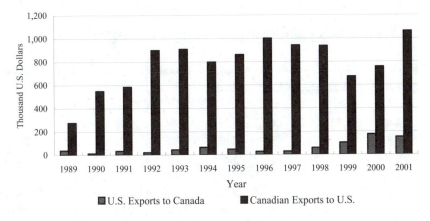

Figure 13.2: Live Beef Exports: United States and Canada
Source: USDA/ERS (2003).

Gray, Schmitz, and Brewin (1999), however, analyze feed-barley prices during the April 1, 1997 to July 31, 1998 period[2] and find neither theoretical nor empirical evidence that the CWB acted, directly or indirectly, in such a manner as to depress the price of Western Canadian feed barley. As a result, the CWB does not provide cheap barley to the Prairie beef industry and therefore it does not give the CWB an advantage over its U.S. counterpart. To the contrary, Gray, Schmitz, and Brewin (1999) find that: (1) prices in Western Canada are very close to prices at a comparable location in the United States, averaging slightly higher in Canada; (2) any action to reduce the domestic price of feed barley is directly contrary to the objective of the CWB for maximizing the pool return for producers; (3) the CWB has some ability to extract a limited premium for feed barley at the port position, and the export basis[3] for CWB grains is less than the export basis for non-CWB grains in Canada; (4) the export basis for West Coast shipments is very comparable to those found just across the border in the United

States; and (5) the CWB inefficiencies alleged by Carter and Loyns (1996) could not be substantiated.

The Western Canadian Feed-Barley Market

During the 1987/88 to 1996/97 periods, 67 percent of Canadian barley production was used domestically, mainly as feed, of which the CWB marketed less than 5 percent. For the remaining 33 percent of barley produced, the CWB sold 6 percent to domestic maltsters, 7 percent to foreign maltsters, and exported 21 percent as feed barley (Table 13.2).[4]

Given the size and structure of the world barley market, the CWB is largely a price taker in this market. Under these conditions, the CWB must offer prices to buyers that are competitive with those offered by firms that export feed barley from the United States. The CWB pooled return should reflect closely the average U.S. grain export prices that exist during the period when CWB sales

Table 13.2: Barley Supplies and Disposition by Crop Year, 1987/88 to 1997/98

| Year | Production | Imports | Domestic Use[a] | | Exports[a] | | Ending Stocks |
			Feed[b] and Seed	Malting Barley	Malt Barley	Feed Barley	
			Thousand Metric Tons				
1987/88	13,916	1	8,282	591	498	4,096	3,794
1988/89	10,326	1	8,027	588	325	2,515	2,790
1989/90	11,784	0	7,811	640	448	4,049	2,056
1990/91	13,441	1	7,662	649	638	3,898	2,646
1991/92	11,617	2	7,584	720	936	2,405	2,614
1992/93	11,032	3	6,941	730	333	2,371	3,266
1993/94	12,972	8	8,275	748	862	2974	3,376
1994/95	11,692	8	9,409	826	1,388	1,622	1,820
1995/96	13,033	10	9,848	922	1,426	910	1,740
1996/97	15,562	19	10,000	938	1,392	2,047	2,919
1997/98	13,527	28	10,905	966	1,276	851	2,457
Average[c]	12,538	5	8,384	735	825	2,689	2,702

[a] 1997/98 Domestic Feed and Seed and Malting use. Malting Exports estimated using the CWB annual report (Designated Barley Pool) (CWB 2003).
[b] Feed refers to feed, waste, and dockage.
[c] This is a ten year average.
Source: Schmitz and Furtan (2000).

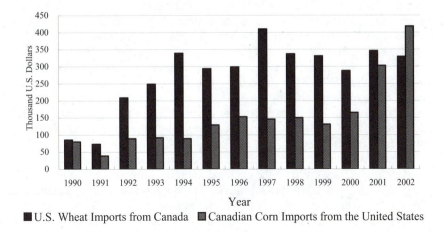

Figure 13.3: Corn and Wheat Trade: United States and Canada, 1990 to 2002
Source: Industry Canada (2002).

are made. The ability of the CWB to provide producers a return that is higher than the average competitive U.S. export price depends on such factors as the ability of the CWB marketing department to select the premium times and locations to sell barley.

Barley competes with corn on the basis of feed value. Corn has less protein but has more digestible energy than does barley. As such, the relative prices of corn and barley can fluctuate with the availability of alternative protein sources. For some customers, barley is preferred to corn. Canada imports sizeable amounts of corn from the United States (Figure 13.3), of which a large portion is used in conjunction with barley as cattle feed. In 2002, U.S. corn exports to Canada exceeded U.S. wheat imports from Canada.

After the 1994/95 crop year, Canadian feed-barley exports dropped because of the removal of the grain transportation subsidy, also called the Crow Rate or the freight-rate subsidy. For example, grain transportation rates increased by CDN $14.20 per metric ton at Lethbridge, Alberta between the 1994/95 and 1997/98 crop years. In effect, this removal of the freight-rate subsidy eliminated an indirect tax from the Canadian livestock industry.

The removal of the Export Enhancement Program (EEP) in the United States also had a major impact on feed-grain prices in the United States and Canada.[5] During the 1985/86 to 1995/96 period, EEP had a tendency to increase U.S. prices while it depressed world prices for Canadian exports.

The CWB and Feed-Barley Prices

Most feed barley is not sold through the CWB. However, those grain producers who do sell their barley through the CWB tender contracts with the CWB for the sale of their feed barley four times during the crop year. At the time of delivery to local elevators, producers receive an initial payment for their crop, the pool-return outlook (PRO) price. Once in storage, the grain companies receive instructions from the CWB to either ship the grain to a port position or to some other location, and the CWB has the responsibility to sell the grain to domestic or to foreign buyers. Revenue from the sale of grain in each crop year is then pooled by the CWB. After deducting all marketing costs and the initial payments made to producers, any remaining revenue is distributed to grain producers in the form of a final payment that is based on the tonnage each producer delivered to the CWB. This process is referred to by the CWB as the estimated pool return (EPR).[6]

The Canadian open-market prices of feed barley are linked to international markets through the CWB. If the open-market price is lower than the producers' EPR derived from CWB pricing signals, producers will tend to contract to deliver their grain to the CWB; if the producers' EPR is less than the open-market price, producers deliver to the open market. The result is that the open-market feed-barley prices will normally track closely the producers' EPR, with the latter acting more or less as a floor to the open-market prices.

When domestic-barley supplies are tight, open-market prices can rise above the producers' EPR. In this situation, domestic livestock producers pay higher prices that often lead to increased imports of corn or barley from the United States (Schmitz et al. 1997; Carter 1999).

Feed-Barley-Price Comparisons

The purchase prices of feed barley in Great Falls, Montana and Lethbridge, Alberta have often been compared. Great Falls is a significant barley-producing area and is located on the Burlington Northern Railway in Northwest Montana. Lethbridge is located approximately 250 miles northwest of Great Falls and is the heart of the beef-feeding industry of Alberta. Given the proximity of Great Falls to Lethbridge, weekly prices for feed barley under a competitive market should be similar.

The prices commercial feed mills paid for feed barley at Great Falls, Montana and Lethbridge, Alberta are given in Table 13.3. Before the review period (July 1996 to March 1997), feed-barley prices in Great Falls exceeded those in Lethbridge by an average of CDN $9.91 per metric ton. During the April to mid-October 1997 portion of the review period, the Great Falls feed-barley prices were much closer to the Lethbridge prices and averaged CDN $5.00 per metric ton above the Lethbridge prices. This situation reversed for the remainder of the review period. From mid-October 1997 until July 1998, the Lethbridge feed-barley price was higher than that in Great Falls by an average of CDN $7.24 per metric ton. For the review period, a simple average of the weekly prices revealed that Lethbridge averaged CDN $2.43 per metric ton higher in their feed-barley prices than did Great Falls.

Lethbridge is specified as the delivery location for the Winnipeg Commodity Exchange for feed barley. Following the review period, Lethbridge feed-grain prices continued to exceed the Great Fall prices to the extent that U.S. feed barley moved into the Lethbridge region from the United States. For the July

Table 13.3: Feed-Barley Prices in Great Falls, Montana and Lethbridge, Alberta: Selected Months, 1996 through 1999

	Before Review	During Review	After Review	Whole Period
	7/96 to 3/ 97	4/97 to 7/98	9/98 to 12/98	7/96 to 12/99
	Canadian Dollars per Metric Ton			
Avg. Price Great Falls, MT	152.28	130.58	98.2	131.91
Avg. Price Lethbridge, AB	142.37	133.01	116.02	133.09
Avg. Lethbridge, AB Premium	−9.91	2.43	17.82	1.18

Source: Alberta Agriculture (1999).

1996 to December 1999 period, the Lethbridge feed-grain prices averaged a premium of CDN $1.18 per metric ton over those at Great Falls. The simple correlation coefficient between the weekly prices in Lethbridge and Great Falls over the July 1996 to December 1999 period was 0.9. Thus markets on different sides of the border move together very closely. Hence even though the Lethbridge market is a feed-barley-deficit market area, and Great Falls is a feed-barley-surplus area, evidence shows synchronous movement even as local supply and demand conditions change, which indicates a feature of normal market behaviour across spatial market points.

Despite the differences in the Canadian and U.S. grain-pricing and grain-handling systems, the price series' closely track one another. This price similarity is consistent with the notion that the reduction in government involvement, the *Western Grain Transportation Act* (WGTA) in Canada and EEP in the United States, has resulted in the convergence of the feed-barley markets of the two countries.

Does the CWB Act in the Interest of Grain Producers?

The objective of the CWB to maximize producer returns is directly contrary to the notion that the CWB is creating cheap feed barley for livestock producers. This stated objective of the CWB has not gone unchallenged. Carter (1999), and Carter, Loyns, and Berwald (1998) develop a theory arguing that the CWB was inefficient. They argue that the CWB fits a stylized Niskanen model of the bureaucratic decision-making process in which the CWB supplies excess marketing services to farmers. With this hypothetical type of behaviour, the CWB could maximize the marketing margins on CWB grains for the benefit of the CWB to the detriment of its producers and producer prices.

Evidence runs contrary to this hypothesis (Schmitz and Furtan 2000). Prior to and during the 1996 to 1999 period, the CWB was under a great deal of public scrutiny. Taking any actions that were not in the interest of producers would have been very short sighted by the CWB. Second, Schmitz and Gray (2000) and Schmitz and Furtan (2000) challenged the added costs attributed to the CWB (Table 13.4) by Carter, Loyns and Berwald (1998).

Both sides of the debate over the operations of the CWB were eventually presented in the Federal Court of Canada. In June 1994, Archibald and several

Table 13.4: Added Costs from the CWB as Estimated by Carter and Loyns, 1996

Cost Item	Barley
	CDN $ per mt
CWB Administration	1.75
Protein and Grade Giveaway	0.00
Delays in Varietal Development	4.00
Excess Malting Barley & Maltster Free Storage	5.50
Excessive Handling Charges	4.00
Overages, Demurrage, Extra Freight and Port Congestion	3.10
Excess Cleaning	2.80
Production Inefficiency	4.00
Delays in CWB Payments	3.35
Taxpayer Costs	9.00
Total Added Costs	37.50

Source: Carter and Loyns (1996).

other farmers, along with the Alberta Barley Commission and the Western Barley Growers, sued the CWB, arguing that the CWB Act "breaches the rights" of the individual plaintiffs under the Canadian Charter of Rights and Freedoms (*Archibald et al. v. HMQ and the Canadian Wheat Board* 1997). The economic arguments presented at the trial in the Fall of 1996 held in Calgary, Alberta, centered on the effectiveness of the CWB as a marketing institution. Carter, Loyns, and others presented evidence that the actions of the CWB resulted in excessive marketing costs and thereby reduced the returns to producers. On the contrary, Schmitz, Furtan, and others presented evidence that the CWB was acting in the general interest of producers and were able to increase the returns to their producers through CWB monopoly-export powers. Judge Muldoon ruled in favor of the CWB, noting that the price-pooling system of the CWB and its monopoly over grain exports are part of the Canadian federal government's economic policy. The Federal Court held that the advantages of the CWB risk-pooling policy, arising from the timing of sales and relieving the farmer of marketing responsibilities, would be lost if the CWB were to lose their monopoly power.

Given the linkage between EPRs and the domestic feed-barley market, it would be contrary to the objectives of the CWB to intentionally lower the price of feed barley by lowering its EPRs. Three studies, Carter (1993), Schmitz, Gray, and Ulrich (1993), and Schmitz et al. (1997) examine systematically the influence of the CWB on the export price of feed barley from Western Canada. Carter (1993) and Schmitz, Gray, and Ulrich (1993) examine the hypothetical consequences of the creation of a "Continental Barley Market" (CBM) whereby the CWB would lose its control over exports, and in particular its ability to export barley to premium world markets. Both studies find that, under the hypothetical CBM, barley exports from Canada to the United States increase. In addition, the domestic price of feed barley falls modestly as exports are re-oriented away from premium external markets. Specifically, Carter estimates that Canadian feed-barley exports to the United States would increase by 400,000 metric tons and domestic prices would fall marginally. Schmitz, Gray, and Ulrich (1993) reveal that an increase in feed-barley exports to the United States will result in a net drop in prices of CDN $2 per metric ton in Canada. Both studies recognize that feed barley must compete in the U.S. market against a very large feed-grain market dominated by corn.

The Schmitz et al. (1997) study compares the CWB marketing system to that of a multiple-seller marketing system using CWB sales and pricing data for barley for the 1985/86 through 1994/95 periods. The model consists of nine market segments including the Japanese feed market and the U.S. 2-row malting-barley market. The impact of the CWB as opposed to a multiple-seller marketing situation is calculated for each year from 1985/86 through 1994/95. Overall, the returns from CWB single-desk selling are found to be significantly greater than if multiple sellers replaced the CWB. The highest priced premiums, however, were earned on malting barley rather than on feed barley. The estimated price premiums for feed barley ranged from a high of CDN $11.36 per metric ton in 1987/88 to a loss of CDN $6.62 per metric ton in 1994/95. The average price premium for the 11 crop years was a modest CDN $3.52 (Schmitz et al. 1997). The positive average premiums revealed by Schmitz, Gray, and Ulrich (1993) and Schmitz et al. (1997) are consistent with the objective of maximizing pool returns. They also imply that the activity of the CWB raises feed-barley prices in Western Canada.

In order to assess the impact of the CWB on Canadian barley producers, these studies had to create a competitive benchmark to facilitate the comparison between the CWB pool returns and the prices that would have prevailed in a multi-seller market. Direct export-price comparisons were not possible given the lack of data on the price at which each metric ton of exports is sold in either the United States or Canada. Furthermore, for much of the last decade, EEP provided a large export subsidy to U.S. export prices making a direct comparison of sales performance between the United States and Canada impossible, which also rendered invalid many of the price comparisons of the performance of the CWB that were used in the analysis cited in Carter (1999).

Performance of the Grain-Handling, Transportation, and Marketing Systems

The net impact of the CWB actions for a producer's pool return is the impact of the CWB on the port selling price minus the impact of the CWB on the export basis. The export basis is defined as all of the transportation, handling, and storage charges involved in getting the grain from the farm gate to the export position. This relationship is well understood and has been pointed out in Carter (1999), Schmitz, Gray, and Ulrich (1993), Schmitz et al. (1997), and Fulton et al. (1998).

Kraft, Furtan, and Tyrchniewicz (1996) compare directly the export-basis charges between non-CWB and CWB grains. Total-export basis charges for CWB grains are significantly lower than they are for non-CWB grains. Canola and flax are non-CWB grains and are predominantly export-oriented crops that use the same handling and transportation facilities, as does wheat. Kraft, Furtan, and Tyrchniewicz (1996) find that the grain-company costs for risk management were CDN $17.00 per metric ton for canola as opposed to CDN $3.85 per metric ton for wheat (the cost would be even lower for barley). This lower cost of risk management in wheat was attributable to fixed initial port prices within the CWB pooling system. The difference between the average port selling price and the producer price on the Prairies was lower for CWB grains than it was for non-CWB grains.

Parsons and Wilson (1999) and Carter and Loyns (1996) argue that the operations of the CWB have caused inefficiencies in the Canadian grain-handling and transportation system. The Parsons and Wilson (1999) study focuses primarily on elevation and the handling of tariffs, and contends that the deregulation of the U.S. grain-handling and transportation system has led to lower basis charges in the United States. Their analysis of basis, however, ignores the much higher rail-freight costs faced by producers in Montana and North Dakota.[7] For instance, the rail-freight rate for a 52-car spot in 1998 was about CDN 5 cents per metric ton per mile in the United States, while Canadian rail-freight rates were less than CDN 3 cents per metric ton per mile (Eley et al., 1996). This pattern of high rail rates and lower elevation charges is consistent with the Fulton et al. (1998) simulation of deregulation within the Canadian system. Carter and Loyns (1996) allege that the CWB system is highly inefficient, which costs Prairie farmers millions of dollars. Specific to barley, they estimate that the additional costs attributed to CWB marketing were approximately CDN $37 per metric ton in 1996 (Table 13.4).

There are three very important oversights in the analysis presented by Carter and Loyns (1996). First, many of the costs (Table 13.4), even if they were excessive, are not the responsibility of nor do they fall within the jurisdiction of the CWB to change. Attributing these costs to the CWB therefore is not plausible. For example, there is no basis for the excess handling charges of CDN $4.00 per metric ton alleged by Carter and Loyns (1996) because handling charges for elevator companies are established by the companies themselves and are not set by the CWB. The cost of CDN $2.80 per metric ton for excess cleaning is required by the Canadian Grain Commission (CGC) to meet export standards. The required grain-cleaning costs of non-CWB grains are even higher than they are for CWB grains. Thus attributing these and other costs to the CWB is simply not appropriate. Second, some of the costs in Table 13.4 tend to increase rather than to decrease the price of feed barley paid by the cattle industry and, therefore, should not be included in this analysis. For example, an additional cost of CDN $4.00 per metric ton for feed barley is attributed to the CWB for delays in varietal development. However, Agriculture and Agri-Food Canada (AAFC), not the CWB, is responsible for the registration of new grain varieties. More importantly, even if these delays could be attributed to the CWB, as alleged by Carter and Loyns (1996), their effect has been to reduce feed-barley production. If this is the case, the CWB actions will serve to raise the price of feed barley to the cattle industry and therefore should not be considered as part of a subsidy, rather it should be considered as part of a tax placed on the livestock industry. Similarly, the CDN $9.00 per metric ton taxpayer cost to cover occasional barley-pool deficits raises the estimated pool return of the CWB, hence it raises feed-barley prices.

Many of the costs listed above are part of the costs of marketing grain in any system, therefore they cannot be attributed as additional costs due to the

CWB. For instance, non-CWB grains in Canada are charged at least the same primary and terminal elevator handling tariffs as are CWB wheat and barley. As an example, primary elevator tariffs reported by the CGC for the Alberta Wheat Pool in 1995/96 were CDN \$9.09 per metric ton for wheat compared to CDN \$11.80 per metric ton for canola. Overages, demurrage, extra freight, and port congestion also occur in the non-CWB grain-marketing system and therefore cannot be attributed solely to the CWB.

CONCLUSIONS

Our empirical analysis on the U.S. dumping case against Canada shows that the impact of the expansion of live-beef exports from Canada to the United States is small. This was demonstrated under several different model assumptions. As a result, there was little or no material injury to the U.S. cattle producers. Therefore, there is no justification under U.S. trade law for the imposition of dumping duties on Canadian barley that is sold in the United States.

In the U.S. countervail complaint against Canada, our major finding is that the CWB did not act in such a manner as to reduce feed-barley prices in Western Canada. Therefore, cattle feeders on the Prairies are not subsidized through grain-input use.

In the final determination, multinationals played a role in both the dumping and countervail cases. Iowa Beef Packers operates both a packing plant and a feedlot in Brooks, Alberta. Cargill, Inc. has a world-scale packing plant in High River, Alberta. It is in the best interests of the multinational companies to keep the borders open. Hence their extremely active defence of an open-border policy in the above border disputes is well documented.

APPENDIX

The Impact of Live-Cattle Imports on the U.S. Cattle Market

The markets for live cattle in Canada and the United States can be described by four equations that depict the demand and supply of live cattle in each market. Because we are interested only in the impact of a shift in supply of imports on the U.S. cattle market, we can characterize the markets by a set of relationships expressed in comparative static form as percentage changes in quantities and prices from the given percentage shift in import supply. The basic equations used to compute the changes in prices and quantities are

$$EQ_m = \eta_{mm}EP_m + \eta_{md}EP_d, \tag{A13.1}$$
(Import demand for Canadian cattle)
$$EQ_m = \varepsilon_m(EP_m + EDM), \tag{A13.2}$$
(Import supply of Canadian cattle)

$$EQ_d = \eta_{dm}EP_m + \eta_{dd}EP_d, \text{ and} \qquad\qquad\qquad\qquad (A13.3)$$
(U.S. domestic demand for U.S. cattle)

$$EQ_d = \varepsilon_d EP_d, \qquad\qquad\qquad\qquad\qquad\qquad\qquad (A13.4)$$
(U.S. domestic supply of U.S. cattle)

in which E denotes the percentage change from the baseline value; P is price; Q is quantity; m is U.S. imports; and d is the domestic U.S. market. The variable EDM is the percentage margin of 5.57 percent. The own-price and cross-price elasticities of demand for imports and U.S. cattle are

$$\eta_{mm} = -(\sigma s_d - \eta s_m), \qquad\qquad\qquad\qquad\qquad (A13.5)$$

$$\eta_{md} = (\sigma + \eta)s_d, \qquad\qquad\qquad\qquad\qquad\qquad (A13.6)$$

$$\eta_{dm} = (\sigma + \eta)s_m, \text{ and} \qquad\qquad\qquad\qquad\qquad (A13.7)$$

$$\eta_{dd} = -(\sigma s_m - \eta s_d). \qquad\qquad\qquad\qquad\qquad (A13.8)$$

where, as indicated in the text, σ is the elasticity of substitution between imports and U.S. cattle and η is the price elasticity of derived demand for all cattle bought in the United States. The import and domestic shares of total production are s_m and s_d, respectively.

The price elasticity of import supply is calculated as the excess supply elasticity according to the formula

$$\varepsilon_m = (1/.4)\varepsilon_c - [(1 - .4)/.4]\eta_c, \qquad\qquad\qquad\qquad (A13.9)$$

where .4 is the share of Canada's supply that goes to the United States as live cattle exports, ε_c is the Canadian domestic supply elasticity that is assumed to be the same as the United States, and η_c is the price elasticity of demand for live cattle in Canada that is assumed to be the same as the United States.

Given values for the various parameters, Equation (A13.1) through Equation (A13.9) were solved numerically for changes in the prices and quantities in the import and domestic market. The following parameter values were assigned to the parameters

- the import share s_m is assumed to be equal to .04 throughout, which implies the domestic share of production s_d is equal to 0.96;
- the elasticity of substitution σ is assumed to equal either 2 or 5. The value of 2 is estimated using import quantities, domestic cattle shipments, and unit values for imports and domestic shipments over the 1989 to 1998 time period;
- the price elasticity of demand for live cattle in the U.S. η is assumed to be either –0.7 or –0.4; the upper bound of –0.7 is

a simple average of –0.65 estimated by Marsh (1992) and –0.76 estimated by Wohlgenant (1989);

- the U.S. domestic supply elasticity of live cattle ε_d is either 0 or 0.1; Marsh (1994) estimates the short-run supply elasticity for fed cattle to be 0.12; and

- the import supply elasticity ε_m is calculated using Equation (A13.9) assuming Canadian domestic supply and demand elasticities are the same as the U.S. domestic elasticities; the values for this elasticity range from 0.6 to 1.3.

NOTES

[1] However, there were difficulties in accessing Canadian slaughter capacity until 1997 and 1998 so that reduced exports from Canada to the United States did not show up until after 1996 (USITC 1999).

[2] This review period differs from the actual period of investigation for the CV investigation that is April 1, 1997 to March 31, 1998. This review period corresponds with other evidence relative to the activities of the CWB, which includes the full 1997/98 crop year. In this report, the term review period will therefore refer to April 1, 1997 to July 31, 1998.

[3] The export basis is defined as all transportation, handling, and storage charges involved when getting the grain from the farm gate into export position.

[4] Table 13.2 does not sum to 100 percent because the net change in the beginning and ending stocks is not taken into account.

[5] The U.S. Export Enhancement Program (EEP) encouraged greater exports of U.S. barley, and caused higher U.S. prices domestically. Since the CWB competed in international markets from 1985/86 to 1995/96, EEP also lowered the Canadian export prices and internal prices of barley. During the review period, EEP for barley was not used.

[6] Pricing signals provided by the CWB include both the Pool Return Outlook (PRO) and the Estimated Pool Return (EPR). These prices are the CWB estimates of what the final price (including all CWB initial, adjustment, interim and final payments) to the producer will be before transportation and handling charges are deducted. The producers' estimated pool return can differ from the PRO- and EPR-price forecasts of the CWB, which are formulated by CWB market analysts, and are quoted at port position.

[7] Other economists have challenged these purported additional costs of transportation. A detailed critique of these costs appears in the Professor Andrew Schmitz statement, September 30, 1996, in Court No. T-2473-93, *Archibald, et al. v. Her Majesty the Queen and the Canadian Wheat Board.* Additional information is contained in Schmitz and Furtan (2000).

REFERENCES

Alberta Agriculture (Alberta Agriculture Food and Rural Development, Economics Research and Logistics Branch). (1999). *AGDATA Series*. Edmonton: Alberta Agriculture, Food, and Rural Development.

Armington, P.S. (1969). "A Theory of Demand for Products Distinguished by Place of Production." *IMF Staff Papers* 16(1): 159–78.

Archibald et al. v. HMQ and the Canadian Wheat Board. (1997). Federal No. T-2473-93. Ottawa: Federal Court of Canada.

Carter C.A. (1999). *Comments on the control of barley exports and prices by the CWB, Countervailing Duty Investigation*. Case No: C-122-834. Washington, DC: U.S. Department of Commerce.

_____. (1993). *An Economic Analysis of a Single North American Barley Market*. Report prepared for the Associate Deputy Minister, Grains, and Oilseeds Branch, Agriculture Canada. Ottawa: Agriculture and Agri-Food Canada (March).

Carter, C.A. and R.M.A. Loyns. (1996). *The Economics of Single-Desk Selling of Western Canadian Grains*. Edmonton: Alberta Agriculture, Food, and Rural Development.

Carter, C.A., R.M.A. Loyns, and D. Berwald. (1998). "Domestic Costs of Statutory Marketing Authorities: The Case of the Canadian Wheat Board." *American Journal of Agricultural Economics* 80(2): 313–24.

CWB (Canadian Wheat Board). (2003). 1997/98 Annual Report. Available at: http://www.cwb.ca/en/about/annual_report/pdf/1997-98_annual-report.pdf.

Eley, R., M.E. Fulton, R.S. Gray, and K. Perlich. (1996). "Freight Rates and Deregulation," *The Economics of Western Grain Handling and Transportation*. Van Vliet Publication Series, Module D-1, Department of Agricultural Economics, University of Saskatchewan, Saskatoon.

Fulton, M., K. Baylis, H. Brooks, and R. Gray. (1998). *The Impact of Deregulation on the Export Basis in the Canadian Grain Handling and Transportation System*. Report presented to Saskatchewan Agriculture and Food. Regina, Saskatchewan.

Gray, R., A. Schmitz, and D. Brewin. (1999). *The Effect of Canadian Wheat Board Policy on the Price of Feed Barley in Western Canada for the Period 04/97 to 07/98*. Report prepared for Agriculture and Agri-Food Canada. Regina, Saskatchewan (April).

Industry Canada. (2002). Available at: http://strategis.gc.ca/sc_mrkti/tdst/tdo/tdo.php.

Kraft, D.F., W.H. Furtan, and E.W. Tyrchniewicz. (1996). *Performance Evaluation of the Canadian Wheat Board*. Winnipeg: Canadian Wheat Board.

Marsh, J.M. (1994). "Estimating Inter-Temporal Supply Response in the Federal Beef Market." *American Journal of Agricultural Economics* 76(August): 444–53.

_____. (1992). "USDA Revisions of Choice Beef Prices and Price Spreads: Implications of Estimating Demand Responses." *Journal of Agricultural and Resource Economics* 17(December): 323–34.

McCalla, A.F. and A. Schmitz. (1979). "Grain Marketing Systems: The Case of the United States versus Canada." *American Journal of Agricultural Economics* 61(2): 199–212.

Parsons, G. and W. Wilson. (1999). *Grain Handling and Transportation Systems: A Canada-United States Comparison*. Study prepared for the Organization for Western Economic Cooperation, Regina, Saskatchewan (January).

R-CALF (Ranchers-Cattlemen Action Legal Fund, United Stockgrowers of America). (2003). Available at: http://www.rcalf.com/.

Schmitz, A. (1996). *Economic Performance of the Canadian Wheat Board: Myth and Reality*. Filed in the court case of *Archibald et al. v. CWB & HMQ,* Federal Court Case No. T-2473-93. Calgary: Federal Court (August 17).

_____. (1996). *Rebuttal to the Affidavit of Dr. Colin Carter*. Filed in the court case of *Archibald et al. v. CWB & HMQ.* Federal Court No. T-2473-93. Calgary: Federal Court (August 17).

Schmitz, A. and W.H. Furtan. (2000). *The Canadian Wheat Board: Marketing in the New Millennium*. Regina: Canadian Plains Research Centre.

Schmitz, A. and R. Gray. (2000). "The Canadian Wheat Board and Feed Barley." *Agri-Business: An International Journal* 16: 491–501.

Schmitz, A., R. Gray, T.G. Schmitz, and G. Storey. (1997). *The CWB and Barley Marketing: Price Pooling and Single-Desk Selling*. Winnipeg: Canadian Wheat Board.

Schmitz, A., R. Gray, and A. Ulrich. (1993). *A Continental Barley Market: Where Are the Gains?* Department of Agricultural Economics, University of Saskatchewan, Saskatoon.

Statistics Canada. (1998). *Livestock Statistics*. Catalogue Number 23-603. Ottawa: Statistics Canada.

USDA/FAS (U.S. Department of Agriculture, Foreign Agricultural Service). (1999). *World Coarse Grains Situation and Outlook*. Washington DC: USDA/FAS. Available at: http://www.fas.usda.gov/grain/circular/1999/99-04/cgra_tbl.pdf.

USDA/ERS (U.S. Department of Agriculture, Economic Research Service). (2003). Available at: http//ers.usda.gov.

USITC (U.S. International Trade Commission). (2003). Available at: http://ia.ita.doc.gov/regs/title7.html.

_____. (1999). *Live Cattle From Canada*. Publication 3255. Washington, DC: USITC (November).

Western Grain Marketing Panel. (1996). *The Western Grain Marketing Panel Report*. Winnipeg: Western Grain Marketing Panel.

Wohlgenant, M.K. (1989). "Demand for Farm Output in a Complete System of Demand Functions." *American Journal of Agricultural Economics* 71(May): 241–52.

Section IV:
U.S. and Other-Country Trade Dispute Case Studies

Chapter 14

Mexico's Antidumping Regime against High Fructose Corn Syrup from the United States

Charles B. Moss,[1] Andrew Schmitz,[2] Thomas Spreen,[3] and David Orden
University of Florida[123]
Virginia Polytechnic Institute and State University

INTRODUCTION

This chapter analyzes the economic issues in the appeals of Mexico's antidumping (AD) findings brought by the United States and high fructose corn syrup (HFCS) producers under the World Trade Organization (WTO) and the North American Free Trade Agreement (NAFTA) dispute-settlement process. The economic issues raised in these appeals involved the measurement of dumping margins and damages to the sugar industry. Mexico found that HFCS was being sold under Sections 1703.40.99 and 1702.60.01 of Mexico's General Imports Tax Law from the United States into Mexico a price less than the average cost of production (ACP) in the United States. The amount of the price discount (the difference between the price in the United States and the U.S. export price or the difference between the export price and the cost of production) is commonly referred to as the dumping margin. Given the finding of a dumping margin, Mexico (under its General Imports Tax Law) can impose an AD duty on imports of HFCS from the United States to offset the dumping margin and, hence, to avoid the implied damages to the country's domestic producers. This chapter examines the U.S.-Mexico HFCS dispute within the contest of U.S. import quotas on Mexican sugar under the U.S. sugar policy. Restricting imports of sugar may well have spurred support for Mexico's action to restrict imports of HFCS.

The imposition of AD duties on HFCS by Mexico began on January 14, 1997, when the National Chamber of Sugar and Alcohol Industries (Sugar Chamber) filed a request for relief under the AD provision with the Secretaria de Comercio y Fomento Industrial (SECOFI) regarding Mexico's importation of HFCS from the United States (NAFTA Appeal Panel 2001). On January 23,

1998, SECOFI made a final determination according to Sections 1703.40.99 and 1702.60.01 of the General Imports Tax Law that both HFCS-42 and HFCS-55 were imported into Mexico from the United States under conditions of dumping and were subject to a dumping quota. Subsequent to this finding, the United States filed appeals with both the WTO and NAFTA Appeal authorities. The basis for these appeals involved eight legal issues (WTO 2000:4–5). Both appellate bodies issued findings concurring with the U.S. position demanding that Mexico remove the AD duty on HFCS. Mexico acquiesced, but it imposed a special-use tax on HFCS that is used in the production of soft drinks in Mexico.

ANTIDUMPING, U.S. SUGAR POLICY, AND NAFTA

While the AD case brought by Mexico against the United States can be viewed in terms of the traditional application of the General Agreement on Trade and Tariffs (GATT), Jamaica and Mauritius stated in a third-party argument to the WTO:

> Jamaica and Mauritius … as third parties, … are cognizant that the issue at hand concerns imports of … HFCS into the market of Mexico … They submit, however, that the issue should also be examined in the broader context in which this dispute is taking place, namely in relation to … NAFTA, a regional trade agreement notified to the WTO, and one which is alleged by the parties to be in conformity with the relevant WTO Rules. (WTO 2000: 164–65)

According to Jamaica and Mauritius, the broader disagreement between Mexico and the United States has spawned other dispute-resolution proceedings, namely:

- this current dispute within the WTO;
- a NAFTA dispute proceeding initiated by Mexico to challenge the limits imposed on its sugar exports to the United States during the implementation of the NAFTA; and
- a proceeding initiated by the United States Corn Refiners Association under the so-called Section 301 procedure of the U.S. law to challenge, as an unfair trade practice, an agreement between the Mexican Sugar Industry and the Mexican soft-drink bottlers pursuant to which the soft-drink industry   has allegedly agreed to limit its consumption of imported HFCS. In the Section 301 proceedings, the United States Corn Refiners Association has requested that the United States impose sanctions on Mexico for its alleged unfair trade practices, and it has been suggested that an appropriate sanction would be to limit or ban U.S. sugar from Mexico.

As developed within this third-party statement, the AD measure brought by Mexico must be viewed within the context of U.S. sugar policy and NAFTA.

U.S. Sugar Policy

Sugar prices in the United States are supported through a variety of policy instruments including the Commodity Credit Corporation (CCC) loan rates and payment-in-kind (PIK) programs (Haley and Suarez 2002). However, given that the United States is a net importer of sugar, the critical policy instrument used to maintain sugar prices for U.S. producers is the tariff-rate quota (TRQ) as depicted in Figure 14.1.

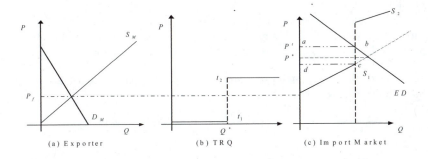

Figure 14.1: Tariff-Rate Quota for Sugar

The excess supply of a commodity (in this case sugar) for a producing country is defined by the quantity of the commodity that will be offered by the country for export at any given price. In Figure 14.1a, this quantity is illustrated graphically by the horizontal distance between the country's supply and demand curves at any particular price. The quantity supplied exceeds the quantity demanded for any price above P_f. Thus, for any price over P_f, the country is willing to export some quantity of the commodity. In general, the excess supply curve for any commodity is an upward-sloping relationship that shows countries are willing to export more as the price increases. The actual quantity exported, however, is affected by any import tariff imposed by the importing country. Countries using a TRQ to control imports impose two different tariffs (Figure 14.1b). The first tier of the tariff t_1 is relatively low (Figure 14.1b), allowing access to the importing country to some threshold level Q^*. After imports exceed this threshold level, imports are subject to a higher tariff or second-tier tariff t_2. This second tariff level is usually prohibitive. This two-tier tariff structure causes the excess supply function for the commodity to be kinked (S_1S_2) as in Figure 14.1c. As a result, imports are typically restricted to the threshold level Q^* resulting in a market price P^t in the importing countries that is higher than the price that would be received in open markets, P^t as opposed to a "free-market" price P^*.[1] In addition, the use of the TRQ yields a tariff rent of *adcb* in Figure 14.1c.

Under the U.S. sugar program, the first-tier tariff t_1 is 0.625 cents per pound and the second-tier tariff t_2 is 15.82 cents per pound (Koo 2002). For the 2003 fiscal year, first-tier imports Q^* were set at 1.117 million metric tons (mmt) raw value (Haley and Suarez 2003) in an effort to support raw-sugar prices at 18 cents per pound. If raw-sugar prices fall below 18 cents per pound, sugar mills may forfeit sugar under the terms of the CCC loan program. However, since the sugar program is mandated to be a zero-cost program under the Dole Amendment (Moss and Schmitz 2002a), any stocks forfeited under the CCC loan program have been used in recent years as PIK payments to sugar producers.

U.S. sugar policy generates quota rents for 40 countries. (In Table 14.1 we show selected countries.) Taking a world futures price for sugar at 7.4 cents per pound in December of 2002 (Haley and Suarez 2003), the quota rents accruing

Table 14.1: U.S. Sugar Imports under Tariff-Rate Quota, Selected Countries, Selected Fiscal Years, 1995 to 2002

Country	10/95–9/96	10/97–9/98	10/99–9/00	10/01–9/02
	Metric Tons, Raw Values			
Argentina	95,867	65,563	45,283	45,281
Australia	185,044	126,552	87,408	87,402
Brazil	323,271	221,084	152,700	152,691
Colombia	53,506	36,593	25,274	25,273
Costa Rica	33,411	22,871	15,797	15,796
Dominican Republic	350,940	268,350	185,346	185,335
El Salvador	57,966	39,643	27,381	27,379
Guatemala	107,014	73,186	50,549	50,546
Honduras	22,294	15,247	10,531	10,530
Jamaica	24,523	16,772	11,584	11,583
Malawi	22,294	15,247	10,531	10,530
Mauritius	26,754	18,297	12,637	12,636
Mozambique	28,983	19,821	13,690	13,690
Nicaragua	46,819	32,019	22,115	22,114
Panama	57,825	44,217	30,540	30,538
Peru	91,407	62,513	43,177	43,175
Philippines	237,422	205,837	142,169	142,160
South Africa	51,278	35,069	24,221	24,220
Thailand	31,213	21,346	14,743	14,743
Zimbabwe	26,754	18,297	12,637	12,636
Total First-Tier Imports	2,167,160	1,600,000	1,135,000	1,117,195

Source: Authors' computations based on data from the USDA/ERS (2003).

to first-tier tariff deliveries becomes 9.975 cents per pound [18 cents per pound (U.S. price for raw sugar) – 7.4 cents per pound (world market price for raw sugar) – 0.625 cents per pound (first-tier tariff duty)].

Interrelationship between Sugar and HFCS in the United States

The TRQ results in significantly higher sugar prices in the United States, which increases the economic rents to sugar producers and sugar mills. (Moss and Schmitz 2002a, 2002b) Also, higher sugar prices may provide protection for other commodities, such as HFCS. It is noted that the HFCS industry is part of the coalition that supports U.S. sugar policy:

> Historically, the [American Sugar Association] ASA, made up of sugar and HFCS interests, has been an effective force in generating support for the U.S. sugar policy. The HFCS-producing group supports sugar import quotas, the key component of U.S. sugar policy, because of the sugar-price umbrella provided by quotas. In addition, corn producers support the program because corn is used in the production of HFCS. Some contend that the domestic sugar program has given sweeteners, such as HFCS, the impetus to develop. (Moss and Schmitz 2002b: 163)

It is this linkage between sugar policy and HFCS that enters the countervail (CV) scenario. Moss and Schmitz (2002c) develop a model in which HFCS is a perfect substitute for sugar in some applications (i.e., the manufacture of soft drinks) but it cannot be used for other applications (i.e., the manufacture of confections). This limited substitutability implies that sugar prices will form an upper bound for HFCS prices. If sugar and HFCS are substitutes at the margin (i.e., sugar is still being used for the production of soft drinks as in Mexico) the HFCS price will be proportional to sugar prices. However, if sugar and HFCS are not substitutes at the margin (i.e., if HFCS has replaced sugar in the production of soft drinks), the dry-weight equivalent price of HFCS will be lower than the sugar price. Moss and Schmitz (2002c) indicate that beginning in 1997 the HFCS price has separated from the domestic price of sugar. Hence, at the margin, changes in the production of HFCS do not affect the economic rents accruing to domestic sugar producers, but HFCS producers benefit from the TRQ for sugar as long as the world sugar price is below the equivalent price for HFCS.

The North American Free Trade Agreement (NAFTA) and the U.S.-Mexico Sugar Trade

The ratification of NAFTA further complicates the implications of U.S. sugar policy. The original provisions of NAFTA subjected Mexico's raw sugar exports to the United States under several conditions:

- During the 15-year transition period, Mexican exports were to be limited to no more than Mexico's net production surplus of sugar (domestic sugar production less domestic sugar consumption). At a minimum, Mexico was allowed to ship duty-free 7,258 metric tons (mt) of raw cane sugar to the United States.

- For the first 6 years of NAFTA, duty-free access was limited to no more than 25,000 mt, raw value. In year 7, the maximum duty-free access quantity of sugar was to become 150,000 mt and, in each subsequent year, was to increase by 10 percent.
- Importantly, NAFTA provided that these maximums could be exceeded if one of two conditions prevailed. The first condition required that Mexico achieve net-production-sugar-surplus status for 2 consecutive marketing years. The second condition specified that Mexico be a net surplus producer for the first year and be projected as a net surplus producer in the second year unless it was subsequently determined, contrary to the projection, that Mexico was not a net surplus producer for that year. (USDA/ERS 2003: 4)

From fiscal years 2001 to 2007, Mexico will have duty-free access to the U.S. market for the amount of its surplus as measured by the NAFTA formula, up to a maximum of 250,000 mt.

The American and Mexican governments exchanged side letters that altered the sugar provisions of the original NAFTA text, which stipulates that projected Mexican sugar production would have to exceed Mexico's consumption of both sugar and HFCS for Mexico to be considered a net surplus producer of sugar. Although Mexico has since rejected the validity of the side-letter agreement, the United States maintains that the side-letter provisions supersede those of the original NAFTA agreement.

The presence of HFCS erodes Mexico's position in NAFTA in two ways. First, increased imports of HFCS displace sugar in the Mexican market, causing lower domestic sugar prices. Second, importing HFCS for use in the manufacture of soft drinks counts against Mexico's net exporter status for sugar, which limits Mexico's duty-free access to the U.S. sugar market.

In addition to the interaction between HFCS and Mexico's status as a net sugar exporter, NAFTA raises additional issues for other countries that hold first-tier import quotas under the TRQ system of the United States. As Mexico's net exports to the United States increase under NAFTA, the United States must decrease its first-tier quotas from other countries to maintain the price of U.S. raw sugar at 18 cents per pound. Table 14.1 also indicates that the total sugar imported under first-tier tariffs has declined steadily since the 1996 crop year, hence Jamaica's and Mauritius's third-party filing with the WTO.

The offer curve of Mexican sugar exports for HFCS imports is given by OS_1 (Figure 14.2). Likewise, the U.S. offer curve of HFCS for sugar is given by OH_1. In equilibrium, Mexico exports S_1 of sugar to the United States in exchange for H_1 of HFCS.

In the course of the sugar dispute, the side agreement with Mexico stipulated that the United States would import an extra 250,000 mt above the Mexican exports of raw sugar to the United States of 10,212 mt TRQ, which is comprised of 7,258 mt under the WTO raw-sugar minimum access commitment (MAC) and 2,954 mt (raw value) of the 38,000 mt of the U.S. refined sugar. In our model, if Mexico becomes a net exporter, it will export S_1 of sugar to the United States, which will be above the import quota amount of 10,212 mt. However, it appears that Mexico has not reached the so-called net exporter status; hence the United States has not imported an additional 250,000 mt of sugar from Mexico (Roney 2003). Consider the sugar data given by the U.S. Department of Agriculture (USDA) for Mexico (USDA/ERS 2003). Note that Mexico imported a sizeable amount of sugar in 2002/03 (Table 14.2). In addition, for each of the three years, 2001/02, 2002/03, and 2003/04, Mexican domestic sugar consumption exceeded production (USDA/ERS 2003). But, there is considerable debate over whether this is the case. Bolivar (2003) contends that at the beginning of the 2002/03 crop year, Mexico had a net surplus of sugar. If this is true, why did Mexico import sugar in 2003 from the rest of the world?

A reduction in Mexico's potential to export raw sugar shifts the offer curve from OS_1 to OS_2. Depending on the change of relative prices between sugar and HFCS, the U.S. offer curve could shift to OH_2, which would result in an increase of HFCS exports H_2 to Mexico from the United States and a decrease in Mexican sugar exports S_2 to the United States. (It is possible that exports of both sugar from Mexico and HFCS from the United States could be reduced to S_2' and H_2'.

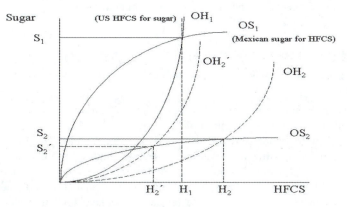

Figure 14.2: Sugar Exports and HFCS Imports

Table 14.2: Mexico: Raw-Sugar Production, Supply, and Distribution, Fiscal Years 1999 to 2004

Year	Production	Imports	Exports	Domestic Consumption	Ending Stocks
		1,000 Metric Tons, Raw Value			
1999/2000	4,979	37	318	4,576	1,063
2000/01	5,220	43	155	4,623	1,548
2001/02	4,168	58	406	5,082	1,286
2002/03	5,038	100	100	5,266	1,058
2003/04	5,200	51	40	5,283	986

Source: USDA/ERS (2003).

As discussed earlier, part of the reason for Mexico bringing AD charges against HFCS exporters was the claim that the United States did not honour the so-called NAFTA side agreement. Yet the United States argues that Mexico never reached the net exporter status required for the United States to import an additional 250,000 mt of raw sugar from Mexico. Questions arise as to why Mexico appeared to use the net-exporter-status argument to block HFCS imports (even though Mexico does not honour the side agreement as a legal document). Due to the side agreement, the original equilibrium of S_1 and H_1 does not exist, but the offer curve OH_1 does exist, but it is not effective largely for political reasons on the part of Mexico. Without political interference, the United States would export HFCS to Mexico, but for this to occur, offer curve OS_1 would be replaced with an offer curve labelled "non-sugar" commodities.

DEFINITION OF LIKE PRODUCTS AND THE RELEVANT MARKET

A critical factor when determining either a dumping margin or the presence of material injury involves the delineation of like markets. The AD duty imposed by Mexico was on the importation of HFCS from the United States. However, it is clear from Mexico's justification that like products includes the sugar market in Mexico. The United States raises objections to this definition on two grounds. First, Mexico's findings neglect the household demand component of sugar. The United States contends that including the household demand for sugar would lessen the impact of HFCS on sugar producers in Mexico:

> In the view of the United States, if SECOFI in fact determined that there were two domestic sugar industries (i.e., one serving industrial users and the other serving household uses), this finding would be utterly inconsistent with its determination that sugar and HFCS were similar. Article 4.1 of the AD Agreement provides that "the term 'domestic industry' shall be interpreted as referring to domestic producers as a whole of the like products or to those producers whose collective output

of the products constitutes a major proportion of the total domestic production of those products..." Therefore, if SECOFI determined that there were two separate domestic sugar industries, it would have to find that sugar for industrial use and sugar for household use were separate like products. However, this like product finding would have been inconsistent with the reasoning that SECOFI used to find that sugar and HFCS were similar, which would apply *a fortiori* to sugar for industrial use and sugar for household use. (WTO 2000: 127)

The United States argues that households would consume part of the sugar replaced by HFCS, so the impact of HFCS on the industrial sugar market would be reduced. Second, Mexico's findings do not address specifically the manufacture of HFCS in Mexico (WTO 2000: 89).

The definition of like products enters the sugar-policy debate in several ways. First, from U.S. perspective, the question of whether HFCS and sugar are like products has been a point of contention in several antitrust actions. Moss and Schmitz (2003) present a synopsis of the legal findings of the case *United States v. Archer-Daniels-Midland (ADM) Co. & Nabisco Foods* (1988). In this case, the U.S. Department of Justice brought legal action against ADM and Nabisco alleging that the HFCS market was noncompetitive. The initial lawsuit was thrown out because ADM and Nabisco claimed that the relevant market included sugar. Given that U.S. farmers produce sugar under the government sugar program, the defendants argued that the market could not possibly be non-competitive. The U.S. Department of Justice appealed the finding and the U.S. Court of Appeals for the Eighth Circuit accepted the contention that HFCS and sugar were functionally interchangeable, but held that the U.S. sugar program implies an economically differentiated market:

> We accept the finding that sugar and HFCS are functionally interchangeable for all uses for which HFCS is suitable, but we cannot ignore the fact that Congress has enacted a sugar program that has artificially inflated the price of sugar. As a result, the domestic price of HFCS has been 10%-30% lower than the price of sugar. Because of lower price, many buyers of sugar have turned to HFCS. As long as an effective price support program is in existence, a monopolist of HFCS will be able to raise the price of HFCS to just below the supported price of sugar before being constrained by the competitive forces of sugar. In other words, the HFCS monopolist is able to exercise excess market power. (*United States v. Archer-Daniels-Midland, Co. & Nabisco Brands, Inc.* 1988: 246)

Moss and Schmitz (2002c) develop an empirical model in which sugar and HFCS are imperfect substitutes for one another (as described previously). In their model, sugar forms an upper bound for HFCS prices where HFCS prices

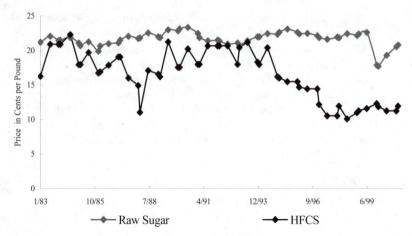

Figure 14.3: Sugar and HFCS Prices in the United States
Source: USDA/ERS (2003).

are determined by sugar prices as long as sugar and HFCS are substitutes at the margin. The HFCS price shown in Figure 14.3 followed sugar from the market's inception until the mid 1990s. However, beginning in the mid 1990s, the price of HFCS became lower relative to the price of sugar. Based on this divergence, using a cointegration approach similar to that applied in Moss and Schmitz (2002c), Moss and Schmitz (2003) conclude that HFCS prices fail to react to changes in the sugar price after 1996. Therefore, HFCS and sugar are no longer like products in the United States.

The fact that sugar and HFCS are not like products in the United States does not imply, however, that sugar and HFCS are not like products in Mexico. The use of HFCS in the soft-drink sector in Mexico increased from 5 percent in 1996 to 7 percent in 2000 (Buzzanell 2002). Most of this increase resulted from

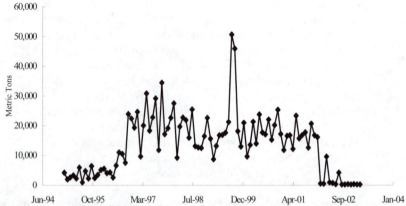

Figure 14.4: Exports of HFCS to Mexico from the United States (Metric Tons)
Source: USDA/ERS (2003).

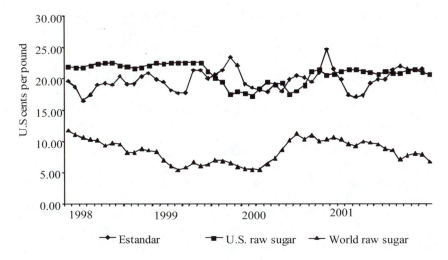

Figure 14.5. U.S. and Mexican Sugar Prices over Time
Source: USDA/ERS (2003).

increased Mexican imports of HFCS from the United States (Figure 14.4). This can be contrasted to the United States where the soft-drink market is dominated by HFCS.

Hence, at the margin, increased imports of HFCS in Mexico displace sugar, or sugar and HFCS are like products in the Mexican sweetener market. Mexico contends that the relevant sweetener market in Mexico includes both sugar and HFCS, which is further supported by the price data in Figure 14.5. The sugar price in Mexico more closely resembles the U.S. price of sugar than it does the world price of sugar.

The conclusion that HFCS and sugar are like products in Mexico raises significant questions regarding the calculation of the dumping margin used in the U.S.-Mexico CV case. Article VI of GATT 1994 defines a like product as:

> ... Throughout this Agreement the term "like product" ("produit similaire") shall be interpreted to mean a product, which is identical, i.e. alike in all respects to the product under consideration, or in the absence of such a product, another product, which, although not alike in all respects, has characteristics closely resembling those of the product under consideration. (GATT 1994, 2.6: 148)

Given the determination of United States Court of Appeals for the Eighth Circuit (*United States v. Archer-Daniels-Midland Co. & Nabisco Brands, Inc.* 1988) and the fact that HFCS and sugar are functionally interchangeable, Mexico would appear justified in its use of sugar as a like product when computing an AD margin for HFCS. If sugar and HFCS are like products, then the AD margin is the difference between the sugar and HFCS prices:

... For the purpose of this Agreement, a product is to be considered as being dumped, i.e. introduced into the commerce of another country at less than its normal value, if the export price of the product exported from one country to another is less than the comparable price, in the ordinary course of trade, for the like product when destined for consumption in the exporting country. (Article VI of 1994 GATT, 2.1: 145)

Given the separation of sugar and HFCS prices observed since 1996 (Moss and Schmitz 2002c; Moss and Schmitz 2003) the evidence appears to support a dumping margin in Mexico. Table 14.3 presents the price of raw sugar on the New York Stock Exchange and HFCS-42 from Mexico. These data could have supported a dumping margin of 7.94 cents per pound in 1996 (the period covered by the initial Mexican lawsuit) if the price of HFCS-42 in Mexico was roughly the same as that charged for HFCS-42 in the United States.

Table 14.3: U.S. Prices for Sugar and HFCS and Price Differences

Year	Raw Sugar Price	HFCS-42 Price	Difference Between Prices
	Cents per Pound Dry Weight Equivalent		
1994	22.04	18.77	3.27
1995	22.96	15.63	7.33
1996	22.40	14.46	7.94
1997	21.96	10.70	11.27
1998	22.06	10.58	11.48
1999	21.16	11.71	9.45
2000	19.09	11.32	7.77
2001	21.11	11.90	9.20
2002	20.87	13.05	7.82

Source: Author's computations based on data from the USDA/ERS (2003).

EVIDENCE OF MATERIAL DAMAGES

Given that the country's trade authority (in this case SECOFI) has established the existence of a significant dumping margin, the next step is to assess whether this dumping margin has resulted in material damage to a local industry:

... A determination of injury for purposes of Article VI of GATT 1994 shall be based on positive evidence and involve an objective examination of both (a) the volume of the dumped imports and the effect of the dumped imports on prices in the domestic market for like products, and (b) the consequence of these imports on domestic producers for such products. (GATT 1994, 3.1: 148)

Evidence of injury can come from a variety of sources:

> ... The examination of the impact of the dumped imports on the domestic industry concerned shall include an evaluation of all relevant economic factors and indices having a bearing on the state of the industry, including actual and potential decline in sales, profits, output, market share, productivity, return on investment, or utilization of capacity; factors affecting domestic prices; the magnitude of the margin of dumping; actual and potential negative effects on cash flow, inventories, employment, wages, growth, ability to raise capital or investments. This list is not exhaustive, nor can one or several of these factors necessarily give decisive guidance. (GATT 1994, 3.4: 148–9)

Thus the evidence is broad that can be used to support injury.

A major contention of the U.S. appeal to the WTO was that Mexico had not developed sufficient evidence of material damage:

> ... Furthermore, the United States argues that, as a consequence of SECOFI's failure to provide an evaluation of the domestic industry's sales, profits, output, and market share, SECOFI also failed to discuss overall trends in, and projections of, consumption of sweeteners (both HFCS and sugar) in Mexico. While SECOFI discussed domestic consumption and market share for sales to industrial sugar consumers, it did not address overall consumption levels. Again, therefore, SECOFI's analysis of consumption in the portion of the industry serving the industrial sugar market is largely meaningless in assessing the overall impact of imports on the domestic industry. As with SECOFI's analysis of sales, it is entirely possible that the domestic industry's share of total domestic consumption would not decline as a result of increasing HFCS imports, if the domestic industry increased its sales to other consumers, such as household consumers of sugar. (WTO 2000, 5:441: 110)

In its initial findings, SECOFI concluded material damages to the domestic sugar industry based on factors such as market share, returns on domestic investment, and profitability for sugar users in the Mexican industrial sector. The United States contends that such a specification overstates the damages to the sugar industry in Mexico by neglecting the household demand for sugar:

> ... While examination of the Article 3.7 factors is required in a threat of injury case, that analysis alone is not a sufficient basis for a determination of threat of injury, because the Article 3.7 factors do not relate to the consideration of the impact of the dumped imports on the domestic industry. The

Article 3.7 factors relate specifically to the questions of the
likelihood of increased imports (based on the rate of increase
of imports, the capacity of exporters to increase imports, and
the availability of import markets), the effects of imports on
future prices and likely future demand for imports and
inventories. They are not, in themselves, relevant to a decision
concerning what the "consequent impact" of continued
dumped imports on the domestic industry is likely to be.
However, it is precisely this later question—whether the
"consequent impact" of continued dumped imports is likely to
be material injury to the domestic industry—which must be
answered in a threat of material injury analysis. Thus, we
conclude that an analysis of the consequent impact of imports
is required in a threat of material injury determination. (WTO
2000, 7.126: 210)

The effect of neglecting household demand for sugar is depicted in Figure 14.6,
which depicts the supply and demand in Mexico considering only industrial uses
of sugar. Before the advent of HFCS from the United States, the supply of sugar
from Mexico S_0 and the industrial demand for sugar in Mexico D_I resulted in a
price of sugar in the domestic market of P_0. Modelling the introduction of
HFCS into this equilibrium yields a downward shift in sweetener supply to S_1.
If we restrict our analysis to the industrial demand alone, this
results in a lower price for sugar (and HFCS) in Mexico of P_1. The economic

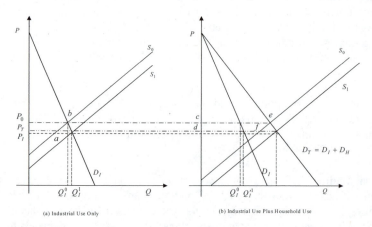

(a) Industrial Use Only   (b) Industrial Use Plus Household Use

**Figure 14.6: The Use of Industrial Demand versus the Total Demand for Sweeteners
in Assessing the Economic Damage to Dumping**
Source: Authors' Computation.

cost of this introduction can be calculated from area P_0P_1ab. Figure 14.6b shows
the interaction between industrial and household users of sugar in Mexico. The
total demand for Mexican sugar D_T is the sum of the industrial demand (held

constant at D_I) and the household demand for sugar D_H. As suggested by the United States in its appeal, including the domestic demand for sugar reduces the price effect ranges from $P_0 - P_1$ to $P_0 - P_T$. However, whether or not this approach yields smaller damages depends on the overall elasticity of domestic supply. As depicted in Figure 14.6b, the economic loss due to dumping becomes *cdfe*, which is actually larger than the original economic loss.

MEXICO'S RESPONSE TO THE NAFTA AND WTO PANELS

On April 22, 2002, SECOFI announced it was establishing a TRQ for HFCS imports. For marketing year 2001/02 (October to September), the in-quota amount was limited to 148,000 mt (dry weight) at a 1.5 percent duty, mirroring "tonne for tonne" the level of Mexico's access to the U.S. sugar market. HFCS imports into Mexico outside the quota face a tariff of 210 percent; the same level that already applies to imports from non-NAFTA countries, which is the maximum allowable under the WTO. Shipments of HFCS to Mexico from the United States have slumped since the implementation of the AD duty (Figure 14.4).

In January 2002, Mexico's government implemented a 20 percent tax on beverages containing HFCS, and although it was suspended by presidential decree in March 2002, the tax was reapplied July 2002 when Mexico's Supreme Court Justice voted to nullify the President's decision to suspend the tax. Mexico's consumption of HFCS slumped in response to its 20 percent tax on soft drinks. Bottling companies in Mexico that were using HFCS in their products then switched to using cane sugar in their product formulas. Almost no HFCS has been sold to the Mexican soft-drink bottlers since Mexico first introduced its tax on HFCS.

CONCLUSIONS

AD and CV cases rarely occur in a vacuum, but are complicated by an array of domestic policies. In the AD case brought by Mexican sugar producers against the United States, the establishment of dumping margins and economic damages are complicated not only by policies directly affecting the commodity named in the action (HFCS), but also by a host of policies affecting the production and marketing of sugar in the United States and Mexico. The U.S. sugar policy maintains a price of raw sugar above the world market price through the operation of a TRQ. However, the effect of the sugar program goes beyond the market for sugar in the United States. The TRQ may create a protected market for HFCS in the United States. From 1997 through 2001 econometric evidence suggests that changes in sugar prices in the United States have no effect on HFCS prices. In the vernacular of imperfect-competition literature, sugar is not included in the relevant market for HFCS in the United States. However, sugar is part of the relevant market for HFCS in Mexico. Thus, the Mexican government appears justified in its contention that the dumping margin for HFCS imports into Mexico can be computed based on the U.S. domestic price of sugar. It is also clear, however, that Mexican estimates of damages based on this dumping margin are misstated because they excluded the interaction between the industrial and household market for sugar in Mexico.

There is an interesting tie between sugar and HFCS. In terms of U.S. imports of sugar from Mexico, the United States argued that it would honour the so-called NAFTA side agreement, but it called for Mexico to be in a net-exporter status position with respect to sweeteners. The United States contends that Mexico never reached this status; hence the United States did not import the 250,000 mt of sugar stipulated in the side letter (ironically, Mexico does not even honour this side letter). The United States has expanded its production of HFCS, and it is natural for the HFCS producers of the United States to expand their HFCS exports to Mexico. This was clearly the case until Mexico introduced AD legislation and imposed a tax on the use of HFCS in the beverage industry in Mexico. Because of this tax, the use of HFCS in Mexico then dropped drastically, and the use of sugar increased. This further takes away from any possibility of Mexico achieving net-exporter status for sugar. It appears unfortunate for the HFCS industry of the United States that a prime reason for AD litigation in Mexico was the refusal of the United States to import additional sugar from Mexico. As we argue, under the U.S.-Mexico NAFTA side agreement the United States is not obligated to buy additional sugar from Mexico, nor is it clear where the sugar would have come from if the United States had decided to increase imports of sugar from Mexico. The resolution of this issue is not likely to happen soon.

NOTE

[1]The exact nature of free-market equilibrium depends on the specification of the free-market tariff structure. The free-market solution in Figure 14.1c assumes that the tariff does not change, or that all imports are subject to the t_1 tariff.

REFERENCES

Bolivar, J. (2003). "Mexico: Net Importer or Net Exporter?" Paper presented at the *F.O. Licht World Sugar 2003: Challenges and Opportunities in a Changing World Conference*. Miami, Florida (September 22–3).

Buzzanell, P. (2002). "The U.S.-Mexico High Fructose Corn Syrup (HFCS) Trade Dispute," in *Sugar and Related Sweetener Markets: International Perspectives* edited by A. Schmitz, T.H. Spreen, W.A. Messina, and C.B. Moss. New York: CABI Publishing: 53–65.

Haley, S.L. and N.R. Suarez. (2002). "U.S. Sugar Policy and Prospects for the U.S. Sugar Industry," in *Sugar and Related Sweetener Markets: International Perspectives* edited by A. Schmitz, T.H. Spreen, W.A. Messina, and C.B. Moss. New York: CABI Publishing: 241–58.

_____. (2003). *Sugar and Sweeteners Outlook*. U.S. Department of Agriculture, Economic Research Service, Bulletin SSS-236. Washington DC: USDA/ERS.

Josling, T. (2002). "The Place of Sugar in Regional and Multilateral Trade Negotiations," in *Sugar and Related Sweetener Markets: International Perspectives,* edited by A. Schmitz, T.H. Spreen, W.A. Messina, and C.B. Moss. New York: CABI Publishing: 13–29.

Koo, W. W. (2002). "U.S. Sugar and Alternative Trade-Liberalization Options," in *Sugar and Related Sweetener Markets: International Perspectives,* edited by A. Schmitz, T.H. Spreen, W.A. Messina, and C.B. Moss. New York: CABI Publishing: 329–47.

Moss, C.B. and A. Schmitz. (2002a). "Coalition Structures and U.S. Sugar Policy," in *Sugar and Related Sweetener Markets: International Perspectives,* edited by A. Schmitz, T.H. Spreen, W.A. Messina, and C.B. Moss. New York: CABI Publishing: 259–80.

_____. (2002b). "Coalitions and Competitiveness: Why has the Sugar Program Been Resilient?" in *Agricultural Policy for the 21st Century,* edited by L. Tweeten and S.R. Thompson. Ames: Iowa State University Press: 160–83.

_____. (2002c). "Price Behaviour in the U.S. Sweetener Market: A Cointegration Approach." *Applied Economics* 34: 1273–81.

_____. (2003). "Relevant U.S. Sweetener Markets: Co-Integration and Substitute Goods." Mimeographed paper, Department of Food and Resource Economics, University of Florida, Gainesville.

NAFTA Appeal Panel (North American Free Trade Agreement Appeal Panel). (2001). Available at: http://www.nafta-sec-alena.org/DefaultSite/home/index_e.aspx.

Roney, J. (2003). "The Future of the US Sugar Industry: An Industry View and a Brief Analysis of the WTO Cancun Ministerial Conference." Paper presented at the *F.O. Licht World Sugar 2003: Challenges and Opportunities in a Changing World Conference.* Miami, FL.

United States v. Archer-Daniels-Midland Co. & Nabisco Brands, Inc. (1988). 866 F.2d 242. Washington, DC: Government Printing Office. Available at: http://www.usdoj.gov/osg/briefs/1988/sg880013.txt.

USDA/ERS (United States Department of Agriculture, Economic Research Service). (2003). "Sugar and Sweetener Policy." Available at: http://www.ers.usda.gov/briefing/sugar/policy.htm.

WTO (World Trade Organization.). (2000). "Mexico–Antidumping Investigation of High Fructose Corn Syrup (HFCS) from the United States." WT/DS132/R. Switzerland: Geneva.

Chapter 15

The Shrimp Import Controversy

Charles Adams, Walter J. Keithly, and Sal Versaggi
University of Florida
Louisiana State University
Versaggi Shrimp Corporation

INTRODUCTION

The warm-water shrimp-harvesting industry in the Gulf of Mexico and South Atlantic (GSA) region represents the most economically important component of all of the domestic commercial seafood-harvesting sectors in the United States. In 2001, the volume and dockside value (i.e., payment received by the vessel) of commercial shrimp landings in the GSA region was estimated to be 176 million pounds (shell-on, heads-off weight) and U.S. $546 million, respectively (USDOC 2002a). The shrimp-harvest sector is reportedly comprised of over 20,000 vessels and crafts that actively trawl for shrimp in near-shore and offshore waters in the GSA region (GMFMC 1994; Swingle 2001; SAFMC 1999). Less than one-half of these vessels operate in offshore waters, while the remainder operates in near-shore bays and estuaries. The vessels are owned by fleet operators who employ on average 3 crewmembers per vessel (the actual number of crewmembers, however, depends on the size of the vessel).

Shrimp are offloaded by shore-side handling facilities, which then set in motion a myriad of economic activities associated with processing, packing, wholesale distribution, and consumer expenditures. Previous studies have suggested that the commercial shrimp industry plays an important role in the economy of the GSA region. Centaur Associates (1984) finds that the shrimp industry created 73,000 jobs, generated approximately U.S. $1 billion in income, and created U.S. $1.4 billion in added value within the GSA region. A more recent study estimates that the commercial shrimp industry in Florida alone creates U.S. $130 million in economic impact to the state's economy (Adams 2002). Thus, the commercial shrimp industry is an important natural resource-based contributor to the economy of the GSA region, and provides an important source of employment and income to the coastal communities in which the vessels homeport.

The domestic market for warm-water shrimp in the United States has undergone significant changes in recent years. Demand for shrimp is at an all-time high. The U.S. supply of shrimp has evolved such that an increasing share is being derived from foreign sources. These foreign sources are themselves becoming more dependent on cultured rather than on wild-caught shrimp. The technology of culturing shrimp in coastal and inland impoundments has become standardized in many regions of the world. The costs associated with the culture process allow shrimp to be produced and shipped to U.S. markets at price levels and volumes that have purportedly exerted strong downward pressure on U.S. domestic dockside prices. Along with high operational costs of domestic shrimp vessels, they have created a cost-price squeeze for many domestic vessels that comprise the commercial shrimp fleet in the GSA region. The eroded profit margin for the vessel operators has resulted in a recent reduction or cessation of trawling operations for many vessels throughout the region. In an effort to alleviate the current fleet-level crisis, representatives of the shrimp-harvesting sector have begun exploring means by which the dockside price of shrimp can be supported, including the use of import controls. Such controls on shrimp-import volumes would have the effect theoretically of boosting dockside prices in the near term. Though fleet operators would favour such quantity controls, other participants in the market may not view such restrictions as beneficial. For example, processors may wish to maintain a steady and consistently high-volume import-augmented throughput to keep average costs down. Similarly, consumers' recent unprecedented demand for shrimp would likely favour any situation that would allow high volumes of low-priced shrimp, as long as product quality is not compromised. Murray (2003) suggests that the economic impact from imported shrimp approaches U.S. \$9 billion in economic output and contributes 138,000 jobs in the United States.

The domestic trawling industry, however, is the industry sector that has experienced a negative impact from an increasing dependence on imported shrimp. Thus, it is this specific sector of the industry that will be the focus of this chapter. The following discussion will: (1) provide an overview of the recent trends and events in the domestic shrimp market; (2) allow insight into the impact shrimp imports have had on dockside price and fleet operations; and (3) review past and current efforts by the domestic shrimp-harvesting sector to control import volumes and increase dockside prices.

TRENDS IN THE DOMESTIC MARKET, LANDINGS, AND SUPPLY

Domestic Market

Seafood, including shrimp products, represents less than 10 percent of the total annual per-capita consumption of all meats by U.S. consumers (USDA 2001). And the annual per-capita consumption of seafood products (edible meat weight) has remained relatively constant over the last 20 years (Figure 15.1). Per-capita seafood consumption increased from 12.3 pounds in 1980 to 16.2 pounds in 1987, most likely as a result of an industry-sponsored generic promotion program and changing consumer attitudes regarding the consumption of red meats. Per-capita seafood consumption, however, remained relatively stable from 1988 to 2001 at an annual average of 15.0 pounds.

Though recent overall consumption of edible meat weight of seafood has been steady on a per-capita consumption basis, the relative importance of various types of seafood products has changed. For example, canned tuna has been a perennial favourite of U.S. consumers. Historically, per-capita consumption of canned tuna has exceeded that for all other individual seafood items, including shrimp (USDOC 2002a). However, per-capita consumption of shrimp products exceeded that for canned tuna during 2001 for the first time since such data have been collected. The per-capita consumption of shrimp products in 2001 was estimated to be 3.4 pounds compared to an estimated 2.9 pounds for canned tuna.

This increased popularity of shrimp products is also reflected in the apparent total U.S. consumption of shrimp. Apparent total consumption (the sum of domestic landings and imports, minus the sum of exports and end-of-year cold-storage holdings) has experienced a dramatic increase (Figure 15.2). Apparent total consumption was somewhat consistent at approximately 800 million pounds (shell-on, heads-off weight) from 1987 to 1996, but then increased at an average annual rate of 9 percent during the 1997 to 2001 period. Total apparent consumption of shrimp products has increased from 851 million pounds in 1996 to 1.3 billion pounds in 2001. The demand for shrimp by the U.S. consumer appears to be insatiable. Interestingly, previous empirical studies have found that shrimp are perceived by consumers as a luxury item, that is, consumption is related directly to real, disposable income (Adams, Prochaska, and Spreen 1987; Keithly, Roberts, and Ward 1993). In addition, these same studies have found that the demand for shrimp products is somewhat price inelastic.

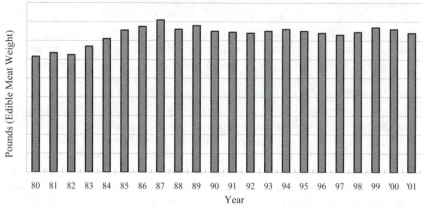

Figure 15.1: Annual Per-Capita Consumption of Seafood, All Species/Product Forms, United States 1980 through 2000
Source: USDOC (2002a).

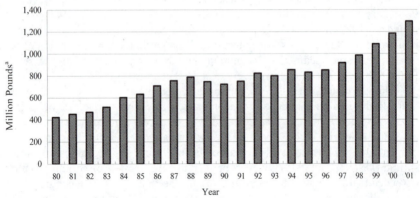

Year

Figure 15.2: Apparent Total Consumption of Shrimp in the United States
[a] Converted to Shell-On, Heads-Off Weight
Source: USDOC (2002a).

World Supply

But where are all the shrimp coming from to meet this unprecedented demand? The worldwide production of warm-water shrimp (shell-on, heads-off weight) has increased from 2.0 billion pounds in 1981 to 4.9 billion pounds in 2001 (Figure 15.3). Prior to the mid-1970s, worldwide warm-water shrimp supplies were provided almost exclusively by wild-catch (capture) methods, primarily by bottom trawls and other forms of nets. However, the worldwide supply of wild-caught shrimp has remained relatively stable over the last 20-year period. But with the advent of the shrimp aquaculture industry around the globe, an increasing share of the total world supply of warm-water shrimp is derived from culture activities. For example, of the total production of warm-water shrimp worldwide during 1981, cultured shrimp represented only 6 percent. By 2001 cultured shrimp represented 36 percent of the total production of shrimp. Wild-caught warm-water shrimp production during this period increased by an average annual rate of 3 percent, while cultured warm-water shrimp production increased by an average annual rate of 15 percent.

Cultured shrimp possesses several characteristics that U.S. buyers find advantageous. They can be harvested at a predetermined, uniform size, thereby allowing growers to target a specific segment of the shrimp market. In the tropical climates where most production occurs, including Southeast Asia, Indonesia, and tropical South America, shrimp can be grown year round, thereby eliminating most of the seasonality inherent in wild-caught supplies. In addition, the economic environment associated with the production, processing, and distribution activities in the countries where the culture occurs may offer distinct comparative cost advantages over the relatively expensive process of shrimp trawling in coastal U.S. waters. These and other characteristics have combined to make cultured shrimp an attractive alternative to the traditional, domestic trawl-caught shrimp in the U.S. market, particularly as the domestic demand for shrimp has increased dramatically.

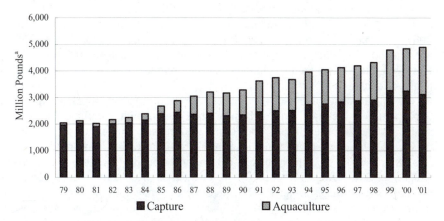

Figure 15.3: Worldwide Production of Shrimp: Capture and Aquaculture
[a]Converted to Shell-On, Heads-Off Weight
Source: USDOC (2002a).

U.S. Shrimp Landings

Domestic landings (i.e., wild caught) of shrimp vary from year to year and are
linked to water-quality conditions found in coastal bays and estuaries where juvenile
shrimp spend most of their life cycle. U.S. shrimp landings are comprised of
cold- and warm-water shrimp. Cold-water shrimp are landed primarily off the
northwest and northeast coasts of the United States, and account for less than 20
percent of annual landings of all shrimp. The majority of domestic landings are
warm-water shrimp, which are landed in the GSA region. Shrimp landings
(shell-on, heads-off weight) in the GSA region exhibited a declining trend from
206 million pounds in 1986 to 146 million pounds in 1997 (Figure 15.4).

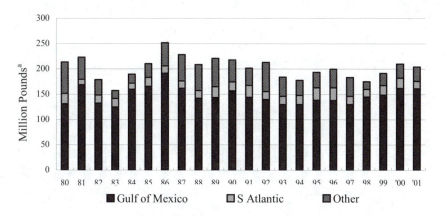

Figure 15.4: U.S. Shrimp Landings (Capture): Regional Production
[a]Converted to Shell-On, Heads-Off Weight
Source: USDOC (2002a).

However, shrimp landings increased to 176 million pounds by 2001. The average annual GSA region production during the 20-year period from 1982 to 2001 was 165 million pounds, and each year the total landings of the Gulf of Mexico and the South Atlantic averaged 90 percent and 10 percent, respectively. However, total shrimp landings in the GSA represent less than 10 percent of the total world landings of shrimp.

Shrimp are cultured in the United States, although in relatively small quantities. Shrimp-culture facilities exist primarily in Texas, South Carolina, Florida, Alabama, and Georgia. These operations produce small amounts of shrimp, mostly as a heads-on product for local markets. Total U.S. shrimp production was estimated to be approximately 6.3 million pounds (shell-on, heads-off weight) in 2001 (Rosenberry 2002). In an attempt to enhance the economic viability of culturing shrimp in the United States, technology has been developed recently to allow the culture of marine shrimp in freshwater systems (McMahon, Baca, and Samocha 2001). Prototype systems are currently being developed in Florida and Alabama. The successful application of this technology will allow the culture of marine shrimp in inland systems, which until now had been hindered by location.

U.S. Shrimp Supply

The total supply of shrimp in the U.S. domestic market expanded dramatically over the last 20 years and imports have increased relative to the total supply. Prior to 1979, domestic landings accounted for more than one-half of the total U.S. supply. During 1978, domestic landings represented 52 percent of the total shrimp supply. Each year since then, imported shrimp volumes have exceeded U.S. landings (on a shell-on, heads-off weight basis), and have exhibited a rapidly increasing share of the total market, particularly since 1996. Shrimp imports have increased from 240 million pounds in 1978 (48 percent of total supply) to 721 million pounds in 1996 (79 percent of the total supply) (Figure 15.5).

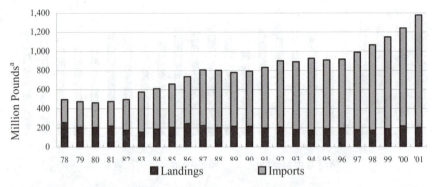

Figure 15.5: U.S. Shrimp Supply: Landing and Import Components
[a]Converted to Shell-On, Heads-Off Weight
Source: USDOC (2002a).

During this period, imported shrimp products increased at an average annual rate of 6.7 percent. However, this annual percentage increase has risen considerably since 1996. Import volumes increased from 811 million pounds in 1997 to 1.2 billion pounds during 2001. During this five-year period, shrimp imports increased at an average annual rate of 10.4 percent. The share of total domestic shrimp supply represented by imports increased from 48 percent in 1978 to 85 percent in 2001. Imported product now dominates the market.

The market for shrimp products is global, and, as the technology of culturing shrimp has become standardized, a shift has occurred in the relative importance of shrimp-exporting countries. Twenty years ago Mexico, Central America, and Northern South America were the predominant exporters of shrimp to the United States and trawling was the most important method of harvesting shrimp. Now, the most important world regions in terms of exporting shrimp to the U.S. market are Asia and Indonesia (Table 15.1). Five of the top ten countries that exported shrimp to the United States in 2001 are located in this global area with combined exports accounting for almost two-thirds of the total shrimp exported to the United States. The leading country of origin for imported shrimp products during 2001 was Thailand (300 million pounds), followed by Vietnam (73 millions pounds), India (72 million pounds), Mexico (66 million pounds), The People's Republic of China (PRC) (62 million pounds), and Ecuador (59 million pounds) (weights expressed on an import product-weight basis). These regions export warm-water shrimp to the United States with the majority of the exported shrimp cultured in saltwater-pond systems, not trawled or otherwise caught.

Table 15.1: Major Countries of Origin for U.S. Shrimp Market, 2001

Country	Volume 1,000 Pounds
Thailand	299,998
Vietnam	73,343
India	72,485
Mexico	66,175
People's Republic of China	61,766
Ecuador	58,995
Indonesia	34,939
Guyana	25,772
Brazil	21,647
Honduras	21,352

Source: USDOC (2002a).

THE PRICE/COST SQUEEZE

Vessel operators in the GSA region have long been recognized as price takers, particularly the independent vessel owners (Adams, Prochaska, and Spreen 1987). The price received at the dock is set by a myriad of factors within a truly global marketplace, over which the independent or fleet-vessel owner/operator has little direct influence in the short term. The same is true for many of the major costs incurred by a typical trawler. Thus, vessels are often at the mercy of the marketplace both in terms of product prices and input costs. While operating costs are increasing, historic periods of declining market prices for shrimp have placed many vessels in the GSA region in financial jeopardy—a situation that appears to be repeating itself in the GSA region shrimp fleet. We discuss these sources of financial pressure below.

Price Trends

The domestic price received by shrimp-vessel owners has been subject to considerable downward pressure from increasing supplies of imported shrimp. Many size classes of shrimp exist and some states specialize in the production of certain size classes of shrimp. For example, Louisiana's catch is dominated by smaller-sized shrimp, which are targeted by the many smaller inshore shrimp vessels that characterize Louisiana's shrimp fleet. In contrast, larger vessels characterize the Texas shrimp fleet, which shrimp further offshore for larger, more valuable (per pound) shrimp. Since 1981, Texas implemented a management program that closed the offshore waters to shrimping for a brief period with the purpose of letting shrimp move offshore from the near-shore habitats to grow to a larger, more valuable size prior to harvest. Regardless of the size class of shrimp, prices at the dock have been trending downwardly during the last several years, particularly since 1999 and 2000 (Vondruska 2001).

Real ex-vessel (dockside) prices (adjusted for inflation using a consumer price index (CPI) deflator index to 1982 as the base year) for shrimp landed by offshore vessels in Texas declined from U.S. $4.57 in 1979 to U.S. $2.47 in 2001 per pound of heads-off tails (U.S. Department of Labor 2003; Haby et. al. 2002) (Figure 15.6). These prices are a weighted average of the various size classes of shrimp caught by the Texas offshore fleet. Prices exhibited a rebound

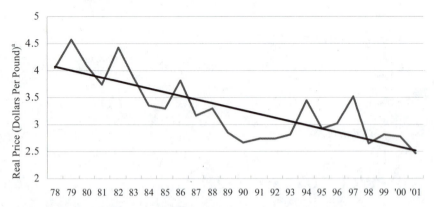

Figure 15.6: Real Ex-Vessel Prices for Shrimp Landed in Texas Ports
[a]Dollars Per Pound heads-off, 1982 dollars
Source: Haby et. al. (2002).

during 1994 (U.S. $3.44) and 1997 (U.S. $3.52), but then declined to unprecedented low levels in 1998 and 2001. Vondruska (2001) reports average ex-vessel prices (expressed in 1999 dollars) in the GSA region declined through 2002.

A current industry perception is that the nominal prices for certain size classes of imported shrimp are below the nominal domestic ex-vessel price, for the same size class of shrimp. Although this may be the case, no formal empirical studies have revealed this relationship. However, the existence of a falling domestic price provides evidence that import volumes are placing downward pressure on domestic ex-vessel prices. A comparison between nominal ex-vessel price of heads-off tail (weighted across all size classes) from Texas offshore trawlers and Thailand cultured imports further strengthens this argument. For example, Texas and Thailand shrimp tails were nominally valued at approximately the same amount during 1997 (U.S. $5.21 and U.S. $5.37, respectively) and have exhibited similar trends until 2001. In 2001, domestic ex-vessel prices dropped below import tail-meat prices (1999 being an exception in both cases) (Haby et. al. 2002; USDOC 2003). Personal communications with several industry representatives suggest that domestic trawl prices are continuing the downward trend begun in 2000.

Trawler Expenses

Concurrent with falling nominal and real ex-vessel prices, domestic trawlers have been forced to deal with rising operating costs. Since 1991, the per-dollar cost of shrimp harvested by offshore trawlers in the Gulf of Mexico has increased from U.S. $0.908 to U.S. $0.962 (Haby et. al. 2002). Thus for every dollar worth of shrimp harvested by domestic offshore shrimp trawlers in the Gulf of Mexico during 1997, more than 96 percent was directed toward covering vessel-operating costs, which was more than the costs that included fuel, ice, crew payments, gear maintenance, and supplies. The slim per-pound profit margin that vessels possess currently can be eroded easily by falling market prices. Thus many commercial shrimp vessels in the Gulf of Mexico region are being forced to tie up due to an inability to cover the costs of a trip.

Rising fuel costs and escalating insurance premiums for vessels are two of the most recent and episodic increases in vessel operating costs. Ward, Ozuna, and Griffin (1995) find that fuel, maintenance, and insurance were the three largest cost items confronted by vessel operators in the Gulf of Mexico. Fuel costs and insurance accounted for 42 percent of the total vessel operating cost. Maintenance costs accounted for an additional 22 percent of the total. Thus, any increases in these major cost categories places additional financial burdens on the vessel business. Vondruska (2003) has shown that fuel costs have been increasing through 2002.

Additional cost increases result from compliance with changes in fishery regulations. Provisions in the *Endangered Species Act* (ESA) require all shrimp vessels in the GSA region to have a turtle excluder device (TED) placed in the trawl throat. This device is designed to ensure that endangered sea turtles do not get caught in trawling nets and drown. A similar device, referred to as a by-catch reduction device (BRD), now required, allows undersized finfish (such as red snapper) to escape the shrimp trawl. Each of these devices represents an investment cost. In addition, the devices contribute to an increase in operating costs because certain amounts of shrimp also escape through the device openings (Griffin and Oliver 1991; Wui, Woodward, and Griffin 2001). The lost shrimp represent a short-term direct-revenue loss, or cost, to the vessel. Thus, individual shrimp vessels must incur the costs associated with species-protection measures and other regulatory constraints, again, without the ability to influence market prices in a manner that might compensate for these costs. In summary, vessel operators are price takers who are unable to pass increasing costs off in the form of higher selling prices for their shrimp at the docks.

EVENTS AFFECTING CURRENT MARKET VOLUME AND PRICE

The utilization of shrimp in the United States involves both static and rapidly changing elements. Relatively stable supplies from domestic sources, intertwined with international economic realities, have created a situation of volatile, yet generally deteriorating financial conditions among domestic participants in the Southeast shrimp fishery. As such, the harvesting and processing sectors are increasingly evaluating actions that could be taken to better position themselves in an ever-increasing global environment.

U.S. Trade Policy Actions

Until recently, the commercial harvesting sector has been the one component of the U.S. shrimp industry that has been unable to meet the needed cost adjustments in light of the growing import base and resulting downward pressure on dockside prices. Not unexpectedly, the origin of requests for relief from perceived problems associated with the increasing imports has been harvesting-sector based.

Since 1975, GSA region shrimp harvesters have sought regulatory relief from burdensome imports on three separate occasions, without beneficial results. In 1975, the U.S. International Trade Commission (USITC) reacted to a petition filed through the public hearing process by the National Shrimp Congress. The subsequent investigation in 1976 sought to determine if shrimp products were being imported in quantities that caused serious injury to the domestic shrimp industry. The analyses and public testimony resulted in a finding of serious injury to the capture fishery. Adjustment assistance permitted under Title II of the *Trade Act* (1974) was approved to allow shrimp-boat operators to obtain loans or loan guarantees. This, it was reasoned, would make domestic shrimp producers more competitive with foreign producers.

Approximately five years later, U.S. Senator Breaux of Louisiana, then a Representative, pointed out that the U.S. Administration actually failed to provide a remedy. Representative Breaux authored a bill to formulate a policy to provide for domestic shrimp industry protection. A temporary five-year import quota combined with a 30 percent ad valorem tariff was proposed. Although the bill failed to attain the support necessary for passage, it was significant because it was introduced at a time when production of cultured shrimp, while in its infancy, was becoming a reality. Like the previous action during 1976, attention was focused exclusively on shrimp harvesting.

In 1985, the focus remained on the shrimp-harvesting sector when the USITC again evaluated the import situation. Renewed supply increases from imported sources, particularly Ecuador, were being experienced. The frequent forecasts of overseas successes of shrimp-farming companies were becoming a reality. The additional shrimp-farming successes in Latin America and Asia loomed on the business horizon. When explaining their situation to the USITC, the U.S. Gulf of Mexico and the South Atlantic shrimp harvesters claimed: (1) harvesting businesses were being harmed as a result of imports; (2) shrimp industries in foreign countries benefited from government assistance, which artificially allowed their products to be more competitive in U.S. markets; and (3) U.S. access to traditionally open foreign shrimping grounds had been restricted, particularly off the coast of Mexico, thus limiting GSA-region harvesters to U.S. waters and increasing the pressure on shrimping activities.

In response to the harvesters claims, foreign shrimp producers contended that: (1) importers had historically provided a large and necessary share of the U.S. shrimp supply since domestic supply could not meet U.S. demand; (2) in many cases, imported shrimp commanded a higher price than domestic shrimp in the U.S. market; (3) tariffs or quotas on U.S. imports of shrimp will increase domestic shrimp prices to the point where the quantity of shrimp demanded and the quantity of shrimp consumed will drop; and (4) there is significant U.S. investment in foreign shrimp operations that fund the exportation of shrimp to the United States, particularly in aquaculture.

Following a staff review of information and a public hearing, the USITC chose simply to issue a report rather than to recommend actions. Given the reluctance by the USITC to take concrete measures to limit imports, it was becoming increasingly apparent that U.S. policy and regulations would not be used to protect the domestic shrimp fishery participants. Certainly, the lack of action by the USITC gave the implication that the shrimp-harvesting sector in the GSA would have to compete with a growing import base and with further price suppression.

The early impetus for trade investigations for shrimp stemmed from the GSA region shrimp-harvesting sector. Other components of the industry, most notably the processing sector, did not actively pursue import restrictions. To a large extent, this points out that the processing sector was, at the time of the 1985 trade investigation, benefiting from the increased import base. Specifically, to meet the growing deficit in raw material caused by the U.S. growth in domestic demand relative to domestic supply, processors turned to foreign shrimp supplies during the 1970s and 1980s. These imports, at least through the late 1980s, served an essential role in filling GSA region processing needs. The farm-raised product (originally from Ecuador and expanding quickly to many of the Asian countries) was particularly attractive to the GSA region processing sector for a number of reasons including: (1) farm-raised shrimp are less seasonal in nature, and are more reliable than its wild counterpart; (2) species and size can be better controlled in a culture-based system than in a wild-based system; and (3) the current trend toward vertical integration in the cultured system lends itself to better adapt to consumer (processor) needs (Csavas 1994). The use and benefits of farm-raised shrimp in the GSA region shrimp-processing sector have been documented in a number of studies including Roberts, Keithly, and Adams (1992) and Keithly and Roberts (1995).

Since the early 1990s, however, exporting countries have pursued value-added activities, particularly peeling, prior to shipment. Increasingly, the U.S. imported product, rather than being used as raw material by the GSA region shrimp-processing sector, competes directly with the domestic-processed product. This has resulted in a declining marketing margin for many of the shrimp products produced by the GSA region shrimp-processing sector. When evaluated on the basis of number of establishments, a rather substantial downsizing of the industry has occurred. Overall, output by the GSA region shrimp-processing sector (in terms of both poundage and current value) has been stagnant since the early 1990s, while the number of firms has fallen by about one-third. This followed a decade in which output (in terms of poundage) increased significantly.

The relevance of the changing structure of the GSA region shrimp-processing sector should not be discounted when discussing potential U.S. trade policy with respect to the GSA region's shrimp sector. Specifically, during the 1985 trade investigation, the processing sector was, at best, passive in attempting to limit imports (many processors likely actively argued against import restrictions). However, much of the processing sector also desired relief from imports and worked with the harvesting sector to achieve a common goal.

The GSA region harvest sector is filing a petition with the USITC to further investigate the potential for the dumping of cultured shrimp on the U.S. market by Asian countries. The petition represents the most recent effort to impose some form of import barrier to reduce the downward pressure on dockside price and to offer relief to the continuing cost-price squeeze afflicting the GSA region's shrimp fleet.

There is little doubt that the global recession is the primary short-term cause for the observed sharp reduction in prices received by GSA region shrimpers. In the world shrimp market, shrimp under normal economic conditions would have been directed toward Japan or the European Union. Because the U.S. prices have been higher than its Japanese and the European Union (EU) competitor's prices, shrimp has been diverted to the United States. This diversion has led to a further suppression in the dockside prices of U.S. shrimp.

Events Relevant to GATT and WTO

At the Uruguay Round of GATT negotiations, the United States proposed that fish and agricultural products be negotiated jointly. While agreeing in principle, the European Community (EC) suggested that the 200-mile Exclusive Economic Zone is a trade barrier and should be negotiated in the Uruguay Round. Disagreement over this EC proposal resulted in the elimination of agricultural and fish products from world negotiations (Wessells and Wallström 1994).

While fish products were severed from agricultural products in the Uruguay Round of GATT, a number of multilateral agreements on trade (MTA) in goods are relevant to fisheries. Where relevant to current and/or historical trade issues impacting the GSA region shrimp fishery, some of these MTAS are examined briefly below.

Tariff Negotiations and the Marakesh Protocol

Commitments among participating countries to eliminate or reduce tariff rates are recorded in the Schedules of Concessions annexed to the Marakesh Protocol. As indicated by the Agency for International Trade Information and Cooperation (AITIC) (1998), tariff reductions agreed upon by Member countries are to be implemented in five equal shares, the first of which became effective January 1, 1995.

Historically, tariff rates that vary considerably among countries (or groups), have been relatively large. At one extreme, the U.S. generally imposes no tariffs on unprocessed seafood. Tariffs on processed products, where applicable, tend to be low (Wessells and Wallström 1994). By comparison, the European Community and Japan practice much more protective policies and tariff rates are frequently substantial.

The issue of tariffs has been the focus of considerable attention by the GSA region shrimp fishery and, at least to some extent, has been related to the tariff reductions agreed upon by Member countries under the framework of the Marakesh Protocol. Consistent with most other seafood products, the U.S. imposes no tariffs on shrimp products. Under its Generalized System of Preferences (GSP), the European Community provided Thailand a voluntary, unilateral reduction on its import tariff equal to 4.7 percent for fresh and frozen shrimp in 1997. Revisions of the GSP in the European Community resulted in Thailand no longer being considered a developing country. As a result, the preferential treatment given by the European Community to Thailand on shrimp duties ended in 1999, and the tariff rate on fresh and frozen product reverted to the bound rate equal to 12 percent (i.e., the rate agreed upon under the GATT Uruguay Round).

As a result of the increased tariff, shrimp exports from Thailand to the European Community reportedly fell by a sizeable amount (some sources claim by up to 60 percent) with much of the product likely being diverted to the U.S. market. Given the fact that shrimp exports from Thailand to the European Community have always been relatively minor compared to Thailand's exports to the United States, it is debatable whether the increased EC tariff rates have a significant impact on the increased Thailand product entering the United States and on the subsequent impact experienced by the GSA region in terms of shrimp-dockside price.

Agreements on Non-Tariff Barriers

As noted by Karnicki (1997), Sanitary and Phytosanitary (SPS) measures and Technical Barriers to Trade (TBT) tend to be interrelated. Generally SPS measures apply to issues of food safety while TBT refers to the issuance of product standards. The SPS agreement affirms the ability of importing countries to impose measures necessary to protect the life or health of humans. Among other aspects, Lupien, Randall, and Field (1997) suggest that the SPS agreement: (1) places a heavy emphasis on "transparency" in the development and application of trade-restriction measures; (2) requires measures to be applied in a nondiscriminatory manner; and (3) strongly presses for "harmonization" between countries based upon the adoption of the standard developed by the international standards-setting bodies.

The SPS agreement has serious implications for the fisheries trade. As suggested by Cato (1998: 34), food-safety problems are often an issue in trade because "it is very easy to make them different, ambivalent or difficult to understand or meet." Because of the vast number of species and product forms, seafood is likely to be susceptible to the use of quality and safety measures as non-tariff barriers to trade.

SPS and Shrimp

In January 2002, the issue of SPS became a trigger point for the GSA region shrimp fishery when the European Community banned imports of shrimp from the PRC temporarily after finding in the shrimp traces of the antibiotic, chloramphenicol. Subsequently, another antibiotic, nitrofuran, was detected in shrimp coming to the European Community from many of the leading Asian shrimp-producing nations, including Thailand, Vietnam, Indonesia, and Bangladesh.

The European Community has a zero tolerance for these two antibiotics. Furthermore, to ensure that products testing positive for either of these two antibiotics do not find their way into the EC food chain indirectly, contaminated products are destroyed at the EC port of entry, which gives no avenue for appeal by the exporters. For a short period of time, the European Community imposed a 100 percent inspection on all shrimp arriving from identified countries.

The Asian Aquaculture Federation, which represents producers and exporters of five Asian countries—Indonesia, Malaysia, the Philippines, Vietnam, and Thailand—alleged that the zero tolerance for these two antibiotics had been made in a non-transparent and discriminatory manner, hence they could be considered a non-tariff barrier. The Asian Aquaculture Federation also claimed that no regulations under the WTO allowed for the destruction of products from other countries without prior approval.

Interestingly, the United States also has a zero tolerance for these two antibiotics. However, due to the methodology employed by the Food and Drug Administration (FDA), detection of the antibiotic chloramphenicol was only accurate down to 5 parts per billion (ppb). By comparison, The European Community could detect chloramphenicol as low as 0.3 ppb. The FDA is working to implement more strict chloramphenicol-detection guidelines, and these should soon be available.

As a result of EC actions, including the finer ability to detect banned antibiotics vis-à-vis the United States, and its policy to destroy product found to be contaminated, many Asian suppliers reportedly curtailed exports of the banned antibiotics to the European Community, redirecting the products to the U.S. market. This adjustment has likely led to further downward pressure on the dockside prices offered to shrimp vessels in the GSA region.

TBT and Shrimp

The objective of the TBT is to prevent countries from using national technical standards or requirements as a barrier to trade (Lupien, Randall, and Field 1997). The TBT is a complement to SPS because it covers all non-SPS standards.

The GSA region shrimp fishery was, at least indirectly, the catalyst for one of the most controversial issues yet to be brought to the attention of the World Trade Organization. The issue involves the use of TEDs. These devices are designed to keep sea turtles from becoming trapped inside a shrimp trawl. Spearheaded by the *Endangered Species Act* in 1987 and in an effort to protect endangered sea turtles, the National Marine Fisheries Service mandated the use of TEDs by shrimp trawlers in the GSA region on a limited basis with the mandate becoming more inclusive by 1989. Shrimpers, particularly in the Gulf of Mexico, contend that TEDs resulted in a loss of catch, thus making operations less viable.

The Southeast shrimp organization argued that they could not compete with foreign operations in which TEDs were not mandated. Environmental groups were concerned that TED regulations, specific to the Southeastern United States, would be inadequate to protect sea turtles due to the turtles' migratory patterns. The two groups combined forces to lobby Congress to extend the use of TEDs to all nations in which shrimp trawling is practiced. Congress complied and in 1989 approved legislation creating a certification program, which had a goal of encouraging other countries to protect their sea-turtle stocks. This required the U.S. Secretary of State to restrict imports of shrimp to the United States from those countries that do not mandate turtle-protection programs comparable to those in the United States (i.e., the use of TEDs in the shrimp-trawl fisheries).

Thailand, Pakistan, India, and Malaysia challenged the U.S. policy. In 1996, they took their case to the WTO. In 1998, the WTO ruled against the United States, partially on technical grounds. In essence, however, the WTO stated that use by the United States of its *Endangered Species Act* of 1973 as a means of banning imports from those countries out of compliance constituted a TBT.

RECENT ACTION TAKEN BY THE GULF OF MEXICO AND THE SOUTH ATLANTIC REGION SHRIMP-HARVESTING INDUSTRY

The domestic shrimp-trawling industry has once again taken steps to create barriers to shrimp products imported into the United States. The Southern Shrimp Alliance (SSA) was formed during 2002 to address a variety of issues of concern to the shrimp-harvesting sector in the GSA region. The issues driving the formation of SSA include the current depressed prices at the vessel level, domination of the domestic market by imported shrimp products, and the possibility of imposing antidumping (AD) actions against the primary countries exporting cultured shrimp into the U.S. market.

The Southern Shrimp Alliance, which is represented by members of the shrimp-harvesting sectors from all states in the GSA region, intends to achieve a variety of goals that include: (1) the recognition by Congress of harm to the U.S. shrimp industry created by increased volumes of cultured shrimp imports; (2) the assurance of the domestic shrimp industry that it maintains at least a 25 percent share of the domestic market; (3) the prevention of cultured shrimp subjected to illegal chemicals and antibiotics from entering the domestic market; (4)

the recognition of the difficulty of assessing the true cost of cultured shrimp exported from PRC and/or Vietnam; and (5) the creation of an advocacy presence in Washington D.C. for ongoing issues confronting the U.S. shrimp-harvesting sector. SSA hopes that achieving these goals will help ensure the economic sustainability of the domestic shrimp-harvesting industry in the GSA region.

Progress by the SSA includes enhanced testing by the FDA for contaminants in imported shrimp, expressions of support by various members of the U.S. Congress and Senate, and the initiation of an investigation into the allegations of dumping by the primary cultured shrimp-exporting nations, which SSA hopes will lead to a formal AD assessment by the USITC. More recently, the General Omnibus Bill passed in January 2003 contained provisions for shrimp industry disaster-relief funds, of which U.S. $35 million was allocated to the shrimp-harvesting sectors in the GSA region. The industry is developing plans to distribute these funds to the appropriate recipients in each state within the region. To what extent the funds should be used for immediate financial relief to individual vessel operators and/or long-term domestic shrimp-product marketing is being debated among industry members.

Finally, during 2003 the U.S. Department of Agriculture (USDA), Foreign Agricultural Service and Farm Service Agency have made relief funds available for agricultural, aquacultural, and commercial-fishing firms whose prices have been influenced negatively by imports of like products (USDA 2003). In the case of commercial-fishing firms, the price decline must be shown to be a result of foreign aquacultured imports. This program is almost tailor-made for the GSA region commercial shrimp-harvesting industry. At present, the shrimp-harvesting sectors in Texas, Florida, Georgia, and South Carolina have submit-ted petitions to be considered as recipients for these relief funds. Again, a moti-vating factor behind this recent relief program with respect to the commercial fishing industry is the widely recognized impact imported products have had on domestic prices, in particular prices received by domestic shrimp vessels in the GSA region.

CONCLUSIONS

The shrimp industry represents the most economically important component of the commercial seafood-harvesting industry in the GSA region. The harvesting sector of the industry historically has been shown to be financially vulnerable to changes in prices for shrimp and to prices of operating inputs. The industry's share of the total U.S. market has declined dramatically as the import volumes have increased. Concurrent with increasing import volumes have been declining dockside prices, which have reached record low points in the recent past. In addition, major operating costs have increased primarily due to rising fuel prices, but also due to costs associated with insurance and more stringent regula-tions. With virtually no ability to influence dockside prices as a means of compen-sating for increased costs, many vessels have been caught in a cost-price squeeze that has left them tied to the docks.

Although previous attempts to construct barriers for imported shrimp have failed, the industry is once again pursuing a strategy for restricting import volumes as a means of placing upward pressure on dockside prices. Given the apparent insatiable appetite for shrimp in the U.S. market, a permanent shift in the structure and conduct of the domestic shrimp market may be a real possibility. How the industry will cope with these changes will likely chart the course of the GSA region shrimp fleet with respect to long-term economic viability.

REFERENCES

Adams, C.M., F.J. Prochaska, and T.H. Spreen. (1987). "Price Determination in the U.S. Shrimp Market." *Southern Journal of Agricultural Economics* 19(1): 103–11.

Adams, C. (2002). "The Commercial Bottom-Trawling Industry in Florida: Balancing Environmental Impact with Economic Contribution." *EDIS* 345. Institute of Agricultural Sciences, University of Florida, Gainesville, Florida.

AITIC (Agency for International Trade Information and Cooperation). (1998). *Uruguay Round Agreements: Implications for Agriculture, Forestry, and Fisheries in the Less Advantaged Developing Countries.* Proceedings of a Workshop Sponsored by the Agency for International Trade Information and Cooperation, and the Food and Agriculture Organization, Geneva, 22–3 (September). Available at: http://www.acici.org/aitic/documents/workshop1/index.html.

Cato, J.C. (1998). *Economic Values Associated With Seafood Safety and Implementation of Seafood Hazard Analysis Critical Control Point (HAACP) Programmes.* FAO Fisheries Technical Paper No. 381. Rome: Food and Agricultural Organization.

Centaur Associates. (1984). *Economic Impact of the Commercial Fishing Industry in the Gulf of Mexico and South Atlantic Regions.* Washington, DC: Centaur Associates, Inc.

Csavas, L. (1994). "Important Factors in the Success of Shrimp Farming." *World Aquaculture* 25(1): 34–56.

Griffin, W.L. and C. Oliver. (1991). *Evaluation of the Economic Impacts of Turtle Excluder Devices (TEDs) on the Shrimp Industry of the Gulf of Mexico.* Final Project Report MARFIN, Agricultural Economics Department, Texas A&M University, College Station.

GMFMC (Gulf of Mexico Fishery Management Council). (1994). *An Economic Assessment of the Gulf of Mexico Shrimp Fishery.* Report prepared by the Economics and Trade Analysis Division, National Marine Fisheries Service, Southeast Regional Office. St. Petersburg, Florida.

Haby, M.G, R.J. Miget, L.L. Falconer, G.L. Graham. (2002). *A Review of Current Conditions in the Texas Shrimp Industry, and Examination of Contributing Factors, and Suggestions for Remaining Competitive in the Global Shrimp Market,* TAMU-SG-03-701. Texas Sea Grant Program, Texas Cooperative Extension Program, Texas A&M University, College Station, Texas.

Karnicki, Z.S. (1997). "The Impact of International Trade and Trade Agreements on Fish Inspection and Quality Control," in *Fish Inspection, Quality Control and HAACP: A Global Focus,* edited by R.E. Martin, R.L. Collette, and J.W. Slavin. Lancaster: Technomic Publishing Co., Inc. (3–11).

Keithly, W.R. and K.J. Roberts. (1995). *Shrimp Closures and Their Impact on the Gulf Region Processing and Wholesaling Sector (Expanded to Include the South Atlantic).* Final Report to the National Marine Fisheries Service, Contract Number NA17FF0376-01, St. Petersburg, Florida.

Keithly, W.R., K.J. Roberts, and J.M. Ward. (1993). *Effects of Shrimp Aquaculture on the U.S. Market: An Econometric Analysis in Aquaculture Models and Economics,* edited by U. Hatch and H. Kinnucan. Boulder: Westview Press.

Lupien, J.R., A. Randall, and C.G. Field. (1997). "Harmonization of Trade and Quality Control Issues," in *Fish Inspection, Quality Control and HAACP: A Global Focus,* edited by R.E. Martin, R.L. Collette, and J.W. Slavin. Lancaster: Technomic Publishing Co., Inc. (12–22).

McMahon, D.Z., B. Baca, and T.M. Samocha. (2001). "First Commercial Inland Farm in Florida, USA Using Zero Discharge in Low-Salinity Ponds." *Global Aquaculture Advocate* 4(5): 66–70.

Murray. T. (2003). *Economic Activity Associated with the Use of Imported Shrimp in the U.S.* Report prepared by Thomas J. Murray and Associates, the American Seafood Distributors Association. Gloucester, Virginia.

Roberts, K.J., W.R. Keithly, and C.M. Adams. (1992). "Determinants of Imported Shrimp and Their Role in the Southeast Shrimp Processing Sector." NMFS Technical Memorandum NMFS/SEFC-305, Silver Spring, Maryland.

Rosenberry, B. (2002). Personal interview. Editor/Publisher of *Shrimp News International* (October 3).

SAFMC (South Atlantic Regional Fishery Management Council). (1999). *Stock Assessment and Fishery Evaluation Report for the Shrimp Fishery in the South Atlantic Region.* Report prepared by the South Atlantic Fishery Management Council, Charleston, South Carolina.

Swingle, W. (2001). *The Physical Environment Affected by Shrimp Trawling in the Northern and Western Gulf (Alabama through Texas).* Paper prepared for the Gulf of Mexico Regional Fishery Management Council, Tampa, Florida.

Trade Act. (1974). Available at:
    http://www.access.gpo.gov/uscode/title19/chapter12_.html.

USDA (U.S. Department of Agriculture). (2001). Food consumption. Available at:
    http://www.ers.usda.gov/data/foodconsumption/datasystem.asp.

_____. (2003). "Trade Adjustment Assistance." Available at:
    http://www.fas.usda.gov/itp/taa.

USDOC (U.S. Department of Commerce). (2002a). *Fisheries of the United States, Current Fishery Statistics No. 2001.* National Marine Fisheries Service, National Oceanic and Atmospheric Administration, Silver Spring, Maryland.

_____. (2002b). Fisheries landings and international trade data website. "National Marine Fisheries Service." Available at: http://www.st.nmfs.gov/st1/.

_____. (2003). "National income and product accounts data." Bureau of Economic Analysis: USDOC. Available at: www.bea.gov/bea/dn/nipaweb/TableViewFixed.asp.

U.S. Department of Labor. (2003). "Producer price index data by commodity." Available at: http://data.bls.gov/servlet/SurveyOutputServlet.

Vondruska, J. (2001). *Southeast Shrimp Markets and Global Market Trends*, Report Number SERO-ECON-01-03. St. Petersburg: National Marine Fisheries Service, Southeast Regional Office.

_____. (2003). *Global Shrimp Market, Update.* St. Petersburg: National Marine Fisheries Service, Southeast Regional Office.

Ward, J.M., T. Ozuna, and W. Griffin. (1995). "Cost and Revenue in the Gulf of Mexico Shrimp Fishery." National Oceanic and Atmospheric Administration, Technical memorandum NMFS-SEFC-371, National Marine Fisheries Service, Silver Springs, Maryland.

Wessells, C.R. and P. Wallström. (1994). "New Dimensions in World Fisheries: Implications for U.S. and E.C. Trade in Seafood," in *Agricultural Trade Conflicts and GATT: New Dimensions in North American-European Agricultural Trade Relations*, edited by G. Anania, C.A. Carter, and A.F. McCalla. Boulder: Westview Press (515–35).

Wui, Y.S., R.T. Woodward, and W.L. Griffin. (2001). *An Economic Analysis of a New Bycatch Reduction Policy in the Gulf of Mexico*. Agricultural Economics Department, Texas A&M University, College Station, Texas.

Chapter 16

Fresh Garlic from the People's Republic of China and U.S. Trade Remedy Law

Fumiko Yamazaki and Mechel S. Paggi[*]

California State University, Fresno

INTRODUCTION

Garlic is used mainly as a food-flavouring ingredient as well as a remedy for a wide variety of health-related conditions. Garlic (Allium sativum) is: (1) a member of the Amaryllis (lily) plant group; (2) related to shallots, onion, leeks, and chives; and (3) produced by 81 countries. Its production reached more than 12 million metric tons (mmt) in 2002 (Figure 16.1). The People's Republic of China (PRC) is one of the world's leading producers of garlic. Its worldwide share of production has increased from 59 percent in 1987 to 71 percent in 2002. The majority of PRC garlic comes from the PRC's Shandong Province, which is located southeast of Beijing. India and South Korea rank second and third with production shares of 4.1 percent and 3.3 percent, respectively. The United States ranks fourth at 2.7 percent of world production in 2002.

On January 31, 1994[1], an investigation of fresh garlic from the PRC was initiated on the basis of a petition filed by the Fresh Garlic Producers Association (FGPA).[2] The FGPA alleged that fresh garlic from the PRC was being sold in the United States at less than fair value (LTFV), and that these imports injured materially a domestic industry. The products covered by this initial investigation were:

> ... all grades of garlic, whole or separated into constituent cloves, whether or not peeled, fresh, chilled, frozen, provisionally preserved, or packed in water of other neutral substance, but not prepared or preserved by the addition of other ingredients or heat processing. The differences between grades are based on colour, size, sheathing and level of decay (59 *FR* 49058 1994).

245

In November 1994, the U.S. Department of Commerce (USDOC) issued an antidumping (AD) duty order on fresh garlic from PRC. U.S. antidumping law is designed to counter international price discrimination, commonly referred to as "dumping." Dumping generally occurs when a foreign firm sells merchandise in a market at a price lower than the price it charges for a similar product sold in the home market. Under U.S. AD law, the USDOC investigates complaints to determine whether "a class or kind of merchandise is being, or is likely to be, sold in the United States at less than its fair value;" at the same time, the U.S. International Trade Commission (USITC) investigates the extent of injury to domestic interests and decides whether a U.S. industry is injured materially by reason of the imports sold at LTFV prices. If dumping is found and the injury is not immaterial, the USDOC assesses duties.

This chapter provides an analysis of the AD case against fresh garlic from the PRC measuring the potential effects to domestic industry of the imposition of the AD duty on PRC garlic. When determining dumping margins and duties, we provide background data on garlic, followed by a discussion of the use of surrogate-country data and conditions for use of best information available (BIA). We use a partial equilibrium trade model with a simple Armington-type specification to examine the potential effects on price, supply, and imports under alternative elasticity assumptions from the imposition of U.S. AD duties on PRC garlic imports (Armington 1969). We conclude with a discussion of questions raised from the analysis and a discussion of additional research required to improve an understanding of the costs and benefits of the application of U.S. AD laws to an import-sensitive agricultural commodity.

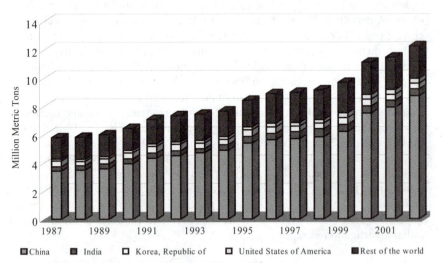

Figure 16.1: World Garlic Production, 1987 to 2002
Source: FAO (2003).

BACKGROUND

U.S. Garlic Industry

U.S. Garlic production has doubled over each of the last two decades. Most of the domestic garlic that enters the fresh and dehydrating product markets are grown in California. In 1999, California's garlic production increased 35 percent to a record 336,000 metric tons (mt), recovering from a 2 percent decline in 1998 (USDA/NASS 2003). During the 1992 to 2002 period, the area harvested for garlic in the United States increased from 23,000 acres to around 33,000 acres. In 2002, California accounted for 84 percent of the U.S. garlic production followed by Oregon at 13 percent. The three California counties of Fresno, Kern, and Monterey provide most of the garlic produced in California, and Fresno County accounts for more than 80 percent of California's garlic production.

Garlic can be separated into three different markets (fresh, seed, and dehydrating). It can be further separated by harvesting methods, growing conditions, and end use. Per-capita consumption of garlic in the United States accelerated in the 1990s due to several factors, including increased demand for ethnic foods, and increased demand from restaurants and the health-supplements industry. While fresh-market garlic is hand harvested, seed and dehydrating garlic are mechanically harvested. In general, these three markets are relatively independent, however, changes in relative market prices and stock levels can result in some shifting in the markets, especially between fresh and dehydrating markets. Garlic can be stored for a relatively long time period. With standard storage, fresh garlic can be marketed for up to 3 months from the time of harvest, up to 6 months with cold storage, and up to a year with a special storage system that controls the atmosphere.

World Garlic Trade

From 1980 to 2001, the value of world garlic exports increased significantly from U.S. $103 million to U.S. $508 million. World garlic exports expanded rapidly during the 1990s, and reached a peak of approximately 892,000 mt in 1999 (Figure 16.2). The PRC emerged as the major contributor to growth in the world garlic export market with a 63 percent share of the market in 2001, up from only 12 percent in 1980. PRC garlic exports have increased 246 percent from 158,000 mt in 1998 to more than 547,000 mt, in 2001.

Many countries around the world import garlic. In 2001, Indonesia was the largest single importer, accounting for approximately 24 percent of world imports, followed by Brazil with 9 percent and Malaysia with 8 percent. The United States is the fourth largest importer, accounting for an estimated 4 percent of world garlic imports (Figure 16.3). The spiked increases in imports in several importing countries are partly reflections of domestic production shortfalls. U.S. imports increased during the 1990s, and accounted for about 23 percent of all garlic used domestically in 2001, both fresh and processed, which is up from 17 percent in the 1980s.

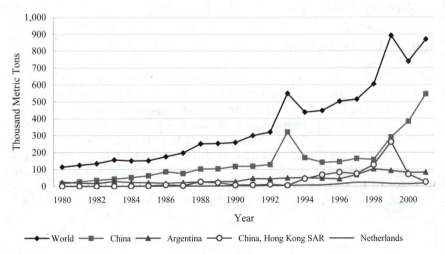

Figure 16.2: World Garlic Exports, 1980 to 2001
Source: FAO (2003).

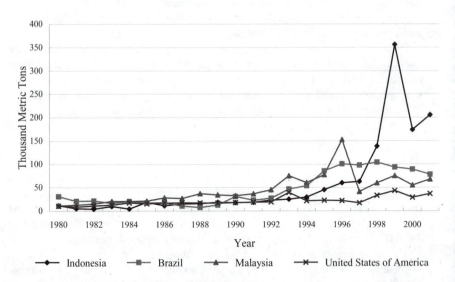

Figure 16.3: World Garlic Imports, 1980 to 2001
Source: FAO (2003).

The Antidumping Case Against Chinese Garlic Imports

In response to the 1994 investigation requested by the FGPA, the USITC notified the USDOC of its final determination on November 7, 1994. The result of the investigation was that the USITC found three like products:

... Fresh garlic, defined as garlic that has been manually harvested and is intended for use as fresh produce; ... dehydrating garlic, defined as garlic that has been mechanically harvested and that is primarily, but not exclusively, destined for non-fresh use; and ... seed garlic, defined as garlic that has been specially prepared and cultivated prior to planting and then harvested and otherwise prepared for use as seed. (59 *FR* 59209 1994)

The USITC determined that the domestic fresh-garlic industry in the United States was injured materially by imports of fresh garlic from the PRC that were being sold at LTFV. The USDOC published its final determination of the investigation of fresh garlic from PRC on September 26, 1994 (59 *FR* 49058 1994) and issued its AD duty order (case A-570-831) on November 16, 1994. Importers of fresh garlic from the PRC were required to post a bond or cash deposit equal to 376.67 percent of the invoice value of the imported product effective July 11, 1994 (59 *FR* 59209 1994). However, the scope of the AD order did not include:[3]

Garlic that has been mechanically harvested and that is primarily but not exclusively, destined for non-fresh use; or garlic that has been specially prepared and cultivated prior to planting and then harvested and otherwise prepared for use as seed. (USITC 1994)[4]

A five-year review was initiated by the USITC on December 1, 1999 (64 *FR* 67315 1999) to determine whether revocation of the AD duty order on fresh garlic from the PRC would likely lead to a continuation or recurrence of material injury to the domestic industry. In five-year reviews, the USITC determines whether or not to conduct a full review that would include a public hearing, the issuance of questionnaires, and other procedures. On March 3, 2000, the USITC decided to conduct a full review of the case (65 *FR* 13989 2000). On December 19, 2000, a hearing was held in Washington, D.C. and the USITC transmitted its determination in the investigation to the Secretary of Commerce on February 21, 2001. The USITC concluded:

... we determine that revocation of the AD duty order on fresh garlic from the PRC would be likely to lead to continuation or recurrence of material injury to the domestic industry producing fresh garlic within a reasonably foreseeable time. (USITC 2001a)

The Structure of U.S. Garlic Imports

U.S. garlic imports increased significantly during the 1990s from a value of U.S. $50 million in 1990 to a peak of U.S. $176 million in 1999. After a decline to approximately U.S. $129 million in 2000, U.S. garlic imports were valued at U.S. $174 million in 2002. On average for the 1989 to 2002 period, over 90 percent of the value of U.S. garlic imports was associated with those categories of garlic included in the AD case (case garlic).[5] The share of total imports accounted for by case garlic increased during the 1990s and accounted for over

93 percent of garlic imports in 2002. Total imports of case garlic grew from U.S. $41 million in 1990 to U.S. $161 million in 2002.

Garlic (fresh/chilled) imports by the United States increased sharply in 1993 to 39,000 mt, which represents a 100 percent increase from the previous year. In 1995, due to changes in the Harmonized Coding System, garlic fresh/chilled was disaggregated into three subheadings; fresh-bulb garlic, fresh-clove garlic, and other fresh garlic. In 1999, U.S. imports of fresh-bulb garlic increased sharply to 39,000 mt, an increase of over 50 percent from the previous year and an almost 200 percent increase from 1997 import levels. U.S. imports of fresh-bulb garlic dropped sharply in 2000, but increased subsequently to 42,000 mt in 2002. There were three significant increases in U.S. imports of fresh garlic from 1989 to 2002 (Figure 16.4). The first sharp increase in fresh garlic reflected increased imports from the PRC in 1993. PRC exports of fresh garlic to the United States increased dramatically from 3,000 mt in 1992 to over 24,000 mt in 1993. The second spike in U.S. fresh-garlic imports was associated with increased fresh-bulb garlic imports from Argentina that increased from over 6,000 mt in 1998 to 20,000 mt in 1999. The third spike came in 2002, once again associated with increased imports from the PRC. Exports of fresh garlic from the PRC to the United States dropped significantly in 1995 to approximately 20 mt after the USDOC issued the AD duty. In 1997 and 1998, there were no imports of PRC fresh-bulb garlic into the United States. However, imports began to increase again in 2000, and reached 18,000 mt in 2002.

Significant increases in U.S. imports of other garlic from the Harmonized Tariff Schedule of the United States (HTSUS) 07 categories in the case, especially frozen vegetables that include garlic, resulted from increased imports of this category from Canada and Mexico. The other type of garlic considered in

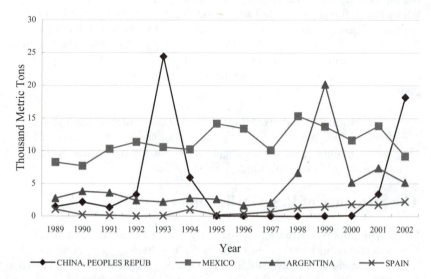

Figure 16.4: U.S. Imports of Garlic Fresh/Chilled (1989-1995) and Fresh Garlic Bulb (1996-2002) From Major Countries, 1989 to 2002
Source: USDA/FAS (2003).

the case was the garlic contained in the other-vegetable categories (HTSUS 2005909500 until 1994 and HTSUS 2005909700 after 1995) (USDA/FAS 2003). The U.S. imported over 50,000 mt of this category garlic in 2002, mostly from Mexico.

The 1994 AD case focused on fresh and chilled PRC garlic (fresh-bulb garlic) imports. For other types of garlic (fresh-clove garlic and other fresh garlic), the PRC played a minor role in the U.S. market. Not surprisingly, imports of garlic categories not considered in the case, especially dry garlic, have increased significantly, and are imported mostly from the PRC (USDA/FAS 2003). The PRC dominates both the garlic powder and dry garlic import markets in the United States with almost a 100 percent share of the market for these commodities.

ISSUES

The AD case against PRC garlic imports provides insight into two interesting issues associated with trade remedy law. The first issue is the procedure and process used to determine when dumping has occurred and how a dumping margin and subsequent AD duty level is determined. Nonmarket designations, the use of surrogate-country data, the use of BIA and the choice of adverse assumptions raise questions concerning the objectivity of the process. Second, despite the imposition of a 376.67 percent tariff on fresh garlic imported from the PRC since 1994, the effectiveness of an AD duty is questionable. Imports of garlic from the PRC are once again increasing in case-garlic categories and further-processed-garlic products. The benefits of the AD duty for the U.S. garlic industry are difficult to measure. To assess the net effect of the AD duty, industry benefits must be weighed against the various administrative costs associated with the investigation and administration of the law, with legal expenses to the industry when bringing the case to the USITC and USDOC, and with consumer costs associated with the barrier to lower-priced PRC garlic.

The Antidumping Investigation Process

Under U.S. Antidumping Law, AD duties will be imposed when two conditions are met: (1) the USDOC determines that the foreign subject merchandise is being, or is likely to be, sold in the United States at LTFV;[6] and (2) the USITC makes a determination that an industry in the United States is injured materially or is threatened with material injury, or the establishment of an industry in the United States is retarded materially by reason of imports of the merchandise under investigation (USITC 1998: 1–2).

Most AD investigations are initiated in response to petitions filed by an affected interested domestic party, including a manufacturer or a union within the domestic producers producing the "domestic-like product" that competes with the imports to be investigated. The petitioner submits available data and information in support of the dumping allegations to the USDOC and the USITC simultaneously.

According to the USITC, the overall AD investigation process has five stages: (1) initiation of the investigation by the USDOC (determination for further investigation within 20 days after the filling of the petition); (2) the preliminary phase of the investigation by the USITC (transmitting preliminary determination within 45 days after the filing of the petition); (3) the preliminary phase of the investigation by the USDOC (preliminary determination within 115 days after the preliminary determination by the USITC); (4) the final phase of investigation by the USDOC (final determination within 75 days after the preliminary determination of the USDOC or, under normal circumstances, within 235 days after the filing of the petition); and (5) the final phase of investigation by the USITC (final determination within 120 days after preliminary determination by the USDOC or 45 days after its final determination, whichever is later) (USITC 2001b: Part II, 3–15).

Based upon the information submitted in the petition, the USDOC has 20 days to evaluate the petition and to determine whether it will initiate an investigation. While the USDOC determines whether and to what extent dumping is occurring, the USITC conducts a parallel investigation to determine whether a domestic industry competing with the allegedly dumped product has been injured materially by such imports. For example, injury may result when unfair low-priced foreign competition reduces the profits and market share of a domestic industry. If the final determinations of both the USDOC and the USITC are affirmative (that is, dumping and injury are confirmed), an AD order is issued. In the order, the USDOC instructs the U.S. Customs Service to collect cash deposits of AD duties on identified products entering the United States or on identified products that are withdrawn from a bonded warehouse. The cash deposit represents an estimate of the actual duties owed. The final amount of duties collected will be the cash deposit or, if an administrative review is requested, it will be the duty established by an administrative review.

Each year, an administrative review may be requested to determine whether the extent of dumping has changed since the order went into effect. Depending on its findings in an administrative review, the USDOC will adjust the AD duty rates so they reflect the actual amount of dumping that occurred for the reviewed period. The U.S. Customs Service is then notified of the change, and appropriate refunds of prior duty deposits or additional duty collections are made. The new rates found in the review will serve as the cash-deposit rates for future entries.

In an investigation or an annual review, the USDOC issues questionnaires to all domestic producers, domestic importers, and foreign producers that reported production or imports of the merchandise in question. According to the USITC, questionnaires for producers generally consist of four parts including: (1) organization/activities of the firm and involvement in petition; (2) data on capacity, production, and inventories; (3) financial information; and (4) sales prices and other price-related information. Importer questionnaires are in three parts: (1) organization activities of the firm; (2) data on imports of the product in question, its quantity, and its value; and (3) data on sales prices and other price-related information. Foreign producer questionnaires also consist of three parts: (1) and (2) are general questions about the firm's operations in the country in question and in the United States; and (3) gives the data on the firm's capacity, production, and sales. Domestic producers and importers must reply to the questionnaires while foreign producers/exporters do not (USITC 2001b: Part II).

Based on their assessment of the initial information, the USITC may request additional information, if required for their investigation. The USDOC generally bases its calculations of margin on information provided by the respondents. If the responding firms fail to provide requested data, the USDOC uses the facts otherwise available, or BIA (prior to the *Uruguay Round Agreement Act* (URAA) of 1995). Under the statute, if the respondent has not acted to the best of his ability by supplying information, the USDOC may make an adverse inference when choosing which facts to use (IA 1998). The potential use of adverse facts available gives the respondents the incentive to cooperate fully with the USDOC proceedings. In addition to the standard sets of questionnaires issued by the USDOC, the record in an investigation or annual review contains numerous documents submitted by the domestic and foreign interested parties as well as the comments on methodology and legal arguments used by the USDOC.

Throughout the proceedings, there are several opportunities to discuss issues. Prior to the final determination, interested parties may request hearings to be held on the arguments addressed in the briefs submitted by the parties. The USDOC makes a price comparison between the price of imports and normal value (NV) based on collected information with some adjustments to ensure the one-to-one correspondence in product for the price comparison. When producers are located in a nonmarket-economy country (NMEC), a comparison is made between a U.S. price and a surrogate NV. In simple terms, the differences between the two prices are the dumping margins, which are calculated and applied on company-specific terms for all firms participating in the investigation or review. In investigations, a weighted-average all-others rate is calculated and applied to firms that did not participate in the investigation. A company covered by the all-others rate continues to receive that rate until a review is requested and completed for that company.

In the 1994 garlic case, the USDOC treated the PRC as a NMEC and considered their prices and costs to be set by the state, thus they were not reflective of market prices. In order to determine the market value of garlic in the PRC, the USDOC obtained factors of production from a surrogate country (i.e., a country with a comparable economy that is a significant producer of the garlic, and in this case they used India. Based on the values from India and other information, the department arrived at a constructed value of the NV of garlic in the PRC market taking into account such costs as materials, energy, packaging, insurance, movement charges, and factory overhead. The PRC market value was then compared to the U.S. price to determine whether dumping had occurred.

When the USDOC determined there had been dumping, the USITC then determined whether the dumped imports caused material injury or threatened material injury to domestic garlic producers. Thus the USITC sent questionnaires regarding the costs and profits of production to domestic garlic producers and importers as well as to PRC producers and exporters of fresh garlic. Given the detailed information required for the calculation of dumping margins, the task became difficult when the PRC firms provided neither accurate nor enough information. It was clear that there was a subjective determination by the USDOC for their process, especially when the PRC producers and/or exporters did not provide sufficient information in a timely manner or did not reply to the questionnaires. For the garlic case, the USDOC employed BIA. There are wide variations when using BIA commerce, from use in some portions of a dumping margin calculation to use as the sole information.

When the USDOC found dumping and the USITC found injury, the USDOC issued an AD-duty order setting out a dumping margin of 376.67 percent on PRC garlic imports. A U.S. importer may continue to import garlic as long as he posts cash deposits equivalent to the dumping margin with the U.S. Customs Service every time he imports garlic into the United States. (The actual dumping duty owed by the U.S. importer is determined during an annual admin-istrative-review investigation in November of each year.) For the next several years, PRC exports of fresh garlic to U.S. markets ceased when the high AD duty was imposed. However, a PRC exporter could attempt to open the market by making a small shipment of garlic to the United States. He then could request a review investigation in an effort to receive a lower cash-deposit rate. Each year, toward the end of October to early November, there is a notice in the *Federal Registry* regarding the "Notice of opportunity to request administrative review of AD or CV duty order, finding, or suspended investigation." Interested parties must make a request for a review before the end of November. There were eight administrative reviews during the 1994 to 2002 period; more than 200 companies were included in these reviews (Chapter 16 Appendix).

Before the implementation of the URAA, there were no time limits on AD-duty review investigations. The USDOC could take several years before announcing its results. Under GATT, the USDOC must finish an investigation in 12 to 18 months. As a result of these reviews, some exporters now have access to a company-specific rate. The URAA also allows new exporters to request a new-shipper-review investigation once they have made a small shipment into the U.S. market, provided they have not been reviewed in a prior investigation. A new-shipper review has a shorter time limit than an administrative review, which allows U.S. importers to post a bond rather than to pay a deposit in cash when they import garlic from a new shipper. Since January 2001, there have been a limited number of new-shipper reviews initiated. For example, in the review for the Jinan Yipin Corporation, Ltd. for the November 1, 2000 to Octo-ber 31, 2001 period, the USDOC published the preliminarily results of its new-shipper review and posted a dumping margin of 15.26 percent (67 *FR* 49669 2002). However, these results were modified based on comments received from interested parties. The final results of the review were changed to "the weighted-average dumping margin for subject merchandise manufactured and exported by Jinan Yipin for the period of review, 0.00 percent" (67 *FR* 72139 2002).

On December 1, 1999, the USDOC and the USITC initiated a sunset review of the 1994 fresh-garlic case (64 *FR* 67247 and 64 *FR* 67315 1999). Both the USDOC, on July 5, 2000, and the USITC, on February 28, 2001, found that revocation of the AD duty order on fresh garlic from the PRC would likely lead to a continuation or recurrence of dumping and material injury to a domestic industry (65 *FR* 41432 2000; 66 *FR* 12810 2001; and USITC 2001a). The sunset-review procedure appeared similar to that of the initial investigation by the USDOC and the USITC (USITC 2001a):

No respondent interested parties that produce the subject merchandise in [the PRC] provided questionnaire responses or participated in this review. Accordingly, we have relied on the facts available in this review, which consist primarily of the evidence in the record from the Commission's original investigation, the information collected by the Commission since the institution of this review, and information submitted by interested parties in this review.

This brief description of the general procedures used by the USDOC suggests that the investigation process for the PRC fresh-garlic case includes a wide range of subjective determinations in the calculation of dumping margins. The subjective determinations include the choice of surrogate country, selection of cost and price data, adjustments for additional costs associated with marketing, and the application of BIA.

There is reason to believe that the discretionary practices used by the USDOC may have resulted in a high dumping margin being calculated for the garlic case. Several studies examined the role of discretionary practices by the USDOC and concluded that the use of BIA leads to dumping margins that are higher than \average margins (Baldwin and Moore 1991; Lindsay 1999). In addition to their subjectivity in the investigation process, the determination process for sales at LTFV or injury is not transparent in the garlic case. For example, it is not clear what value of export price or constructed-export price was used for the determination, what the determined values for NV or constructed NV were, or what types of adjustments were made during the investigation process.

We compare the AD investigation process for fresh garlic from the PRC by the United States to the more transparent process applied by Canada. Canada initiated an AD investigation on fresh garlic from the PRC in August 1996 and the final determination was rendered on February 1997 (Table 16.1). The AD case was re-investigated in October 2000 with a final determination in April 2001. The initial AD duty of CDN $0.99 per kilogram (kg) was re-calculated in the re-investigation process to CDN $1.82 per kg. The NV was determined using a surrogate country with an open-market economy (Mexico), and their investigation process displayed more transparent results.

In addition to problems associated with the investigation process, AD cases have high administrative costs including information gathering, publication of notices, and the hearing process. Since the initiation of the AD case on fresh garlic from PRC from February 1994 to March 2003, approximately 72 *Federal Registry* (*FR*) notices have been published regarding this case (*FR* 1994 to 2003). Costs associated with publication, investigation, and administration by the government, the FGPA, and consumers, need to be defined in order to measure the net benefits of the AD case on fresh garlic.

Table 16.1: Calculation of Dumping Margin by Canada: Fresh Garlic Exported From the People's Republic of China

Initiation of Investigation: August 23, 1996

Final Determination: February 19, 1997

Finding: March 21, 1997
    AD duty of CA $0.99/kg on fresh garlic imported from the PRC for July 1 to December 31 of each calendar year.
    AD duty (CA $0.99/kg) = the Normal Value (CA $1.91/kg) – Export Price (CA $0.92/kg)

Re-investigation of the case: October 31, 2000

Final Determination: April 2, 2001

Finding: May 2, 2001
    AD duty (CA $1.82) = the Normal Value[a] (CA $2.50/kg) – Export Price[b] (CA $0.68/ka)

[a]Normal Value: Determined in a surrogate country with an open-market economy (Mexico), on the basis of profitable domestic sales or the full cost of the goods plus an amount for profit
[b]Export Price: Declared selling price by PRC are considered to be unreliable, thus the export price will be determined to be $0.92/kg. This amount represents the average selling price of fresh PRC garlic derived from reliable evidence.
Sources: CCRA (1998; 2001); CITT (1997; 2001).

Effectiveness of Antidumping Policy

When the AD duty was applied to PRC garlic, an increase in the import price of PRC garlic (assuming no change in the exchange rate) was expected and the quantity of garlic imported from the PRC declined. This decline in PRC garlic imports might be filled by U.S. domestic production and/or by increased shipments from foreign exporters of "like products." One of the problems associated with the effectiveness of AD duties on garlic is the potential for circumvention of the duty by the importation of garlic, originating in the PRC and coming circuitously from another other country (transhipment). According to FGPA, some PRC garlic appears to be entering the United States after being transhipped through other countries. In January 2002, the FGPA complained that PRC garlic was being imported at low prices with labels indicating it was produced in countries such as Thailand, Vietnam, and Spain, thus circumventing a 376 percent tariff. For example, on March 2, 2000 in a letter to the Secretary of Commerce, William Thomas (a member of the U.S. Congress) wrote:

> I am informed by the California fresh garlic industry that Commerce is investigating a Spanish company for possible violations of the anti-dumping duty order on fresh garlic from [the PRC]. Representatives of this Spanish company have told California interests that this [garlic was] shipped repacked [from the PRC] through Puerto Rico in boxes stamped "product of Spain."

PRC fresh-garlic exports to Spain increased from 225 mt in 1995 to over 1,900 mt in 2001. PRC fresh garlic exports to Vietnam increased significantly from 3,400 mt in 1995 to 67,000 mt in 2002. PRC exports to Thailand also increased from 135 mt in 1995 to 7,100 mt in 2002. The PRC's largest export destination for the fresh and chilled garlic was Indonesia (244,000 mt in 2002). Exports to Indonesia increased significantly over the 1995 to 2002 period. However, as discussed earlier, increases in imports by some of these countries might be the result of domestic shortfalls in their own domestic fresh-garlic production. The Food and Agricultural Organization of the United Nations (FAO) production data has no entry for the countries of Malaysia and Vietnam. Further analysis is needed to identify proven cases of PRC garlic transhipment.

Effects of Antidumping Duty

The imposition of the AD duty by the United States on imports of PRC fresh garlic could lead to an increase in the supply available from domestic producers (Armington 1969). The extent of change in domestic-garlic production and market share depends on many factors, especially on the degree of substitutability between domestic and imported garlic. Traditional trade analysis often assumes imports and domestic goods are perfect substitutes. This assumption leads to difficulties when understanding the observed continued demand for PRC garlic despite changes in its relative price over time. When an AD duty is applied to imports of garlic from the PRC, the price of garlic increases. However, the effect of the change in the price of imports on the price of domestically produced garlic depends on the effects of domestic resource allocation. If the imported garlic is an imperfect substitute, the price of the domestic garlic may not change by the same proportion as that of the import (Figure 16.5).

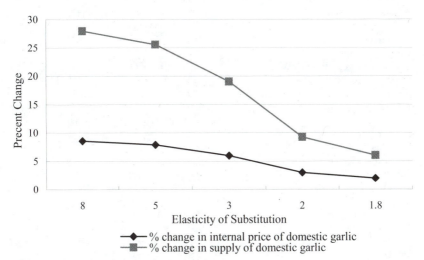

Figure 16.5: Antidumping Duty and Domestic Garlic: Sensitivity to Armington Specifications
Source: Authors' Computation.

Thus, the impact an AD duty has on the structure of domestic production depends on the degree of substitutability between domestically produced and imported garlic, the so-called Armington elasticity.

The elasticity of substitution between imported and domestic garlic can be defined as the proportionate change in the ratio of quantities divided by the proportionate change in the marginal rate of substitution in demand between these two goods: the higher the value of this parameter, the closer the degree of substitution. In other words, a high value of this parameter implies that imports and domestic supplies are considered by consumers to be identical, but they would be exactly identical if the parameter was infinite. Conversely, a low value of the parameter implies that PRC garlic and domestic garlic are dissimilar.

In this section, we provide examples of the effect of the imposition of the AD duty on imports of garlic from the PRC, on domestic prices, and on the quantity of garlic from the results of a simple partial equilibrium Armington model developed by J. Francois and H.K. Hall (1997). The model is a nonlinear system of equations with three supply sources of garlic: domestic, PRC imports, and imports from the rest-of-the-world (ROW). Benchmark 1994 values for sales and/or imports are taken from USITC values (Tables 16.2 and 16.3).

Table 16.2: Fresh Garlic: U.S. Shipments of Domestic Product, U.S. Imports, by Sources, and Apparent U.S. Consumption, Crop Years 1991 to 1994

	1991	1992	1993	1994
Item	Quantity (1,000 Pounds)			
U.S. Producer shipments	42286	58137	74520	82102
U.S. Imports from -				
The People's Republic of China[a]	6055	3540	9395	63532
Others	37279	34474	33527	34677
Total	43334	38014	42922	98209
Apparent consumption	85620	96151	117442	180311
	Value (1,000 U.S. Dollars)			
U.S. Producer shipments	32538	39766	53191	52966
U.S. Imports from -				
The People's Republic of China[a]	2474	1446	3719	20014
Others	20778	20227	17915	17697
Total	23252	21673	21634	37711
Apparent consumption	55790	61439	74825	90677
	Share of the Quantity of U.S. Consumption (Percent)			
U.S. Producer shipments	49.4	60.5	63.5	45.5
U.S. Imports from -				
The People's Republic of China[a]	7.1	3.7	8.0	35.2
Others	43.5	35.9	28.5	19.2
Total	50.6	39.5	36.5	54.5
	Share of the Value of U.S. Consumption (Percent)			
U.S. Producer shipments	58.3	64.7	71.1	58.4
U.S. Imports from -				
The People's Republic of China[a]	4.4	2.4	5.0	22.1
Others	37.2	32.9	23.9	19.5
Total	41.7	35.3	28.9	41.6

[a] PRC imports include imports from Hong Kong.
Source: USITC (1994).

Table 16.3: Fresh Garlic: U.S. Shipments of Domestic Product, U.S. Imports, By Sources, and Apparent U.S. Consumption, Crop Years 1991 to 1994

Item	1991	1992	1993	1994
	Quantity (1,000 Pounds)			
U.S. Producer shipments	42286	58137	74520	82102
U.S. Imports from -				
The People's Republic of China[a]	6055	3540	9395	63532
Mexico	20615	22721	25059	26565
Argentina	7886	5147	5024	5511
Chile	2826	2018	2264	1543
Taiwan	4712	2973	947	711
All other	1239	1615	233	346
Subtotal	37277	34474	33527	34677
Total	43334	38014	42922	98209
Apparent consumption	85620	96151	117442	180311
	Value (1,000 U.S. Dollars)			
U.S. Producer shipments	32538	39766	53191	52966
U.S. Imports from -				
The People's Republic of China[a]	2474	1446	3719	20014
Mexico	9222	12499	12203	12065
Argentina	6106	3627	3241	3640
Chile	2634	1813	1946	1496
Taiwan	1792	1241	382	206
All other	1025	1047	142	290
Subtotal	20778	20227	17915	17697
Total	23252	21673	21634	37711
Apparent consumption	55790	61439	74825	90677
	Unit Value (Per Pound)			
U.S. Producer shipments	0.77	0.68	0.71	0.65
U.S. Imports from -				
The People's Republic of China[a]	0.41	0.41	0.40	0.32
Mexico	0.45	0.55	0.49	0.45
Argentina	0.77	0.70	0.65	0.66
Chile	0.93	0.90	0.86	0.97
Taiwan	0.38	0.42	0.40	0.29
All other	0.83	0.65	0.61	0.84
Average	0.56	0.59	0.53	0.51
Average	0.54	0.57	0.50	0.38
Apparent consumption	0.65	0.64	0.64	0.50

[a]PRC imports include imports from Hong Kong.
Source: USITC 731-TA-683 (1994).

The base rate of specific import duties on garlic (HTSUS 0703.20.00) of 1.7 cent per kg[7] is converted to cents per pound and then is converted to an ad valorem rate (percent) (USDA/FAS 2003). Changes in quantity and price are calculated based on the imposition of a dumping duty on imports of fresh garlic from the PRC.

Several studies have estimated supply elasticities and Armington elasticities for agricultural products. The estimated values for these elasticities depend on several factors, specification of model, level of aggregation, time period, and others. In this analysis some default values are considered for the initial calibration.[8] Then, two types of sensitivity analysis are performed for the model with different elasticities of substitution and different assumptions on the elasticity of supplies. The resulting analysis indicates the sensitive nature of the movements in price and quantity to the different substitution elasticities applied in the model (Figures 16.5, 16.6, 16.7, and Table 16.4).

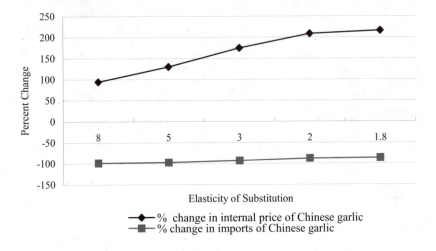

Figure 16.6: Antidumping Duty and Garlic from the People's Republic of China: Sensitivity to Armington Specifications
Source: Authors Computations.

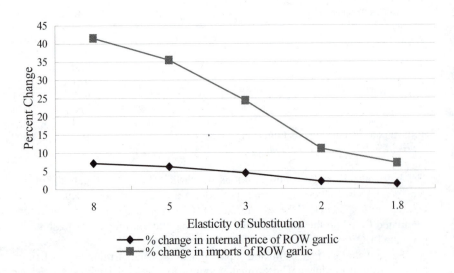

Figure 16.7: Antidumping Duty and Garlic from The Rest of the World: Sensitivity to Armington Specifications
Source: Authors Computations.

For example, Figure 16.5 shows that a high value of elasticity of substitution of 8 percent leads to an 8.57 percent increase in the internal price and a 28 percent increase in the supply of domestic garlic, which results in an AD duty on PRC garlic. With this high level of elasticity of substitution, the import price of PRC garlic will increase by over 94 percent and the quantity of PRC garlic imports will decline by 99 percent. ROW import prices will increase by 7 percent and imports will increase by over 41 percent. This large increase in price and quantity for imports from the ROW is based on the elasticity of supply used in the base model. Thus, the results of the model are not only sensitive to the value of elasticity of substitution but also to the value of elasticity of supply applied in the model.

Table 16.4: Sensitivity Analysis with Different Armigton Elasticities[a]

Elasticity of Substitution	8	5	3	2	1.8
	Benchmark Data				
Elasticity of Domestic Supply	3	3	3	3	3
Elasticity of PRC[b] Import Supply	5	5	5	5	5
Elasticity of the ROW Import Supply	5	5	5	5	5
	Simulation Results Price, Quantity and Tariff Revenue Effects (Percent Change)				
Internal Price of Domestic Garlic	8.57	7.89	5.98	2.99	1.97
Supply of Domestic Garlic	27.96	25.58	19.03	9.24	6.03
Border Price of PRC Garlic	−58.6	−50.95	−41.5	−34.34	−32.66
Internal Price of PRC Garlic	94.29	130.2	174.51	208.13	216
Imports of PRC Garlic	−98.78	−97.16	−93.15	−87.8	−86.16
Internal Price of ROW Garlic	7.2	6.26	4.45	2.13	1.39
Imports of ROW Garlic	41.59	35.49	24.39	11.1	7.14
	Change in Tariff Revenue				
For PRC Garlic	−57.96	2040.08	8203.49	17654.48	20741.63
For ROW Garlic	352.1	299.03	203.03	91.53	58.63
Total Change	294.14	2339.11	8406.51	17746.01	20800.26
	National Income Effects of AD Duty on PRC Garlic				
Welfare Triangle	−63043.5	−73581.4	−84146.7	−88984.3	−89537.4
Terms-of-Trade Effects	−125.61	422.71	1399.47	2321.56	2547.44
Trade Diversion Effects on ROW	282.76	241.33	165.40	75.46	48.51
Net Welfare effect	−62886.3	−72917.4	−82581.8	−86587.3	−86941.4

[a]In order to avoid the composite price effects to dominates cross-price effects; substitution elasticities are chosen to be greater than the composite elasticity of demand of 1.5 (assumed in this analysis). For example, for the elasticity of substitution of 1.5 will lead to no changes in domestic and ROW markets. With relatively low substitution elasticities, the composite price effects related to increased duty on PRC imports will dominate cross-price effects, thus, the net effect of an AD duty will be a decrease in demand for the domestic and ROW garlic caused by decreased expenditures on garlic.
[b]People's Republic of China.
Source: Authors' Computation (2003).

Table 16.5 Sensitivity Analysis with Different Elasticities: Selected Cases

Example 1: Elasticity of Substitution = 3.0

	Case 1	Case 3	Case 5	Case 7	Case 9	Case 11
	Benchmark Data					
Elasticity of Dom[a] Supply	3	3	3	1.5	1.5	5
Elasticity of PRC Import Supply	5	3	1.5	1.5	1.5	5
Elasticity of ROW Import Supply	5	1.5	1.5	3	1.5	1.5
	Simulation Results (Percent Change)					
Internal Price of Dom Garlic	5.98	5.73	4.59	6.43	6.64	4.44
Supply of Dom Garlic	19.03	18.2	14.41	9.79	10.12	24.28
Border Price of PRC Garlic	−41.5	−51.19	−62.12	−62.03	−61.96	−41.51
Internal Price of PRC Garlic	174.51	129.05	77.74	78.18	78.53	174.49
Imports of PRC Garlic	−93.15	−88.37	−76.69	−76.6	−76.53	−93.15
Internal Price of ROW Garlic	4.45	7.72	6.16	4.78	6.64	8.03
Imports of ROW Garlic	24.39	11.79	9.39	15.05	10.12	12.29
	National Income Effects of AD Duty					
Welfare Triangle	−84146.7	−66114	−44091.5	−44152.9	−44201.4	−84142.6
Terms-of-Trade Effects	1399.47	3226.11	8438.36	8460.56	8478.12	1398.94
Trade Diversion Effects on ROW	165.40	80.19	63.84	102.30	68.80	83.57
Net Welfare Effect	−82581.8	−62807.7	−35589.3	−35590.0	−35654.5	−82660.0

Example 2: Elasticity of Substitution = 8.0

	Case 1	Case 3	Case 5	Case 7	Case 9	Case 11
	Benchmark Data					
Elasticity of Dom Supply	3	3	3	1.5	1.5	5
Elasticity of PRC Import Supply	5	3	1.5	1.5	1.5	5
Elasticity of ROW Import Supply	5	1.5	1.5	3	1.5	1.5
	Simulation Results (Percent Change)					
Internal Price of Dom Garlic	8.57	9.37	7.93	10.22	11.11	7.01
Supply of Dom Garlic	27.96	30.82	25.74	15.72	17.12	40.33
Border Price of PRC Garlic	−58.6	−64.47	−70.29	−70.02	−69.78	−58.67
Internal Price of PRC Garlic	94.29	66.73	39.45	40.7	41.83	93.94
Imports of PRC Garlic	−98.78	−95.52	−83.8	−83.58	−83.38	−98.79
Internal Price of ROW Garlic	7.2	10.92	9.24	8.77	11.11	9.72
Imports of ROW Garlic	41.59	16.83	14.18	28.68	17.12	14.92
	National Income Effects of AD Duty					
Welfare Triangle	−63043.5	−51759.5	−37595	−37843.1	−38066.3	−62938.4
Terms-of-Trade Effects	−125.61	1113.13	6325.87	6404.39	6474.8	−131.36
Trade Diversion Effects on ROW	282.76	114.42	96.42	195.03	116.43	101.46
Net Welfare Effect	−62886.3	−50532.0	−31172.7	−31243.7	−31475.1	−62968.3

[a] Domestic.

Source: Authors' Computation (2003).

The results of the sensitivity analysis on different supply elasticities applied in the model are provided in Table 16.5. The results of the sensitivity analysis suggest that the benefit to domestic producers depends on the flexibility of domestic supply and depends on PRC imports and imports from the ROW.

Thus, in order for the domestic producer to benefit from the AD duty on fresh garlic imported from the PRC, the following conditions must hold:

- *A relatively high elasticity of substitution.* Domestic and PRC garlic are similar products, thus the changes in PRC imports will influence the domestic supply;
- *A relatively high elasticity of PRC import supply.* Large increases in the import price of PRC garlic and large declines in the quantity of imported PRC garlic, thus an AD duty on imports of fresh garlic from the PRC will lead to a decline in the market share of PRC imports; and
- *A relatively elastic domestic supply with respect to the ROW supply.* Domestic producers will make up for more of the changes in the PRC supply than will the ROW producers.

CONCLUSIONS

There are several factors that need to be considered in order for the U.S. domestic garlic industry to benefit from the changes in market share resulting from the imposition of an AD duty on fresh garlic imports from the PRC. Without understanding market characteristics, including the degree of substitutability between domestic garlic and imported garlic, the imposition of an AD duty on PRC garlic may have an adverse effect on the U.S. domestic garlic industry. A comprehensive market analysis, which includes identifying a supply and demand structure and identifying the presence of substitutability between imports and the domestic like product, is required.

Prior to the URAA, AD orders were not subjected to comprehensive automatic review; however, international agreement and U.S. law with respect to AD orders now requires sunset reviews. For the case of garlic, the sunset review was undertaken in a systematic manner and it is difficult to find a modification in the investigation process relative to the initial investigation. For example, in the initial investigation, the product focus was "fresh garlic" (HTSUS 0703.20.00), and there was no discussion of other garlic classified in the HTSUS (0710.80.7060, 0710.80.9750, 0711.90.6000 and 2005.90.9500). What is the implication of defining many products rather than specifying the fresh-garlic product of HTSUS 0703.20.00, as considered in the AD case by Canada or South Africa (USDA/FAS 2003)?[9] As discussed in the previous section, BIA is employed in the sunset review. This implies that the USITC and the USDOC did not have enough information even for the sunset review. The USITC concluded in their in the five-year review:

> ... Overall, we conclude that the likely volume of subject imports would be significant both in absolute terms and relative to consumption in the United States if the order is revoked. We base this conclusion on a number of factors, including: the demonstrated ability of producers in the PRC to increase their U.S. market penetration rapidly; the existence of the PRC's very large capacity to produce fresh garlic; the demonstrated export-orientation of the PRC industry; the existence of third-country restrictions which limit market access for exports from the PRC; the restraining effect that the order has had

on subject import volumes; and the attractiveness of the growing U.S. market as an outlet for PRC production. (USITC 2001a: 11–12)

USDOC is required to initiate the next five-year review of the garlic case no later than February 2006 (66 *FR* 14544 2001). It will be interesting to see if USDOC defines the PRC as a non-market economy for the coming review. A more transparent investigation and review process in addition to a less-systematic approach would make it easier to modify existing dumping margins. For the five-year review, the investigation should include an in-depth analysis of developments in the domestic industry during the review period that would identify clearly what effects may be attributed to the AD order relative to other factors.

To determine the effectiveness of AD duties as a mechanism to deal with unfair import competition, additional research and analysis will be required. A measure of benefits to the domestic industry relative to increased market share, including prices and returns, must be established. The net benefit to society, if any, of AD duties can be determined only when the full costs of conducting the investigation by the USITC and by the USDOC are accounted for. Thus the legal costs to the domestic garlic industry of pursuing the case along with the costs to consumers must also be accounted for.

If AD duties will be the main instrument of trade remedy law available to domestic producers, the development of a more streamlined and transparent process may be advisable. A less-complicated, more-transparent process is needed that reduces the industry costs of filing complaints against suspected unfair competition. This will protect those less-prosperous industry sectors from unfair trade practices that their more-prosperous counterparts can afford.

APPENDIX

Table A16.1: Administrative Reviews (AR) of Fresh Garlic from the People's Republic of China

Notice of Opportunity to Request AR and AR Number		Period of Review	Notice of Initiation of AR and AR Number		No. of AR Companies
11/01/95	60 FR 55540	07/11/94 to 10/31/95	12/15/95	60 FR 64413	158
11/04/96	61 FR 56663	11/1/95 to 10/31/96	12/16/96	61 FR 66017	9
11/07/97	62 FR 60219	11/1/96 to 10/31/97	12/23/97	62 FR 67044	1
11/12/98	63 FR 63287	11/1/97 to 10/31/98	12/23/98	63 FR 71091	3
11/16/99	64 FR 62167	11/1/98 to 10/31/99	12/28/99	64 FR 72644	4
11/08/00	65 FR 66965	11/1/99 to 10/31/00	12/28/00	65 FR 82322	6
10/30/01	66 FR 54750	11/1/00 to 10/31/01	12/19/01	66 FR 65470	21
11/01/02	67 FR 66612	11/1/01 to 10/31/02	12/26/02	67 FR 78772	11
			Total Number Reviewed for the eight ARs		213

Source: Authors' Compilation (2003).

NOTES

*Fumiko Yamazaki is senior research economist and Mechel S. Paggi is Director, Center for Agricultural Business, California State University, Fresno. The California Department of Agriculture's Buy California Initiative and the U.S. Department of Agriculture (USDA) provided funding for this analysis. All interpretations and conclusions in this chapter are entirely those of the authors and reflects the position of neither the California Department of Agriculture nor the USDA.

[1] The investigation period was August 1, 1993 to January 31, 1994.

[2] Fresh Garlic Producers Association (FGPA), at the initial petition, consisted of the following 7 members in California: the A&D Christopher Ranch, Gilroy; Belridge Packing Co., Wasco; Colusa Produce Corp., Colusa; Denice & Filice Packing Co., Hollister; El Camino Packing, Gilroy; The Garlic Company, Shafter; and Vessey and Company, Inc., El Centro (59 *FR* 6043, February 9, 1994). For the 5-year review, the FGPA consists of 10 members; five of the initial members (in bold above) and Crinklaw Farms, King City; Dalena Farms, Madera; Frank Pitts Farms, Five Points; Spice World (Jenner Fresh), Orlando, FL; Thomson International, Inc, Bakersfield (65 *FR* 41432, July 5, 2000).

[3] The subject "garlic" as classified in the initial investigation was under subheadings 073.20.0000, 0710.80.7060, 0710.80.9750, 0711.90.6000, and 2005.90.9500 of the Harmonized Tariff Schedule of the United States (HTSUS) (USDA/FAS 2003). Some of the subheadings under the HTSUS were changed in 1994 to the following:

> 0703.20.0000 to 0703.20.0010
> 0703.20.0020
> 0703.20.0090
> 2005.90.9500 to 2005.90.9700

[4] Fresh Garlic from the People's Republic of China (PRC), Inv. No. 731-TA-683 (Final), USITC Pub. 2825 (November 1994) (USITC 1994).

[5] For the purpose of data extraction/analysis, case garlic is defined in this analysis as HTSUS of following: 0703.20.0000, 0703.20.0010, 0703.20.0020, 0703.20.0090, 0710.80.7060, 0710.80.9750, 0711.90.6000, 2005.90.9500, and 2005.90.9700. Non-case garlic is 0712.90.4020 and 0712.90.4040 (USDA/FAS 2003).

[6] Selling at LTFV, or dumping, is defined by the U.S. Department of Commerce (USDOC) in Section 771(34) of the *Tariff Act* of 1930 (19 U.S.C. § 1677 (34))(USDOC 2003) as "the sale or likely sale of goods at less than fair value." In specific terms, dumping is defined as selling a product in the United States at a price that is lower than the price for which it is sold in the home market (the "normal value"), after adjustments for differences in the merchandise, quantities purchased, and circumstances of sale are made. If home-market sales are not sufficient, the price for which the product is sold in a surrogate "third country" may be used. In the absence of sufficient home-market and third-country sales, "constructed value," which uses a cost-plus-profit approach to arrive at normal value, may be used (USITC 2001b: 1–3).

[7] The base-rate duty is taken from the World Trade Organization (WTO) Uruguay Round Agreement (URAA), Schedule XX – Unites States of America, Part I – Most-Favoured-Nation Tariff, Section I – Agricultural Products, Section I – A tariffs.

[8] Elasticities considered for the initial calibration are: composite elasticity of demand of 1.5; elasticity of domestic supply of 3; elasticity of PRC import supply of 5; and elasticity of rest of the world import supply of 5.

[9] South Africa also considered dried garlic of 0712.90 for their case.

REFERENCES

Armington, P.S. (1969). "A Theory of Demand for Products Distinguished by Place of Production." *IMF Staff Papers* 16(1): 159–78.

Baldwin, R.E. and M.O. Moore. (1991). "Political Aspects of the Administration of the Trade Remedy Laws," in R. Boltruck and T.E. Litan, eds., *Down in the Dumps: Administration of the Unfair Trade Laws*. Washington, DC: The Brookings Institution Press: 253–80.

CCRA (Canada Customs and Revenue Agency, Customs and Excise). (1997 to 2002). "Fresh Garlic, Originating in or Exported From the People's Republic of China." *Customs Notice* N-230, N-362, N-380, *Memorandum* D15-2-10. Ottawa: Antidumping and Countervailing Directorate.

CITT (Canadian International Trade Tribunal). (2001). *Garlic, Fresh or Frozen, Originating in or Exported from the People's Republic of China and Vietnam, Excluding Fresh Garlic Subject to the Finding made in the Canadian International Trade Tribunal Inquiry No. NQ-96-002*. Inquiry No. NQ-2000-006. Ottawa: CITT.

_____. (2000). *Fresh Garlic Originating in or Exported from the People's Republic of China*. RD-99-002. Ottawa: CITT.

_____. (1997a). *The Dumping in Canada of Fresh Garlic Originating in or Exported from the People's Republic of China*. RD-97-002. Ottawa: CITT.

_____. (1997b). *Fresh Garlic Originating in or Exported from the People's Republic of China*. NQ-96-002. Ottawa: CITT.

FAO (Food and Agriculture Organization of the United Nations). (2003). *Agriculture Data*. Available at: http://www.fao.org/waicent/.

FR (*The Federal Register*). (1994 to 2003). Various issues on antidumping case A-570-831 by Department of Commerce (USDOC), International Trade Administration, and the Investigation No. 731-TA-683 by the U.S. International Trade Commission (USITC). National Archives and Records Administration, Office of the Federal Register. Available at: www.access.gpo.gov/su_docs/aces/aces140.html.

Francois, J.F. and H.K. Hall. (1997). "Partial Equilibrium Modelling," in *Applied Methods for Trade Policy Analysis: A Handbook*. Cambridge: Cambridge University Press: 122–55.

Global Trade Information Service, Inc. (2003). *Global Trade Atlas*. Available at: http://www.gtis.com/gta.

IA (Import Administration). (1998). *Antidumping Manual: 1997 Edition* International Trade Administration, Department of Commerce. Washington D.C. Available at: http://www.ia.ita.doc.gov.

Lindsay, B. (1999). *The U.S. Antidumping Law: Rhetoric versus Reality*. Trade Policy Analysis No. 7. Washington, DC: Cato Institute (August).

USDA/FAS (U.S. Department of Agriculture, Foreign Agricultural Service). (2003). *U.S. Trade Imports – HS 10 Digit Codes*. Available at: http://fas.usda.gov/ustrade/USTImHS10.asp?QI=.

USDA/NASS (U.S. Department of Agriculture/National Agricultural Statistics Service). (2003). Available at: http://www.usda.gov/nass/.

USDOC (U.S. Department of Commerce). (2003). Available at: http://www.commerce.gov/.

USITC (U.S. International Trade Commission). (1994). *Fresh Garlic from the People's Republic of China.* Investigation No. 731-TA-683 (Final), Publication 2825. Washington, DC: USITC (November).

_____. (1998). *Summary of Statutory Provisions Related to Import Relief,* Publication 3125. Washington, DC: USITC (August).

_____. (2001a). *Fresh Garlic from the People's Republic of China, Determination and Views of the Commission.* Investigation No. 731-TA-683 (Review), Publication 3393. Washington, DC: USITC (February).

_____. (2001b). *Antidumping and Countervailing Duty Handbook, Ninth Edition.* Publication 3482. Washington, DC: USITC (December): 3–15.

WTO/URAA (World Trade Organization/Uruguay Round Agreements Act). (2003). Available at: http://www.wto.org/english/docs_e/legal_e/legal_e.htm#goods.

Chapter 17

Summary

Andrew Schmitz
University of Florida

INTRODUCTION

Trade disputes over agricultural products have received considerable political attention and have escalated in recent years. For example, U.S. President George W. Bush and Canadian Prime Minister Paul Martin met in the spring of 2004 to discuss agriculture and trade disputes between the two countries. These agricultural trade disputes include softwood lumber, wheat, country-of-origin labelling (COOL), the threat of the United States imposing duties on hog imports from Canada, and trade liberalization in live beef cattle, following the outbreak of the Bovine Spongiform Encephalopathy (BSE) in Canada and the United States. According to Prime Minister Paul Martin, "we have to find a way in what is a very, very important set of commercial flows between our two countries to have better ways of settling our disputes" (Elliott 2004a).

CONTROVERSIES

This volume is focused on the controversial economic and legal aspects of anti-dumping (AD) duties, countervailing (CV) duties, and import safeguards. At least in the United States and Canada, the procedures are straightforward for filing AD and CV cases. For example, in the United States, all preliminary AD and CV duties are determined by the U.S. Department of Commerce (USDOC). However, before they can become permanent, it is necessary for the government to show that unfair foreign competition imposes significant material injury on import-competing producers. The U.S. International Trade Commission (USITC) decides whether or not material injury has taken place.

The interface between the resolution of CV and AD cases and appeals to the World Trade Organization (WTO) is less clear than are the internal workings of trade dispute cases. Often cases are referred to the WTO when disputing countries cannot resolve disputes between themselves. Two examples in this volume are the U.S.-Canada dairy dispute and the Canada-U.S. softwood lumber case. One element of the WTO process is the extent to which countries comply with decisions made by the WTO. For example, in the lumber dispute, the WTO argued that the United States was correct when it imposed duties on softwood lumber from Canada. However, according to the WTO, the imposed duties were excessive because the United States used the wrong methodology when calculating the material injury. But even with the WTO decision, controversy remains over the size of duties that should be imposed on U.S. imports of softwood lumber from Canada.

In many disputes, private-sector interests, including special interest groups, are the litigants. These groups invest money to bring cases against competitors in an attempt to enhance their own welfare through higher commodity prices that result when border measures are imposed on imports. This so-called "rent-seeking" behaviour is influenced by the nature of the commodity groups or by the private firms seeking subsidy relief from foreign competition. Multinational corporations often play a role in dispute resolutions. This is very apparent in the United States' AD beef case against Canada. Tyson Foods, Inc. and Excel Beef, Inc. were very instrumental in persuading the U.S. government not to impose duties on live cattle imports. However, in May of 2003 with the outbreak of BSE, the United States closed the border to imports of Canadian live beef cattle. It is less clear that these same packers support the reopening of the border between the United States and Canada on the live beef cattle trade. In fact, due to border closings, the profits to the packers in Canada have skyrocketed:

> ... the [packing] companies have been under considerable pressure from farmers and politicians in recent months for what critics claim is profiteering following the BSE discovery. Researchers at the George Morris Centre in Guelph, Ontario, Canada, have estimated packers took in an extra CDN $227 million in profits between October 6, 2003 and February 16, 2004, according to members of parliament. (Elliott 2004b)

From a rent-seeking perspective, it is clear that for many products there are no CV or AD duty actions, since the products are not produced in the importing country. For example, rarely do you see cases in Canada in which duties are imposed on the importation of lettuce and fruits and vegetables from the United States.

A new twist has been added to U.S. rent-seeking activities with the passage of the so-called "Byrd Amendment" of the *Continued Dumping and Offset Act* of 2000, in which producers and processors, in certain instances, are allowed to keep the tariff revenue. Thus there are additional monies available to producers and processors for rent-seeking purposes to restrain trade. Tariff revenues normally go to the federal government.

One major trade dispute is the role state trading enterprises (STE) play. For example, the Canadian Wheat Board (CWB) is an STE that is strongly opposed by many U.S. commercial interests. The United States has brought numerous lawsuits directly against Canada over imports of Canadian grain, but most of these have been unsuccessful (Schmitz and Furtan 2000). The United States has been successful when imposing punitive import tariffs on only one type of Canadian wheat. However, in this case, Canada brought an appeal through the NAFTA dispute-settlement process. Also, U.S. interests filed through the federal government a complaint with the WTO charging that the CWB unfairly prices wheat in certain key markets in an attempt to gain world market share. Up until this point, legal challenges had been held in national courts and tribunals. The Bush Administration initiated a WTO trade-dispute panel as part of a strategy to deal with the U.S. wheat industry's complaints about the CWB's trading practices. The CWB won a major victory when the WTO ruled that the CWB's practices were not in violation of WTO trade law. The United States failed to establish its claim that Canada breached its obligations under Article XVII:1 of the 1994 General Agreement on Tariffs and Trade (GATT). The WTO Panel also ruled against the Bush Administration's claim that Section 87 of the *Canada Grain Act* (1985) violated WTO rules. The WTO Panel argued that the United States failed to establish its claim that Section 87 of the *Canada Grain Act* is inconsistent with Article III:4 of the 1994 GATT and Article 2 of the *Trade-Related Investment Measures Act* (1994). However, concerning grain segregation, the WTO Panel found that parts of the *Canada Grain Act*, Canada Grain Regulations, and the *Canada Transportation Act* (1996) violated WTO rules because under these regulations/acts Canadian grain is given preferred treatment over that of competitors.

Controversies often exist because rent-seeking behaviour deals with more than one particular commodity under investigation. For example, in the high fructose corn syrup (HFCS) case, which is discussed in chapter 14 of this volume, Mexico attempted to impose duties on HFCS imports from the United States largely in retaliation to Mexico's allegation that the United States had not honoured the so-called Side Agreement under the North American Free Trade Agreement (NAFTA). Under this Side Agreement, the United States was to import a minimum of 200,000 tons of raw sugar from Mexico, provided that Mexico could achieve net-export status for sugar. While Mexico was unsuccessful imposing duties on HFCS, it was able to restrict the use of HFCS through other means, including direct taxes on the use of HFCS in the beverage industry. There are other cases in which factors of a general nature are taken into account when resolving trade disputes. For example, in early trade disputes between Mexico and the United States over tomatoes, duties were often not imposed by the United States because they did not want problems over oil imports from Mexico (Schmitz, Firch, and Hillman 1981). Also, in the tomato cases between the United States and Canada, which are discussed in Chapter 11 of this volume, the U.S. case against Canada was lifted partly as the result of the Canadians bringing an AD case against the U.S. tomato industry over Canadian imports of tomatoes.

Countries like the United States provide subsidies to producers, and these subsidies have been sore points in negotiating freer trade worldwide. Yet these subsidies are not taken into account when an individual commodity group brings trade action against a competitor. For example, in U.S. cases against Canadian grain imports, the issue is not whether the United States is exporting wheat below the cost of production, but whether Canadian producers are exporting and selling grain below the Canadian cost of production.

Often, less-developed countries are hurt by unfair agricultural subsidization by developed countries, which results in products being exported below the cost of production. However, there are very few cases in which less-developed countries bring legal action against high-income countries, such as the United States and Canada, because the less-developed countries do not have the means to bring such legal action.

Dealing with issues over AD and CV duties and related trade law is much easier than having to deal with border disputes where safeguards are involved. In recent years, controversies over safeguards have increased as evidenced by the COOL debate and by border closings of trade in live cattle and beef products as a result of the outbreak of BSE in Canada. COOL has been put on hold until 2006. However, the controversy over BSE continues. There is disagreement in the scientific community over whether all beef cattle have to be tested in order for a country to be considered BSE-free or whether only a percentage have to be tested. So far, it appears that science has been unable to help in the freeing up of trade in live beef cattle. Until now, Japan, for example, has argued that future beef imports from the United States have to be from animals that have been tested and certified as being BSE-free. But this stance may be changing, as statements are being made that by the Fall of 2004 the Japanese may resume imports from the United States without 100 percent testing for BSE.

DISCREPANCIES BETWEEN ECONOMICS AND TRADE LAW

One of the shortcomings of applying trade law to perishable commodities is that the law cannot accommodate normal business conduct. The criterion that dumping occurs if a product is sold below the full cost of production plus 6 percent is inconsistent with normal business practices. Producers of commodities such as lettuce will often sell the commodity at prices below the full cost of production as long as prices are sufficient to cover certain variable costs such as picking and packaging. To adequately deal with perishable products, the law should be changed to recognize that even though a product is sold below its cost of production for a certain period of time, this does not necessarily constitute dumping.

In certain instances, suspension agreements are used to resolve trade disputes. In these agreements, exporters cannot sell below an agreed upon minimum price. In the tomato trade controversy between Mexico and the United States, producers in both countries benefited from the suspension agreements between the two countries (Schmitz, Furtan, and Baylis 2002). However, the degree to which suspension agreements lead to a competitive environment has not been investigated. If suspension agreements resulted in a form of price fixing, that certainly would be a matter of concern for U.S. authorities who deal with anticompetitive behaviour.

Since the 1990 book entitled *Canadian Agricultural Trade: Disputes, Actions and Prospects* edited by Lermer and Klein was published, new avenues have arisen through which Canadian litigants can file CV and AD complaints. This volume, *International Agricultural Trade Disputes: Case Studies in North America*, edited by Schmitz, Moss, Schmitz, and Koo (2004), highlights the various avenues by considering the HFCS case brought by Mexico against the United States. Litigants now can go outside the domestic channels and use the WTO trade-dispute panel process and/or the NAFTA trade-dispute settlement procedures. The payoffs to litigants vary according to the dispute mechanism chosen.

Under U.S. trade law, U.S. producers can file a complaint to the USDOC if they feel they are injured by unfair competition from competing exporters. But these lawsuits are generally brought by import-competing U.S. producers. Thus importers are suing exporters. And there really is no avenue for export-competing producers to sue for unfair practices by importers. However, with the advent of the WTO trade-dispute-panel process, the latter is now possible. For example, there is an interesting case in which the Philippines challenged Australia through the WTO over Australia's high trade barriers to the importation of fresh fruits and vegetables from the Philippines (Javelosa 2004).

With the WTO trade-dispute resolution in place, countries are given a wide range of opportunities to file trade grievances, which would otherwise not be available. For example, Brazil, a cotton exporter in 2003, brought a case against U.S. cotton growers for alleged unfair subsidization of U.S. cotton exports by way of U.S. farm policy. In April of 2004, the preliminary ruling by a WTO panel supported Brazil's allegations of dumping. Traditional lawsuits generally involve an importer bringing a case against subsidized exports. This was also an important case because it appears to be the first time that U.S. farm policy has been challenged by way of complaints through the WTO mechanism.

U.S. agricultural trade policy, as reflected in both historical and current negotiating positions, argues for international agreements that will result in reduced subsidies and increased market access. U.S. law, on the other hand, continues to subsidize agriculture at significant levels and often operates to limit market access for imports. Several features of the U.S. Constitution and the historical context in which U.S. laws affect agriculture and trade have developed over time and have contributed to this discontinuity. First, there is the basic constitutional division of powers between the executive and legislative branches of the U.S. government, granting the executive branch the power to negotiate treaties while giving the legislative branch sole power to lay duties and to regulate commerce with foreign nations. Second, the U.S. Constitution created a bicameral-legislative scheme under which rural and agricultural states are represented to a degree disproportionate to their populations. And third, U.S. trade policy in favour of liberalization is largely a post-World War II phenomenon.

Before either an AD or CV duty can be imposed, WTO rules require that the importing country should determine if:

> ... the effect of the dumping or subsidization, as the case may
> be, is such as to cause or threaten material injury to an
> established domestic industry, or is such as to retard materially
> the establishment of a domestic industry. (Featherstone and
> Uhm 2000)

This requirement is known as the material-injury test. However, the concept of what constitutes material injury is nowhere specifically defined (Sykes 1997). The new WTO antidumping and subsidies codes indicate that an analysis shall include an evaluation of all relevant economic factors and indices that have a bearing on the state of the industry. Such factors include sales, profits, output, and market share. Neither the WTO antidumping codes nor the subsidies codes indicate how the various factors are to be weighed, nor did they know what quantum of injury is required for "material injury." From an individual country perspective, Canada, for example, provides a definition that injury means material injury to a domestic industry; however, there is no specific mention of a threshold of how much injury constitutes material injury. The U.S. trade remedy laws also do not provide a more specific meaning of material injury. The U.S. law defines material injury as "harm, which is not inconsequential, immaterial, or unimportant." Also, an ambiguity arises with respect to the required causal relationship between material injury and unfair trade practice. The USITC is not necessarily instructed to determine whether or not the unfair trade practice is the cause of material injury. However, this does not appear to be the case for the WTO codes where the determination of causality is necessary (Sykes 1997). One might ask the question of why countries and the WTO cannot have a standard code and methodology for dealing with AD and CV cases.

THE DEBATE OVER MEASUREMENT AND DETERMINATION OF TRADE INJURY

The USDOC determines duties when it finds competitors are subsidizing production (CV duties) and/or selling below the full cost of production plus 6 percent (although other criteria are also used, including selling in the home market at a price above the export price). Generally, what constitutes a subsidy is not clear. Also, conducting a complete and full cost-of-production accounting in many instances is difficult. This is especially true in cases involving the People's Republic of China (PRC) (Chapter 16, this volume, which deals with U.S. imports of garlic from the PRC) in which data are extremely scarce. In addition, as stressed in Schmitz, Firch, and Hillman (1981), the law should be changed to deal with perishables in which the concept of a "normal business practice" should be taken into account. Often U.S. farmers, for example, will sell perishables below the full cost of production during periods when the price of the commodity is only slightly above the cost of picking and shipping. However, when an exporter to the United States also follows this practice, dumping is alleged. Why the law has not been changed to deal with perishables remains a mystery.

It is not clear how changes in exchange rates play into decisions on trade-dispute resolutions. For example, some have argued that because of the Mexican devaluation of the peso, Florida tomato producers suffered financially. The Florida tomato producers sought relief through the AD duty-action process, while arguing that exchange-rate devaluations were not in the spirit of NAFTA. However, this is a contentious issue, and will not go away when examining future trade disputes. Many argue, that the large increase in Canadian grain exports to the United States was due to the depreciation of the Canadian dollar. But why is monetary policy an issue in trade-dispute resolutions? Interestingly, in the final resolution of the Mexico-Florida trade dispute over tomatoes, a suspension agreement was reached, which has since been renewed. The United States and Mexico once again agreed to a minimum price for tomatoes below which Mexico cannot sell their product in U.S. markets.

When examining the market impacts from import duties, how one defines a market is critical to determining the economic impacts from alleged dumping (Schmitz and Sigurdson 1990; Barichello, this volume Chapter 11). The greater the degree of substitutability among products, the less is the material injury from unfair competition. In this volume, several chapters deal with the problems of defining "like markets." The notion of market definition in quantifying the impact of market duties is very different than "like markets" in antitrust-merger cases. In the latter, even if markets are highly substitutable, the U.S. Department of Justice argues that this does not rule out the potential for price fixing from merger activity (Moss and Schmitz 2004). Also the notion of "like markets" once again comes into play in the 2004 USDOC investigation into U.S. complaints over live hog imports from Canada. The United States is expected to impose preliminary CV and AD duties on live hog imports. The importation of pork is not under investigation.

Once preliminary duties have been established by the USDOC, it is necessary to prove that there is material injury before these duties can be put into effect. We present results in this volume on the methodology generally used by the USITC, but this methodology has been challenged by certain academics, including researchers of the International Trade and Policy Center at the University of Florida. These researchers argue that the methodology used biases the results in favour of the defendant. There is ongoing research on how different models generate different results. Also, in AD and CV cases, trade lawyers handle the disputes, using their own expert witnesses to conduct analyses on the economic impact of a specific trade-dispute case. This may lead to results that may or may not be consistent with those generated by the USITC. Also, it is difficult to interpret the meaning of "material injury." For example, is a 10 percent reduction in gross revenue caused by unfair competition considered material injury, or would a 5 percent reduction be sufficient?

When in consultation with private attorneys, economists use various models to estimate the impacts of subsidization and/or dumping. These economic models differ widely from those of the USITC. And the approach by the USITC appears to be different than that used by other countries. Regardless of the approach used, however, in most cases full-fledged econometric analysis is not carried out to determine the impact from subsidization and/or dumping. Even if this analysis is used, the determination of material injury still remains a problem.

REFERENCES

Canada Grain Act. (1985). Available at: http://laws.justice.gc.ca/en/G-10.

Canada Transportation Act. (1996). Available at: http://laws.justice.gc.ca/en/C-10.4/.

Elliott, Ian. (2004a). "Beef to be Topic for Bush-Martin Meeting." *Feedstuffs* April 19: 5.

Elliott, Ian. (2004b). "Canadian Packers Ordered to Deliver Financial Records." *Feedstuffs* April 5: 1.

Featherstone, Dennis and Ihn Ho Uhm. (2000). "Trade Disputes: The Antidumping and Countervailing Duty Laws and the Role of Quantitative Economic Analysis." Paper presented at the *Challenges in Agricultural Trade Under the U.S.-Canada Free Trade Agreement (CUSTA) Conference*, Fargo, North Dakota (October 26–7).

Javelosa, Josyline C. (2004). "The Philippine-Australian SPS Case on Fresh Fruit and Vegetables: What is there to Gain from the WTO Dispute Settlement System?" Working Paper, Department of Food and Resource Economics, University of Florida, Gainesville, Florida.

Lermer, G., and K. K. Klein (Editors). (1990). *Canadian Agricultural Trade: Disputes Actions and Prospects.* Calgary: University of Calgary Press.

Moss, Charles B. and Andrew Schmitz. (2004). "Delineating the Relevant U.S. Sweetener Markets."*Journal of Agricultural and Food Industrial Organization* 2(1): 1–19.

Schmitz, Andrew, Robert S. Firch, and Jimmye S. Hillman. (1981). "Agricultural Export Dumping: The Case of Mexican Winter Vegetables in the U. S. Market." *American Journal of Agricultural Economics* 63(4): 645–55.

Schmitz, Andrew and H. Furtan. (2000). *The Canadian Wheat Board: Marketing in the New Millenium.* Regina: Canadian Plains Research Centre (September).

Schmitz, Andrew, W. H. Furtan, and K. Baylis. (2002). *Agricultural Policy, Agribusiness, and Rent-Seeking Behaviour.* Toronto: University of Toronto Press.

Schmitz, A., C. B. Moss, T. G. Schmitz, and W. Koo. (2004). *International Agricultural Trade Disputes: Case Studies in North America*, this volume.

Schmitz, A. and D. Sigurdson. (1990). "Stabilization Programs and Countervailing Duties: Canadian Hog Exports to the United States," in *Canadian Agricultural Trade: Disputes, Actions, Prospects*, edited by G. Lermer and K .K. Klein. Calgary: University of Calgary Press (73–92).

Sykes, Alan O. (1997). "The Economics of 'Injury' in Antidumping and Countervailing Duty Cases," in *Economic Dimensions in International Law: Comparative and Empirical Perspectives*, edited by Jagdeep S. Bhandari and Alan O. Sykes. Cambridge: Cambridge University Press.

Trade Related Measures Act. (1994). Available at: http://www.wto.org/english/docs_e/legal_e/ursum_e.htm#eAgreement.

Index

INDEX